CLIMAX AT GALLIPOLI

CAMPAIGNS & COMMANDERS

GREGORY J. W. URWIN, SERIES EDITOR

CAMPAIGNS AND COMMANDERS

GENERAL EDITOR

Gregory J. W. Urwin, *Temple University, Philadelphia, Pennsylvania*

ADVISORY BOARD

Lawrence E. Babits, *East Carolina University, Greenville*
James C. Bradford, *Texas A&M University, College Station*
Robert M. Epstein, *U.S. Army School of Advanced Military Studies, Fort Leavenworth, Kansas*
David M. Glantz, *Carlisle, Pennsylvania*
Jerome A. Greene, *Denver, Colorado*
Victor Davis Hanson, *California State University, Fresno*
Herman Hattaway, *University of Missouri, Kansas City*
J. A. Houlding, *Rückersdorf, Germany*
Eugenia C. Kiesling, *U.S. Military Academy, West Point, New York*
Timothy K. Nenninger, *National Archives, Washington, D.C.*
Bruce Vandervort, *Virginia Military Institute, Lexington*

CLIMAX AT GALLIPOLI

The Failure of the August Offensive

Rhys Crawley

UNIVERSITY OF OKLAHOMA PRESS | NORMAN

Library of Congress Cataloging-in-Publication Data

Crawley, Rhys, 1985–
  Climax at Gallipoli : the failure of the August Offensive / Rhys Crawley.
    pages cm. — (Campaigns and commanders ; volume 42)
  Includes bibliographical references and index.
  ISBN 978-0-8061-4426-9 (cloth)
  ISBN 978-0-8061-5206-6 (paper)
   1. World War, 1914–1918—Campaigns—Turkey—Gallipoli Peninsula. 2. Gallipoli Peninsula (Turkey)—History, Military—20th century. I. Title.
  D568.3.C73 2014
  940.4'26—dc23
                    2013037472

Climax at Gallipoli: The Failure of the August Offensive is Volume 42 in the Campaigns and Commanders series.

The paper in this book meets the guidelines for permanence and durability of the Committee on Production Guidelines for Book Longevity of the Council on Library Resources, Inc. ∞

Copyright © 2014 by the University of Oklahoma Press, Norman, Publishing Division of the University. Paperback published 2015. Manufactured in the U.S.A.

All rights reserved. No part of this publication may be reproduced, stored in a retrieval system, or transmitted, in any form or by any means, electronic, mechanical, photocopying, recording, or otherwise—except as permitted under Section 107 or 108 of the United States Copyright Act—without the prior written permission of the University of Oklahoma Press. To request permission to reproduce selections from this book, write to Permissions, University of Oklahoma Press, 2800 Venture Drive, Norman OK 73069, or email rights.oupress@ou.edu.

Interior layout and composition: Alcorn Publication Design

Contents

List of Illustrations	vii
Preface	ix
List of Abbreviations	xiii
Introduction	3
1. Planning	12
2. Mobility	47
3. Fire Support	69
4. Combined Operations	93
5. Lines of Communication	119
6. Supply and Transport	157
7. The August Offensive	188
8. Subsequent Phases	214
Conclusion	242
Appendix 1. MEF Order of Battle, 6 August 1915	247
Appendix 2. Artillery Available for the Offensive	255
Appendix 3. Range/Distance	259
Notes	261
Bibliography	323
Index	351

Illustrations

Figures

Request, Acquisition, and Disembarkation Cycle	121
Lieutenant-General Sir William Birdwood, GOC ANZAC, outside his dugout	149
Looking north from Anzac at the foothills of the Sari Bair Ridge	150
Gunners of the 7th Indian Mountain Artillery Brigade	150
Commodore Roger Keyes, Vice-Admiral John de Robeck, General Sir Ian Hamilton, and Major-General Walter Braithwaite	151
Ships anchored in Mudros Harbour, with a British airship overhead	152
Field guns being brought ashore at Anzac Cove	153
Australian soldiers in trenches on Pope's Hill on 6 August	153
The dead littering the trenches on 6 August	154
Troops unloading supplies from motor lighters at Suvla Bay	155
Chunuk Bair, with the Dardanelles in the distance	156

Maps

1. The Dardanelles defenses and 25 April objectives	4
2. Key features of Birdwood's proposal	34
3. Objectives of the August Offensive	42
4. Main cable routes	61
5. Allied lines of communication	123

6. The offensive in the Anzac and Sari Bair sectors   193
7. The offensive at Suvla Bay   196
8. Positions after Ottoman victory   209
9. Ottoman lines of communication   228

Tables

1. War Establishment and Effective Strength of the Mediterranean Expeditionary Force   53
2. Effective Artillery Strength, Mediterranean Theater, August 1915   78

Preface

In the historiography of the Gallipoli Campaign, the August Offensive—the largest and last major effort to break the deadlock and defeat the Ottoman Empire at Gallipoli—is invariably portrayed as a "near miss" or "near success." Victory was assured, the story goes, "if only" the Allies had pushed a little harder, or had been the recipients of some simple good luck. Apart from glossing over the fact that the August Offensive was an utter failure, this view has prevented an objective analysis of the offensive. This book addresses this historical imbalance by reexamining the operational capabilities of the Mediterranean Expeditionary Force (MEF), and indeed, the true potential for success in a prolonged offensive operation at Gallipoli in August 1915.

In this sense, the August Offensive must be viewed within the wider context of Allied operations during the First World War. Despite its differences in location, scale, and enemy, the war fought at Gallipoli was similar to that fought on the Western Front. In 1915, both the MEF at Gallipoli and the British Expeditionary Force (BEF) on the Western Front were trying to adapt to a new form of warfare—one where static defense had replaced the maneuver and offensive warfare that formed prewar British doctrine. The August Offensive at Gallipoli, like the battles at Neuve Chapelle and Loos on the Western Front, was another example of this adjustment. All three aimed for too much, and all three failed. By focusing on the operational level of war, and examining aspects such as planning, command, mobility, fire support, interservice cooperation, and logistics, this book contends that the August Offensive was not a near success or, indeed, even a viable operation. The offensive never approached success, nor could it.

Methodology

Empirical in nature, this book is built to a significant degree on archival research conducted at thirteen repositories across the UK and Australia. Research at these localities enabled a thorough survey of the relevant files of organizations such as the War Office, Admiralty, and Dardanelles Committee. Aside from providing an understanding of what issues were discussed between the theater and London, these records also placed the August Offensive within the context of a wider British war effort. In addition, the war diaries of *every* Allied unit involved in the August Offensive were examined to gain an insight into the concerns and actions prior to, during, and after the August Offensive. So that these issues could be understood, the personal papers of those individuals who held positions of responsibility—whether political, operational, or administrative—were also examined. Further adding a personal element to the book are the 1,686 pages of evidence heard by the Dardanelles Commission, which provided a useful commentary of the issues faced, and the personalities concerned.

Copies of the operational files of the New Zealand Expeditionary Force, including unit war diaries and the personal papers of key participants, were available in Australia and the United Kingdom; research in New Zealand was therefore not required. Although comprising a significant component of the Allied force at Gallipoli, the Corps Expéditionnaire Français des Dardanelles was not actively involved in the August Offensive, and as such, French records were not examined. Similarly, given the book's focus on Allied capabilities, and because of the difficulties of researching Ottoman script—a skill that few possess—no archival research was undertaken in Turkey.[1] Research conducted on the Gallipoli Peninsula in 2008, 2011, and 2012, however, provided an understanding of the theater of operations, the terrain, and the supply routes. When it comes to style, I have retained hyphens in military ranks (and their abbreviations) and have referred to military units as they were treated at the time of the Gallipoli Campaign.

This book, like all others, could not have been written without the support and encouragement of many people. I should first like to express my sincere gratitude to my doctoral supervisor, Dr. Craig Stockings, who, despite advocating the keys to completion as poverty, chastity, and obedience, somehow got me through it. Behind Craig were the staff and students at the Australian Defence Force Academy, including Emeritus Professor Peter Dennis, Professor Jeffrey Grey, Professor David Lovell, Dr. John Connor, Dr. Eleanor

Hancock, Dr. Sinisa Marcic, Jo Muggleton, Marilyn Anderson-Smith, Shirley Ramsay, Bernadette McDermott, Derrill de Heer, and Kerry Neale. This book is a product of their guidance and a wonderful learning environment. Similarly, I would like to thank my co-supervisors, Professor Robin Prior of the University of Adelaide, and Nigel Steel of the Imperial War Museum, London, who humbled me with their expertise.

I also benefitted from words of wisdom and advice from many others, for which I am thankful. These included Associate Professor John McQuilton, Professor David Horner, Dr. John Blaxland, Professor Brian Holden-Reid, Dr. Jenny Macleod, Dr. John Moremon, Professor Gary Sheffield, Dr. John Bourne, Dr. Peter Stanley, Dr. Peter Pedersen, Dr. Edward Erickson, Professor Tim Travers, Dr. John Shephard, Dr. David Cameron, Peter Hart, Brigadier Chris Roberts, Ashley Ekins, Anne-Marie Condé, Meleah Ward, Kim Doyle, Lachlan Coleman, Dr. Jen Roberts, and the members of the YMMHA, Dr. Peter Dean, Dr. Karl James, Michael Molkentin, Aaron Pegram, and Tristan Moss. I would also like to thank my colleagues in the Strategic and Defence Studies Centre, School of International, Political and Strategic Studies, at The Australian National University, for their encouragement and support, and for making SDSC such a wonderful place to work.

In addition to thanking the staff of the various repositories in which I sat, tired-eyed, for the good part of two years, I would also like to thank the following for permission to quote material from their collections: the Australian War Memorial (who also provided the photographs); Churchill Archives Centre; the Trustees of the Liddell Hart Centre for Military Archives; Mrs. F. Oglander, for permission to quote from the papers of Cecil F. Aspinall-Oglander; the National Army Museum; and the Imperial War Museum.

I would like to thank Professor Gregory Urwin, Chuck Rankin, Emmy Ezzell, Emily Jerman, Amy Hernandez, Kelly Parker, and the rest of the staff at the University of Oklahoma Press for accepting a manuscript from the antipodes, and doing such a fantastic job to turn it into the product you see. Similarly, Jennifer Sheehan from Multimedia Services, ANU College of Asia and the Pacific, did a wonderful job with the maps.

I was also fortunate to be the recipient of a number of grants from the University of New South Wales. Special appreciation, however, is reserved for the Australian Army History Unit, whose generous grant enabled me to burrow away in the archives of the United Kingdom in 2008. Without this financial assistance the book could never have become a reality. Particular thanks must go to Roger Lee, Dr. Andrew Richardson, and Nick Anderson.

Despite the funding made available, this book would also have failed without the generosity and support of two absolute gems, Fred and Joyce Carr. They opened their home to a stranger, young enough to be their grandson, with open arms. They gave me a home, fed me, took me for a pint when necessary, and gave me that support I required when away from family and friends for six months. I am forever in their debt, and they will forever be in my heart.

Lastly, I would like to thank my friends and family (you know who you are), who constantly remind me that there is much more to life (and indeed, more to conversation) than military history and the Gallipoli Campaign. Mum, Dad, and Lachlan—I could not ask for a more supportive family. Final appreciation, however, is reserved for my wife, Jen. This book, which she proofread, lived with, supported, and accepted, is as much hers as it is mine. It is for these, and many other reasons, that I dedicate this book to her.

Abbreviations

AA&QMG	Assistant Adjutant and Quartermaster General
ALH	Australian Light Horse
ANZAC	Australian and New Zealand Army Corps
AQMG	Assistant Quartermaster General
Bde.	Brigade
BEF	British Expeditionary Force
BGRA	Brigadier-General, Royal Artillery
BLC	breech-loading, converted
Bn.	Battalion
CCS	casualty clearing station
CGS	Chief of the General Staff
CID	Committee of Imperial Defence
CIGS	Chief of the Imperial General Staff, War Office
CO	commanding officer
CRA	Commander, Royal Artillery
DA&QMG	Deputy Adjutant and Quartermaster General
DAG	Deputy Adjutant General
Div.	Division
DMS	Director of Medical Services
DQMG	Deputy Quartermaster General
DST	Director of Supplies and Transport
EMS	Eastern Mediterranean Squadron
FAB	Field Artillery Brigade
FOO	forward observation officer
FSR	*Field Service Regulations*
GHQ	General Headquarters
GOC	General Officer Commanding
HMS	His Majesty's Ship
HMT	His Majesty's Transport
HQ	headquarters
HTO	Hospital Transport Officer
IGC	Inspector General of Communications

IMA	Indian Mountain Artillery
L-of-C	lines of communication
MEF	Mediterranean Expeditionary Force
MR Regt.	Mounted Rifles Regiment
NZ&A Div.	New Zealand and Australian Division
NZMR Bde.	New Zealand Mounted Rifles Brigade
PBM	Principal Beach Master
PDMS	Principal Director of Medical Services
PMLO	Principal Military Landing Officer
PNTO	Principal Naval Transport Officer
QMG	Quartermaster General
RANBT	Royal Australian Naval Bridging Train
Regt.	Regiment
RFA	Royal Field Artillery
RGA	Royal Garrison Artillery
RNAS	Royal Naval Air Service
SAA	small arms ammunition
SNO	senior naval officer
STO	Superintending Transport Officer

Climax at Gallipoli

Introduction

The opening stages of the First World War did not unfold as either side had envisaged. Both sides' failed flanking maneuvers during the "Race to the Sea" (September–October 1914) and the subsequent fighting during the first battle of Ypres (October–November 1914) resulted in the cessation of mobile warfare across the Western Front. Maneuver was replaced by deadlock and stalemate. The British Expeditionary Force (BEF), a relatively small army by comparison to those of its major ally, France, and its principal enemy, Germany, found itself in the uncomfortable position of fighting a prolonged, continental land war—the antithesis of Britain's long-standing strategic preference, which, like all the major combatants of this war in its early years, stressed the importance of the decisive attack.

In 1915, a year characterized by failed offensives on the Western Front, the BEF attempted to rebuild and adapt to this new form of static warfare. Efforts were made to reintroduce tactical mobility, but neither side could find a solution to the overall problem of the trenches. The massing of British artillery at the Battle of Neuve Chapelle (March 1915), for example, could not break the impasse, nor could the use of chlorine gas by the Germans at the second battle of Ypres (April–May 1915).[1] Perhaps, at least according to some influential voices in Whitehall, the most vocal of whom was First Lord of the Admiralty Winston Churchill, the answer lay elsewhere.

The concept of the Royal Navy forcing the Dardanelles and proceeding to the Ottoman capital of Constantinople (modern-day Istanbul) was, in itself, not a novel idea. It had been debated within British political and naval circles since the early nineteenth century, but the operation was generally discounted as being too perilous.[2] Following an appeal from the commander in chief of the Russian army, Grand Duke Nicholas, on 2 January 1915, however, the British government decided to accept the risk. A naval operation against the Ottoman Empire was ordered to alleviate some of the strain being placed on Russia.[3] A fleet consisting of old surplus warships would attempt to methodically destroy the Ottoman defenses of the Dardanelles and then proceed to Constantinople.[4] This, it

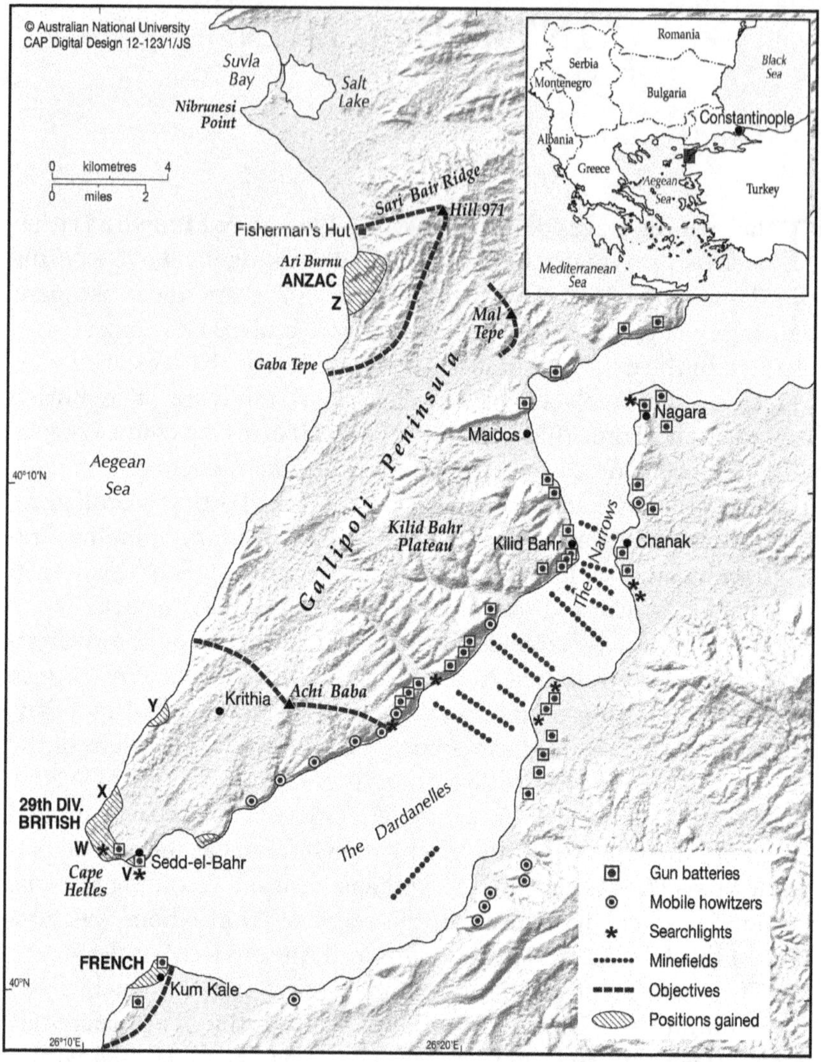

4 CLIMAX AT GALLIPOLI

Map 1. The Dardanelles defenses and 25 April objectives

was hoped, would remove the Ottoman Empire from the war, thus opening a much-needed logistic route to Russia (for imports and exports), as well the possibility of acquiring new allies in the Balkans, and securing British interests in the East. At the very least, the Committee of Imperial Defence (CID) in London, which was responsible for defense planning and strategic advice, thought that

Allied occupation of Constantinople could be used—when discussing peace—as a bargain against German gains on the Continent.[5]

Prelude to the August Offensive

The Dardanelles Campaign commenced with an Allied naval bombardment of the outer forts of the Dardanelles defenses at 9:51 A.M. on 19 February 1915. By 5:30 P.M., when the firing ceased, little had been accomplished, but there remained a confidence that the navy would ultimately be victorious.[6]

Over the next month attempts were made to silence the outer, intermediate, and inner defenses of the Dardanelles through a series of naval bombardments, all of which failed in achieving the overall objective of enabling the fleet a safe passage into the Sea of Marmara.[7] It was soon made clear to the British naval command, however, that long-range naval fire was inaccurate, especially when combined with the inadequate aerial spotting, which was not able to precisely report the fall of shot. Further, the Ottoman mobile howitzers and searchlights hindered operations against the intermediate and inner defenses, including the clearing of the minefields. Demolition parties were landed on both shores of the Dardanelles throughout this period to combat the threat but were met with stiff opposition and made minimal impact. The naval attempt to force the Dardanelles culminated on 18 March, with the loss or destruction of six Allied warships during the failed attack on the Narrows.[8] Concerned that the operation was beyond the means of the navy, Vice-Admiral John de Robeck—who had recently been appointed commander of the Eastern Mediterranean Squadron (EMS)—decided to abandon any further single-service attempts, and to prepare for a combined operation with the army.[9] General Sir Ian Hamilton, described by the German General Staff at the time as the world's most experienced soldier, had arrived in the theater just days beforehand as general officer commanding (GOC), Mediterranean Expeditionary Force (MEF), and, after witnessing the failure of 18 March from on board HMS *Queen Elizabeth*, agreed that the army was required to land on the Gallipoli Peninsula to assist the navy.[10]

The subsequent land campaign, known as the Gallipoli Campaign, commenced at dawn on 25 April 1915. The Australian and New Zealand Army Corps (ANZAC), commanded by Lieutenant-General

Sir William Birdwood, landed on and around the small point of Ari Burnu (subsequently known as Anzac Cove).[11] Birdwood's force, consisting of two infantry divisions, was given the task of holding the enemy within its vicinity from moving south to reinforce against the main thrust of the British landing at Cape Helles. To achieve this, the ANZAC was to secure the precipitous hills that fronted it and thence press on across the peninsula to Mal Tepe, thereby splitting Ottoman defensive capabilities and severing Ottoman supply routes, which ran down the peninsula to Helles.[12]

Shortly after dawn, the British 29th Division, commanded by Major-General Aylmer Hunter-Weston—who had previously commanded the 11th Brigade on the Aisne and was known to all as an aggressive officer, or "thruster"—began landing at five separate beaches surrounding Cape Helles (code named S, V, W, X, Y).[13] Despite being a smaller force than Birdwood's, it was Hunter-Weston's regular army division—albeit with no experience fighting as a formation—that was assigned the main objective: to seize the height of Achi Baba, which overlooked the entire area, and to push forward to the Kilid Bahr Plateau, thereby securing the tip of the Gallipoli Peninsula for future combined operations with the navy.[14]

At the same time as the British were pouring ashore, the 6th Colonial Regiment (consisting of one Colonial and two Senegalese battalions) of the 1st French Division commenced its landing at Kum Kale on the Asiatic coast of the Dardanelles. Although successful in achieving its objective, during which the regiment captured five hundred prisoners, this landing was merely a feint to draw attention away from the 29th Division and ensure that the Ottoman command did not send all its forces across the Narrows to meet the British attack. Having succeeded, the French were withdrawn from Kum Kale the following morning and placed alongside the British on its right flank, where they would operate for the remainder of the campaign. By the end of April, the ANZAC had secured a half-mile beachhead, known as the Anzac sector, and the British and French had advanced approximately two miles, securing the tip of the Gallipoli Peninsula.[15] None of the initial main objectives were achieved.

May 1915 was a period of consolidation and defense in the Anzac sector. On 19 May the Ottomans launched their first major counteroffensive but were defeated with heavy losses. The stench and health implications of up to three thousand rotting Ottoman corpses lying in no-man's-land led to an armistice on 24 May—where, in addition to burying their dead, both sides used the truce as a useful intelligence-gathering opportunity.[16] At Cape Helles, British and French troops remained on the offensive, striving to reach their first-day objective, Achi Baba (a target that remained elusive throughout the entire campaign). The most notable action in this period was the second battle of Krithia (6–8 May) in which an advance was made by British and dominion forces over open ground during daylight. Gains were minimal and casualties high.[17] Meanwhile, a new menace appeared; on 25 May a German U-boat sank HMS *Triumph*, followed by HMS *Majestic* two days later.[18]

Despite some Allied advances during the third battle of Krithia, June and July were, to all intents and purposes, a stalemate. Life in the trenches was monotonous. At Anzac, much work was done to extend the trench lines to the south, while at Helles, the period was categorized by marginally successful, if unambitious "bite and hold" tactics.[19] Meanwhile, satisfied by reports that there was a possibility of turning the enemy's right flank and reintroducing mobility to the battlefield, General Hamilton shifted his focus from the Helles to the Anzac sector. The result was the August Offensive. It is this offensive, which failed and was the last major offensive action before the evacuation of the peninsula in December 1915–January 1916, that is the focal point of this book.

Historical Bias and Mythology

The August Offensive was, and continues to be, considered the defining moment of the Gallipoli Campaign. Writing to his naval counterpart on the eve of battle, General Hamilton referred to the offensive as "our second great adventure": the MEF's second—and largest—attempt to advance across the Gallipoli Peninsula.[20] Similarly, the Australian official historian of the First World War, Charles Bean, described the offensive as "the greatest effort of the campaign" and "the climax in Gallipoli."[21] Not only was it "one of the greatest offensives of the war," but for the enemy it also represented "a glorious page in the history of the Turkish army."[22] The offensive's failure led to dramatic alterations in the political and strategic policies towards the Dardanelles, including the recall of General Hamilton and the eventual evacuation of the Gallipoli Peninsula. It is therefore critical that these battles are analyzed within their correct context—not as an example of Australian or New Zealand prowess, but as one of the many failed attempts by the Allies to break the deadlock during 1915.

Like most battles of the First World War, the historiography of the August Offensive is influenced or warped by various national mythologies.[23] Indeed, the Gallipoli Campaign is generally considered one of the greatest "what ifs" of the war, and the August Offensive has been described as a lost opportunity that nearly succeeded and only just failed because of some simple bad luck.[24] General Hamilton was the foremost proponent of this view. On 10 August 1915, Hamilton informed King George V's private secretary, Clive Wigram, that despite capturing trenches and guns and taking prisoners during the offensive, "the thought of how very near we were to carrying through a real decisive coup makes me feel as depressed as it is in my nature to be."[25] That the general underlined "very near" for added emphasis should not be discounted. Hamilton was already trying to salvage something positive from the utter failure that was the August Offensive, while also conveying the idea that his plan was a credible and sound operation of war. At least one member of the Dardanelles Committee realized this. At the committee's meeting on 19 August, Secretary of State for Colonies Andrew Bonar Law commented that Hamilton "was always *nearly* winning."[26] Others, representing all levels of command, and from both the army and navy, echoed Hamilton's troubled sentiment. By dwelling on the apparent near success and missed opportunity, such views ignore the inherent difficulties of the August Offensive and the fact that it never even approached success. The myth has permeated from such self-serving origins, where it was used to downplay the failure, into the subsequent historiography of the offensive.[27] This dominant interpretation is faulty.

While such myths generate public interest in the offensive, they also lead to a narrow and uncontested interpretation of the past.[28] In her deconstruction of mythology and the Australian soldier, historian Jane Ross contended that the mythmaker is concerned with presenting a particular representation of the truth.[29] This select view has certainly been the case for the August Offensive, where the genesis of the myth was often self-serving. The case of the author of the two British official histories of the Gallipoli Campaign, Cecil Aspinall-Oglander, is a prime example of this bias. As chief operations officer on Hamilton's staff at General Headquarters (GHQ), Aspinall

(Aspinall's name was hyphenated after he adopted his wife's maiden name in 1927) was responsible for planning the August Offensive and thus had a vested interest and his own agenda in writing about it. The underlying bias and drive to protect himself and his fellow staff officers from criticism pervade his account of the offensive, and deeply affected his objectivity. In shielding himself, Aspinall-Oglander, as author in the early 1930s, attributed the failure of the offensive to the inability of the commanders to carry out his plan, rather than the defects of the plan itself.[30] An example of this can be seen in his choice to deliberately omit evidence that contradicted his viewpoint and implicated his own plans as a reason for failure.

Meeting shortly after the failed offensive, a committee at the War Office reluctantly concluded that "the whole series of tasks planned for IX Corps [at Suvla Bay] is open to criticism," but without more information "we do not feel justified in suggesting such criticism."[31] While Aspinall-Oglander acknowledged this (the official view), he ignored the attached appreciation by Lieutenant-General Sir Archibald Murray, deputy chief of the imperial general staff (CIGS)—written at the request of the CIGS to give the committee's critical, but "unofficial" view—which confidently concluded that Suvla Bay was "not a thoroughly sound practical operation of war."[32] Until now, this appreciation, with its obvious criticism of GHQ's plan, has remained tucked away in Aspinall-Oglander's papers on the Isle of Wight. He saw it but chose not to use it.

Given Aspinall-Oglander's bias, and the subsequent focus by historians on the political, social, strategic, and tactical levels of the Gallipoli Campaign, there remains no balanced or thorough analytical study of the August Offensive at the operational level of war.[33] The term "operational level of war" refers to the area between tactics and strategy—the level where generals fight—and encompasses the planning, direction, and performance of the offensive.[34] As such, and despite bookshelves crammed with texts on Gallipoli, the August Offensive has still not received the same analysis accorded to other campaigns of the First World War, particularly those on the Western Front. Misunderstandings of this failed enterprise, therefore, remain deeply embedded in both the historiography and public consciousness.

By adopting a previously untried approach, issues such as planning, intelligence, command, mobility, fire support, joint operations, administration, and logistics come to the fore. The failure of any one of these aspects creates difficulties, and can singularly cause defeat.[35] What then are the chances of success if they all go awry, as was the case in August? Moreover, by analyzing the operational proficiency and capabilities of the MEF, and challenging some of the key historical myths surrounding the August Offensive, this book will answer and provide evidence for some previously unanswered questions. To what extent, for example, was the MEF actually able to embark on a large-scale offensive at Gallipoli in August 1915? Was success really possible? Or was the attempt futile, and another example of Britain's flawed offensive model of the decisive breakthrough? By answering these and other questions, this book provides the first detailed account not only of what occurred during the August Offensive but also of how and why events turned out as they did.

Layout

Given its focus on assessing the performance, potential, and capabilities of the MEF during the August Offensive, this book is structured thematically, with each major aspect of the operational level of war getting its own chapter. Unique among histories of the Gallipoli Campaign, this approach allows a more in-depth study of these important historical events than hitherto produced, and enables robust scrutiny and analysis.

Chapter 1 examines the evolution of the planning process. Its aim is to determine what form the plans took, what influenced them, what the operational objective was, and whether the plans were feasible. The second chapter examines the mobility of the MEF, bringing into focus the health and number of troops available, and the tasks required of them. It also focuses on command, communications, terrain, and the impact that all could, and did, have on the force's mobility during the offensive.

Chapter 3 looks at the Allied fire support available for the offensive. It begins by examining the role that the artillery played, with a particular focus on the number of guns and the amount of ammunition available. The chapter then moves to an examination of the technical capabilities of the artillery pieces available, and the level to which artillery observation—both land and air—impacted upon the accuracy of their fire. Comparisons to artillery preparations on the Western Front are a crucial element of this analysis.

Chapter 4 addresses another previously neglected aspect of the August Offensive: combined operations.[36] Key proponents examined include the role of the fleet in the new amphibious landing at Suvla Bay, naval gunfire support for the troops ashore, submarine warfare, and the relationship between the services, particularly the command relationship between Hamilton and de Robeck.

Chapter 5 is the first of two chapters dealing with logistics. It offers an introduction into the importance of logistics in war—an aspect that has been too often ignored in the historiography of the August Offensive. It then looks at the lines of communication and the administrative processes of acquiring supplies and transporting these from the UK to the beaches at Gallipoli. Following this, chapter 6 examines the disembarkation of these items at the various advanced bases, and the subsequent distribution of these to the units. This chapter concludes with a brief examination of the logistic elements of medical evacuation, and what, if any, impact this had on operations.

The seventh chapter is a narrative of the August Offensive. It brings together the aspects discussed in the previous chapters to show how they shaped, impacted, and contributed to the failure of the offensive. Unlike previous chapters, this one is structured chronologically; it is also more descriptive than analytical. This chapter can also be read as a prelude for those wanting an understanding of how the offensive unfolded, before delving into the more detailed chapters.

The final chapter deals directly with the incorrect assumption that the offensive "nearly succeeded." Its purpose is to analyze what would have been required had the Allies achieved any of their objectives and progressed across the Gallipoli Peninsula in accord with the subsequent phases of General Hamilton's operational objective. Topics discussed include whether the MEF was mobile enough and capable of advancing across the peninsula, against a determined enemy; whether the guns and their ammunition were suitable (in quantity, efficiency, and accuracy) and whether they could have been moved to support the offensive as it progressed; whether the navy was willing or able to launch offensive operations in August and therefore bring the offensive to a successful close; and whether sufficient supplies could be landed for a prolonged action and then transported to the troops as they fought for their next objective.

CHAPTER 1

PLANNING

Planning for the August Offensive was a long and complex process. At its conception, the plan was limited to strengthening the perimeter of the Anzac sector. This localized attack, however, ultimately developed into a breakout offensive, the aim of which was to "secure a position astride the Gallipoli Peninsula" and to defeat the Ottoman enemy on land.[1] This chapter focuses on the motives, conception, and evolution of the plans. How and why did a multiphase, large-scale offensive come into existence? What influenced the high command to change its mind and expand its ambitions? Was the plan, in its final form, asking too much? And in what ways did the planning process itself sow the seeds of failure?

The Situation in London

It is first necessary to understand the politico-military system (as it pertained to the Dardanelles) that operated in London. The two principal bodies concerned with operations were the War Office and the Admiralty, whose duty it was to ensure that the respective services were prepared for war. Each department contained advisory boards, the members of which were selected to give expert advice regarding the most appropriate methods to approach a particular situation. Importantly, the advice of these boards was often not sought—or was disregarded—by their departmental heads throughout the Dardanelles Campaign.

As secretary of state for war, and therefore responsible to Parliament for all business of the Army Council, Lord Kitchener regularly took matters into his own hands.[2] Although he met with the various departmental heads of the War Office every day (all of whom were members of the Army Council), formal meetings of the Army Council were infrequent and held in the main to record decisions already made.[3] Kitchener, who should have concerned himself solely with the political machinations of the War Office, often made operational decisions without consulting his subordinates.[4] According to the CIGS, Lieutenant-General Sir James Wolfe Murray (who was also on the Army Council), Kitchener too often usurped the proper roles and duties of his subordinates by acting more as commander in chief—a position that had actually been replaced by the formation of the Army Council—than as the political head of the War Office. Wolfe Murray noted that because of Kitchener's influence, the position of CIGS was much different in practice from what it should have been in theory, and what it had been in the past. Rather than consulting his military experts, Kitchener "acted very much as his own Chief of Staff," thus informally relegating his advisors to mere staffing roles.[5]

Similarly, Major-General Charles Callwell, the director of military operations (and intelligence), stated that the British General Staff was unable to undertake its proper duties due to Kitchener's personal influence and penchant for secrecy.[6] Indeed, Lord Haldane (secretary of state for war, 1905–1912) believed that Kitchener's domination of his departmental heads was a consequence of his "old school" view that a General Staff was not actually required—despite the powerful example set by the German equivalent in the second half of the nineteenth century. By shutting out his advisors, Kitchener ensured that his decisions were not thrashed about or debated.[7] The result was that the War Office and the Army Council "revolved around [Kitchener's] sense of priorities and whims," and operations, such as the August Offensive, were not subjected to the opinions and influence of the military's experts in London.[8]

It was a similar story at the Admiralty. The Board of the Admiralty (the naval equivalent of the Army Council) was responsible for naval administration.[9] The reluctance of First Lord of the Admiralty Winston Churchill to call meetings, however, resulted in the board falling largely into abeyance. As was the case at the War Office, a layer of secrecy consequently grew within the Admiralty. Without such meetings, the sea lords, who were responsible for strategic planning and various operational aspects, "were never informed of what was going on" and "basically knew nothing of the operations" beyond what they heard as rumor and gossip.[10] Again, this situation was largely the result of the personality of the departmental head.

In theory, Churchill required the agreement of the first sea lord (Admiral Sir John Fisher) and the chief of the naval staff

(Vice-Admiral Sir Henry Oliver) to make any decisions, but an order in council theoretically gave all control to the first lord of the admiralty.[11] Churchill used this control. Oliver, who should have been involved in all aspects of the decision making process, recalled: "I more or less carried out the instructions of the First Lord and the First Sea Lord."[12] Like Kitchener, Churchill dominated his department. Because of this, plans were not subject to widespread expert scrutiny, and, as a result, were too often uninformed and inadequate. The situation improved under Arthur Balfour, who replaced Churchill as first lord in May 1915, but it remained far from perfect.[13]

As noted, the War Office and the Admiralty were responsible solely for those matters affecting their particular service. If there was an overlap between departments, and a need for interservice cooperation—as was constantly the case in the Dardanelles theater—the departmental head was to consult the War Council.[14] This council of cabinet ministers, consisting of Herbert Asquith (prime minister), Lord Haldane (lord chancellor), Lord Kitchener, David Lloyd George (chancellor of the exchequer), Sir Edward Grey (secretary of state for foreign affairs), Churchill, and Lord Crewe (secretary of state for India), with Lieutenant-Colonel Maurice Hankey as secretary, met on an ad hoc and informal basis to discuss the conduct of the war.[15] The War Council relied entirely on information from the various departments, and after examining this information, conveyed its decisions directly to the head of the relevant department, leaving that particular department to work out the details.[16]

Due to the unhealthy reliance on predigested but underscrutinized departmental evidence and, as has previously been discussed, a reluctance of the experts to contradict the heads of their department, the War Council too was, to all intents and purposes, run by Kitchener and Churchill. Wolfe Murray, who attended as a military expert, *never* expressed his opinion "as Kitchener was the War Office spokesman," while First Sea Lord Fisher recalled that it was primarily the politicians who spoke at meetings, while the soldiers and sailors remained "almost invariably mute."[17] Despite the lack of expert advice proffered to it, the War Council was fundamental in determining what direction the war in the Dardanelles would take, particularly with regard to reinforcements.[18]

After the failure of the April landings at Gallipoli to achieve their objectives, the War Council was left considering its options: should Britain continue with, or abandon, its commitment to the

Dardanelles theater?[19] At a council meeting on 14 May 1915, less than three weeks after the campaign started, Kitchener spoke of his doubts as to whether strategic success was possible, commenting that the Ottomans could not be driven from their positions on the peninsula. He remained, however, opposed to an evacuation, believing that the only way for the British to free themselves from the Dardanelles was to push on. The contradiction seemed lost on him. Lloyd George agreed with Kitchener but cautioned that the same mistake of underestimating the enemy must not be made again. He therefore requested that the council "examine the whole situation and see what we could reasonably expect to accomplish." Any decision, Lloyd George continued, as to whether the force be withdrawn, maintained at its present level, or reinforced in order to end the business, should be based on an appreciation of what force was required to ensure success. Kitchener agreed to ask Hamilton.[20] Hamilton's answer was four more divisions.[21]

Resignation, Reinforcements, and a New Committee

The following day (15 May) Admiral Fisher—who disagreed with Churchill's methods and was opposed to a continuation of the Gallipoli Campaign—resigned from his post as first sea lord.[22] Fisher's resignation, combined with the "shell crisis" on the Western Front, forced Prime Minister Asquith to form a coalition government. During the reshuffle, Balfour replaced Churchill as first lord of the admiralty, and the War Council was dissolved and replaced with the aptly named Dardanelles Committee.[23] Upon receiving news of this change, General Hamilton wrote to Churchill for the first time since 12 March. Knowing that Churchill maintained his position on the committee, and that he would continue to advocate for an increased effort in the Dardanelles, Hamilton, with a clear and understandable agenda, wrote: "Certainly there are enormous difficulties. Here we are, after all, only an expeditionary force, though a strong one, fairly lodged within easy striking distance of the enemy's Capital and head-power. This enemy, though much fallen away from his high state, is still a great empire on a continental scale possessing vast resources. Hence our troops have had to contest against three successive armies. As soon as one lot are defeated they are reinforced.... Still, by putting a bold face on it and pushing forward whenever we can, we are advancing slowly not withstanding all these fresh reinforcements received by the enemy."[24]

The Dardanelles Committee convened for the first time on 7 June 1915. Despite its title, the Dardanelles theater was never the committee's sole focus, but given the necessity of interservice action in the theater, it remained a high priority. Having received Hamilton's projection that four additional divisions would be required to see the campaign through to success, the committee discussed whether such a reinforcement was possible. The nine members present (three were absent) decided to send three New Army divisions and additional naval units that would be less vulnerable to submarine attack. Kitchener, who just two weeks previously had opposed troop number increases in the Dardanelles, now gave his full support.[25] Churchill's persistence was no doubt a key factor in Kitchener's reversal.[26]

The committee's overall motivations for increased support to the Gallipoli Campaign were varied. High on the list was the fact that the BEF on the Western Front had to remain on the defensive until sufficient ammunition could be stockpiled to allow for a renewed offensive in Flanders.[27] Resources could therefore be diverted, for the time being, to the Dardanelles. The feeling of frustration caused by the inability of the MEF to break through the Ottoman lines cannot be discounted, nor can the enthusiasm of the Dominions, especially Australia and New Zealand, who were raising new divisions for service.[28] There was also the standing belief that evacuation or defeat in the Dardanelles would damage British prestige and interests in the East.[29]

The British War Cabinet met on 18 June to discuss this offer of further reinforcements. It was initially concerned that such reinforcements would mean a large increase in the scale of operations at the Dardanelles but was soothed by talk that the additional forces would be used in a "starving" rather than "storming" operation.[30] This was untrue. Any advance across the Gallipoli Peninsula necessitated storming before starving the enemy by cutting their supply routes.[31] As shown throughout the remainder of this chapter, the politico-military system in London had a direct and significant impact on the progression of the August plans from a tactical attack designed to improve the security of the Anzac sector into a large-scale offensive operation.

Intelligence and Its Use in Operational Planning

Another issue that requires examination before discussing the evolution of the August plans in a direct way is the means by which intelligence was gathered in the Dardanelles. The value of intelligence in this war was clear to all, especially General Joseph Joffre, commander in chief of the French army on the Western Front, who noted that adequate intelligence enabled senior officers to determine the obstacles to an attack, how they should be dealt with, and by whom.[32] The importance of intelligence was not lost on the decision makers in London, where both the War Office and the Admiralty had their own intelligence branches. The War Office's foreign intelligence department, MO2, fell under the realm of the directorate of military operations and its head, Major-General Callwell. The Admiralty's intelligence service reported to the director of the intelligence division, Captain William "Blinker" Hall.[33] These branches focused on strategic intelligence, whereby, through the use of attachés, consuls, foreign diplomats, agents, code breakers, and the foreign press, they constructed a picture of the war within its wider political context.[34] With regard to the Dardanelles, these intelligence branches' principal focus was on the attitude of the Balkan States, particularly Bulgaria, and the political situation in Constantinople. The War Office and Admiralty then passed this information on to the intelligence branches of the MEF and the EMS respectively. There was precious little collation and cooperation between the War Office and Admiralty, with the MEF and EMS receiving separate, and often conflicting, intelligence.[35]

The intelligence branches at the Dardanelles added to the strategic-level information they were provided by analyzing, interpreting, and evaluating their own information gained through the use of reconnaissance (air, naval, and land), enemy documents (found or captured), and enemy interrogation (deserters, prisoners, and the local population), in order to create an operational and tactical picture of the enemy's defenses, order of battle, supply routes, and morale.[36] This information was then used in the development of operational plans.[37]

Reconnaissance in the Dardanelles theater, however, was hindered not only by the technical, physical, and atmospheric constraints that beset all fronts in 1915 but also by the nature of the terrain on the peninsula itself. The air service, which was portrayed in *Field Service Regulations* as a subsidiary of the cavalry for reconnaissance purposes, was still in its infancy in 1915.[38] While aerial photography for mapping purposes was being developed at the Dardanelles, the poor quality of the photographs, and a lack of people with experience in interpreting the images taken, rendered the product unreliable at best. Cameras were, for example, fixed to the side of the aircraft, and because they were not truly vertical at the moment the image was taken, the exact scale of the photograph was always difficult to determine. Importantly, terrain appeared much flatter from the air, thus reducing the perceived size and significance of gullies and ridges. Scrapes in the ground, for instance, were often read as enemy trenches.[39] There is no doubt that aerial photography had improved by August 1915, but it was still not without its problems. It is also noteworthy that aerial reconnaissance was only one of the duties of the Royal Naval Air Service (RNAS), which was always stretched for resources in the Dardanelles theater.

The main impact of the RNAS on the development of the operational plans for August was its reconnaissance patrol missions. Through such flights the RNAS was able to provide information to the army and navy on enemy troop movements; transportation of Ottoman supplies (both land and sea); and the whereabouts of enemy camps, bivouacs, and artillery positions.[40] Again, however, technological and atmospheric conditions hindered operations. The seaplanes of the RNAS did not have the engine capacity to fly high enough to avoid the enemy's antiaircraft and machine-gun fire, and were therefore of very limited utility as reconnaissance machines.[41] The airplanes, which could reach a higher altitude than the seaplanes, were few in number and only reliable for short-range reconnaissance patrols in fair weather. They too, therefore, could only provide limited information.[42] Brigadier-General Hamilton Reed, chief of staff to IX Corps, for example, was as a consequence always skeptical about the reliability of aerial intelligence. Based on his experience on the Western Front, Reed noted that it was difficult for pilots and observers to report findings accurately, especially if the enemy remained stationary, or if enemy guns were well concealed and did not fire.[43] The usefulness of aerial reconnaissance was further limited by the constant need for secrecy. Flights had to be made at extremely high altitudes to avoid arousing Ottoman suspicion as to where an attack might be mounted.[44] This obviously added to reconnaissance difficulties. Indeed, frequent aerial reconnaissance was forbidden over Suvla Bay prior to the August Offensive for this very reason.[45] Such limitations, whether due to technology or the need for secrecy, directly impacted upon the quality of aerial reconnaissance, and as will become clearer later in the chapter, in turn significantly influenced the evolution of the August plans from the tactical to the operational level.

For its part, the navy relied on the RNAS for much of its intelligence. RNAS flights informed the EMS of any alterations or increases in the armaments of the Ottoman forts along the Dardanelles. Additionally, the RNAS searched for enemy howitzers and guns that could be used against the ships and minesweepers, as well as for the presence of enemy submarines. In order to aid the passage of friendly submarines through the Dardanelles, the RNAS kept watch on Ottoman submarine defenses at Nagara (above the Narrows).[46] Furthermore, Allied naval forces carried out reconnaissance patrols in the theater, with a particularly keen eye for enemy submarines and foreign ships carrying contraband. In addition, and in line with the *Manual of Combined Naval and Military Operations*, the navy reconnoitered the coastline to determine potential anchorages and harbors for transports and warships, as well as highlighting appropriate landing places for future amphibious operations.[47]

The EMS was also crucial for reconnaissance from the sea. Prior to the August Offensive, ships were used as a principal means of surveying the topography north of the Anzac sector. While this gave military planners and commanders a feel for the terrain in which they would operate, this method of reconnaissance limited the knowledge of the terrain to what could actually be seen from on board the ship. What lay beyond the Sari Bair Ridge, for example, could only be understood through aerial reconnaissance and was therefore still largely unknown when the August Offensive was launched. Like the RNAS, the navy was required to maintain a high level of secrecy surrounding the August operations, and thus reconnaissance of the coast was undertaken infrequently and at long distances.

For land commanders at Gallipoli, the importance of reconnaissance was made clear in *Field Service Regulations*. Officers were reminded (in bold font) that "time spent in reconnaissance is seldom wasted." Good reconnaissance would enable surprise, and each commander was also warned that he should never commit a formation or unit "to an engagement until he has made a personal survey of the ground before him." While somewhat outdated in that it expected the commanders to carry out their own reconnaissance personally, the message was clear: reconnaissance was an essential element of the planning process. However, due to the difficulty of the terrain and the close proximity of the enemy on the Gallipoli Peninsula, where reconnaissance patrols could not survey the ground beyond the enemy's defenses, land reconnaissance was only ever useful for tactical intelligence. These patrols, usually consisting of an officer, numerous scouts, and an interpreter, would survey the land to determine the topographical features of the country and the movements and disposition of the enemy.[48] Their reports were then sent to the various headquarters and used in formulating tactical plans of attack. This was the primary method of land intelligence gathering at Gallipoli. Such patrols throughout May, June, and July, and their resultant reports, greatly influenced the plan of operations for the August Offensive.

The final source of intelligence available to Allied planners in the Dardanelles was the enemy. Prisoners, defectors, dead bodies, and Ottoman documents provided useful information concerning the enemy's disposition, strength, and morale. While these sources may on occasion have presented new information, their value was often more in confirming or refuting preexisting intelligence pictures. Such high importance was placed on this source of information that by late July 1915 there were eleven officers and forty-seven native interpreters attached to the MEF, whose sole duties were concerned with gathering intelligence from enemy sources.[49] After being captured (or voluntarily capitulating), Ottoman prisoners were escorted to an area selected by divisional headquarters, allocated a serial number, and interrogated by an officer and his interpreter. If the prisoner was wounded, he was interrogated at the hospital.[50] Interrogators, who were issued with a set of standard questions to ask prisoners, were encouraged to provide the prisoners with a meal and a cigarette to calm their nerves, thus increasing the reliability of the information provided.[51]

A daily summary of prisoners captured (and their regiments) was forwarded to corps headquarters, who then passed it on to the deputy adjutant general (DAG) at GHQ.[52] The usefulness of information received from the enemy generally depended on the soldier's rank. Noncommissioned officers (NCOs) were considered the best sources of information, as they were better informed than the soldiers and, unlike commissioned officers, often did not object to sharing what they knew. Answers were uniform at times, particularly with regard to supplies and ammunition, but it was believed that prisoners rarely supplied false information with the deliberate intent to mislead.[53] To the contrary, captured soldiers were deemed a rich and plentiful source of information. From the commencement of operations at Gallipoli in April until the end of July, a total of 2,376 Ottoman prisoners were captured.[54] A further 702 were captured between 6 and 14 August.[55]

Enemy documents were also useful for intelligence purposes. There were six types of documents that Allied intelligence gatherers expected to find: copies of orders; diaries and notebooks; field reports and memorandums; maps and plans; private letters; and military certificates. Of these, field reports and memorandums were the only sources that were examined as soon as they were discovered. This was done to ascertain whether there was anything of immediate military value to the Allies. When found, every Ottoman document was first sent to a native interpreter, who, under the supervision of his officer or the first-class interpreter attached to the division, translated the headings, dates, first few lines, and signature of the document. Documents were then sorted according to their level of importance.[56] Any urgent information was forwarded to GHQ by telegram.[57] Those marked as "immediate importance" were translated in more detail. The others, with the exception of those marked "of personal value to the prisoner"—which were sent directly to GHQ—were sent to the various corps headquarters, along with a daily intelligence summary.[58]

The picture constructed from all sources of intelligence was crucial to the development of the August Offensive. However, the credibility of the information gained and accepted was, at times, distorted. Prior to the August Offensive, two themes were common. The first (and correct) was that the enemy's right flank was open and vulnerable to a sweeping maneuver from the Anzac sector. As will be seen, this was the original opportunity that motivated the entire conception of the offensive. The second (and incorrect) theme was that the enemy were weak, demoralized, short on supplies, and about to crumble.[59] On 6 July, for example, GHQ informed VIII Corps that information from a "reliable source" stated that the enemy were "disheartened," and would surrender en masse if guaranteed proper treatment.[60] Major-General Granville Egerton, GOC

52nd (Lowland) Division commented on this line of thought, noting that from the beginning of the Gallipoli Campaign, the staff at GHQ "have been obsessed by one idea, that the Turk was near the end of his tether and that we had only to push, push, push, and he would collapse suddenly. Thus our continual costly bites into his granite wall. They wanted to believe all this, and on this they have gone from the start; but bar diminution of R[oyal] A[rtillery] fire, I see no sign of any weakening on the part of the Moslem; on the contrary . . . I seriously fear that they [GHQ staff] have fallen into the same error again, in these operations to the North [Sari Bair and Suvla] and have attacked with inadequate forces."[61] The naval chief of staff in the Dardanelles theater, Commodore Roger Keyes, concurred, and deplored the obsession with an "apparent" low level of enemy morale. Shortly after the failure of the August Offensive, Keyes wrote to Vice-Admiral de Robeck: "How far the Military reckoned on the reported loss of morale by the Turks is hard to say, but the result of the fighting has shown that the Turk is still full of fight."[62] As unrealistic as the intelligence picture may have been, understanding it is crucial for an examination of the planning process.

The Appeal of a Large-Scale Offensive

Those responsible for planning the August Offensive were experienced, intelligent men. Their previous appointments had established them as competent military professionals. Both Birdwood and Hamilton, who lay at the center of the development of the August plans (at the tactical and operational levels respectively), had proven their capabilities in the Boer War. Surely such men realized that up to August all attempts to break through the enemy's defensive lines at Gallipoli had failed, and while they no doubt viewed their Ottoman enemy as racially inferior, there can be no doubt that they respected the enemy's tenacity, bravery, and ability to defend against frontal attacks.[63] How did these Allied generals, then, expect to succeed?

The fact was that the combined picture of a weak enemy with an exposed right flank greatly appealed to the Allied command at the Dardanelles. The continual failure to break through the enemy's defensive positions by way of frontal assaults had reaffirmed to Hamilton and Birdwood the fruitlessness of this type of attritional warfare.[64] Such a stalemate was an uncomfortable and relatively recent phenomenon for these men. They had been conditioned throughout their careers to strive for maneuver and the decisive battle—both of which were seen as crucial to success. Such Clausewitzian themes were deeply embedded as an institutional belief within the British Army, and carried into the First World War.[65] *Field Service Regulations*, for example, stressed that "decisive success in battle can be gained only by a vigorous offensive."[66] When confronted with the reality of a positional war of attrition, both Hamilton and Birdwood reverted to the comforting notion of a decisive battle through maneuver as a means by which to escape the morass of the trenches. They were not alone.

On the Western Front, the initial success at Neuve Chapelle, for instance, had also reaffirmed the British belief in the decisive victory.[67] In 1916 General Sir Douglas Haig adopted this basic principle for the Battle of the Somme, whereby he hoped to break through the German defenses and restore maneuver and mobility to the battlefield.[68] "Open warfare," as espoused in *Field Service Regulations*, always remained the goal.[69] The transformation to static warfare in 1914 was abrupt.[70] In 1915, the commanders at the Dardanelles, like those on the Western Front, were still attempting—although unsuccessfully—to adapt.[71] For Hamilton and Birdwood, news that the enemy's flank was open offered a tantalizing opportunity for a return to a comfortable mode of thought and action. Maneuver, it was felt, would allow them to bypass the enemy's strongpoints and—by way of surprise, deception, and speed—attack Ottoman weakness and envelop and defeat their adversary.[72] However, again like their counterparts on the Western Front, these men did not yet realize that current technology and tactics were insufficient to break the impasse. Indeed, it was not until the advances of the Hundred Days Offensive in 1918 that the British Army was in a position to force a return to mobile warfare.[73] However, 1918 was a world away from the realities of 1915.

In addition to their enduring belief in the power of the maneuver, the Allied commanders at Gallipoli remained convinced that their force was structurally, physically, and morally stronger than their foe. This basic assumption underpinned the very reason for an offensive in August. By attacking the enemy's right flank, Hamilton believed that he would force the Ottomans from the protection of their trenches, after which they would be easily defeated. He expressed this in a letter to Field Marshal Sir John French, commander in chief of the BEF:

> In a manoeuvre battle of old style our fellow here would beat twice their number of Turks in less than no time but, actually, the restricted peninsula suits the Turkish tactics to a "T." They have always been good at trench work where their stupid men have only simple straightforward duties to perform, namely to stick on and shoot anything that comes up to them. They do this to perfection; I never saw braver soldiers in fact than some of the best of them. When we advance, no matter the shelling we give them, they stand right up firing coolly and straight over their parapets. Also they have unlimited supplies of bombs, each soldier carrying them, and they are not half bad at throwing them.[74]

For Hamilton, the "wish to fight and [the] will to win are the surest victory getters in the pack."[75] In his opinion, war would be won by the stronger race, not necessarily the stronger army.[76]

There was, in addition, one last reason for an offensive. Beyond his belief in the possibility of ultimate victory, Hamilton recognized the importance of maintaining morale among his own force. The August Offensive was, to some measure, a means of avoiding a defensive spirit and a subsequent decrease in morale.[77] For Hamilton, an offensive spirit was crucial to the fighting capability of his force. Keeping his men idle, Hamilton believed, would lead to depression, sickness, and discouragement and at the same time would boost Ottoman spirits.[78] It was this desire to maintain a high level of morale, combined with the attractive possibility of victory through maneuver, that led the Allied command at the Dardanelles to embark on a large-scale offensive in August 1915.

The Origins of the August Offensive

With insight into the assumptions and thought processes of senior British commanders, the chapter now turns to the evolution of the plans themselves. How did the scheme for the August Offensive alter and adapt to the political situation, the intelligence gathered, and the will of the commanders?

Within days of failing to achieve its initial objective in April, the ANZAC was locked into trench warfare. Yet its commanders remained firmly set on a return to maneuver warfare, and they looked for ways to reintroduce mobility. On 3 May 1915, just eight days after the initial landing, Rear-Admiral Cecil Thursby (commander,

No. 2 Squadron, EMS) wrote to Lieutenant-General Birdwood stressing the importance of occupying the Sari Bair Ridge. Such a position, he reminded Birdwood, would, with naval gunfire support, enable an advance across the peninsula to Mal Tepe.[79] The significance of this was not lost on Birdwood or his staff. They had already detailed one raiding party—the previous morning—to land at Nibrunesi Point (the southern point of Suvla Bay) and reconnoiter the ANZAC left flank, and would the following day land another party on their right flank, just north of Gaba Tepe.[80] Both raids met with enemy resistance, but the raid on Nibrunesi Point highlighted the relative dearth of enemy troops to the north of the Anzac sector.

By 13 May, Birdwood's headquarters (HQ) had received enough tactical information to draw and hold its attention to the north. A report from a Greek deserter stated that while enemy patrols watched the area north of the Anzac sector and reported (by telephone) any Allied movements to Ottoman headquarters at Maidos and Gallibolu (the village from which the peninsula got its name), there was no strong Ottoman presence between the Anzac sector and Taifur Keui.[81] Birdwood, who now increasingly believed that the enemy's flank was exposed, wrote to Hamilton, requesting that the 29th Indian Brigade be sent to Anzac. Birdwood wanted to improve the position held by his force: "I feel I want more troops to get into a better position than I now occupy, as what I hold is by no means satisfactory on the lower slopes of this big hill. I am absolutely blind where I am, as it is impossible to scout through this thick scrub—the seaplanes can never give me any movements of troops in this scrub, and I am overlooked all round. We have necessarily had to sit tight all this time, as we have not been strong enough to advance, and I have only been able to consolidate myself and dig in.[82]

It had been less than three weeks since the initial landings, and Birdwood had already begun to understand that he could not break through the multiple lines of trenches that confronted his position. The only area free of the enemy's control was Birdwood's extreme left flank. He therefore proposed, with the 29th Indian Brigade, to "make a sweeping movement round my left" toward Biyuk Anafarta (east of Suvla Bay) and take Hill 971 and the Sari Bair Ridge. With this, Birdwood stated, "I should feel in a satisfactory position, as I should overlook the whole of the valley towards the Straits." Such a task, he admitted, would be difficult and perhaps beyond the capabilities of his force. The enemy would counterattack in strength, and Allied troops on the Sari Bair Ridge would be subject to heavy fire from the Straits. Even if the position could not be retained, Birdwood noted that he would be content with removing some of the enemy's guns near Hill Q and southeast of Chunuk Bair.[83] The aim, after all, was to improve the security of the Anzac sector.

Such a movement to the north, however, did not initially appeal to GHQ because it contradicted the initial instructions (from April) to push across the peninsula south of the Anzac sector, from Gaba Tepe. On the copy of Birdwood's 13 May letter retained by GHQ, a staff officer wrote, "Why left [i.e., north]? Right [i.e., south] is the way we want him to go."[84] Birdwood understood the importance of cutting the enemy's communications to the south, but also realized, from the failed raid at Gaba Tepe on 4 May, that the Ottomans were too strong in this direction. He therefore proposed, as an aside, that if it were possible, a large force should be landed secretly at Anzac Cove and placed in a position to cover Kilia Liman (the Bay north of Maidos). Birdwood did not specify the locality of this position but mentioned that if heavy guns could be emplaced there, the enemy's land and possibly sea communications would be severed. This would, however, necessitate the use of a searchlight for spotting, which he admitted "would be a great target to the enemy's guns."[85]

Meanwhile, Birdwood's subordinate commanders were also thinking about the next move. On 14 May, Lieutenant-Colonel William Malone, commanding officer (CO) of the Wellington Infantry Battalion, discussed his ideas for a future offensive with Major-General Archibald Paris, GOC of the Royal Naval Division. Much like Birdwood's proposal, rather than continuing with costly frontal attacks, Malone proposed to strengthen the Anzac position and maneuver around the enemy's right flank, attacking Hill 971 from Nibrunesi Point.[86] While the conception of an attack on the Sari Bair Ridge may be attributed to Birdwood and his staff (especially his chief of staff, Lieutenant-Colonel Andrew Skeen, whom Hamilton described as "the father of the Anzac idea"), Birdwood's opinion was no doubt influenced by conversations with and among subordinates like Malone.[87]

At 5:00 A.M. on 15 May 1915, without the knowledge of ANZAC headquarters, Major Percy Overton and Corporal John Denton of the Canterbury Mounted Rifles commenced a reconnaissance patrol of the country north of the Anzac sector. Overton, who was second in command of his unit, had earned his reputation as a scout during the Boer War. Leaving No. 1 Outpost, they traveled up the Sazli Beit Dere and along the lower slopes of Rhododendron Ridge. By 1:00 P.M. Overton's patrol had arrived at an area near what later became known as the Apex (just below Chunuk Bair). From here Overton spotted, at a distance of approximately four hundred yards, what appeared to be an Ottoman observation post or Maxim machine-gun position. Farther north, on the ridgeline, Overton observed three trenches, which he estimated could accommodate no more than ninety men. If the two smaller trenches could be taken, he noted, the enemy at Chunuk Bair and Battleship Hill could be outflanked. His report concluded that the country, while difficult, was denuded of enemy troops, and the routes, though complex, were passable. Major-General Alexander Godley, GOC of the New Zealand and Australian Division (NZ&A Div.), was informed of the findings, and passed the information onto Birdwood. This further stimulated Birdwood's desire for a maneuver to the north of his position, and he ordered additional patrolling in that area.[88] With this type of information, the initial concept began to turn into a plan.

The following day, 16 May, Hamilton visited the Anzac sector to check up on Birdwood, who had been slightly wounded the previous day. There is little doubt that the two men discussed Birdwood's proposal of 13 May. That Hamilton was being sent an additional division (the 52nd Lowland) must also have been mentioned, for later that day Birdwood wrote to Hamilton, giving specifics as to his proposed plan of operations and expressing how he intended to use another division (in addition to the 29th Indian Brigade already requested) if it was available. Birdwood proposed a three-pronged attack on the Sari Bair Ridge. Two brigades would assault Hill 971 via Damakjelik Bair; two battalions would advance up Bauchop's Hill and attack Chunuk Bair; and two brigades would attack from Russell's Top up along the main ridge. In addition to holding the ridge, Birdwood hoped to capture some of the enemy's guns. This force, if successful, would then advance southwest from Sari Bair down Third "Gun" Ridge toward Gaba Tepe, in conjunction with an attack from the right flank of the sector by the newly arrived division (Birdwood had originally wanted to use this division in the attack on Sari Bair but reworked his scheme because of Hamilton's doubts as to whether an extra division could be supplied with food, water, and ammunition in such difficult country).[89] The defense of this area against enemy counterattacks would, Birdwood believed, require the entire force at his disposal. He therefore proposed to only attempt the first phase with his own troops or, if others were available, then to wait "and go for the whole thing at once."[90] Someone at GHQ remarked: "Don't wait the date may be distant."[91] In three days Birdwood's plan had expanded from strengthening the Anzac sector by capturing the Sari Bair Ridge to include the subsequent capture and consolidation of Third Ridge.

The Plans Take Shape

Intelligence received after the failed Ottoman attack of 19 May—with its ten thousand casualties—suggested that the majority of the thirty-five thousand enemy troops employed against the Anzac sector were "untrained or elderly reservists" and that many of them "have no heart in their work."[92] This apparent low morale (which seemed at odds with the stalwart defense thus far offered by the Ottomans), coupled with new reconnaissance reports—which showed that the enemy were only lightly present in the northern foothills—further impressed Birdwood as to the potential of a large attack to his north.[93] Birdwood, however, was now faced with a new issue. As he pondered his embryonic offensive, the Ottomans were extending and strengthening their own positions along the Sari Bair Ridge, and new trenches were evident every day.

In addition, a far more pressing problem was the presence of an enemy gun on the W Hills (east of Suvla Bay). This gun, which had the range of the Allied positions at Walker's Ridge and Russell's Top, was causing significant casualties. As a further hindrance, on 29-30 May the enemy retook a position that the Allies had captured the previous day. This post (later known as Old No. 3 Post) overlooked two of the routes to the Sari Bair Ridge, and blocked an advance on Rhododendron Ridge—the principal approach to Chunuk Bair. After the loss of Old No. 3 Post, Major Overton, who knew the ground better than anyone, suggested that the whole plan be dropped, as surprise was no longer possible.[94] Birdwood and his staff, however, saw nothing but potential success and continued with their plans. On 28 May, nine days after it had first been requested, Birdwood was reminded to send an estimate to GHQ of the reinforcements required to successfully achieve the objectives of the initial landing in April: GHQ were not yet fully convinced of the idea of a left-hook maneuver to capture the Sari Bair Ridge, but remained interested in an advance across the peninsula toward Maidos.[95] After discussing the scheme with Hamilton during his visit to Anzac on 30 May, Birdwood accompanied Hamilton back to GHQ and presented his appreciation that evening.[96]

Birdwood's appreciation confirmed all but one of the objectives mentioned in his letter of 16 May. Personal reconnaissance, from both sea and land, had incorrectly convinced Birdwood that Hill 971 was separated from the remainder of the Sari Bair Ridge by a deep chasm. Hill 971, the highest point of the Sari Bair Ridge, was therefore dropped as an objective. This memorandum, however, went into much greater detail than any past correspondence. It acknowledged that the terrain was "far more [difficult] than any we have occupied so far," and therefore proposed, for purposes of surprise, that the attack take place over a broad front at night. Birdwood expected that three infantry brigades would be sufficient to capture and consolidate the Sari Bair Ridge from Hill Q to Battleship Hill, whence one brigade would, in combination with another from within the Anzac sector, launch a pincer movement on Baby 700. Another brigade would then be used to take the enemy's trenches opposite Anzac from the rear, thus allowing the entire force, including an additional division, to break forward to Third Ridge. Gaba Tepe would also be taken during this action. Due to the size of Third Ridge and the difficulty of getting artillery onto the Sari Bair Ridge, Birdwood acknowledged that he might not be able to achieve this, even with an additional division.[97] But he was willing to try.

The situation was much the same throughout June. Reconnaissance patrols continued to report on the enemy's low but increasing presence to the north of Anzac, while intelligence constantly portrayed the Ottoman enemy as weak—both in morale and defensive capability. Birdwood and his staff continued to work out the details of their plans, and vague objectives were replaced with detailed tactical specifics. On 7 June, for example, it was proposed that in order to draw the enemy's attention away from the Sari Bair Ridge, two battalions should launch a feint against the 400 Plateau (Lone Pine and Johnston's Jolly). This should occur just before dusk, thus allowing sufficient light for the attack but also making the enemy's defense more difficult as darkness fell. An additional two battalions would then be used to occupy and consolidate the position.[98] Another appreciation by ANZAC HQ in early June, however, questioned the feasibility of a feint: "There is no good ground for supposing that the enemy draws off troops from one place to meet threatened attacks at another." This feint, whether successful or not, would be followed by another attack the following morning against Baby 700, which, according to Birdwood, "is essential to draw off attention from and co-operate with the main enveloping movement" against Sari Bair. Other aspects of the attack that were discussed in detail included clearing the foothills below the Sari Bair Ridge and the advance along Third Ridge.[99] While Birdwood's plans increased in detail, GHQ received news from London. As a result of this news, GHQ's attitude toward Birdwood's proposed attack underwent a massive shift.

GHQ Warms to the Plan

As noted, at its first meeting on 7 June the Dardanelles Committee decided to send three New Army (10th, 11th, and 13th) divisions and naval reinforcements to the Dardanelles. Hamilton was informed that the last of these divisions should arrive in mid-July. Lord Kitchener also advised Hamilton to refrain from any premature risks in the meantime, thus allowing him to attack with his full force once these reinforcements had arrived.[100] Hamilton replied that this good news "has inspired us with fresh confidence" and reminded Kitchener that staff for two corps would be required to manage such a number.[101] Hamilton was subsequently told that only one corps staff, designated IX Corps, would be sent, and asked whether Lieutenant-General Sir Bryan Mahon was a suitable commander.[102] Hamilton responded in the negative, considering Mahon "quite hopeless" for such a role, and instead, requested either Lieutenant-General Sir Julian Byng or Lieutenant-General Henry Rawlinson, who were commanding corps on the Western Front: "Both possess the requisite qualities and seniority; the latter does not seem very happy where he is, and the former would have more scope than a Cavalry Corps can give him in France." These two men, however, could not be spared from the Western Front, and they were both junior to Mahon, who would now join IX Corps as GOC 10th Division. Kitchener therefore suggested the "fit and well" Lieutenant-General Sir John Ewart, who, at fifty-four years of age, had had a distinguished career as director of military operations (1906–1910) and adjutant general to the force (1910–1914).[103] After rejecting Ewart because he was overweight, Hamilton then suggested Lieutenant-General Sir Frederick Stopford.[104] Hamilton wrote to Field Marshal Sir John French, commander in chief of the BEF, that while he did not know who would get the job, "we have had one or two terrifying suggestions from home."[105] Stopford, whom Hamilton included as one of these "terrifying suggestions" (but whom Hamilton had, in fact, actually suggested) was eventually chosen.

Meanwhile, news of the three additional divisions reinvigorated GHQ's discussions about Birdwood's plan. On 11 June Hamilton and his chief of the general staff (CGS), Major-General Braithwaite visited Anzac to discuss the outline of the proposed attack with Birdwood. At this stage, even with reinforcements, the basic plan was not expanded—its objective remained Third Ridge and the strengthening of the Anzac sector. The views of Lieutenant-General Hunter-Weston, now commanding VIII Corps at Cape Helles, and General Henri Gouraud, commanding the Corps Expéditionnaire Français des Dardanelles, were sought, and both approved.[106]

The next day, buoyed by an admission from Birdwood that if the Bulair Lines were attacked the enemy's supplies could be cut and "the fighting in this peninsula should be over in about a week," the Dardanelles Committee convened to discuss the matter.[107] Birdwood's remark, combined with a memorandum from the British journalist Ellis Ashmead-Bartlett (recently returned to London from the Dardanelles) formed the basis of the meeting. Ashmead-Bartlett's memorandum stated that due to the enemy's strength, victory would not come at Helles or Anzac but rather from actions against the Bulair Lines (in the northern part of the Gallipoli Peninsula). Prime Minister Asquith and Lord Kitchener were unconvinced by Ashmead-Bartlett's arguments, but his ideas appealed to Churchill and Lord Selborne, president of the Board of Agriculture and a member of the Dardanelles Committee. The committee concluded, therefore, that Kitchener should telegraph Hamilton and inquire into the possibility and most appropriate means of "starving" the enemy, whether at Bulair or elsewhere.[108] This he did. Similarly, Balfour, who had replaced Churchill as first lord of the admiralty in May, asked Vice-Admiral de Robeck for his opinion.[109] Hamilton's reply was to the point: both he and de Robeck were opposed to the idea of action at Bulair and the best means of cutting the enemy's communications was to push forward from Anzac.[110] Despite Bonar Law's conclusion that there was an underlying apprehension in Hamilton's telegrams, the Dardanelles Committee supported the plan, and the likelihood of Birdwood's scheme being put into action rose once more.[111]

Gaining Momentum

The pace quickened at GHQ. By 17 June, Captain Orlo Williams, the chief cipher officer at GHQ noted that "appreciations and preparations for the big move at Anzac . . . are progressing."[112] Kitchener also reaffirmed his support for such an action by stating, "Your proposed advance on the Australasian front would have the most excellent effect."[113] Not everyone, though, was confident of success. Upon hearing of the scheme, Lieutenant-Colonel Arthur Bauchop, CO of the Otago Mounted Rifles Regiment (MR Regt.), who would later die of wounds suffered while leading his unit on 6–7 August, noted that it was "fraught with difficulty. I do not feel hopeful of our prospects at all here."[114] Similarly, the CO of the Wellington Battalion, Lieutenant-Colonel Malone, who had originally supported the movement to the north and who would also die leading his unit at Chunuk Bair, now felt that there was insufficient ammunition and artillery for an attack and that the enemy were now much stronger numerically and their positions well entrenched.[115] Objections aside, the planning continued.

The way in which Hamilton might employ his expanding force underwent a further change on 22 June when Kitchener asked whether he would like a fourth division.[116] Naturally, Hamilton accepted, noting that it "might just be needed to turn the scale." With such an increased force, he hoped "to strike a blow which if successful would bear greater fruit than the mere winning of any one enemy position."[117] Despite seriously considering the Anzac plan, GHQ had still not yet made a definite decision as to how exactly to employ the new force.[118] This, however, did not stop Birdwood's staff from continuing with their plans. On 23 June, a proposal, outlining the objectives, the troops that would be used, the strength of the enemy, and the plan of attack, was circulated among the ANZAC staff. It also noted that contrary to appearances, there was no break in the Sari Bair Ridge, and Hill 971 was therefore reinstated as an objective.[119] GHQ encouraged Birdwood to continue planning for an offensive and reminded him that he should keep any undue attention away from his left flank.[120]

Beyond Third Ridge

The following day, 26 June, Kitchener asked Hamilton whether he could manage a fifth division.[121] News of this potential expansion again directly impacted upon existent plans—and for the first time Birdwood proposed going beyond Third Ridge. These reinforcements, he stated, could be used to push across the peninsula from Anzac to Maidos—in accord with GHQ's desires to attack the enemy's southern flank. Birdwood also mentioned the possibility of capturing the guns near the W Hills, which continued to harass his sector. The capture of these guns, Birdwood stated, would assist his attack on Hill 971.[122] The decisions of the Dardanelles Committee in London were therefore directly shaping and encouraging an expansion of the plan. On 28 June, Hamilton officially decided that an attack would be launched from Anzac.[123] He informed Kitchener of his intention to use the first three divisions in an advance across the Gallipoli Peninsula, with the fourth and fifth in reserve—to be thrown in at Anzac in the case of nonsuccess or, if successful, to be used at Helles or landed on the Asiatic shore of the Dardanelles. He concluded, "I think I have reasonable prospects of eventual success with three divisions, with four the risks of miscalculation would be minimised, and with five . . . success would be generally assured."[124] In summary, in less than a month the plan had evolved from one where Birdwood would try, but was not confident of being able, to advance successfully on Third Ridge to a scheme that included an additional five divisions and an advance across the Gallipoli Peninsula. This expansion also saw operational command transfer from Birdwood to Hamilton, with the former and his corps being relegated to a tactical role. Birdwood's staff continued planning, but Hamilton would now oversee the entire offensive.

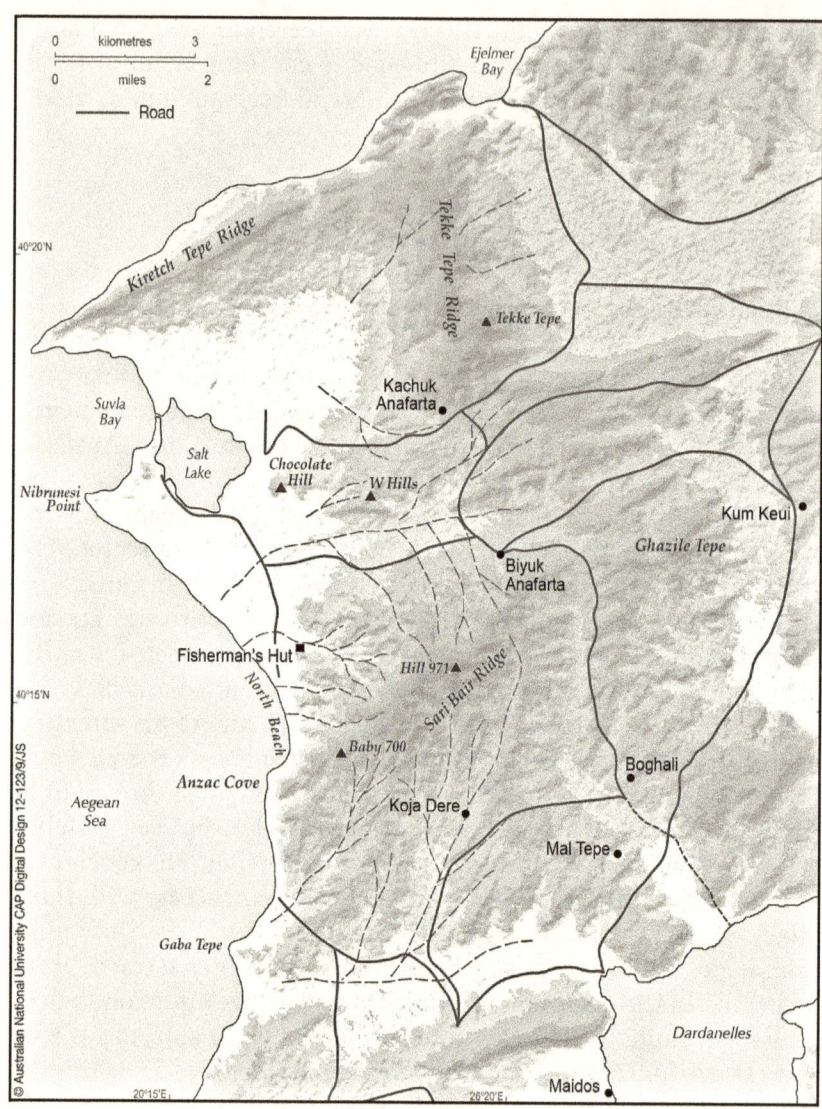

Map 2. Key features of Birdwood's proposal

Suvla Added to the List

The evolution of the plans was most significant throughout July. On 1 July, Birdwood proposed a change to his initial plan of 30 May. In conjunction with the attack on the Sari Bair Ridge, one brigade would be landed in Suvla Bay, then would proceed eastward and capture the enemy's guns in the W and Chocolate Hills. This, he believed, was "necessary to prevent the powerful guns located there from enfilading operations against" the Sari Bair Ridge and Baby 700. After successfully pushing the Anzac sector forward to Third Ridge, the force would, in accord with Hamilton's wishes, advance "in the direction of Mal Tepe and Maidos, so as to completely command the country between [Anzac] and the Narrows." News of possible reinforcements had increased the force to be used overnight from twenty-one thousand to thirty-five thousand rifles.[125]

For his part, Birdwood remained unsure of how to best employ a third division. He realized that it would not fit within the confines of the Anzac sector but could perhaps be landed at Suvla Bay to create a "secure base for supplies." This force, Birdwood proposed, should advance and occupy the Tekke Tepe Ridge from Ejelmer Bay to Kuchuk Anafarta. Rather than holding a continuous line, Birdwood believed that the ridge could be held by "strongly entrenched detachments," therefore leaving a striking force to move against Ghazile Tepe (which overlooked Kum Keui and controlled Ottoman land supply routes) or, alternatively, to move toward Koja Dere and Boghali from Hill 971 and Biyuk Anafarta. Suvla, however, was just one option. He also proposed landing the additional troops slightly north of Anzac Cove at Fisherman's Hut, or, if Greece decided to join the MEF, have the Greek army occupy the Tekke Tepe Ridge "so as to give us a secure base for a large force in Suvla Bay."[126]

Importantly, Birdwood and the GHQ staff relied on a 1:40,000 scale map of the Gallipoli Peninsula when drafting these proposals. This map, which had been produced before the campaign commenced, was inaccurate and imprecise and did not adequately depict the real difficulties of the terrain. As such, the conception of the August Offensive and the subsequent planning (tactical and operational) was based on a map that provided nothing more than a strategic blueprint of the peninsula from which it was not possible to develop intricate plans with any level of accuracy. Fortunately for the MEF, a new 1:20,000 map, which clearly highlighted the terrain (in ten-meter contours), was published in late July and was used during the August Offensive (as distinct from during the planning process). While not accurate for artillery fire, it at least gave some indication of the intricacies of the terrain that would have to be crossed during the operations.[127] The new map, however, was no substitute for the ambitious plans that had been based on its predecessor. If anything, the 1:20,000 map showed that the objectives were even more difficult than first thought. Such observations, if made, had little effect.

Kitchener officially offered Hamilton the fourth and fifth (53rd Welsh, and 54th East Anglian) reinforcement divisions (without artillery) on 5 July.[128] "Hurrah," Hamilton replied, "this means one less anxiety."[129] At this point, the suggestion that additional troops could be landed at Suvla Bay was given more credence. Suvla Bay's central purpose, though, remained its usefulness as a base of supplies. By way of some "real good piers and fine strong breakwaters," Birdwood envisaged Suvla Bay as providing a satisfactory embarkation point for supplies during bad weather.[130] Yet, when news of the two additional divisions reached him, Birdwood's proposal changed. Now, rather than securing Suvla Bay for purely logistic purposes, Birdwood proposed that the extra divisions should be landed at Suvla Bay and employed in an offensive role there. One division should push through the Anafarta Gap and seize Ghazile Tepe (the northeastern summit of the Sari Bair Ridge), and the other should hold the Tekke Tepe Ridge, which overlooked the Suvla plain. With this, Birdwood wrote, "I feel that we should have a complete domination over the Turkish forces." Birdwood's position began to change. He now stressed that without offensive action at Suvla, the Allies may find it too difficult to push across the peninsula.[131]

At this time Birdwood also submitted what he described as a "wild cat scheme." In this fanciful plan, which he admitted was likely to be dismissed immediately, Birdwood proposed that on the first night of the offensive a regiment of mounted Australian light horsemen should gallop from Anzac to the north, wheel to the right, outflank the enemy, and return to the Anzac right flank. This, he felt, would confuse the enemy. In all, the regiment would be required to cover over seventeen miles during the night. Birdwood wrote: "Such a raid with small numbers would I think most probably have an extremely demoralising effect upon the Turks, for they would absolutely have no idea what was intended, while in the moonlight the noise of galloping horses would probably exaggerate the numbers enormously. . . . The moral damage to the enemy would I fancy be considerable, as also should be the material damage, as the Light Horse might in all probability be able to account for small Turkish encampments, or small bodies of men, while there would be little chance of large bodies forming up to beat them."¹³² As a sign of its absurdity, nothing more was heard of the scheme.

Given his role as GOC of the ANZAC, Birdwood left the planning of the Suvla project to GHQ and concentrated on the role to be played by his own corps. Reconnaissance of the routes to Sari Bair continued, with special attention paid to enemy defenses in the area. There was so much importance placed on this reconnaissance, and those who undertook it, that Birdwood's HQ issued a precautionary order to those who had partaken in it to leave the peninsula: they "know too much now, and therefore should not be sent out again. It is imperative that they be available" as guides for the coming offensive.¹³³ Units resting at Imbros Island were ordered to commence practicing night marching and attacking over hilly ground.¹³⁴ Intelligence reports confirmed a depleted enemy force in the Anafarta Section, with only two Ottoman regiments covering the whole area north of Battleship Hill.¹³⁵ Preparations continued within the Anzac sector, and owing to the increased sea traffic in the area, an order was issued banning bathing in Anzac Cove after 7:00 P.M.¹³⁶

GHQ Plans the Suvla Operation

By now, GHQ was frantically working out the details for the new landing at Suvla Bay. The nights of 6–8 August were chosen as potential dates for the general offensive as they were deemed the most suitable for landing new troops because the moon would not rise until 2:00 A.M., thus allowing more time to embark under the cover of darkness and thereby maintaining surprise for as long as possible.¹³⁷

By 17 July the operations staff at GHQ had completed a series of tables showing in detail the men, animals, vehicles, stores, and other supplies to be landed at Anzac Cove prior to the attack and at Suvla Bay during the offensive. These were then sent to Vice-Admiral de Robeck for his perusal and comment.¹³⁸ Reconnaissance of Suvla Bay from the sea reported that the enemy had improved their defenses, but they were still not considered to be of a number that might thwart the operation.¹³⁹ Intelligence reports focused on the arrival of enemy reinforcements and predicted that the Ottomans were about to undertake a large-scale attack of their own with some one hundred thousand troops. GHQ hoped that the Ottoman attack would be launched prior to their own offensive, thereby allowing the Allies to inflict heavy losses on the enemy and greatly enhance the Allied chances of success.[140] This Ottoman attack never materialized.

Detailed plans for IX Corps operations at Suvla were drawn up by Hamilton's staff and issued to Lieutenant-General Stopford on 22 July. The objective of the wider offensive was made clear: after capturing the Sari Bair Ridge and forcing the enemy to vacate their current position, the Allies would seize a position across the peninsula from Gaba Tepe to Maidos "with a protected line of supply from Suvla Bay." The objective at Suvla was also clear. Its purpose was for "the capture and retention of Suvla Bay as a base of operations for the northern army." Stopford's first task was to secure the beaches and, to ease Birdwood's concerns, capture the W and Chocolate Hills. This latter task was "of first importance." Stopford was told that these hills "should be captured by a coup-de-main before daylight in order to prevent the guns which they contain being used against our troops on [Hill 971] and to safeguard our hold on Suvla Bay." Birdwood's proposal for one division to advance through the Anafarta Gap and seize Ghazile Tepe while the other held Tekke Tepe Ridge was *not* adopted. Rather, a watered down version was chosen. It was "hoped" that those units not employed in holding the hills would be able to assist Birdwood's force by moving up the eastern spurs of Hill 971, but this was *not* to be their primary objective.[141]

The Opinions of a Corps Commander

After viewing his objectives from the left flank of Anzac, and after discussions with his staff, Stopford submitted a revised plan to GHQ.[142] Stopford has been criticized by many authors for revising the plans, but this was the regular process. The corps commander reserved the right, as is evident in Birdwood's role during the planning process, to express his concerns and have the plan altered (subject to the final approval of GHQ). Indeed, Stopford was informed that apart from gaining Hamilton's final approval, he was left "an entirely free hand in the selection of your plans and operations."[143]

Due to the fact that no artillery would be landed with the first troops at Suvla, Stopford doubted whether he could take his first objectives before dawn. He believed that this task would consume all available troops and therefore stated that he would not be able to advance through the Anafarta Gap to aid Birdwood. He also altered some tactical aspects of the plan, including where units would be landed. Again, this was his right as a corps commander. Despite these changes, the primary objective of the Suvla landing remained the same. Suvla Bay would be secured as a base first, and only then were the W and Chocolate Hills to be captured. This secondary objective (assisting Birdwood's force), however, would only be attempted if it would not prejudice the safety of Suvla Bay. These changes were unquestionably accepted by GHQ and new orders were issued accordingly on 29 July.[144]

GHQ's new orders acknowledged the difficulty of the task allotted to IX Corps and reaffirmed that the primary objective was to secure Suvla Bay "as a base for all the forces operating in the northern zone." After securing the bay, Stopford was reminded that if "it is possible, without prejudice to the attainment of your primary objective," his force should remove the threat posed by any Ottoman guns, thus further securing the bay and "greatly facilitating the capture and retention" of Hill 971.[145] Stopford replied, noting the importance of capturing the high ground east of Suvla Bay, but acknowledged that in order to secure the bay and support Birdwood's attack he must first capture the W and Chocolate Hills. Any further assistance to Birdwood was beyond his corps' limits. Stopford wrote, "I fear that it is likely that the attainment of the security of Suvla Bay will so absorb the force under my command as to render it improbable that I shall be able to give direct assistance to [Birdwood] in his attack on [Hill 971]. If, however, the operations above referred to meet with such slight opposition as will free a portion of the troops engaged, you may rely on my giving him every assistance in my power."[146]

The plans were set. Stopford's concerns were taken on board, and the "offensive" elements of his plan were removed. On 30 July, Birdwood was informed that his scheme of 1 July had been approved.[147] Hamilton, now the operational commander, had received approval from Kitchener, who stated that the operations had the full support of London and asked whether anything else was required. Kitchener concluded, "In the short time available before the bad weather intervenes the Dardanelles operations are now of the highest importance."[148] The plans were then given to divisional and brigade headquarters, which were left with determining the specific tactical movements of their respective units. These orders were then issued to battalion commanders immediately prior to the operations.

The Operational Objective

The great majority of literature concerning the August Offensive has focused on the tactical aims of battles within the offensive (such as the fight for the Sari Bair Ridge and the creation of a base at Suvla Bay) and has inaccurately viewed them as the ultimate operational aim. In reality, these battles were only the first objective of a multi-tiered operation. In focusing on the first phase of the August Offensive (which was in fact only the first tactical objective) and the events as they unfolded, such histories have ignored the overall operational goals and their inherent difficulties and have concluded that the offensive was on the "brink of complete victory."[149]

While some histories of the August Offensive acknowledge the four separate operational phases and their inherent difficulties, there remains no single account of what these various phases consisted of, or what they hoped to achieve. Given the absence of a single operational order that clearly outlines the various phases of the August Offensive, this is understandable. But it is incorrect. The absence of such an order was, in fact, not abnormal and is no real surprise. Being a summary of discussions (many verbal), operational orders acted as a guide for commanding officers and, as was made clear in Britain's *Field Service Regulations* (*FSR*), which formed the basis of how the British (including the MEF) operated in the first two years of the war, orders "should contain just what the recipient requires to know and nothing more."[150] They were therefore, by their very nature, simple and concise.

In war it is important to have loosely defined objectives so that the plan can be adapted to circumstances as they evolve. Detailed plans, according to the Prussian field marshal Helmuth von Moltke (the Elder), "should not extend beyond the first encounter with the enemy."[151] *FSR* adopted a similar principle, directing that "it is seldom necessary or desirable to endeavour to look far ahead in stating intentions."[152] Specific plans would become obsolete as soon as the offensive commenced owing to the inability to predict what the situation would be at the end of the first phase. This was clearly the attitude taken by Hamilton and his staff prior to the August Offensive. In discussing the subsequent phases of the Helles attack on 6 August, for example, GHQ informed the GOC of VIII Corps that if the operations at Helles were successful they could perhaps be followed by the capture of Krithia, and "plans for this action should be prepared beforehand. But as the launching of this further attack must be entirely dependent on unknown factors, a definite decision on this point cannot be arrived at beforehand."[153] Flexibility was essential, but so too was secrecy; any definite orders were at risk of being captured by the enemy, either found on a dead body or obtained from a prisoner of war. Such an instance, it was realized, "would render the whole operation abortive."[154]

In the absence of a definite multiphase order for August, this book has used various sources such as operational orders, memorandums, appreciations, telegrams, letters, and diaries at all levels of command, as well as recollections, to reconstruct a picture of what the Allied high command expected the MEF to achieve during the August Offensive.

The Four Phases of the August Offensive

There were two principal objectives of the first phase of the August Offensive. The secondary, and less important, of these was the creation of a safe harbor at Suvla Bay, which would offer better protection from the weather and submarines than the beaches in the Anzac sector could.[155] From here, Hamilton imagined a railway line being constructed from the bay up to the Sari Bair Ridge, thus providing an effective and reliable means of supplying the force during the second phase of operations—the starvation of the enemy.[156] The primary objective of the first phase, and what Lieutenant-Colonel Maurice Hankey, secretary of both the CID and the Dardanelles Committee, described to Prime Minister Herbert Asquith as an "offensive conception," was to seize the Sari Bair Ridge.[157]

This position, it was believed, would offer a view of the enemy's beaches at Kilia Liman and Maidos, as well as the Narrows, and the roads leading northward to Bulair and Constantinople.[158] Once Sari Bair had been seized, the troops were to dig in, traverse the trenches, create communications trenches, and consolidate for the expectant enemy artillery fire and counterattack.[159] The troops themselves were aware that the offensive did not cease here. Birdwood himself had informed them that driving the enemy from its position on Sari Bair was but the first move: "It is then that our hardest work, and possibly the greatest determination, will be required, as we not only have got to turn the enemy off his present position, but having

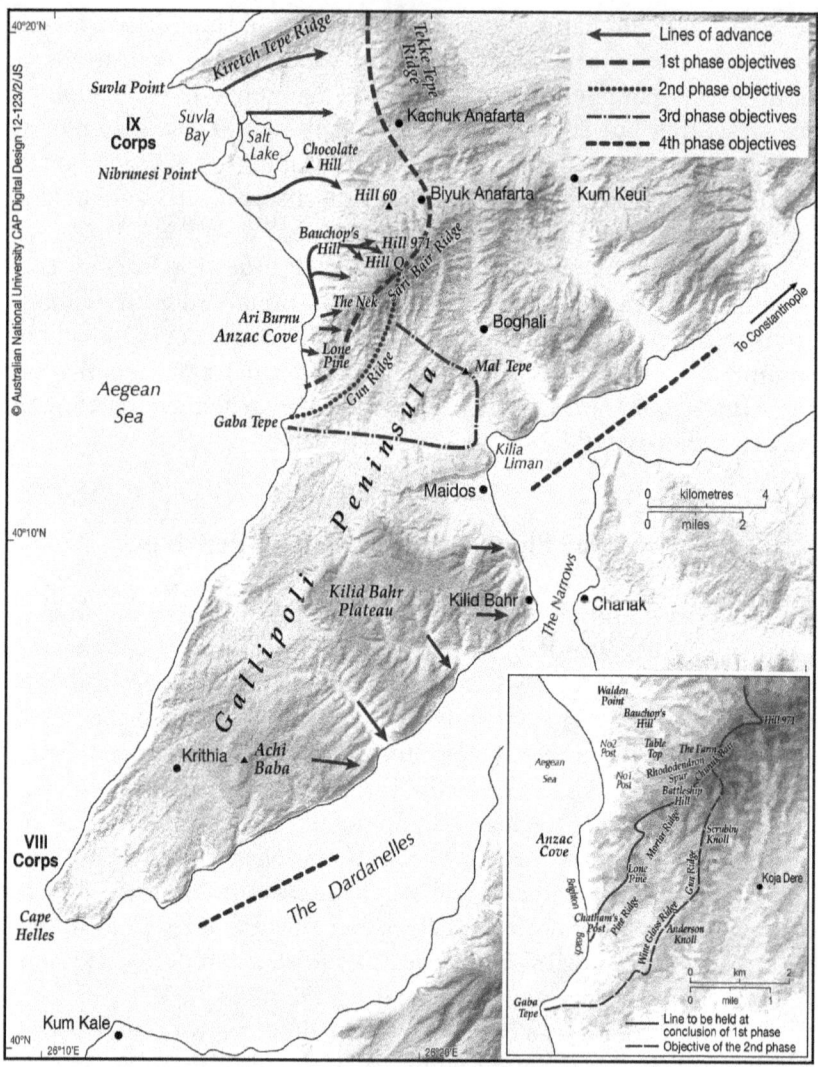

Map 3. Objectives of the August Offensive

once shifted him from his front trenches, we have to keep running him out of them as far as we possibly can, capturing we hope everything he possesses, and giving him no rest until he is completely defeated here."[160] Once the position had been consolidated, a pincer movement would be made on Battleship Hill in conjunction with an attack from Anzac against Baby 700. This would require the force at Chunuk Bair to "advance South West along the Ridge against BATTLESHIP HILL and down the Southern slopes of SARI BAIR."[161]

The second phase of the August Offensive was to begin once the enemy had been cleared from Battleship Hill and Baby 700. There was then to be a determined effort to clear the ground east of the present Anzac sector. This would involve a flank attack from Quinn's Post to the crossroads near Scrubby Knoll.[162] This move would then allow the Chessboard trenches to be taken in reverse and the enemy's reserves from the direction of Koja Dere to be dealt with.[163] The force would next "advance and occupy a line extending from the neighbourhood of Gaba Tepe along the main spur marked approximately by the track 82–67–165–Chunuk Bair, and thence along the Chunuk Bair Ridge to and including Hill 305."[164] In other words, the forces were to occupy a line, beginning east-northeast of Gaba Tepe and along the track on Wine Glass Ridge in front of Anderson Knoll, continuing along Gun Ridge, in front of Scrubby Knoll, northward, past Su Yatagha to Chunuk Bair, and then along the Sari Bair Ridge to Hill 971. The breakout to Gun Ridge, from Scrubby Knoll to the sea, was to be made by the 1st Australian Division.[165] Hamilton then intended to place heavy guns along Sari Bair and Third Ridge and shell the Ottoman land and sea communications, thus starving the enemy.[166] This information filtered through the services, with a senior medical officer of VIII Corps recognizing that one of the aims of the offensive was to "secure sites for which artillery could cut off sea traffic whether with [the] Dardanelles, Constantinople or with Asia."[167] Indeed, the navy saw the capture of this ridge as "of vital importance" because it would allow for observation stations to be established, and "the reduction of the Chanak Forts could be at once undertaken with sure chances of success."[168]

The third phase of the offensive would begin after the protracted period of bombardment from the Sari Bair Ridge and the establishment of a protected line of supply from Suvla Bay. The aim of this phase was to "secure a position astride the Gallipoli Peninsula from the neighbourhood of Gaba Tepe to the straits north of Maidos."[169] It was believed that this advance from Gaba Tepe to the Straits, a distance of eight thousand yards, not only would cut off all the land communications between the enemy and their supply routes from the north (and hence Constantinople) but also would make sea communications very difficult, thus effectively cutting off the already-starved enemy and separating their northern and southern forces.[170]

The successful completion of this phase would mark the end of the land-only component of the offensive and open the way for the navy to revert to the type of operations undertaken in February and March.

The final or fourth phase of the August Offensive would begin when the Allies controlled the waist of the peninsula between Gaba Tepe and Maidos. In this instance, the objectives would return to those strived for in April. In what would see a resumption of combined operations, it would be the role of the army to destroy the forts and silence any mobile Ottoman artillery lining the shores of the Dardanelles, thus allowing the fleet to begin minesweeping operations. This phase was, effectively, the operational objective of the entire campaign. It was necessary to reach this objective so that the EMS could prepare for an attack on the strategic objective: Constantinople.

With the objectives of the four phases of the offensive in mind, it is clear that the August Offensive is an example of an attempt at the large-scale breakthrough offensives common of the First World War. The offensive was styled around the doctrine of maneuver warfare that dominated British military thought, and it was hindered by the same structural problems faced by the BEF on the Western Front. One cannot help but be reminded in this regard of the "one more ridge" thinking of the British high command, as exemplified at Neuve Chapelle in 1915, the Somme in 1916, and through to the Flanders campaign in 1917.[171] In this regard, the August Offensive, like those battles that followed, could not have been labeled a "success," or even have been seen to approach success, until the objectives of *all* four phases had been obtained.

British operational command and planning did not limit itself to one phase. Yet the historiography of the August Offensive has treated this operation as something significantly different from similar large-scale offensives in France and Belgium. In doing so, by focusing only on the first phase, a mythology of "near success" has developed and prospered. In reality, the August Offensive was an increasingly impossible task. In subsequent chapters this book will analyze the Allied potential to successfully prosecute a large-scale offensive in the Dardanelles theater during August 1915, thus debunking the near success myth and proving that, like the failed offensives on the Western Front in 1915, the August Offensive could not succeed.

The Evolution of the Planning Process

Over a period of two and a half months, the plans for offensive action in August at Gallipoli had evolved from a local operation, the aim of which was to strengthen the Anzac sector, into a large-scale offensive involving five additional divisions. With this change, the plan had, in fact, grown into something that resembled the initial plans of April 1915. This was no longer a tactical battle—but rather a climactic operation aimed at deciding the issue in the Dardanelles theater. The political support of London, by way of sending additional reinforcements and supplies, combined with an attractive (if inaccurate) intelligence picture of a weak and sparse enemy, greatly appealed to the preconceptions and prejudices of the Allied command. A flanking maneuver from the Anzac sector would allow for a breakout offensive, thus introducing the maneuver warfare that senior British officers craved.

In this sense, the August Offensive was little different from the battle of Neuve Chapelle in France. Upon General Haig's (GOC of the First Army) insistence, Neuve Chapelle was to be a breakthrough offensive.[172] Like the Sari Bair Ridge, the village of Neuve Chapelle was but the first objective.[173] After capturing the German lines at Neuve Chapelle, Haig intended to exploit the momentum and drive the enemy off Aubers Ridge.[174] Like the August Offensive, the battle of Neuve Chapelle was a multiphase operation that stalled at its first objective. Hamilton, like Haig, was a product of the British military establishment—and at this stage in the war, both were yet to realize that this type of offensive was beyond the capabilities of their respective forces.

With hindsight, there can be no doubt that the plans for the August Offensive were too ambitious. The objectives were beyond the scope and capabilities of the Allies in 1915. They expected too much from the sick, exhausted, and inexperienced troops (and their officers); they were based on an inaccurate knowledge of the terrain; and they were shrouded in secrecy. The architect of the tactical plans for action from the Anzac sector, Lieutenant-General Birdwood, later realized this and admitted that the task "was a most difficult one—more difficult, indeed, than I myself had realised."[175] As will be seen in chapter 7, some minor tactical gains were achieved during the first phase of the August Offensive, but the Allies were never able to attempt the subsequent phases of the operational plan. The August Offensive, therefore, never approached success. In effect, the objectives, which developed around a series of cascading misreads, were too many and too large.

CHAPTER 2

MOBILITY

Mobility is one of the key elements for maneuver warfare. The term encapsulates not only the method of movement (whether on feet, hooves, or wheels) but also the condition of the roads, soil, and terrain.[1] Without mobility, the enemy cannot be outflanked, their positions cannot be turned, and local success cannot be exploited. This was especially the case for the August Offensive, where the aim was to capture the heights of the Sari Bair Ridge, eject the enemy from their positions opposite the Anzac sector, and advance across the Gallipoli Peninsula, thus cutting the enemy's supply lines and allowing naval forces to begin the process of forcing their way through the Dardanelles defenses. Mobility was therefore vital for success. The offensive would not succeed if the ground force could not advance. It is crucial, therefore, to evaluate the mobility of the MEF in order to judge whether it stood any chance of accomplishing the objectives set. Answering this question implies an analysis of the impact that secrecy, command, force size and structure, health and morale, communications, terrain, and, not least, the impact that the Ottomans had—and would continue to have—on the mobility of the force should it proceed as planned across the peninsula.

Secrecy, Surprise, and Their Impact on Operations

Hamilton understood the importance of surprise. With it, he could attack the weaknesses of an unprepared and nonexpectant enemy. Without it, there would be little chance of success in the forthcoming operation. He also realized that surprise could only be maintained through strict secrecy (something that had been lacking for the initial landings on 25 April), deception, accurate intelligence, and speed.[2] Such a view was the accepted norm. General Joffre noted that "the higher command should . . . take every necessary precaution to ensure secrecy, thus allowing for surprise."[3] What was peculiar about Hamilton, however, was his acute anxiety to retain the element of surprise for the August Offensive at all costs. Fearful that information about the operation would leak to the enemy, Hamilton had the following message sent to the inspector general of communications: "Secrecy, so far as it is possible, is of utmost and vital importance, and it should be explained to all officers and men how much they can contribute towards the success of the next general action by maintaining absolute silence about anything connected with the movement of troops which comes to their knowledge . . . and by avoiding the slightest discussion of these movements, even amongst themselves. The whole Lines of Communication is infested by spies and one incautious conversation may be worth 50,000 men to the enemy."[4] As a further measure designed to quash all discussions of future movements, Hamilton had maps of the Asiatic coast printed in Egypt. These, he hoped, would instill the belief that the offensive would take place on the Asiatic shore, and if there were "spies," such false information would inevitably make its way back to the Ottomans.[5]

To ensure the secrecy of his plans and objectives for August, Hamilton took few officers into his confidence. Secrecy, he stated, was "so ultra-vital that we are bound to keep . . . [knowledge of the operations] within a tiny circle."[6] Even some of his senior commanders were kept at bay until it was deemed absolutely necessary that they should be briefed. Upon learning that Lieutenant-General Birdwood had discussed some aspects of the plans with his divisional generals, Hamilton wrote to him disapprovingly: "I am sorry you told your Divisional Generals[,] I have not even informed Stopford or Bailloud [GOC of the Corps Expéditionnaire d'Orient]. Please find out at once how many Staff Officers each of them have told and let me know. Now take every opportunity of telling your Divisional Generals that the whole plan is abandoned. I leave it to you to invent the reason for this abandonment. The operation is secret and must remain secret."[7] Birdwood acceded and retracted his statements.[8] As it eventuated, Hamilton had the opportunity to discuss his plans with Stopford upon the latter's arrival at GHQ on 11 July, but, according to Stopford, Hamilton refused to provide any details, such was his penchant for secrecy. It was eleven more days before Stopford, who was to command the troops at Suvla Bay, received an outline of the August operations.[9] It was not only Hamilton's subordinates, however, who remained in the dark. So too, he refrained from informing his political superiors on the Dardanelles Committee of his intentions. "If any hint or inkling gets about that I am meditating a large operation," he explained to Lord Kitchener, "my coup may completely fail."[10]

Hamilton's approach, at least as far as the Ottomans were concerned, bore fruit. While suspicious of a new landing, the Ottomans did not, in fact, know where the attempt would be made. In mid-July, Marshal Liman von Sanders, the GOC of the 5th Ottoman Army, received a report from Salonica that the Allies had accumulated 50,000–60,000 troops and 140 ships at Lemnos Island for an attack. But he could only guess where they would be used.[11] An order was then issued to the Ottoman forces warning that the Allies would attack in early August. In accord with von Sanders's fears, a landing of British and Italian troops was expected in either the Gulf of Xeros or on the Asiatic coast.[12] Hamilton's deception had worked. Marshal von Sanders deployed his reserves to defend the Bulair Lines. It must also be noted that the enemy's knowledge of an impending attack varied. Ottoman prisoners captured on 7 August stated that they had heard ten days previously that the Allies would attack soon and that it would be the decisive battle of the campaign. Others, however, stated that they had not heard about it and that the attack came as a complete surprise.[13] In terms of deceiving the enemy and maintaining surprise, the secrecy surrounding the operations was a success.

On another level, though, the degrees of secrecy demanded by Hamilton significantly hindered the conduct of Allied operations. By limiting those with preknowledge of the operation, the plans themselves could not be scrutinized, discussed, or debated. In addition, the plans were not divulged to lower level commanders—or the troops for that matter—until, on some occasions, the day of the offensive. Brigadier-General Monash, the CO of the 4th Australian Bde., for example, did not explain the plans to the officers and non-commissioned officers of his brigade until 6 August. It was then left to these men to determine the specific tactics to be employed and to explain the operation to all ranks under their command—all on the day of battle.[14] The product of this secrecy, where commanders, and the men under them, had little knowledge of the wider scheme or even their objectives, had a profoundly negative impact on operations.

Many officers, particularly those of IX Corps, did not see a map of the area of operations before landing. Commodore Oliver Backhouse, the CO of the 2nd Royal Naval Brigade, Royal Naval Division (RND), who witnessed the landings at Suvla Bay, noted that "troops and officers seemed to have only [a] vague idea of their orders."[15] Similarly, Arthur Beecroft, a signal officer attached to the 34th Infantry Brigade (11th Division) revealed that prior to landing at Suvla Bay, "no attempt was made to explain the object to the troops.... We knew practically nothing."[16] This was a direct result of the level of secrecy imposed by Hamilton. Divisional commanders were advised to refrain from divulging information until the last moment and then only to release those portions of the orders that were of particular concern to a specific unit.[17] In addition, any information concerning future plans or movements—the subsequent phases—was to be kept from those lower than brigade staffs.[18] Troops and their immediate commanders were therefore prevented from fully grasping their tasks and objectives. Aside from creating confusion, such secrecy also minimized the ability of the attacking units to build on any momentum gained and to exploit local success. Mobility would inevitably and fundamentally be hindered by the need to determine subsequent plans and then explain these to the attacking units.[19] Time was necessary for such work, but any pause in the assault would doubtless reduce the element of surprise necessary for continued successful maneuvers. Secrecy therefore had already had an impact on the MEF's mobility, and would have increasingly had a profound impact on the mobility (and operational proficiency) of the MEF should it have attempted to cross the peninsula.

Command Structure

Another key aspect that would directly impact upon the ability of the MEF's ground forces to succeed in the type of mobile warfare demanded in the second and third phases of the August Offensive was command structure and styles. A style of "open command" was adopted (in theory at least) in the Dardanelles, where plans were produced to allow for subordinates to use their tactical initiative.[20] Initiative, however, came with experience and a working knowledge of higher command intent. Without experienced and resolute commanders, there would be little direction and drive, and even less initiative. That this issue might impair success was recognized in the theater of operations. With the aim of avoiding any unnecessary delay, the divisional and brigade commanders at Anzac were ordered by corps headquarters to select successors to replace them should they become casualties during the August Offensive. Recognizing that the ability to command was not something one was born into, the order also stated that these commanders' choices need not depend on seniority, but rather should focus on those most suitable to command in an emergency.[21]

Much has been written about the inability of certain commanders, particularly those of IX Corps, to perform during the August Offensive, some of which has merit. There is little doubt that for many, the rigors of command at the levels expected was beyond them. But it must also be acknowledged that these men were easy targets (especially for those with reputations and careers to protect) upon whose vulnerable shoulders the failure of the offensive nicely fit.

It is also important to note that by August 1915 there was a collection of experienced commanders at Helles and Anzac, accustomed to the conditions that they had faced over the preceding months. This, though, did not necessarily fashion them into being "effective" commanders—however one might measure such a term. What can be measured is these commanders' familiarity with maneuver warfare. Given that Gallipoli had not yet offered such experience, one must look elsewhere. Of those commanding a brigade or higher during the August Offensive, 78 percent had served in the Boer War (see appendix 1). The vast majority, therefore, inevitably looked to their past experience as a model of how to act in a particular situation—this was natural, and they cannot be blamed for doing so.[22] The lessons of South Africa, however, were largely outdated by the new technologies that dominated the battlefields of the First World War.[23] Such men were in many ways doomed to apply obsolete experiences to a new problem. They were neither prepared nor experienced in the type of warfare they would have to perfect in order for the August Offensive to be successful.

The commanders' ability to influence the outcome of the offensive was further limited by the fact that communication with their troops ceased once the attack commenced.[24] Those commanding brigades, the level at which there was still some element of personal influence possible, were as a group perplexed as to whether they should remain behind or join their troops.[25] During the August Offensive, the majority of brigadiers accompanied their formations, but sensibly established their headquarters in rear of the firing line. The most influential level of command during the August Offensive, however, was at the battalion level, where officers physically accompanied their men into battle. The application of command in this instance was limited to how far one could shout and how long one could remain in action without being wounded.[26]

Force Size

The Allied force available for the August Offensive was nearly double the size of that for the initial landings in April. Yet, of the eleven divisions available, only five (plus an additional two brigades) were utilized for the offensive. On paper, and not including the two half-strength divisions (53rd and 54th) proceeding from the UK or the 2nd Mounted Division in Egypt—which combined to give Hamilton a general reserve of 19,000 men—Hamilton's force numbered 120,000.[27] In spite of the overall increase in troop numbers, the MEF remained 1,202 officers and 36,025 other ranks short of war establishment (excluding the French).[28] This incomplete force was required to attack the enemy, defend against counterattacks, undertake fatigues, hold the lines of communication, and advance across the peninsula in accord with Hamilton's operational objective. For his attack on the Sari Bair Ridge, Birdwood received an additional 15,200 men.[29] At the commencement of operations, Birdwood commanded 37,000 men—16,000 rifles below "war establishment."[30]

Inclusive of the force reserve, there were a total of twelve British and Dominion divisions at the Dardanelles in August 1915—a number overshadowed by the thirty-six British divisions on the Western Front and the twenty-six (thirteen Regular and thirteen Territorial) divisions in the UK. In other words, there were more than twice as many divisions in the UK being fitted out and trained as there were committed to the Dardanelles theater. With the two French divisions, the Allied force at the Dardanelles represented a mere 11 percent of the 126 *Allied* divisions on the Western Front.[31] A more pressing comparison can be made when examining the figures for September 1915. The MEF had a total strength of 191,682 (encompassing all forces in the Mediterranean *and* Egypt, including the

Table 1. War Establishment and Effective Strength of the Mediterranean Expeditionary Force

Formations	War Establishment		Effective strength, including details attached as in War Establishments		Surplus (Sur.) or deficiency (Def.)			
					Officers		Other ranks	
	Officers	Other ranks	Officers	Other ranks	Sur.	Def.	Sur.	Def.
GHQ and GHQ Troops	85	460	141	991	56	—	531	—
Army Troops	7	238	7	110	—	—	—	128
Royal Naval Division	391	10,494	269	8,667	—	122	—	1,827
10th Division	365	11,406	344	10,347	—	21	—	1,059
11th Division	492	15,118	413	12,080	—	79	—	3,038
13th Division	533	16,111	335	10,619	—	198	—	5,492
29th Division	604	17,981	439	14,503	—	165	—	3,478
42nd Division	555	15,673	450	11,304	—	105	—	4,369
52nd Division	540	15,987	307	9,347	—	233	—	6,640
ANZAC	1,463	40,547	1,133	30,449	—	330	—	10,098
Indian Contingent	153	7,072	148	6,645	—	5	—	427
Total at the Front	5,188	151,087	3,986	115,062	—	1,202	—	36,025

Source: "State of the MEF according to returns prepared by GHQ, 3rd Echelon, MEF," 31 July 1915, TNA, WO 162/69.

French divisions and reinforcements). This accounted for only 20 percent of the 916,605 *British* troops on the Western Front, or 13 percent of the 1,383,114 Territorial and Regular troops at home. The Gallipoli Campaign was clearly (and quite rightly) a subsidiary operation, constituting but 7 percent of the total British forces, yet the objectives set for the August Offensive were strikingly similar in terms of scope and scale to the ambitious tasks attempted in France and Flanders.[32] In terms of men alone, the August Offensive was drastically short.

While many of the old hands or originals from the April landings remained in August, there were also many new faces within the ranks—inexperienced drafts and fresh reinforcements, many of whom had only received minimal basic training. The divisions of IX Corps had not yet experienced active service. They were inexperienced and unaccustomed to the realities of war, and their reactions were not yet instinctive.[33] Moreover, since answering Kitchener's call for enlistments they had undergone ten months of training—but, because of the stalemate that had developed on the Western Front, this training was in trench warfare rather than the maneuver operations expected of them once they landed at Suvla Bay.[34] Their shooting may have been "good," and they may have been "well trained . . . fine personnel," but IX Corps was not at all practiced in mobile warfare.[35] How could they be expected to adapt successfully to this new warfare untrained and unprepared? Lieutenant-General Stopford realized this problem, writing that, after the failure to build on the surprise gained during the initial landing on 6–7 August, "the chances of our getting through with only raw troops and quite inadequate field artillery were very remote."[36]

In addition to the lack of experience in maneuver warfare among the attacking units, the general reserve available to Hamilton for his August Offensive was also insufficient. The 53rd Welsh and 54th East Anglian Divisions were at his disposal as a general reserve, to be employed where Hamilton deemed necessary.[37] It must be remembered, however, that the Dardanelles Committee regarded the 54th Division primarily as a draft pool to replace casualties, and not as a formation to be used in a general offensive.[38] Furthermore, the troops of these two divisions had received similar training as those of IX Corps and were therefore better prepared for static trench warfare than for the operations that would be expected of them during the offensive. Moreover, according to Lieutenant-Colonel

Thomas Forster, the assistant adjutant and quartermaster general (AA&QMG) at the Intermediate Base (Lemnos), who had closely observed two battalions of the 53rd Division during his voyage to the Dardanelles, the troops of these units were unfit for service, and a large proportion of them were underage. He had no hesitation in stating before the Dardanelles Commission in 1917 that these units should not have been sent to the Dardanelles in the first place.[39] Hamilton did not know that the 2nd Mounted Division in Egypt was at his disposal until Kitchener informed him on 28 July.[40] Upon learning of this, Captain Orlo Williams, responsible for deciphering telegrams at GHQ, retorted that, while it was good news, "we should have liked this information earlier."[41] Lieutenant-General John Maxwell, the GOC of the Force in Egypt, was also shocked by this sudden offer, stating that the news was "very disquieting" as he could only afford to part with four thousand yeomanry.[42] The yeomanry were trained in mobile war—of the mounted variety—and were commanded by Major-General William Peyton, a cavalry officer with little experience of unmounted maneuver. Therefore, like the attacking units, Hamilton's force reserve was also inexperienced and untrained in the type of operations planned for August at Gallipoli.

More importantly, however, were the barriers limiting the way in which Hamilton's reserve could actually be used. Hamilton had no definite plans on how to employ his reserve, preferring not to commit them, but to adapt his plans to the situation as it evolved and to throw them in where necessary. They were, to all intents and purposes, a reactionary force. If all went to plan, Hamilton did not even expect to use them at Anzac for the push across the peninsula. This feat, he thought, could be accomplished by the attacking force alone. Rather, he believed the reserve would be of best use if landed on the Asiatic shore of the Dardanelles, despite at the same time noting that there were not enough of them to affect any real advantage.[43]

Aside from this conceptual problem, as was made clear by the events on 9 August, the reserve could *not*, in fact, be employed where they were most required.[44] As the offensive unfolded, Birdwood was forced, purely due to logistic problems, to decline Hamilton's offer of the 54th Division to aid the attacks against the Sari Bair Ridge. There was simply no room for these reserves in the cramped confines of the Anzac sector until the heights of the Sari Bair Ridge were held. This achievement, of course, did not eventuate. That the reserve could not be accommodated at Anzac until the heights were held meant that even if Sari Bair was successfully gained, the reserve could never be in a position to build quickly on this success and push forward from Anzac for the second and third phases of the offensive. This delay, combined with their lack of training in mobile warfare, would render such a task impossible. Indeed, as it eventuated, one of the reserve divisions—the 53rd—was, at the admittance of its own GOC, incapable even of defense.[45] The force reserve was insufficient—in number, experience, and ability—to be relied on to defend a position, let alone to advance 4.6 miles across the peninsula. Even had the first phase succeeded, the subsequent phases would have stalled due to a lack of reinforcements capable of carrying out Hamilton's overly ambitious plans.[46]

Health and Morale in the MEF

Numbers, experience, and ability aside, the attacking units were in a number of other ways unfit for the type of warfare required of them. After more than three months on the peninsula, many troops were sick, exhausted, and demoralized.[47] Constant work, lack of sleep, and a monotonous diet had taken its toll. Prior to the offensive, according to the Australian official historian, Charles Bean, whose brother was a medical officer with the 3rd Australian Infantry Battalion, the men "were almost without exception sickening with intermittent diarrhoea, and their physical strength was slowly but obviously decreasing."[48] Dysentery and paratyphoid were rife.[49] By the end of July, the ANZAC was losing as many men per fortnight through sickness as they would from a general assault.[50] In fact, throughout the first four days of August, sick cases accounted for nearly *83 percent* of ANZAC losses.[51] This was clearly not a force capable of prolonged action.

The impact that sickness was having on Birdwood's force in the lead-up to the August Offensive was evident at all levels of command. Lieutenant-Colonel William Malone, the CO of the Wellington Battalion, informed his wife on 1 August that the men of the New Zealand Infantry Brigade—tasked with seizing Chunuk Bair and then proceeding southeastward through Battleship Hill and onto the rear of Baby 700—were so exhausted "that really they could not do themselves justice in fresh hard work."[52] Hard work, however, was exactly what was required. Similarly, Brigadier-General John Monash, who was tasked with seizing Hill 971, noted that "the men's health was below normal and getting worse."[53] But he was hopeful that the prospect of an advance would improve their morale and physical condition. Monash later admitted that the tasks of August were beyond the capacity of his worn troops.[54]

Birdwood too realized that all was not well. Sickness was having a debilitating effect on his troops and on the numbers available for the forthcoming offensive. He expressed his concern to Hamilton:

> I am afraid that I am not too happy about the state of the health of the men here. There is no epidemic, and [Colonel Neville] Howse, the Australian DDMS [sic, assistant director of medical services (ADMS)], tells me it is only what is to be expected at this time of the year, but at the same time he considers that the Australian Division with a fighting strength of 14,000 could not from a medical point of view be regarded as containing more than 10,000 fighting men in it. He is a very good man, and far from being an alarmist, so his words carry weight. There is no complaint against the rations in either quantity or quality, but, as he says, men want a change, and many of them have got run down and are weak from diarrhoea.[55]

While the determination to succeed was strong among his troops, Birdwood noted, "I fear that in many cases the flesh is rather weak."[56] He later admitted that his troops were too unfit to advance more than a couple of miles.[57] Yet, overall success was *many* miles distant. Despite informing Kitchener on the eve of the offensive that Birdwood's troops were in a poor state, Hamilton failed to recognize the implications that this would have on the combat effectiveness of the force, and by extension, on its real chances of successfully carrying all objectives for the upcoming operations.[58] Determination was not enough to succeed, especially for troops in such a debilitated state.

The physical condition of IX Corps, despite the men having only recently arrived, was no better than that of the troops in the Anzac sector. The voyage from the UK to the Dardanelles was long, hot, and cramped. Rest was minimal and dysentery rife. Additionally, many were still unwell as a consequence of recent cholera inoculations.[59] This was hardly a fresh force ready for action. According to Arthur Beecroft,

Suvla was already lost in Imbros. We had hell in that Island. We knew little about sanitation or the dangers of a tropical climate, and water was so scarce that armed guards had to be detailed for water-carts. . . . Instead of training the troops in open warfare, CO's spent their time trying to get sufficient water, and in trying to cope with diarrhoea. We had a crude saying that the 11th Div. went into battle grasping a rifle in one hand and holding up its trousers with the other. There was hardly a man who was not so troubled, and I need not add what a depressing and devitalizing effect such a malady has. Spirits become lower and lower, and there was already discontent. In the whole of my life I have never felt so down. . . . When one is rushing for the latrines dozens of times a day, as most of us were, esprit de corps soon oozes away.[60]

Such was the condition of Hamilton's attacking force before the commencement of the offensive. While supposedly the men were buoyed by the prospect of attacking the enemy, once the fighting got under way and the troops were further laden by the physical hardships of battle, their poor condition began to have a marked impact on their ability to advance. Marching and attacking had a profound effect on a state of health that was already unsatisfactory. Lieutenant Reginald Savory of the 14th Sikhs, tasked with seizing Hill Q, noted, "None of us is very hardy after three months of enforced inactivity in the trenches, and consequently when attacking up a very steep slope we all get so done up that we have to stop for a bit to rest."[61] Similarly, the men of the 4th Australian Bde. were so exhausted after their march on the night of 6–7 August that they abandoned attempts toward Hill 971 and spent the majority of 7 August resting. Birdwood later realized that further attacks on the Sari Bair Ridge were at that moment impossible owing not only to Ottoman resistance, but more importantly to "the increasing exhaustion of the troops."[62] The human elements of war (health, exhaustion, morale) cannot be underestimated in this regard. All had a direct impact on the performance of the MEF in August. Such troops were in *no* condition to wage a prolonged offensive—as would have been the case had the first phase of the offensive succeeded.

In addition to those becoming sick, battle casualties must also be considered. According to the Committee of Imperial Defence, it was necessary to have an additional 25 percent of any attacking force as reinforcements ready to be thrown in immediately to make up for casualties and to avoid delay.[63] Such a possibility, however, never existed at the Dardanelles. Rather, it took six weeks for drafts to arrive to fill vacancies caused by casualties.[64] The IX Corps, for example, had no arrangements for replacing wastage.[65] Lieutenant-General Stopford was therefore forced to accommodate this factor by reducing the effective strength of each unit by 20 percent and retaining the balance as a corps reserve.[66] The battalions of IX Corps, therefore, went into action even further below their deficiency in war establishment as outlined in table 1. The system was problematic, the solution even more so. Further evidence of the insufficiency of the system can be seen in the case of the ANZAC. Of the 5,800 casualties suffered by the corps (not including sick or attached units) from 6 to 10 August, only 34 percent (1,981) were replaced by reinforcements arriving at the same period: 66 percent of casualties therefore could not be immediately replaced. By 21 August, Birdwood's force of 37,000 had been reduced to 23,000.[67]

By October, the total size of the MEF was 105,705 rifles, some 86,453 men below war establishment.[68] The realization that "only by regardless sacrifice of men can we put this show through to any chance of success" was offset by the shortage of troops and the shortage of replacements.[69] Without men to replace casualties, any advance during the subsequent phases of the offensive would inevitably stall and lose its momentum. This is but one more example of the difficulty of large-scale, maneuver warfare. It is also further evidence against the opinion that the August Offensive nearly succeeded.

Signals Communication

Without adequate modes of intercommunication (telephone, telegraph, wireless, visual, orderlies, runners, and liaison officers), there could be no control or cohesion between units, whether in attack, defense, or retreat. The importance of the signal service in maintaining mobility was clearly recognized in *FSR* as being essential for the passing of orders, but more importantly, for the ability of subordinate commanders to keep their superiors, as well as neighboring commanders, informed of the progress of events in their vicinity, and any alterations to the tactical situation.[70] The role of the signal service was therefore complex and wide-ranging. Aside from the very important work of maintaining communication with the artillery, navy, and RNAS, the signal service had to establish and hold communications to the front and rear (between attacking units and their headquarters) and laterally (between flanking units).[71]

In addition to this work, the signal service was also responsible for laying and maintaining cables and systems on Imbros and Lemnos Islands, and liaising with the Eastern Telegraph Company.[72] Its task was further hampered by the physical separation of the three sectors in August (Helles, Anzac, Suvla) and by the fact that GHQ was located at Imbros Island—fifteen, eighteen, and nineteen miles from the respective sectors.[73] For the ambitious operational objective of Hamilton's offensive to be met, however, it was necessary that the signal service not only overcome these extant difficulties but also establish and maintain intercommunication systems at the earliest possible moment, thus allowing for the timely reporting of information, and for any advantages to be exploited.

While aspects of the signals communication system at the Dardanelles were the same as those employed on the Western Front—such as its structure and the equipment used—the amphibious nature of the campaign, the uniqueness and difficulty of the terrain, and the cramped confines in which it was fought necessitated some variations in how these systems were applied and adapted to suit local conditions.[74] For the August Offensive, the Helles and Anzac sectors would rely on the systems and structures already in place. The signallers would continue to maintain communication with brigade headquarters, who would then pass the information onto divisional headquarters, and so on, until it reached the GHQ Signal Company, under the command of the MEF director of army signals, Colonel Michael Bowman-Manifold.[75] The system in place, however, would not allow interdivisional (lateral) communication, and therefore any communication to a formation's flank had to be made through the corps HQ signal office, which then relayed the message to its intended recipient.[76] This limitation increased the time that it took to communicate with flanking units and resulted in delay and confusion. Because Suvla Bay was a new front, there was no existing communication system. This necessitated the development of an entirely new system allowing for communication from Suvla Bay to GHQ, ANZAC, and the supporting ships.

Basic signals communication was established at Suvla Bay by the morning of 7 August. A submarine cable laid between Kephalos Harbour (in Imbros Island) and Nibrunesi Point, which was then continued to A, B, and C Beaches, connected GHQ with the central

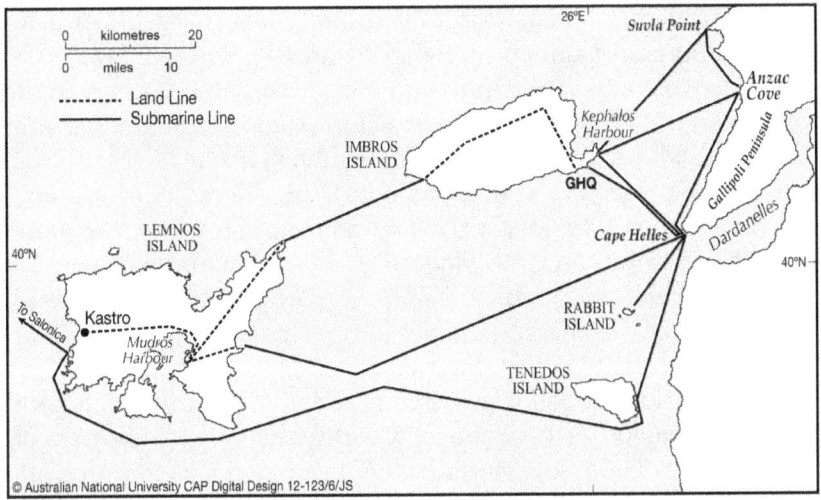

Map 4. Main cable routes

signal office south of Suvla Bay. Cables were then run inland to the infantry headquarters. Communication between shore and ships was made by visual signaling and two wireless transmission stations (W11 and W10). A third station (W9) situated on Imbros Island allowed GHQ to receive the messages between shore and ships, but this station was only to be used in a great emergency because of the resultant congestion and interference it caused. A cable was also run from Suvla to the south, thus connecting IX Corps with ANZAC.[77] This system was basic and far from efficient. Lateral communication between sectors was always problematic. Messages to GHQ were few, and there was great delay in using the wireless sets.[78] Indeed, many of the initial problems at Suvla were a direct result of the lack of communications.[79]

The communications problems at Suvla were exacerbated by the placement of IX Corps headquarters. It was initially planned for Stopford and his staff to remain at Imbros until communications had been established at Suvla Bay. This, it was felt, would ensure contact with GHQ and coordination with ANZAC HQ. But Stopford wanted to be close to the action and close to his troops.[80] Without warning GHQ, he, and the remainder of IX Corps HQ, boarded HMS *Jonquil* and embarked for Suvla on 6 August. This resulted in serious problems as no communication arrangements had been made for this scenario.[81] In addition, HMS *Jonquil* was incapable of handling the increased amount of signals required because of Stopford's decision. Not only was it now home to Stopford's HQ but, more importantly, HMS *Jonquil* was the flagship of Rear-Admiral Arthur Christian, who was supervising the landing—a role that required constant communication with the supporting ships, transports, and landing officers.[82] At Stopford's own admittance, this "was more than [the signallers on HMS *Jonquil*] could satisfactorily manage."[83] Stopford's chief staff officer, Brigadier-General Hamilton Reed agreed, noting, "It was impossible for the signallers with all their power to do more."[84] Delay ensued.

Stopford and his HQ was therefore effectively out of touch with the formations under his command during the first crucial days of the offensive. The result was a lack of command and control from the corps commander and inexperienced subordinate formations acting with little guidance. Stopford later defended his decision to remain on board *Jonquil*, noting that it was his only option if he was to remain in contact with GHQ and the navy. It was not for his comfort, he stressed, but for necessity of control.[85] In reality, there was little control.

Stopford and his staff finally left the *Jonquil* and took up a position at Suvla Point on the evening of 8 August.[86] This did not improve the situation. According to the director of army signals, the location chosen was "very inconvenient as regards communications, which became precarious owing to the amount of traffic crossing the cable along the beach." Its positioning also necessitated transferring the submarine cable from Nibrunesi Point to the signal office at Suvla Point so that IX Corps HQ could communicate with GHQ. This was not completed until 6:00 P.M., on 9 August.[87] The first three days of the battle at Suvla therefore passed with little guidance from Stopford or GHQ. The impact that this had on the fluidity and mobility of operations was marked: without communication there was no coordinated effort, and attacks were often launched in isolation rather than in tandem.

Another aspect that hindered the work of the signal service at the Dardanelles (and also on the Western Front) was a lack of signals personnel.[88] In the Anzac sector, for example, the NZ&A Divisional Signals Company struggled to scrape together enough men to accompany the advance toward Chunuk Bair on 6 August. It was only through improvisation and cooperation with the 13th

Divisional Signal Company that "no faults occurred and lines remained through all night." The shortage in personnel continued throughout the offensive. By the end of August it was noted that signals "personnel [are] still wasting faster than replaced."[89] There was also a shortage of operators to receive and relay all messages at the signal office.

By 9 August the NZ&A Divisional Signals Company communications responsibilities had expanded to include the Sari Bair force (minus the 13th Division) and the light horse brigades within the "old" Anzac sector. The company's diary exclaimed that all of this work was "a large order with only 12 operators!" The task was made even more difficult by the decision to move divisional headquarters two hundred yards north of its original position to No. 2 Outpost. To further add to its difficulties, the NZ&A Divisional Signals Company suffered from a lack of officers. Lieutenant Edward Hulbert, officer commanding (OC), New Zealand Mounted Rifles Brigade (NZMR Bde.) Signal Section, was evacuated sick prior to the offensive. Captain Henry Edwards, OC of the NZ&A Divisional Signals Company, was evacuated wounded on 10 August, followed two days later by Lieutenant Gavin Alexander, OC of the New Zealand Bde. Signal Section. The evacuation of all three men resulted in there being no signals officer available for the attack on 21 August against Hill 60, thus forcing Brigadier-General Monash to make the communications arrangements himself.[90] Back at Suvla the situation was so dire that GHQ sent operators and linesmen, thus depleting their own numbers, to alleviate the strain on Stopford's ailing headquarters.[91]

During the August Offensive, the Allied signal service also suffered due to the breakdown and congestion of lines. Maintaining communications was one of the principal difficulties during the advance toward the Sari Bair Ridge. Prior to the advance, officers leading columns were reminded that because of the potential of causing panic, no messenger was to be sent to the rear of a column any faster than the movement of that column forward. If the message was urgent, the messenger was to be dropped to await the arrival of the recipient.[92] Despite the NZ&A Division GOC Major-General Godley's praise of the linesmen who through "bravery and devotion to duty" maintained communication between his headquarters and his various columns, the reality was much different.[93]

In spite of the huge effort made by linesman, units constantly lost touch (or never had it) with each other and their headquarters.

Godley later acknowledged as much, stating that communication difficulties were to blame for the confusion surrounding the failure of a combined attack against Sari Bair to eventuate on 8–9 August (see chapter 7).[94] This case was but one example of the difficulty of maintaining the flow of tactical information between scattered units, where important messages too often became lost in a maze of "Chinese whispers."[95] In this instance, Godley's HQ was forced to communicate with brigade headquarters, rather than with the battalion directly (due to the absence of a direct line connecting the two).[96] Information was expected to filter down the chain of command, but this was not possible, as the 1/6th Gurkhas—who were to attack the enemy at Hill Q—were not in direct touch with their brigade headquarters.[97]

Another similar example existed at Chunuk Bair, where the Allied troops were essentially isolated—their signal lines and approaches being under constant enemy fire—from the direction or orders of the commanders at divisional and corps headquarters. Repairing these lines was both difficult and dangerous. Indeed, the only individual awarded a Victoria Cross for actions at Sari Bair—and the only New Zealander during the whole campaign—was Corporal Cyril Bassett for connecting divisional headquarters with the units at Chunuk Bair and then repairing cables while under heavy fire.[98]

Terrain as an Obstacle to Mobility

Aside from making it difficult to establish and maintain signals communications, the terrain at Gallipoli was also a significant physical obstacle to the movement of the attacking units themselves. While not the sole reason for the Allied failure in August, terrain was a very important aspect.[99] The Ottomans held all of the favorable ground, thus compensating to some extent for their deficiencies in fire support and munitions. Unlike the flat fields of France and Flanders, Gallipoli was rugged and mountainous, and the most precipitous terrain was the approach to Sari Bair Ridge—the precise area through which the Allies attacked on 6 August.[100] In the words of the war correspondent Henry Nevinson, "No analysis or map or description can adequately express the roughness and complexity of that desert jungle, the steepness of its cliffs and spurs and edges, or the bewilderment of its dry watercourses, creeks, fissures, and ravines."[101]

Hamilton described it as more difficult than the Khyber Pass, while Major-General Frederick Shaw, GOC of the 13th Div., stated that it would be "a difficult nut to crack."[102] Kitchener was informed that the ground "was far worse than anything the [Australian and New Zealand] Army Corps had to negotiate when it first landed . . . [and] probably the most difficult and hazardous ever undertaken by a body of troops of this size."[103] Major-General Godley had the last word. After revisiting the area in 1925, he admitted that it "was more desperately difficult than we ever realised."[104]

It was this very difficulty that Birdwood hoped would help ensure victory. Writing to his wife two days before the offensive, he stated that the best chance of success was to attack the strongest part of the natural defenses—where the enemy would least expect it.[105] It is certainly true that the Ottomans did not expect an attack in this region—but for good reason. An attack could not be sustained through such terrain. The fact that the Ottomans did not consider the area worthy of defense is itself significant in this regard. Purely in terms of the inevitable limitations imposed on mobility by the terrain, the idea of attacking the Sari Bair Ridge was always destined to prove a fundamental mistake. In terms of terrain alone (and by no means was terrain the only problem encountered), it was not a good plan that nearly succeeded, but rather it was an implausible task from its conception. But how did terrain impact upon the movement of the force?

Prior to the offensive Lieutenant-General Birdwood was conscious of the fact that the difficulty of the terrain would prevent him using his force to its best advantage.[106] The guides and officers leading the attack against the Sari Bair Ridge were warned that, in such broken country, the maximum speed of advance could not exceed more than one mile per hour.[107] It was this broken country that delayed the early stage of operations on 6–7 August. The ground was so difficult to traverse that the task allotted to the clearing force, the NZMR Bde., could not be completed in time. Similarly, terrain was the primary factor in the Canterbury Battalion arriving late at its rendezvous on Rhododendron Ridge on the morning of 7 August. The route taken by the left assaulting column (4th Australian Bde. and 29th Indian Bde.) was so difficult and confusing, that even with the newly issued 1:20,000 scale maps—which clearly showed the terrain in ten-meter contours—Monash and his subordinates were perplexed as to their actual whereabouts. The delay caused by the terrain was sufficient to remove the element of surprise that Hamilton had always thought essential, and the very difficult going prevented a cohesive Allied attempt to take the Sari Bair Ridge.

Although dwarfed by comparison with the difficulty of the terrain at Sari Bair, the ground at Suvla was no easy feat on its own terms. The bay itself was overlooked by a series of small hillocks that proved to be decisive barriers during the Allied landing on 6 August. As was confirmed by the events on the following day, the Salt Lake, despite being dry, was also a formidable obstacle to any forward advance. Similarly, while appearing rather flat on a map, the Suvla plain itself was deceptively difficult: the whole area, according to Aspinall, was "a lot of scrub jungle with rocks . . . a typical country for sniping."[108] Moving inland, according to Stopford's chief of staff, the ground became "very difficult with thick scrub and not very easy I should say for a goat to get through."[109] A ring of hills, strewn with Ottoman defensive posts, dominated the entire area. Kiretch Tepe Ridge, the northernmost ridge—where much heavy fighting occurred during the early stages of the offensive—was so rocky that it was impossible to dig adequate defensive positions.[110] Should the offensive have progressed into its subsequent phases, the Suvla sector would prove to add little beyond a base of operations (as was the original intention). The geographical features of the sector, which was situated at the widest part of the Gallipoli Peninsula, offered little advantage for maneuver. Any attempt to cut the enemy's lines of communication would require holding a line with both flanks exposed "ten miles" long from Suvla to the Straits, all the while defending against strong enemy counterattacks.[111] In reality, Suvla was too far from the Narrows to have any effect on operations.

Ottoman Defensive Capabilities

Overlaid on top of all of the not inconsequential barriers to Allied mobility thus far discussed is one common aspect: the enemy. Ottoman forces on the peninsula were the most fundamental obstacle to Allied mobility. While facing many, if not more, of the same difficulties as the Allies, the Ottomans had two major advantages: terrain and troop numbers. Furthermore, sickness was not as rife as it was for the Allies, morale was generally high, and the Ottomans were prepared to defend every inch of ground.[112] Nonetheless, British senior officers still tended to underestimate the capabilities of their Ottoman enemy, whom they saw as the remnants of a militarily weak and declining empire.[113] For Hamilton, the mobile soldier was far better than the static one—and soldierly potential itself was linked to race. Hamilton therefore wanted to fight the enemy in the open, where he was sure that his force would excel over his ethnically and fundamentally inferior enemy. On 14 June he wrote to Kitchener, "Let me bring my lads face to face with Turks [sic] in the open field, we must beat them every time because British volunteer soldiers are superior individuals to Anatolians, Syrians or Arabs and are animated with a superior ideal and an equal joy in battle."[114] Hamilton was, however, forced to concede the defensive abilities of the Ottomans. Five days later he wrote to the commander in chief of the BEF, Sir John French: "In a manoeuvre battle of old style our fellows here would beat twice their number of Turks in less than no time, but, actually, the restricted Peninsula suits the Turkish tactics to a 'T.' They have always been good at trench work where their stupid men have only simple, straightforward duties to perform, namely, in sticking on and shooting anything that comes up to them."[115]

To Hamilton, the Turkish soldier was "stupid, but exceedingly brave."[116] "Toe-to-toe," he informed Kitchener, "the individual Turk is a better fighting man than the same German," especially when fighting for his homeland.[117] Birdwood agreed, reminding his troops before the offensive that "there is no doubt that they [the enemy] will always fight well when behind trenches": getting them into the open was the only way to combat this.[118] Allied command respected the Ottomans' defensive ability, but it had not yet grasped the reality of static industrial war. In this regard the promise of August was an answer to an outdated question.

The Inability of Progressing across the Peninsula

A large-scale offensive such as the August Offensive at Gallipoli was beyond the abilities of the MEF. A force much smaller in number than those on the Western Front was expected to attain an objective that was as ambitious, complex, and difficult as those being undertaken in France and Flanders in 1915. Indeed, the battle at Neuve Chapelle had shown that, while it was possible to break into the enemy's defenses, it was not possible to break through and beyond them at this stage of the war.[119] The August Offensive was further evidence of this. As was later acknowledged in the British Fourth Army's *Tactical Notes* of 1916, a soldier could only contribute so much before fatigue took over. There was a limit to human endurance, and men were not physically capable of more than one decisive assault without sufficient rest.[120]

For a breakout offensive such as that planned for August, mobility was essential. Yet it was not possible at Gallipoli in any meaningful sense. Sick and exhausted men, with little knowledge of their objectives and insufficient in number, were required to advance under a detached command and control system. An overworked and poor intercommunication system compounded these difficulties, and all the while the Allies faced terrain that was too complex to allow for a coordinated maneuver. Against all of these factors was a capable and determined enemy. Even had the MEF overcome its own structural and physical deficiencies, mobility would have withered under such difficulties. There was, in reality, little chance of success. The assumption that success was assured once the heights of the Sari Bair Ridge were in Allied hands is incorrect. The August Offensive did not even approach success. This was as true for mobility as it was for artillery. But was Allied fire support sufficient and adequate enough to protect the MEF's ground forces should they have attempted to advance across the peninsula?

CHAPTER 3

FIRE SUPPORT

Fire support at the Dardanelles was peculiar. The amphibious nature of the campaign, and the complexity of the terrain that confronted the Allies, necessitated an array of fire support techniques. This was especially evident during the August Offensive, in which artillery tactics differed markedly between the various sectors. Helles was, like the Western Front, experiencing a type of siege warfare; the terrain at Anzac (and Sari Bair) highlighted the need for high-angle howitzer fire; and, being a new amphibious landing, Suvla was initially entirely dependent on the navy for its fire support. The complex systems employed in all sectors, which relied on interservice cooperation (for observation), adequate and timely communications, and a flexible command and control system, were, however, still stuck in the lessons of previous wars.[1]

In 1915 British doctrine and operational theory viewed artillery as an accessory (and subsidiary) to the infantry, rather than an autonomous arm.[2] Its function, as made clear in *FSR* was "to assist the other arms in breaking down hostile opposition."[3] The emphasis on "assisting" tended to mean, at the very outset, that fire support had to mold and adapt to the infantry's plans, rather than those plans being developed in accordance with the strengths (and weaknesses) of the fire-support resources available. Indeed, it was not until 1917 that the British realized the full potential of artillery and adapted their plans and planning processes accordingly.[4] As the war progressed it became clear that fire support was much more than an accessory. It was "the lord of the battlefield" and it was essential for success.[5]

But, within this doctrinal context, was the Allied land-based artillery available during the August Offensive sufficient to enable the infantry to achieve the operational objectives set? To answer this, and therefore objectively assess the true operational capabilities of the MEF, this chapter examines the quantity and quality of fire support available for the August Offensive. It also analyzes the application of this fire support—particularly the coordination and cooperation between the infantry, artillery, and air service—all of which were crucial if the plans were to have any chance of succeeding (for an examination of naval fire support, see chapter 4).[6]

This chapter begins with a brief examination of the Allied artillery at Gallipoli in preparation for and throughout the August Offensive, followed by an in-depth analysis of the difficulties faced during operations. Such an appreciation will provide a framework for a subsequent discussion in chapter 8 on the predicted barriers (based on an understanding of the plans and limitations) that would have been encountered by Allied artillery during the subsequent phases—should they have ever been attempted.[7]

Artillery Support during the August Offensive

Typical accounts attributing the start of the August Offensive to 6 August largely neglect the work of the artillery. The artillery offensive actually commenced much earlier. For five days preceding the initial feint at Cape Helles, Allied artillery spent time and effect registering fire onto Ottoman trenches and attempting to silence hostile guns.[8] With the preparations complete, the preliminary bombardment, consisting of three batteries of French 75mm field guns (twelve guns) and one howitzer battery (six howitzers), commenced at 2:29 P.M., 6 August. For an hour the British and French howitzers directed their fire onto the Ottoman frontline trenches. The field batteries (sixty 18-pounders and eight 15-pounders) and thirty Vickers machine guns joined in an hour later. The rate of fire increased as zero hour approached.[9] The aim of this fire was to subdue the Ottomans' machine guns in order to give the infantry a clearer approach. At 3:50 P.M.—the moment of attack—Allied guns lifted their fire onto the enemy's reserve trenches and guns.[10] This, it was hoped, would form a *tir de barrage* to cover the infantrymen while they consolidated their newly won positions.[11] But the bombardment was not effective. When their assault commenced, British infantrymen were immediately cut down by Ottoman machine-gun and artillery fire. Allied artillery at Helles had, in this case, failed to support the infantry.

In the Anzac sector the preliminary bombardment was focused on the Ottoman positions at Lone Pine, the Chessboard, the Nek,

German Officers' Trench, Baby 700, and Battleship Hill.[12] The plan was that the shrapnel of the 18-pounder field guns would destroy wire entanglements, while the 4.5-inch and 5-inch howitzers directed their high-explosive shells on to the Ottoman trenches.[13] In the case of Lone Pine, the bombardment was successful. It inflicted numerous casualties upon the enemy and forced the remainder of the Ottoman defenders to take cover, thus leaving the parapets only lightly manned to meet the oncoming Australian attack.[14] Once the assault on Lone Pine commenced, Allied fire support shifted its attention from the Ottoman front lines onto their communication trenches, guns, and approaches to the firing line.[15] Counterbattery fire was important to try and reduce the amount of Ottoman artillery fire.[16] This tactic was doubly important due to the short distances to be covered by the attacking infantry, and the need to avoid friendly fire, but at the same time it essentially meant that from zero hour the attacking troops were without fire support.[17] The Heavy Battery (Australian Divisional Artillery), consisting of one 4.7-inch gun and two 6-inch howitzers, was especially successful in neutralizing the fire of the enemy's batteries south of Lone Pine but could not completely destroy them.[18] The success of the infantry at Lone Pine can largely be attributed to the fire support provided.[19] Writing on 10 August, Brigadier-General Joseph Talbot Hobbs, commander, Royal Artillery (CRA), of the Australian Divisional Artillery, noted, "There is one thing every one of us must never forget, that is, the enormous self sacrificing assistance the Infantry have received throughout from every gun."[20]

Fire support for the other feints in the Anzac sector on 7 August was less successful. With the actions at Lone Pine within sight, subsequent Allied bombardments merely warned the Ottomans that more attacks were imminent. The bombardment at the Nek, for example, did little except highlight the Allies' intention to attack in that region—an intention that was made all the more obvious as the intensity of the bombardment increased throughout the night of 6–7 August.[21] This warning, combined with poor communications and the failure of the bombardment to destroy the enemy's machine guns, had a profound effect on the attacking force.[22] Largely unharmed by the shelling, and able to man their guns, the Ottomans immediately opened fire on the Australians, quelling the attack. In this instance, as in those at the Chessboard and German Officers' Trench, fire support, especially its practical application, was found wanting.

The situation was profoundly different for the attack against the principal objective of the first phase of the August Offensive—the Sari Bair Ridge. Due to the need for surprise, and the fear of raising suspicion of an impending attack, none of the guns in the Anzac sector had even registered their fire on the ridge, or its approaches, prior to the offensive.[23] This meant that there was no preliminary bombardment for the attack on Sari Bair, and should there be a problem, the field artillery at Anzac could only fire indirect, unregistered rounds in support—a practice that dramatically decreased its accuracy and increased the chances of misdirected friendly fire.[24] The exception to this was the "destroyer program," which occurred nightly for three weeks preceding the offensive.[25] This program, undertaken by HMS *Colne* and HMS *Chelmer*, aimed to lure the Ottoman defenders at Old No. 3 Post into becoming complacent and accustomed to shellfire, with the hope that the Ottomans would not suspect anything when firing opened on 6 August. While it worked, and directly assisted the NZMR Bde. in its task of clearing the foothills below Sari Bair, the naval shelling itself was minimal and cannot be described, in any meaningful sense, as a bombardment. Moreover, the destroyers ceased firing once first contact was made with the Ottomans on 6 August and offered no further protection to the attackers.

Thus, on the morning of 7 August, with the element of surprise gone and the preliminary phases over, the land-based fire support available for the troops attacking Sari Bair proved lacking. Having failed to reach their objectives before daylight, the Allied infantrymen were greatly exposed and vulnerable to Ottoman fire from both flanks, and fire support was urgently required. Lieutenant-Colonel George Johnston, CRA of the NZ&A Divisional Artillery, later stated that the most senior artillery officer of the MEF, Brigadier-General Richard Fuller, and the General Staff at GHQ had failed to consider the implications of the attack not succeeding, and therefore, had not thought of how to support the now static and pinned-down Allied troops throughout the day.[26]

The minimal covering fire available from within the Anzac sector was not sufficient, with troops having to rely on Maxim machine-gun fire to protect their local advances.[27] Some early support was available in the form of naval gunfire and eight obsolete 10-pounder mountain guns of the 21st Kohat and 26th Jacob's Mountain Batteries—of the 7th Indian Mountain Artillery (IMA)

Brigade—which accompanied the advancing columns. Because of their close proximity to the troops, these mountain batteries were forced to employ crossfire techniques, firing in support of their flanking column rather than their own. There was little communication or cooperation between the two batteries, which as a consequence of their physical separation caused them to fire on those targets they *presumed* to be of importance to the other column, rather than what was necessarily required.[28] Realizing that eight obsolete mountain guns were insufficient to protect the exposed troops, all batteries of the Australian Divisional Artillery that could fire in a northeasterly direction were ordered during the afternoon of 7 August to register fire on the Sari Bair Ridge.[29]

For the next three days, these batteries, in conjunction with those of the New Zealand Divisional Artillery, provided indirect fire on the summits and approaches to Sari Bair, as well as maintaining fire in support of counterattacks at Lone Pine. Should the troops ever have managed to reach Sari Bair in sufficient numbers to hold the crest for an extended period, Lieutenant-Colonel Johnston was convinced that there were not sufficient guns to support them on their objective. The planners of the offensive should, he believed, have recognized this and landed more guns at Anzac as a precaution in case the attack did not succeed in the first instance.[30]

The situation was much the same at Suvla Bay. The need for secrecy removed the possibility of a preliminary bombardment, and, like the attackers at Sari Bair, IX Corps was supported by an insufficient number of guns. As an amphibious operation, fire support at Suvla Bay differed from that employed elsewhere. Unlike the other fronts, there was no field artillery to support the infantry. Rather, troops landed ashore solely under the "protection" of the ships' guns. It was the task of the infantry to advance first, and thereby create a rear area into which guns could be safely placed and operated. Hamilton specifically noted that "an advance has to be made to enable the field guns to open fire."[31] The problem was that the infantry found it difficult to advance at Suvla in the absence of artillery support.[32] The slow progress of the infantry, combined with a lack of small landing craft, rough seas, and the need to land field ambulances and supply mules, all delayed the landing and deployment of the field artillery at Suvla.[33] Only one battery of 18-pounders—"A" Battery from the 59th Brigade, Royal Field Artillery (RFA)—and one battery of 10-pounder mountain guns—the Argyll Battery of the

4th Highland Mountain Brigade—managed to land at Suvla in the first twenty-four hours of operations. These guns had the responsibility of engaging hostile guns *and* supporting the infantry attacks.[34] The three remaining batteries of the 59th Brigade, RFA, which were meant to land shortly after dawn on 7 August, did not actually arrive until the afternoon of 8 August.[35] The unit's war diary noted that, as such, they were "too late to take any serious part in the action."[36]

The next guns to arrive at Suvla were four 60-pounders of the 15th Heavy Battery, Royal Garrison Artillery (RGA), on 10 August. Those of the 10th Heavy Battery, RGA, which had been earmarked for Suvla but which had landed at Anzac, remained at the latter throughout the offensive due to an absence of suitable positions at Suvla and the difficulty of moving them between sectors. Another battery of 18-pounders—the 58th Battery, RFA—which had also been disembarked at Anzac, did not arrive at Suvla until 11–12 August.[37] Thus, for the first two and most crucial days of the operations at Suvla, only eight guns supported the entire infantry push. This was exceedingly short of the normal establishment of one hundred guns that would usually (and doctrinally) accompany a force of such size.[38] These eight guns were not capable of dealing with the nineteen well-hidden Ottoman artillery pieces, which were spread out along the Kiretch Tepe and Tekke Tepe Ridges, and which had been positioned and preregistered so as to bring fire on all ground between the Ottomans' defended localities.[39] Additional Ottoman guns also arrived much faster into the area around Suvla than those of IX Corps. There were fifty-four Ottoman pieces in position by 8 August, and one hundred by 21 August.[40] On the same dates there were only twenty-four and thirty-six opposing Allied guns respectively.[41] Contrary to the belief that it was a superior force to its Ottoman enemy, IX Corps was outgunned at Suvla Bay. While there was naval gunfire support available, due to a range of practical and procedural shortcomings to be discussed later in this and the following chapter, the ships' guns had little material effect in supporting the infantry at Suvla.

Across the board, the Allied efforts to provide adequate fire support for the August Offensive could not prevent the movement or massing of Ottoman reserves, as was shown in their ability to mount large-scale counterattacks at Suvla on 8–9 August and at Chunuk Bair on 10 August. The reasons for this went beyond the simple lack of guns already discussed. Allied artillery plans also suffered from a largely inept command structure that did not provide for proper consultation between headquarters and divisional artillery commanders and that left the gunners with little knowledge of the objectives they were supposed to suppress or destroy. The MEF also had insufficient ammunition to support an offensive of the scale envisaged. Moreover, many of the guns that were available were of an inferior quality and not suitable for action in the type of terrain encountered. Furthermore, naval fire, while available, was largely ineffective due to its flat trajectory, and there were numerous problems associated with spotting for all forms of fire support. Added to this was the safer and superior positions occupied by the enemy and their guns. The chapter will now examine each of these aspects, and how they had an impact upon the fire support available for the August Offensive.

Artillery Planning and Command Structure

It was acknowledged during the planning process for the August Offensive that "the provision of adequate artillery support will be a great difficulty" as suitable positions for the construction of gun emplacements were scarce and a great deal of ammunition would be required.[42] Such a realization, however, did not deter the planners. The lessons of March 1915 at Neuve Chapelle, which showed that concentrated fire and detailed artillery preparation was essential for initial success, were ignored. At Gallipoli, plans developed without due consideration of the firepower situation and irrespective of the opinions and concerns of the artillery experts. Lieutenant-Colonel Johnston later testified before the Dardanelles Commission about the dangers of such a situation: "If the CRA of an Army does not express himself strongly he may be dominated, and the Chief of the Staff, not being a gunner, may not realize what is absolutely necessary."[43] Such was indeed the case at the Dardanelles. The CGS of the MEF, Major-General Braithwaite, directed the head artillery commander, Brigadier-General Fuller, in what was necessary and what was expected of the artillery. Artillery formations and units were then left to develop plans and timetables in accordance with the objectives selected by Braithwaite and his staff. The offensive was thus conceived and developed as an infantry operation, and the artillery was expected to fit in with the infantry plan. This was not cooperation, and the offensive suffered accordingly.

Aside from the lack of communication between the infantry and the artillery during the planning process, the artillery organization itself also suffered from a lack of internal cooperation. High-level plans were predominantly developed at army and corps level, with the CRAs at divisional level being left out of the process until the last moment.[44] This was especially pronounced in the Anzac sector. Charles Cunliffe Owen, brigadier-general, Royal Artillery (BGRA) of the ANZAC, took on a greater than usual role prior to the August Offensive, working out the specifics of the artillery timetables—a task previously (and properly) allotted to his subordinates. There was, therefore, a clear divide between those who planned the operations and those who were to carry them out. Some details managed to slip through the web of secrecy to divisional level, but these were only segments of the whole scheme.[45] Detailed plans were not formally explained to the CRAs at Anzac until 2 August.[46] Their subordinates at brigade level were informed and issued orders the following day.[47] Conferences were then held on 4 August to explain the targets and schemes to the battery commanders.[48] This rushed process allowed neither much time to study the ground nor enough time for the procurement of necessary ammunition or the registration of fire.

At the commencement of the August Offensive, Allied artillery was organized and administered on an ad hoc basis. According to Lieutenant-Colonel Johnston, "There was no arrangement about it." Indeed, there was little supervision of individual artillery formations. Johnston, for example, rarely saw his superior, Brigadier-General Fuller.[49] This was particularly the case at Helles where there was no corps-level artillery officer—the most important level of artillery command.[50] Instead, command of all British artillery in the Helles sector fell to the divisional artillery commander, Brigadier-General Hugh Simpson-Baikie, CRA of the 29th Div. Artillery.[51] Such a force was too large to fall under the responsibility of a single CRA, though, and Fuller realized that the situation would further deteriorate if the force were called on to advance from its present position. Fuller therefore suggested that an officer be appointed BGRA of the VIII Corps, thus restoring the normal system of command.[52] The change, however, did not occur until the appointment of Brigadier-General Cecil de Rougemont on 17 August.[53] A general reorganization then took place in VIII Corps, which both simplified the artillery command structure and improved cooperation within the artillery and with the infantry.⁵⁴ This modification was too late to have any effect on the offensive.

The amphibious nature of the operations at Suvla had a profound impact on the application of fire support. While a more standard organizational structure was in place at Suvla Bay, the artillery command system quickly broke down. Believing that he could better cooperate with the navy and control his artillery from offshore, Sydenham Smith, BGRA of the IX Corps, remained on board HMS *Talbot* throughout the offensive.⁵⁵ In doing so he was plagued by the same communications problems that troubled Stopford and his staff on HMS *Jonquil* and was therefore largely out of contact with both his artillery ashore and the infantry commanders who required his support. The problem was further compounded on 9 August, when one of the two battery commanders ashore at Suvla, Major Henry Cowell, OC of "B" Battery, 59th Brigade, RFA, was mortally wounded. The command structure was dealt another blow on the morning of 13 August when Brigadier-General Edward Granet, CRA of the 11th Divisional Artillery, was also wounded. Stopford's corps could ill afford such losses, especially considering that an enemy situated in better terrain, with superior observation, and with pre-registered fire outgunned it. Many of these issues were fixed by a reorganization of IX Corps' artillery, but again this did not occur until after the failure of the operations of 21 August.⁵⁶

Like IX Corps, the artillery of the ANZAC was organized along standard lines but was not without its own complications. The increase in guns for the offensive, for instance, was not matched by a commensurate increase in senior officers to command them. Lieutenant-Colonel Johnston, for example, commanded twice as many guns than someone of his rank usually did.⁵⁷ His command and responsibility therefore doubled, without a doubling of his staff. Similarly, the command responsibility of Lieutenant-Colonel Charles Rosenthal, CO of the 3rd Australian Field Artillery Brigade (FAB), increased to include twenty-nine guns/howitzers—an increase of 241 percent from what he doctrinally ought to be commanding.⁵⁸ Such increases in responsibility without equivalent increases in staff meant that more work had to be transferred to subordinates.⁵⁹ These issues aside, Johnston was of the opinion that while his preparations for the August Offensive were affected by this, it had little impact on the overall result—as far as he was concerned he had too few guns to achieve anything anyway.⁶⁰

Table 2. Effective Artillery Strength, Mediterranean Theater, August 1915
Allied artillery pieces per sector up until 10 August 1915

Weapon type	Helles	Anzac	Anzac for Suvla	Suvla	(Egypt/ Mudros)	Total
60-pounder field gun	8	—	4	4	—	16
6-inch howitzer	4	3	—	—	4	11
5-inch howitzer	8	24	—	—	—	32
4.5-inch howitzer	4	4	—	—	16	24
12-pounder naval gun	4	—	—	—	—	4
4.7-inch naval gun	—	1	—	—	—	1
18-pounder field gun	84	28	16	16	64	208
15-pounder BLC gun	20	—	—	—	—	20
10-pounder mountain gun	—	12	—	8	—	20
6-inch siege gun	—	—	—	—	4	4
9.2-inch naval gun	—	—	—	—	2	2
15-inch howitzer	—	—	—	—	1	1
75mm field gun (French)	48	—	—	—	—	48
65mm field gun (French)	20	—	—	—	—	20
120mm long (4.7-inch) howitzer (French)	4	—	—	—	—	4
155mm long (6-inch) howitzer (French)	4	—	—	—	—	4
155mm short (6-inch) howitzer (French)	6	—	—	—	—	6
Total	214	72	20	28	91	425

Artillery Strength and Its Deployment

But were there too few guns? Were the plans developed outside the parameters of what could realistically be achieved by the Allied fire support available for the August Offensive? Historian Tim Travers does not think so. Rather, he states, "Gallipoli was *probably* supplied with *just enough* artillery and ammunition to achieve Allied success."[61] It is important to examine the validity of such a claim. Because nothing is certain in war, it is necessary to determine the specifics and make comparisons with similar offensives. Although much smaller in size (frontage and attacking force), but blessed with much more ammunition, the British attack at Neuve Chapelle in March 1915, for example, was very similar in its conception. Like the August Offensive at Gallipoli, the enemy trenches at Neuve Chapelle were only the first objective of a multiphase operation, which aimed to break through the enemy's lines and reintroduce mobility to the battlefield. That plan too, was a failure.

The MEF had an effective strength of 425 artillery pieces in the Mediterranean theater in August 1915—82 of these belonged to the French, who, apart from allotting 18 pieces to the British for their actions at Cape Helles, took no further part in the offensive. This reduced the total available for the offensive to 334 pieces.[62] There were a further 91 pieces located throughout Egypt and Mudros, but due to limitations of space on the cramped peninsula, it was neither intended nor possible to utilize these weapons during the early stages of the August Offensive.[63] This then reduced the total to 270 artillery pieces available on the peninsula—150 at Helles, 72 at Anzac, 28 to be landed at Suvla, and an additional 20 at Anzac awaiting transportation to Suvla (for a further detailed breakdown of weapon types and numbers per sector see appendix 2).[64]

This total—the amount of artillery pieces available for the largest offensive at Gallipoli—was well under war establishment. At the commencement of the war, the artillery establishment for each British division contained seventy-six pieces.[65] If this establishment figure is applied to the eight complete divisions available for the August Offensive (excluding the two French divisions, the Royal Naval Division, and the two reserve divisions), the MEF should have had 608 pieces available.[66] It must be acknowledged, however, that because of production limitations the British could only equip the New Army and Territorial divisions with four-gun batteries.[67]

With this in mind, at this reduced establishment the MEF should still have been equipped with a minimum of 416 pieces. Even if one includes the 91 pieces at Egypt and Mudros, the MEF was still 55 pieces (13 percent) below establishment. It should be reiterated, however, that it was not possible to employ these 91 until the force had advanced and thus created sufficient space for additional gun emplacements. Further conclusions can be drawn when one examines the artillery deficiency in each sector. Helles was largely at establishment with a deficiency of only 3.8 percent.[68] Suvla was substantially worse, with a deficiency of 44.2 percent.[69] Anzac, however, was the worst, with a deficiency of 62.1 percent.[70] Despite this, the Allies still outgunned the Ottomans overall, who in August had a total of 163 guns and howitzers.[71] As shown by the deficiencies, though, superiority in numbers did not necessarily mean superiority in practice.

Compounding the problems associated with deficiencies in numbers, the tactical deployment of the Allied firepower was also skewed. The proportion of guns in each sector did not match the proportion of troops. Despite representing only 36 percent (not including the French divisions) of the available troops and the least significant sector for August, Helles contained 55.5 percent of the artillery. Suvla was roughly proportional with 20 percent of troops and 17.8 percent of the artillery. Anzac, however, was well below par in this regard with 44 percent of the troops but only 26.7 percent of the artillery.[72] The result was a clear deficiency in the artillery available to support the two main sectors: Sari Bair/Anzac and Suvla. This would be troublesome, especially if the Allies proceeded into the second and third phases of the offensive—where the role of the artillery would increase, as would its responsibilities should Hamilton attempt to push across the peninsula with the two reserve (and artillery-less) divisions.

As noted previously, many similarities appear if comparisons with the tactical employment of fire support during the August Offensive are made with that of the first British set piece offensive of the war (against an entrenched enemy), the battle of Neuve Chapelle. In both instances the 18-pounders were used to destroy the wire entanglements, the howitzers to fire on the trenches, and the heavy artillery to bombard distant targets and engage in counter-battery work.[73] The artillery plans were also similar, both containing numerous phases and new roles for the artillery as the offensive progressed. Despite the conceptual similarities of the two offensives, however, the fire support available was significantly different.

In spite of being a much smaller operation than the August Offensive, there were far more artillery pieces available for Neuve Chapelle. With approximately 340 artillery pieces to support four divisions (only three brigades were actually involved in the initial attack) the fire support at Neuve Chapelle was 11 percent in excess of establishment (compared to the 13 percent deficiency at the Dardanelles).[74] With a frontage of two thousand yards, or one artillery piece for every six yards of trench, Neuve Chapelle had the heaviest concentration of British artillery fire at the time, and was not surpassed until 1917.[75] This ratio of pieces per yard employed during Neuve Chapelle was considered an optimal amount for a preliminary bombardment that aimed to "crush and demoralise the enemy's infantry," yet numbers alone did not ensure success.[76]

The preliminary bombardment at Neuve Chapelle, while successful in destroying the majority of wire entanglements, was less successful, especially on 23rd Brigade's front, in hitting the German trenches.[77] The British infantry was eventually successful in obtaining its first phase objectives, but as a result of artillery limitations (primarily the lack of preregistered targets) and the defensive resilience of the Germans, the offensive could not proceed beyond this phase. Neuve Chapelle showed that target registration and powerful artillery support was essential for offensive operations.[78] Neither of these, however, was available at the Dardanelles. The fire support available for the Helles operations equated to one piece per twenty-eight yards of front (a ratio similar to that later employed at Loos).[79] At Anzac/Sari Bair, it was worse with one piece for every *111 yards* of frontage.[80] The situation at Suvla was absolutely dismal. For the first three days of operations, there was one piece ashore for every *833 yards* of frontage. With the arrival of additional pieces, the ratio improved, but only to one for every 416 yards.[81] With the example of Neuve Chapelle in mind, from an artillery perspective, it is small wonder the August Offensive failed to achieve even the first phase of its objectives.

Despite the deficiencies in artillery pieces available in the Dardanelles, it is important to note that the MEF's artillery, as a percentage of *total* British artillery, was roughly proportional to the percentage of *total* British troops sent to the Dardanelles. In other words, the Dardanelles represented approximately 7 percent of both the total British troops and artillery.[82] The 73 artillery batteries at the Dardanelles, for example, represented 13 percent of those in the United Kingdom; 23 percent of those on the Western Front; and 7 percent of the total 1,024 on all fronts. Similarly, the four siege batteries at the Dardanelles represented 13 percent of those in the UK; 17 percent of those on the Western Front; and 7 percent overall. The MEF, however, was proportionally lower in terms of heavy batteries. Of the ninety-three heavy batteries on all fronts, the four at the Dardanelles accounted for *only* 4 percent; 7.5 percent of those in the UK; and 12.5 percent of those in France.[83]

Furthermore, the proportion of personnel to man the MEF's guns was deficient. With an effective strength of 9,976 artillery personnel, the MEF's artillery strength represented a mere 3.3 percent of the total British artillery manpower.[84] Such comparisons show that the MEF was *never* given adequate resources—whether in troops or guns—for the task that was expected of it (however, the same can be said of the BEF on the Western Front). With only 7 percent of total British artillery resources, the August Offensive, and indeed the Gallipoli Campaign as a whole, was drastically understrength in terms of gunnery.

Ammunition Availability

The MEF, like the BEF, was restricted in its access to ammunition in 1915. Proportionally, though, there was less ammunition available at Gallipoli than on the Western Front.[85] That said, artillery ammunition supplies for the August Offensive were in excess of what had previously been available in the theater.[86] For example, the increase in supplies available for the 9th Battery (of the 3rd Australian FAB) enabled them to expend more ammunition in August than the previous three months combined.[87] Such increased supplies, which Hamilton described as a "handsome dollop," could not, however, be maintained for long, as they had an impact on the BEF's ammunition supply on the Western Front.[88] On 24 July 1915, Lieutenant-General Sir Henry Wilson, principal liaison officer with the French army on the Western Front, wrote to Andrew Bonar Law, secretary of state for the colonies (and member of the Dardanelles Committee), criticizing the drain that Gallipoli was having on the BEF's resources: "The Dardanelles is crippling us a good deal in high explosive shells for certain guns, and of course in men and guns and ammunition."[89] Wilson was right to be concerned. The ammunition shortage on the Western Front, which had (incorrectly) been given as the reason for the failure at Neuve Chapelle in March, had still not improved by August. By 5 August the BEF was 1,200 shells below war establishment for their 18-pounders; 1,300 rounds for 4.5-inch howitzers; and 300 rounds for 60-pounders.[90] The Dardanelles Campaign, however, was not the reason for this shortage. With its eye firmly set on maneuver warfare, prewar British military planning had not anticipated the need for the enormous quantities of artillery ammunition that would be required.[91] Production had not yet caught up to demand.

Despite the overall increase in ammunition sent to the Dardanelles, the MEF was predominantly given shrapnel shells (in lieu of high-explosive shells).[92] Shrapnel, though, particularly that fired by 18-pounder field guns, was of little value for offensive operations in mountainous terrain such as that found in the Anzac and Sari Bair sectors.[93] Shrapnel was also designed for firing on troops in the open, which meant that it did little damage to the Ottoman artillery batteries, the trenches, or the men in them—all of which were well protected by defensive works or favorable terrain.[94] This was problematic given the destructive purpose of 1915 artillery barrages, which aimed to destroy obstacles and keep the enemy in their trenches until the attacking troops arrived. For these tasks the artillery required high-explosive lyddite shells. Due to the complexities of production, however, lyddite shells were only really used by howitzers and remained in short supply for the field artillery throughout 1915.[95] Indeed, the first supplies of 18-pounder high-explosive shells did not arrive in the Anzac sector until 2 August; and then, this amounted to a paltry 150 rounds per battery.[96] Similarly, prior to August only *eleven* 18-pounder high-explosive shells *in total* had been fired at Helles.[97]

The shells available for the August Offensive were not appropriate for the task set. When one examines the artillery expenditure at Helles in more detail, it is clear that high-explosive shells were not sufficiently available.[98] Only 12 percent of all shells fired from 6 to 10 August were high-explosive. For the two heaviest days (6–7 August), the principal guns—18-pounders—were responsible for only 17 percent of all high-explosive shells expended. Furthermore, this figure represented only 3 percent of all shells fired by the 18-pounders during this period.[99] The reasons why the preliminary bombardment at Helles failed to subdue the enemy therefore become apparent—shrapnel shells could not destroy the enemy's trenches, machine guns, or batteries, all of which remained as substantial obstacles for the infantry when it attacked.

It was a similar, yet more dismal, story for the 9th Battery (of the 3rd Australian FAB) at Anzac. Of all the shells fired by this battery throughout August, only 10 percent were high-explosive. This figure was even lower during the principal period of the offensive (6–10 August), amounting to a mere 8.6 percent of all shells fired.[100] This was insufficient, especially given the battery's key task of counter-battery work to the southeast of Anzac. While successful in periodically silencing the enemy's guns, the 9th Battery could never destroy them.

It is also clear from these above figures that there was much greater demand, availability, and expenditure of artillery ammunition during the five days of the August Offensive than during the remainder of the month. Of the 47,476 rounds fired by VIII Corps at Helles throughout August, 74.7 percent were fired during the period 6–10 August.[101] Similarly, over half (55.8 percent) of the rounds fired by the 9th Battery were expended during this period. Indeed, half of the entire monthly expenditure of 9th Battery was fired on 6 August alone.[102] Such spikes in expenditure, though, could not be maintained for long. GHQ reminded VIII Corps of this, stating that there were *only* a total of 30,000 18-pounder rounds available for all artillery in the Helles sector (i.e., 3,750 rounds per gun), and these had to last for an indefinite period.[103] It was imperative that VIII Corps, like the remainder of the MEF, maintain a substantial number of shells, in the vicinity of six thousand to ten thousand rounds, in reserve—to defend against Ottoman attacks.[104]

While exact figures are not available for the Anzac or Suvla sectors, it is evident that the expenditure at Anzac worried GHQ. On 11 August, after only five days of firing, GHQ informed Birdwood's staff, "Your expenditure [of] gun ammunition [is] causing great anxiety."[105] The following day GHQ reported that there were only fifty rounds of 10-pounder ammunition left on the MEF's lines of communication, and stocks of 60-pounder, 4.5-inch howitzer, and 6-inch howitzer ammunition were "very low."[106] Two days later, 5-inch howitzer ammunition was added to the list.[107] The first phase of the August Offensive had used the majority of the ammunition available, and yet success was no closer.

If artillery stocks were insufficient for the incomplete and unsuccessful first phase of the offensive, there is little chance they would have been adequate for subsequent phases if launched. There was just not enough ammunition available to support such a prolonged multiphase operation. This is evident in the anxiety of GHQ and the subsequent limitations placed on the rounds allotted to each battery per day. Contemplating the possibility of a renewed effort on 11 August, Lieutenant-General Francis Davies, the GOC of VIII Corps, noted that "much larger" ammunition expenditure would be required if a similar attack was to be made.[108] Similarly, Captain Guy Dawnay of Hamilton's General Staff—and one of the officers responsible for drawing up the plans for the August Offensive—recognized that in future attempts, "a very large supply of ammunition will certainly be essential to success."[109] Yet, this was not available during August. Limited ammunition, combined with the lack of artillery pieces per yard of frontage, hamstrung the artillery fire-support capabilities of the MEF. Should the offensive have continued into the second, third, and fourth phases, it would have been without effective artillery support, and the result, insofar as the contingencies of history might allow, a conclusive failure.

Poor-Quality Artillery Pieces

Ammunition shortages aside, the offensive faced an additional disadvantage in that many of the artillery pieces used by the MEF were unreliable or obsolete. The 10-pounder mountain guns, for instance, dated from the Second Afghan War of 1879 and were described by Brigadier-General Hugh Simpson-Baikie as "of an obselete [sic] pattern and hopelessly inaccurate."[110] It was still in service due to the lack of an alternative. By 1915 the 10-pounder mountain guns at Gallipoli were worn out. Six of the twelve guns belonging to the 7th IMA Brigade had to be exchanged during the campaign due to wear. Their replacements from India, however, were also old and worn. Incredibly and indicatively, four of the 7th IMA Brigade's *discarded* guns were actually used to bring the 4th Highland Mountain Artillery Brigade up to strength for the August Offensive. The value of this weapon was further reduced due to the regular failure of its shrapnel shells to "break up" when fired. This, along with the lack of sufficient "common" shells (casings filled with explosives rather than shrapnel), dramatically reduced the fire effect of the 7th IMA Brigade in its support of the advance on the Sari Bair Ridge.[111] Given that these problematic guns were the only ones able to accompany the advance on Sari Bair, and that until the afternoon of 8 August they represented more than a quarter of all artillery at Suvla Bay, it becomes even clearer that the fire support available for the first phase of the August Offensive was inadequate.

Despite being the longest ranging Allied gun on the peninsula, and the workhorse of British heavy artillery throughout the remainder of the war, the 60-pounder (Mk. I) gun used at Gallipoli was plagued by a flaw in its design, rendering it unreliable. In his assessment of the 60-pounders at Gallipoli, Simpson-Baikie described the Mk. I model as "practically useless" as "the recoil was too great for the carriages and consequently the latter broke down hopelessly. No amount of repair in the workshops could keep them in action."[112] In particular, due to a lack of spare parts, and an absence of artificers to repair them, there were lengthy delays in returning the carriages to action at Gallipoli.[113] Of the eight 60-pounders at Helles, at least half were out of action prior to the August Offensive due to problems with the recoil springs, which broke under pressure.[114] By mid-August only two 60-pounders remained in action in this sector; by 23 August only one was in service, and it too had a damaged inner spring case.[115]

It was a similar story for the 15th Heavy Battery at Suvla, all guns of which were out of action on 21 August with similar problems.[116] The flawed Mk. I 60-pounder design, which was reported back to London, led Major Frederick Hunter, the chief inspector of ordnance and munitions from the Army Ordnance Department, to conclude that "the recoil of firing these guns is always violent... and I am consequently led to believe that the charge used here with these guns is too large for the carriage as at present designed."[117] The unreliability and absence of these guns meant that 18-pounder field guns had to be used to silence Ottoman artillery—something which, as noted, due to a lack of high-explosive shells, necessitated a great deal of ammunition expenditure and even then was ineffective.[118] This added expenditure, which itself could hardly be afforded, had an impact on the otherwise reliable 18-pounders, the recoil system of which was also prone to break due to the pressure of continuous action.[119]

Besides the 10- and 60-pounders, there were also problems and complaints about some of the other artillery weapons. The twenty

15-pounder BLC guns used at Helles were in fact weapons originally used by the British during the Boer War. They were old and worn and proved next to useless in modern war. After firing an average of only one thousand rounds, their bores became so pitted by corrosion that they were no longer safe to fire. The fuses on the ammunition were also inaccurate and therefore could not be used for supporting fire close to the troops.[120]

The worn-out 15-pounder BLCs were not the only outdated guns pressed into service at Gallipoli. The 5-inch howitzers that arrived to supplement the howitzers available at Anzac for the offensive were considered old seventeen years earlier at the battle of Omdurman.[121] "They made a lovely noise," Birdwood wrote, but "were ... far from accurate weapons" owing to their badly worn bores. Rather, he would have preferred more 4.5-inch howitzers, which he considered "of incalculable value on that hilly country."[122] This mixture of obsolete and unreliable weapons further reduced the effectiveness of artillery support at Gallipoli during the August Offensive. Effective fire support for a large-scale multiphase attack, and therefore a successful offensive in August, was beyond the capabilities of the MEF in 1915.

Gun Emplacements

Difficulties associated with weapon numbers, and types of ammunition, were further compounded during the August Offensive by the lack of suitable positions for gun emplacements, and the dominating positions occupied by the Ottomans. No location was safe from Ottoman observation or fire. This was especially problematic for the heavy artillery. Indeed, upon visiting Helles in July, the chief artillery advisor to GHQ, Brigadier-General Fuller, noted that there were no more positions, either in the British or French sectors, for additional heavy artillery.[123] Even had they been available, however, they would not have remained hidden from Ottoman observation and fire for long owing to the smoke and dust thrown up upon firing.[124] It was a similar case in the shallow confines of the Anzac sector. Likewise, there were actually only two places available for artillery in the ground held by the Allies at Suvla: on the lower southeastern slopes of Kiretch Tepe Ridge and in the vicinity of Lala Baba. More positions would have become available should the Allied force advance, as in accord with the objectives set, but even then there were the ongoing problems of insufficient ammunition and the difficulty of actually employing *accurate* fire.[125]

Hitting the Target

Artillery was not a precise weapon in 1915. Accuracy was limited by the guns themselves (many of which, as discussed, were obsolete and unreliable), the ammunition, the accuracy of observer reports and maps, the wind, the temperature, the barometric pressure, and even the rotation of the earth.[126] Methods of dealing with these considerations, however, were still in their infancy in 1915. A British training booklet published in 1915 recognized the limitations to accurate fire, noting, "In the conditions of war, such accuracy as is promised by the range tables will seldom be reached. Sights may shift or be slightly out of adjustment, the layer may not invariably manipulate the gears correctly and so introduce an error due to the play of the gears, or other mistakes may be made due to the personal factor."[127]

Actually hitting an intended target was difficult, as no two shells fired from the same gun would fall in the same place. Lieutenant-Colonel William Rettie, who commanded the 59th Brigade, RFA, at Suvla, noted that even if a target could be seen and located, it was "very difficult to hit an actual piece" and put it out of action.[128] Indeed, only 50 percent of all 18-pounder shells fired at a range of three thousand yards would actually fall within ten yards of the intended target, with the remainder landing up to forty yards away. Accuracy decreased as the range increased. At five thousand yards 50 percent would fall within twenty-five yards, with the remaining shells falling up to ninety yards away.[129] It was a similar case for the 60-pounder and the 4.5- and 6-inch howitzers. Therefore, direct hits, especially on small targets such as trenches or guns, were always difficult to accomplish.[130] At Gallipoli, accuracy was further hindered by the mountainous terrain on the peninsula, where it was difficult to burst shrapnel over the ridges, and, because of the close proximity of the enemy's elevated positions, Allied howitzers often fired too low to have the desired effect and the rounds regularly hit the ground upon reaching their apex.[131] This was especially the case in localities such as Anzac and Sari Bair where little distance separated friend and foe. Accuracy would become increasingly problematic during the second and third phases of the offensive, as close quarter fighting continued, but where ranges would inevitably increase.

One means of accommodating for the lack of accuracy at Gallipoli was the extensive use of forward observation officers (FOO). The FOO, who was placed into a favorable position to observe the fire of his battery, was tasked with reporting the fall of the shot with reference to the target. Corrections were then made to improve accuracy, and the next round was fired.[132] The FOO was therefore extremely important prior to the offensive in assisting with the registration process—the importance of which the failure at Neuve Chapelle had clearly demonstrated—as well as during the offensive when adjusting his battery's fire. Spotting and reporting, however, was a slow and difficult process, especially if numerous guns were firing at the same time. In such cases it was nearly impossible to distinguish which shots belonged to a particular battery. It was also dangerous. A FOO was an attractive target and therefore received much attention from Ottoman snipers and riflemen.[133] The entire task required advantageous terrain for the FOO, as well as adequate and constant communication between the FOO, the guns, and the infantry commanders.[134]

The importance of maintaining communication between the infantry and artillery was not lost on those responsible for planning the August Offensive. Observation officers accompanied the infantry advance and were instructed to report back via telephone lines, which would be pushed forward during pauses in the fighting.[135] Because of the physical vulnerability of these lines, orderlies were also allotted to units, and at Helles at least, visual signaling was established as a contingency.[136] Such preparations, though, did not ensure successful communication and fire-support coordination. The 8th Battery (of the 3rd Australian FAB), for example, lost communication with its FOO during the Australian attack at Lone Pine when its telephone lines were severed, despite burying them prior to the offensive.[137] Similarly, men of the New Zealand FAB noted that once communication with their FOO was lost they could do little except watch the battle, presumably for fear of firing on their own troops.[138] In addition to the physical breakage of lines, communications could also be interrupted by ground conditions. The Salt Lake at Suvla, for instance, interfered with the insulation of the telephone lines.[139] Where FOOs could not be used, because of a lack of appropriate observation positions or a breakdown in communications, the artillery had to revert to indirect or unobserved fire. This happened during the offensive.

Unobserved fire, which relied principally on grid shooting and aerial observation rather than on preregistering or adjusting by a FOO, was inaccurate in 1915. Artillery survey—the task of accurately locating a gun, whether friendly or hostile—which was crucial for such a method, was also difficult at Gallipoli due to the absence of an accurate large-scale artillery map.[140] Despite containing ten-meter contour lines, which should have been sufficient, and despite giving an indication of the nature of the ground, the 1:20,000 operational maps used by the Allies for the August Offensive were not technically correct.[141] This meant that when fired on a grid reference alone, shells would not actually land where intended. Aerial spotting and photography was used to ameliorate this problem, but due to technological limitations, a lack of sufficient aircraft, and a dearth of experience, this was far from effective.[142] The artillery, for example, especially that at Suvla, had no prior experience in working with aerial wireless telegraphy, nor did the aircraft observers, who were often recruited based on their light weight rather than on operational expertise, have experience in spotting for land artillery. This was further complicated by the inability of the wireless stations ashore to actually signal the aerial observers.[143] Brigadier-General Simpson-Baikie commented on the communication breakdown between the aircraft and the ground as follows: "Few of the aeroplanes were fitted with wireless and the receivers on the ground could not take in messages over a distance longer than 5,000 yards. Consequently, each aeroplane had to return within this radius of the receiver, before its observation could be delivered, thus immensely curtailing the usefulness and efficiency of the aeroplane observation."[144] The result was that the Allies could seldom hit those targets that could not be seen—which happened to be the majority of the enemy's guns. This made counterbattery work difficult and ineffective.

Counterbattery fire—the task of subduing the enemy's guns—was particularly important during the August Offensive. Once the offensive commenced and the enemy's guns began retaliating, counterbattery fire was the only means of fire support available to the infantry. The lack of target registration, due to the desire for surprise, combined with the absence of precise maps, made it difficult to locate, let alone silence the enemy's artillery.[145] Terrain and more accurate maps enabled the Ottomans to apply far more effective counterbattery fire despite their numerical artillery inferiority.¹⁴⁶ The superiority of the Ottomans' positions, which afforded them greater protection and observation, combined with a lack of suitable positions for Allied gun emplacements at Suvla, forced three of the 15th Heavy Battery's four guns, for example, to remain concealed by day and to fire by night.¹⁴⁷ Lieutenant-Colonel Rettie, later commented, "Only occasionally could we spot the dust kicked up by the discharge of a gun tucked into some depression amidst the scrub high above us. But the hillsides and tops were such a tangled mass of ridges and nullahs it was very difficult to say exactly where the pieces were."¹⁴⁸ With the enemy's artillery positions hidden on the reverse slopes of ridges, or well camouflaged, the Allies found it difficult to ascertain their exact location, and therefore most often left the Ottoman guns free to fire on them (as much as Ottoman ammunition supplies would allow).¹⁴⁹

The Allies also found it difficult to determine the actual effect of their own limited counterbattery fire. Their task was made further difficult by the fact that the enemy's guns were mobile and frequently changed positions, as well as by the Ottoman tactic of employing dummy flashes and smoke balls to mislead Allied spotters.¹⁵⁰ Although actually able to see the flashes of the Ottoman guns, the Allies were able to do little more than search for these guns by firing on various squares of their map (known as "grid shooting").¹⁵¹ While such a measure reduced the enemy's fire, it rarely silenced their guns.¹⁵² The Ottomans were therefore able to maintain effective counterbattery fire (and fire in support of their troops), which would not wane as long as they had ammunition. Such fire support from the Ottomans, which could continue without significant interruption, would no doubt prove to be a considerable obstacle to an Allied advance toward Maidos during the third phase of operations. Allied counterbattery work was largely ineffective at Gallipoli, and it was not until technological advances, such as sound ranging and flash spotting were employed in 1917, that the British were able to fire on the enemy's guns with any real accuracy.¹⁵³

Insufficient Fire Support

From all that has been discussed thus far, it is evident that the land-based artillery support available to the MEF was insufficient in quantity, quality, and application to successfully support the August Offensive. It is not enough simply to criticize the War Office in London for not sending more guns, and it must be remembered that shortages were also affecting the BEF on the Western Front. Numbers alone could not ensure victory. Indeed, there was no room for additional guns on the peninsula should more have been sent. That the MEF suffered from a lack of artillery pieces, especially in comparison to the smaller offensive at Neuve Chapelle in France, however, should not be discounted. It is clear that there were insufficient guns for an operation of this magnitude, especially one in unfavorable terrain like that confronting the troops at Gallipoli. The plan for August was developed in (willful) ignorance of this point and without consideration of the limitations of the available fire support. Put simply, if only from an artillery point of view, the objectives and expectations set by Hamilton and his staff were unrealistic and too ambitious. This is particularly evident when one examines the suitability of the guns available. The inadequacies of the obsolete and unreliable artillery pieces aside, the August Offensive was marred by a disproportionate spread of artillery pieces per sector, which was then further hampered by a lack of sufficient and suitable ammunition. Accuracy was also a problem. The superiority of the Ottomans' positions largely negated effective direct fire, replacing it with the more difficult task of indirect and unobserved fire. A lack of precise maps and the ineffectiveness of aerial spotting combined to ensure that the Allies often could not locate, let alone silence, the hostile batteries. Such factors helped doom the first phase of the August Offensive to failure. It was a similar story for the navy.

CHAPTER 4

COMBINED OPERATIONS

The role of the naval forces is a largely neglected aspect of the history of the August Offensive. Too many authors have forgotten that the Gallipoli Campaign was a combined amphibious operation. Eventual success at the Dardanelles relied upon *both* the army and the navy. This was especially the case for the August Offensive. While the majority of the offensive was confined to the Gallipoli Peninsula—and therefore the army—it should not be forgotten that the operational objective of the August Offensive was to destroy the Ottoman forts skirting the European shore of the Dardanelles, thus enabling the navy to commence minesweeping and offensive operations. The overall success of the August Offensive therefore rested with the navy's ability to partake in offensive warfare (rather than merely supporting and supplying the army) and to successfully carry out the fourth phase of the offensive. But were Allied naval forces in this theater capable, or indeed willing, to conduct such offensive operations in August 1915?

Despite the plethora of texts on the Gallipoli Campaign, this fundamental question has thus far escaped appropriate scrutiny. This chapter addresses this critical issue by analyzing the operational proficiency of the naval component of the Allied force with respect to the August Offensive. To accomplish this, it examines numerous factors including the actual role played by the naval forces during the offensive; the extent of naval involvement in the planning process; the relationship between the army and navy—both at the organizational and operational level; the impact that this had on the operations; and the limitations of a 1915-style "joint command" system.[1]

Preliminary Role and Fleet Composition

Before beginning a close examination of the capability and willingness of the EMS to partake in offensive warfare at Gallipoli in August

1915, it is first necessary to consider the role undertaken by and the composition of the fleet in support of the August Offensive. The primary and most demanding function of the navy at the Dardanelles throughout the campaign was the task of transporting men and supplies. Because the campaign was amphibious, the MEF relied exclusively on the naval forces to deliver everything necessary for living and fighting. Not least of these needs were troops themselves. The navy's importance in this regard is clear and was demonstrated conclusively in the disembarkation of IX Corps at Suvla Bay. In order to secure the sea routes to the peninsula, and thus to ensure the safety of the transports, the EMS conducted submarine patrols and searched foreign ships for contraband that might be en route to the Ottomans.[2]

Leaving these largely logistic tasks to one side for the moment, the naval forces were also of fundamental importance in deceiving the Ottomans prior to the August Offensive—and, in doing so, directly assisted the MEF during the first phase of operations. Such deception took the form of nightly shelling the area around Lone Pine "to give the impression . . . that [the Allies] are after all [the] information they can [get] about this flank."[3] Another task in this regard was the nightly program undertaken by HMS *Colne* and HMS *Chelmer*, which, as already mentioned, through a combination of searchlight placement and predictable bombardments, successfully deceived the Ottoman defenders at Old No. 3 Post to become lax and abandon their front line, thus enabling the NZMR Bde. to capture the post—largely unopposed—and commence clearing the approaches to the Sari Bair Ridge on the night of 6 August (see chapter 7).[4] Allied naval forces were also engaged throughout this period in their usual duty—so as not to arouse suspicion among the enemy—of providing fire support for the MEF, particularly counter-battery work such as that given, for example, by HMS *Theseus* and HMS *Endymion*, in their attempts to knock out as many Ottoman batteries as possible on the afternoons of 2 and 3 August.[5]

While the Allied fleet available for the August Offensive was larger and better suited to action in the Dardanelles (in terms of gunnery and limited protection from hostile submarines), it was "less imposing" than that available in April.[6] Having lost the principal battleship, HMS *Queen Elizabeth*, which had returned to home waters, and an additional four battleships (plus four cruisers), which were sent to join the Italian fleet in the Adriatic, the navy had, in fact, *fewer* battleships available in August than there had been in April.[7]

The loss of these battleships meant a loss of the largest caliber guns, with greater range than any others in the theater. It also reduced the EMS's capacity for offensive action.

By August the Allied fleet consisted of eighty-four warships (battleships, cruisers, monitors, and destroyers), eighteen submarines, and a flotilla of auxiliary vessels (trawlers, drifters, tugs, lighters, transports, and supply ships).[8] Another four 9.2-inch monitors were on their way from the UK but would not begin arriving until mid-August.[9] In terms of the overall size of Vice-Admiral de Robeck's force, the Admiralty considered him as being "fairly well provided."[10] Yet, based partly on his reservations about unnecessarily subjecting his fleet to the danger of German submarines and partly on the necessity of maintaining a reserve, de Robeck in fact utilized *less than one-third* of these warships for the August Offensive (five cruisers, ten destroyers, thirteen monitors—separated into three squadrons).[11]

Command of the 1st Squadron, which was tasked with supporting the army at Helles, was given to Rear-Admiral Stuart Nicholson. Captain Algernon Boyle commanded the 2nd Squadron in support of the Anzac sector, with the 3rd Squadron, in support of the landing at Suvla, under Captain Fawcet Wray.[12] The IX Corps at Suvla could also call upon the 2nd Squadron for additional support during the offensive, thus increasing the potential naval support for Suvla to twelve warships. While this increase improved matters at Suvla, it hardly amounted to the "forty ships" claimed by Compton Mackenzie, an author and member of the intelligence staff at GHQ.[13] The remaining vessels of de Robeck's force, including his temporary flagship, HMS *Chatham*, were relegated to reserve, transport, or escort duties.[14] It is important to note that the composition of the squadrons was, like the allocation of field artillery, tactically *disproportionate*. There were more warships, and therefore guns, in support at Helles, for example, than there were at the more significant sectors of Anzac and Suvla.

Despite the Admiralty's claim that he was "fairly well provided," de Robeck held significant concerns about the strength of his fleet. In July he warned the Admiralty that unless reinforcements were sent from England the fighting efficiency of the fleet would be reduced.[15] He was also concerned about the rate at which his officers were falling sick and their being posted to supply and transport billets.[16] These issues, however, caused less distress than his concerns about the state of the fleet. The small 6-inch monitors, which represented 31.5 percent of all the EMS's monitors, began developing serious engine-room defects immediately prior to the August Offensive.[17] Vice-Admiral de Robeck believed that his destroyers required a rest, and many a refit.[18] After the failure of the offensive, he reiterated his concern for the destroyers, noting that "many are sadly in need of a visit to a dockyard," but could not be spared.[19] On a positive note, de Robeck was happy with the general health of his crews, and felt that the remaining ships were in "a satisfactory order."[20] It was this limited fleet, and its anxious commander, that supported the land forces during the August Offensive.

The first actions of the navy *during* the offensive were, like their previous bombardment programs, an effort to deceive the Ottoman command about the true nature of the Allied operations. This involved two feint landings, the first by a flotilla of trawlers to the south of Anzac, the second by HMS *Jed* and HMS *Minerva*, which together disembarked 350 Greek irregulars at Chana Ovasi on the night of 6 August.[21] Neither landing, however, was successful, and the Ottomans were not fooled.

Delivering IX Corps to Suvla

Deceptive efforts aside, the genuine test for the navy came in applying the lessons of April to a new landing at Suvla Bay. The landing of IX Corps, like that of the ANZAC in April, was undertaken in complete darkness, and therefore faced similar difficulties—especially with regard to disembarking troops at the correct location. The general conduct of these new landings (as distinct from the provision of fire support) was assigned to Rear-Admiral Arthur Christian, who had little experience in the Dardanelles theater and *none* in the peculiarities of amphibious warfare. The main obstacle facing Rear-Admiral Christian, and therefore the successful commencement of the offensive, was the quick disembarkation of men, munitions, and supplies. He was helped in this regard by eleven motor lighters, otherwise known as "beetles," which began arriving in July. These vessels enabled a much quicker and safer journey to the peninsula than the rowboats of April. Built for Admiral Fisher's Baltic project, the "beetles" could carry five hundred men (or forty horses) at a rate of six to seven knots, and disembark them dry (in theory), by way of a long ramp that extended onto the beach.[22] It was largely because of these motor lighters, which traveled back and forth between the peninsula and the transports, that the navy was successful in disembarking IX Corps at Suvla Bay.

The Suvla landing itself was spread over three beaches: A, C, and B (see map 7). The 11th Division was to land in two waves on 6 August, followed by two brigades of the 10th Division the following morning. The majority of the force was to land at B Beach (C Beach was to be used for landing guns and supplies), while a small portion would land inside Suvla Bay itself, at A Beach.[23] The 11th Division left Imbros Island on the evening of 6 August and proceeded toward Suvla. Ten destroyers, each carrying 530 men and each towing a motor lighter (which carried a further 500 men), formed the first wave of attack. They were followed by the cruisers HMS *Endymion* and HMS *Theseus*, as well as the sloop HMS *Aster* and six trawlers, which formed the second wave.[24] The landing at B Beach went to plan.[25] After disembarking their first load of 3,500 men in one trip, the seven motor lighters involved returned to their partner destroyers and ferried a further 3,710 men to B Beach.[26] The first wave of the 11th Division (32nd and 33rd Brigades) was ashore, as a covering force, by midnight, 6–7 August.[27] The motor lighters then returned to the cruisers and support vessels to begin landing the second wave. The landing of the 34th Brigade at A Beach, however, which was to act as a covering force for the 10th Division, did not fare so well.[28] Troubled by shallow water and confusion among the ships, it was 5:00 A.M., 7 August, before all troops were ashore.[29] The rest of 10th Division began arriving in armed boarding steamers from Port Iero and Mudros at dawn on the same morning.[30] Due to the confusion on shore, though, there was a delay in landing many of the six thousand remaining troops of 10th Division.[31] Despite the difficulties experienced inside Suvla Bay, the EMS was largely successful in getting the troops ashore in a quick manner, thus maintaining the element of surprise so essential for an amphibious landing.

Naval Fire Support

As was discussed in the previous chapter, there were limited numbers of artillery pieces available for the August Offensive, and even fewer positions to situate them. As such, the naval forces were required to provide added fire support for the MEF. For this to occur, however, some changes were necessary. Because of the dangers posed by German submarines, in May 1915 de Robeck decided to recall all battleships—which were not submarine proof and therefore vulnerable to being sunk—from open waters to the safety of Mudros Harbour (the cruisers remained offshore in support of the army).[32] As such, the land forces lost the support of the biggest caliber naval guns available. Reflecting on the changed circumstances, Brigadier-General Simpson-Baikie, the CRA of the 29th Div. Artillery, wrote, "The poor Navy—one feels quite sorry for them—their ships look so imposing and yet they are so impotent in the face of the new submarine peril—so they have to leave the Army to its fate and we suffer from the constant shelling."[33]

The navy understood the impact this had on the army, and was anxious to improve the situation. Indeed, de Robeck was so delighted upon receiving notice that new monitors, fitted with a bulged hull and therefore somewhat better protected from submarine torpedoes, would arrive in time for the offensive that he informed Major-General Alexander Godley, the GOC of the NZ&A Div., of their usefulness, especially compared to the "poor old battleships [which] cannot stand the modern torpedo and turn over like a tired cow."[34] While de Robeck was confident that the EMS could now provide a level of fire support that had been lacking since May, the MEF's senior artillery officer, Brigadier-General Richard Fuller was less certain, noting less than two weeks before the offensive that the entire "question of naval support" could "collapse at any moment" with the presence of enemy submarines.[35] That it did not collapse was because there were no enemy submarines in the vicinity of Allied ships during the August Offensive—not as a consequence of the new monitors or other improved naval circumstances.

With regard to fire support, de Robeck's ships were crucial both in terms of the preliminary bombardments provided at Helles, Lone Pine, and the Nek, as well as providing fire-in-depth during the actual battles. A conference was held on board the flagship HMS *Triad* on 2 August at which the MEF and EMS discussed the plans for naval fire support during the offensive.[36] After indicating what ships would be available to provide fire, it was made clear to both services that the MEF, through the BGRA (at corps level), would decide how the naval guns could be best used to assist their corps and would then have control of these guns during the offensive.[37] The army could therefore incorporate the fleet's guns into its own fire-support plans. The downside to this system, however, was that it prevented the army's divisional commanders from having immediate control over their naval fire support, despite the fact that they were the ones who controlled the field artillery equivalent. Such a system proved problematic and was further limited by the signals difficulties already discussed.[38]

Despite adding to the fire support available to the ground forces, the ships' guns, in fact, did little to alter or improve the overall situation. The effectiveness of naval gunfire support was limited by various factors including the availability of ammunition; the inability of the guns to reliably hit their targets, especially due to the inaccuracy of the guns and the hilly terrain; and observation difficulties tied to the lack of reliable spotting. Of course, there were some examples of successful naval gunfire support, but in the overall scheme of the August Offensive naval fire had little real impact apart from improving Allied and perhaps lessening Ottoman morale.

The first problem was ammunition. Apprehension about naval shell stocks and expenditure were so pressing that de Robeck advised the fleet to husband its ammunition during the offensive. He informed his subordinates that there was no reserve of ammunition for the monitors, which represented the greatest proportion of the supporting ships, and therefore firing was to be limited, where possible, to 6-inch ammunition (less than ideal for counterbattery work). The monitors received further guidelines, limiting their expenditure during the first twenty-four hours of the August Offensive to thirty rounds per 14-inch monitor (limited strictly to "suitable" targets), forty rounds per 9.2-inch monitor, and sixty rounds per 6-inch monitor.[39] While only guidelines, these instructions were a clear indication of de Robeck's concerns and the problems associated with insufficient ammunition.

In the absence of detailed records of the fleet's actual expenditure of ammunition during the principal period of the offensive (6–10 August), it is difficult to come to a valid conclusion about the impact of these guidelines on the fleet's readiness to support the army. From the limited information available, however, two things are clear. When the MEF was undertaking offensive action, the ships fired in excess of their recommended allotment. In times of relative "inaction" (on the army's part), they fired very little. On 6–7 August, for example, the nine British ships of the 1st Squadron at Helles (excluding the ships at Rabbit Island) fired an average of forty-one shells each. Similarly, between 7 and 9 August, the three cruisers in support of the Suvla operations expended an average of 133 shells per day, per ship.[40] While the figures were no doubt considerably less for most of the monitors, HMS *M30*, for which good records remain, nonetheless fired 108 shells (well in excess of its 60-shell limit) on 7 August.[41] The records for the days after the main portion of the offensive are much more detailed, and show that during the period of marked inactivity (12–17 August) the fleet fired a total of 1,404 shells—at an average of only 8 shells per ship, per day. This increased during the offensive action later in the month with 4,416 during the attacks on W and Scimitar Hills (18–22 August) and 5,035 during the attacks on Hill 60 (23–38 August).[42] This said, the *type* of ammunition fired provides a greater insight into the impact that the ships' guns could and did have on land operations.

Of the 10,855 shells fired by the fleet from 12 to 28 August, 51.6 percent were common shell; 38.3 percent, lyddite (high-explosive); 9.2 percent, shrapnel; and an almost negligible 0.9 percent, armor piercing.[43] During peak periods of fighting, when the number of shells fired increased, this increase consisted almost entirely of common and lyddite shells. But as the tactical situation and therefore targets changed, and the fleet's stocks became depleted, there was a decrease in common and shrapnel shells, and an increasing reliance on lyddite. In terms of technical quality, lyddite was the superior and more effective shell. Yet, despite having a great morale effect when fired on troops in the open, lyddite shells caused little damage unless a direct hit was achieved. Common shell, which was still used in large quantities, was less effective still, especially when fired at long ranges. Its pointed nose, for instance, had "a tendency to bury and dig a furrow" before bursting, thus reducing the severity of its explosion. The difficulty of spotting the graze of shrapnel, combined with the poor quality of the shells themselves (the oldest of which dated back to 1897 and the most recent, 1908) and the limited quantities available, meant that shrapnel—the principle means of killing troops in the open—was even less useful than lyddite or common shell.[44] The navy, therefore, could be relied upon neither to inflict large enemy losses nor to prevent the movement of Ottoman troops.[45] Rather, their focus, as a result of both ammunition availability and tactical responsibility (in delivering preliminary bombardments), was to destroy obstacles such as defensive works and guns.

Moreover, even with regard to providing destructive fire (its principal task, and that which accounted for the majority of shells fired), the navy was still largely unsuccessful. As the historian Tim Travers has noted, "Allied naval fire was of little value against precise targets like trenches, machine-guns or enemy batteries, due to sheer technical inability."[46] Vice-Admiral de Robeck himself acknowledged these technical difficulties prior to the offensive, writing, "Though effective in keeping down the fire of the enemy's batteries—when it is a question of trenches and machine guns, the Navy is of small assistance."[47] Even when it could keep down the enemy's artillery fire, the navy could not silence it. Indeed, in September 1915 Brigadier-General Fuller noted that even after the experience of the August Offensive, "There appears to be no definite scheme of registering ships on enemy's guns with a view to silencing them, or driving them further afield."[48] The reasons for this were twofold: the inaccuracy of the guns, especially when firing while moving, and the impossibility of observation in terrain such as that at Suvla and Anzac.

By August the wear on the fleet's guns in the Dardanelles theater was significant.[49] The guns of the 6-inch monitors were beginning to weaken due to constant use and had to undergo repairs.[50] Such wear was inevitable, especially given the old age of the majority of the guns and their constant use since February. With such wear came inaccuracy and an increasing inability to hit a target reliably. The newly arrived 14-inch monitors were similarly inaccurate at long ranges, though in this case due to problems with their projectile rather than the gun.[51] This issue was compounded by the necessity of firing at long ranges in order to remove the danger of being shelled by the enemy's field artillery.[52] A further hindrance to the overall accuracy of the ships' fire was the difficulty of hitting a target while the ships were moving.[53] These technical deficiencies, however, were themselves surpassed by the problems posed by the geography of the peninsula.

Observation and Directing Naval Fire

Accurate naval shellfire was particularly difficult in undulating terrain due to problems with observation and the inaccuracy of maps.[54] Because direct observation was not possible, naval guns, like their land-based equivalents, were forced to search the broken ground for hidden targets.[55] However, in his evidence to the Dardanelles Commission, Lieutenant-Colonel Johnston, CRA of the NZ&A Divisional Artillery, made it clear that despite their hard work, the fleet's guns fired at such a low trajectory that they were of little support, especially in hitting hidden Ottoman guns.[56] Put simply, naval shells could not be fired at a high enough angle to both clear the ridges and then drop onto their targets.

Johnston added that experience in France (gained after the Dardanelles) had taught him that in order to properly bracket and then neutralize a target, an observer had to be placed within 110 yards of that target in order to relay accurate adjustments.[57] Placing an observer (naval or otherwise) that close to the intended target was just not possible during the August Offensive. Without the advantage of the high ground, the EMS had to rely on aerial observation. While the air service had improved its effectiveness by August, aerial spotting for naval fire was still in its infancy.[58] Aircraft could only spot for one vessel at a time, and their usefulness was reduced by a lack of experience among spotters and poor signaling equipment.[59] Even when correction reports were signaled to the fleet, there was then the added difficulty of timely adjustments.[60] There were also problems with the aircraft themselves. Seaplanes were unable to fly at high altitudes, and there was an insufficient number of serviceable land-based aircraft capable of flying at any one time. Then there was the problematic issue of airborne spotters keeping a fixed target while their airplane constantly moved around. This was made even harder by the glare from the sea and sand, which proved a severe strain on the observers' eyesight.[61]

To overcome some of the problems associated with seaplane and land-based aircraft naval gunfire spotting, kite balloons were occasionally used. These platforms made observation much easier, they could remain in the air for unlimited periods of time, and communications were rapid (usually an average of 20–30 seconds) between the observer and the firing ship via the use of a direct telephone link between the balloon and ship.[62] Despite the kite balloons' advantages, their overall usefulness was largely negated by the fact that their presence immediately drew the enemy's fire, and, as was the case on two occasions on 10 August, they became principal targets for Ottoman aircraft. With a maximum height of three thousand feet, the kite balloons were always vulnerable to enemy fire and were often forced to move farther from the shore, thereby further reducing their effectiveness.[63] Their usefulness was also limited by external factors. The thirteen ascents made by No. 1 Kite Balloon Section from 7 to 10 August, for example, were largely ineffective due to unfavorable weather conditions—with mist hindering observation—as well as the difficulty in spotting the fall of shot and the inaccuracy of the ship's fire.[64] The fleet, therefore, like the Allied field artillery, was most often forced to fire blind.

The range of limitations examined thus far all combined to reduce the effectiveness of naval fire during the first phase of the August Offensive. As has shown to be the case for other aspects, the situation would have invariably been worse had the second and third phases been implemented, with the navy required to fire across the peninsula with the view of cutting the enemy's lines of communication and bombarding the rear of the forts that guarded the Narrows. While Allied occupation of the Sari Bair Ridge would have no doubt provided an excellent observation station, it must be noted that the key Ottoman fort at Kilid Bahr would have remained obscured from direct view by the Kilid Bahr Plateau. Even if this problem could have been overcome through a combination of aircraft spotting and land-based forward observers, the task of neutralizing such targets would continue to be hampered by the suitability and availability of naval ammunition and the technical limitations of the ships' guns. Overall, aside from potentially buttressing Allied morale, and at times terrifying the enemy, the naval forces could never offer real or effective fire support during any phase of the August Offensive.

Submarine Warfare

Leaving aside the problems associated with naval gunfire support, it is true that Allied naval forces did play significant alternative offensive roles throughout August. In particular, in addition to the RNAS, which undertook sporadic air raids on Ottoman shipping and logistic hubs—including an air torpedo attack on 12 August by Flight Commander Charles Edmonds and subsequent attacks on 17 August by Edmonds and Flight Lieutenant George Dacre—the EMS took the battle to the enemy through the use of submarines.[65] Vice-Admiral de Robeck believed in the potential of this platform, writing to the first lord of the admiralty that "with three submarines in [the Sea of Marmara] our attack on any sea-borne supplies that the Turks are sending to the Peninsula should prove most effective."[66] He was correct.

Throughout August three Allied submarines, *E14*, *E11*, and *E2*, wrought havoc upon the Ottoman lines of communication. From 6 to 12 August the first two submarines, *E14* (under Commander Edward Boyle, and on its third voyage in the Marmara) and *E11* (under Commander Martin Nasmith, and on its second voyage in the Marmara) worked in conjunction in the Sea of Marmara.[67] During this time they observed at least twenty-eight enemy vessels and destroyed thirteen, including a battleship and a five-thousand-ton supply ship. They also searched a hospital ship, which they incorrectly suspected of carrying reinforcements. The pair also spent a couple of hours on 7 August shelling Ottoman troops proceeding along the coast road toward the town of Gallipoli. The impact of this particular action is contested. Nasmith stated that while the submarines' fire did not completely stop the column of troops, it did force them to briefly scatter for cover, and "a large number of dead and wounded appeared to be left alongside the road."[68] The Ottoman General Staff, however, reported, "There were no casualties and no damage to men, horses or material as a result of this gunfire. The troops changed their route and moved along a road further inland."[69] What can be known with certainty is that the overall impact of this type of minor shelling was minimal. *E14* left the Sea of Marmara on 12 August and was replaced by *E2* (under Lieutenant-Commander David Stocks). It too rendezvoused with *E11* and between them they destroyed at least another twenty-four Ottoman vessels by the end of the month.[70]

There is no question that Allied submarines were successful in destroying a number of Ottoman craft. Rear-Admiral Rosslyn Wemyss, the senior naval officer (SNO) at Mudros, was so impressed by their success that he described them as playing "a conspicuous part in the general offensive."[71] But while successful in causing delay in supplies and harassing the enemy (in this case by sinking a small proportion of food supplies and causing the variation of supply routes), there was no significant or sustained impact on Ottoman operations. Maurice Hankey—and the naval and military intelligence officers who advised him—fully realized this. On 5 August, the day before the offensive, Hankey informed the first lord of the admiralty that "though the Turks are hampered by our submarines, the [Ottoman] sea route of communications is not entirely interrupted, and, I fear, is never likely to be."[72] To combat Allied submarines, the Ottomans transported seaborne supplies (usually food and ammunition) in shallow draught craft (which were generally safe from torpedoes) under the cover of darkness, while also staying close to the shore.[73] Even Keyes, who had immense faith in the ability of submarines (having previously commanded the British submarine service), later acknowledged that in such circumstances, "too much cannot be expected of' the Allied submarines."[74] While Ottoman troops traveled by safer land routes, smaller craft, according to the Ottoman General Staff, still "guaranteed the daily needs" of the army.[75] Therefore, despite the successes of the Allied submarine operations throughout August (and indeed, the entire campaign), the submarines were not able to alter the course of the campaign.[76] General Hamilton knew this, noting that completely stopping Ottoman seaborne supplies was impossible: "The swiftness of the current; the shallow draft [sic] of the Turkish lighters; the guns of the forts, made it too difficult even for our dauntless submarine commanders to paralyse movement across these land-locked waters."[77]

While the offensive operations undertaken by the RNAS and the submarines in August were important, it must be stressed that these actions were part of a larger campaign effort and were not specific to the August Offensive. In other words, they would have gone ahead even if there was no corresponding land offensive planned for August. Therefore, while the naval forces undertook offensive action in conjunction with the August Offensive, these actions were not factored in as a component part of the offensive. At Arthur Balfour's admittance, the navy had been relegated to a supporting role since March.[78] But why was this? Given the overall purpose of the August Offensive—to clear a path through the Dardanelles for the navy—how could this be? The place to begin searching for an answer is in the navy's role in the planning process for the August Offensive.

Naval Planning

As the August Offensive was, at its heart, a multiphase land affair, and given that the EMS was required for the all-important task of transporting and disembarking IX Corps at Suvla, it seems sensible that Vice-Admiral de Robeck's staff spent the majority of its time planning for the disembarkation of troops, naval gunfire support, and, as Commodore Keyes referred to it, the ongoing requirement for "hewing of wood and drawing of water."[79] Such administrative work, combined with naval reconnaissance, kept the naval staff more than busy, especially Keyes, who after an unusually long time between letters, explained to his wife on 5 August: "I don't think I have ever spent quite such a strenuous time as I have the last few days—in my life before—I really have not had time to write."[80] All of this planning, which required close cooperation with the army's general staff at GHQ, focused on support for the MEF—not the navy's offensive operational role in the coming August attack.

Despite the important offensive role that the navy was required to play should the first three phases of the August Offensive succeed, the naval staff was not involved in any offensive planning. In this regard, the plans for August were significantly different from those issued in April, which stipulated that, after landing the troops and supporting them until the position was secure, "the Navy will attack the fortifications at the Narrows." In April, minesweeping was to commence while the troops were disembarking, and naval demolition parties were to land and destroy the guns of the forts, once the area had been cleared of Ottoman resistance.[81] In August, however, there was no mention of any naval action at all apart from landing and supporting the army. Therefore, while the August Offensive was conceived and envisaged as a combined operation, with the operational objective requiring naval action, the planning process was devoid of any combined operational planning. Joint plans were issued for the August Offensive, but only because there was an amphibious landing planned for Suvla Bay. The August Offensive, therefore, was a combined operation only insofar as the MEF relied on the EMS to land troops and supplies, but it was *not a combined offensive*. There was no offensive naval plan.

One may contend that, like the MEF's operational orders, which specified only the first of four phases, the navy was holding off from making offensive plans until the third phase was complete. After all, the naval orders for April stated that "Orders . . . dealing with the attack on the Narrows and further progress of the Fleet will be issued in due course."[82] Under this line of reasoning, naval plans were not made due to the failure of the land forces to progress beyond the first phase. The problem with this logic, however, is that it was clear that senior naval officers were thinking about their future offensive role, even in an absence of orders. Vice-Admiral de Robeck, for example, briefly wrote of future operations to the first sea lord, Admiral Henry Jackson: "The big ships . . . will all be ready when the army make their next big effort early next month. Then I think we should do all in our power to support them, first of all by attacking the forts with the monitors, holding the battleships in readiness to take advantage of any success."[83]

Similarly, Commodore Keyes informed his wife that if the army achieved its objectives, the navy "shall not have to wait long."[84] Again, this gave away little in terms of detail. That Keyes, the foremost proponent of a renewed naval offensive at the Dardanelles, did not mention the existence or discussion of offensive naval plans is significant and out of character. In truth, a detailed examination of the papers of all key naval and military personnel involved in the planning process for August indicates that little detailed thought, or discussion, was given to what precise action the EMS would undertake should Hamilton's troops succeed. Indeed, there had been no detailed correspondence at all between the Admiralty and the EMS on the matter of future operations.

The first lord of the admiralty himself believed that nothing should be discussed before the results of the army's offensive were known.[85] Success, he believed, was "at present remote, since there seems little hope of destroying the heavy batteries until the heights commanding them are taken." This task, he admitted, was "a very stiff nut to crack."[86] It is therefore clear that both the Admiralty and de Robeck were waiting to see the result of the army's attack before considering what their future operations should be. The point is, however, that without previous planning there would be little time to forewarn, prepare, and train the fleet, and the EMS could no longer rely on experience gained in March 1915, as the situation was different than it had been then. In reality, the lack of naval plans for August was a consequence of more than a desire to wait and see how the land forces went. There was, in fact, an underlying reluctance from some sections of the Admiralty and the EMS, including de Robeck, to embark on any offensive naval warfare at all at Gallipoli in August.

Interservice Cooperation

The first aspect of this reluctance can be seen in the relationship between the two services, both in London and in the Dardanelles. By and large, the two services worked well together in theater.[87] Both stood by the *Manual of Combined Naval and Military Operations*, which espoused the importance of working together for the common goal.[88] Naval and military staffs helped each other and personal relationships were close.[89] In spite of the cordial relations between the services leading up to August 1915, and the close cooperation of the staffs, it was clear that by this time both services (and particularly their commanders in chief) were tiptoeing around each other to avoid any confrontation. By August the relationship between the navy and the army was beginning to sour.

All remained rosy on the surface, with both services working exceptionally hard to maintain good relations. But despite personal courtesy, professional frustration flowed underneath. Hamilton, who as August approached walked on eggshells to avoid upsetting the navy, informed Lord Kitchener, "Any sort of statement . . . that they [the navy] are short of anything is regarded [by the navy] not, as it might be, or as it is intended to be . . . but always as a reflection on the Navy." While individual relationships remained strong, by this stage of the campaign, professional rapport was strained by what Hamilton described as the "totally differently constituted" service cultures and traditions.[90] In the context of a long campaign that to this point had been frustrated at every turn, both services competed and compared systems without really understanding the other. Symptomatic was the fact that from the departments in London to the commanders in the theater, both institutions kept information from the other, and both maintained attitudes of superiority.[91]

In London, for example, the War Office and Admiralty rarely consulted each other. There were no interdepartmental conferences, and there was no joint planning committee like that established after the First World War.[92] If interdepartmental discussion did occur, it took the form of private conversations between departmental heads (Kitchener and Balfour) rather than formal meetings.[93] This situation was a consequence, more than anything else, of service tradition and pride. Admiral John Godfrey (who spent time at the Admiralty Plans Division in 1914, and as a lieutenant served as a navigation officer at the Dardanelles) later recalled, "Naval leaders felt no need to consult the generals on how to conduct the Naval war, and it would not have occurred to the War Office to turn to the Admiralty for advice on how to wage their land campaigns." It was not that the service representatives in London did not want to meet, but that "they unconsciously saw no need to cross Whitehall." This culture of there being a distinguishable "land war and the sea war and that was that" was ingrained deeply in both services and was maintained in the Dardanelles despite the joint or combined nature of the theater.[94] Indicative of a lack of cooperation was the fact that the services never consulted each other on a strategic direction for the campaign should the August Offensive succeed.[95] There was, of course, the Dardanelles Committee, which discussed operations that affected both departments. But this committee was reliant upon the service heads for information—the same individuals who had been educated and operated firmly within the parameters of their own service's traditions—and as a result was largely incapable of providing either strategic or operational guidance on combined operations.[96]

Interdepartmental consultation and cooperation in London was also limited by the personalities of departmental heads. As discussed previously, Lord Kitchener acted more as a commander in chief than a secretary of state for war.[97] His poor opinion of the British general staff resulted in his paying scant attention to his advisors, and rather making his own decisions.[98] In effect, Kitchener was the War Office and his word was final. His Admiralty equivalent, Arthur Balfour, was the polar opposite. He relied heavily upon his advisors, was generally rather lethargic, and was happy to delegate.[99] Outside of the Dardanelles Committee meetings, these two men (and therefore their departments) had little contact. The Admiralty, for instance, knew very little about the August Offensive and complained specifically in mid-July about the lack of detailed information. Incredibly, naval planners in London claimed they still did not "quite know the situation" by 25 August.[100]

Joint Command

The impact of these insular cultures came to a head in the joint command system in place at the Dardanelles. This system, which had a profound influence on the August Offensive, differed from that of continental powers, which subordinated the admiral to the general during combined operations. In the Dardanelles, however, Hamilton and de Robeck shared *equal* responsibility for operations in the theater. While Hamilton commanded the land operations—and therefore held more overall responsibility than de Robeck, who commanded the subsidiary sea-based operations—neither had authority over the other. Such a command system, according to the British naval strategist and historian Sir Julian Corbett, "could only work by mutual goodwill and understanding between the two officers concerned."[101] Goodwill was in abundance at the Dardanelles—understanding was not. Cross-institutional correspondence between each commander and their opposite department did not exist.[102] Both commanders also misunderstood the basic operational conceptions of the other: Hamilton's objective was to pursue offensive warfare and enable combined operations, while de Robeck was content to wait.[103]

The joint command system in place actually *prevented* one commander from imposing his will on the other. Neither had the authority to overrule or direct the other service even if such action was required to ensure a unity of purpose or direction. In addition, neither Hamilton nor de Robeck felt it his place, as a consequence of their institutional cultures, to inform the other what he wanted (or hoped for) from the other service. Neither suggested action or encroached on the other's command. As such, there was no true unity of command, and no real coordinated direction toward a common goal at Gallipoli in August 1915.[104]

Despite the efforts of their respective chiefs of staff to encourage shared command and effective cooperation, neither Hamilton nor de Robeck could bring himself to discuss his wishes with the other. To both men, the other service was outside his realm, and was therefore best left alone.[105] In Hamilton's opinion, "If a sailor on land is a fish out of water, a soldier at sea is like a game cock in a duckpond."[106] Hamilton did not see it as his place, despite his desire for a combined military and naval assault in August, to get involved in naval matters, and continually resisted the temptation to suggest such a move to de Robeck—even though it was required.[107] For example, after discussing the upcoming offensive with Rear-Admiral Wemyss on 27 July, Hamilton wrote, "What would it not be to me were the whole Fleet to attack as we land at Suvla! But obviously I cannot go out of my own element to urge the Fleet to actions, the perils of which I am professionally incompetent to gauge."[108]

The issue was still on Hamilton's mind on 3 August when he noted that despite the wishes of some, he could not broach the subject of a naval offensive in August because he had "neither the data nor the technical knowledge which would justify me to my conscience in doing so."[109] Hamilton even refrained from giving his opinion to de Robeck on 20 August when de Robeck mentioned the possibility of Admiralty support for a renewed naval offensive. Hamilton recorded: "Every personal motive urges me to urge him on. But I have no right to shove my oar in—no right at all . . . so I fell back on the first principles and said he must attack if he thought it right from the naval point of view but that we soldiers did not call for succour or ask him to do anything desperate."[110] Hamilton refused all further pleas to request naval action for the remainder of the campaign, and refrained to comment on such actions for the remainder of his life.

Similarly, de Robeck did not feel qualified to discuss military matters. In commenting on the failure of the Suvla operations, he refused to remark on the reasons for failure, noting that "this is not my business" but that of the army.[111] His chief of staff, Commodore Keyes, believed that de Robeck did not like to interfere, and "is very diffident about putting his views to the general [i.e., Hamilton] in anything to do with land operations."[112] As Sherman Miles, U.S. military attaché to Ankara, 1922–1925, noted, both Hamilton and de Robeck "scrupulously, perhaps over-scrupulously, avoided meddling in the other's province."[113] Aside from not actually having the authority to order the other to action, neither wanted to dabble in the other's business. They were, in this regard, hamstrung by their respective traditions and by a joint command system, which did not vest overall authority with one man. This is not to suggest, as have other authors, that such problems would have been avoided if there had been one supreme commander rather than two coequal commanders at Gallipoli. Such a conclusion is both anachronistic and ignorant of the impact that tradition had on these men's actions.[114] There is no evidence, for example, that Hamilton would have overruled de Robeck even if he had the authority to do so. Nor is it fair to criticize Hamilton or de Robeck alone for their reluctance to discuss interservice operations, for in this, they were not the only culprits.[115] It is clear, however, that the joint command system, combined with the cultural differences of the army and navy, had an impact on the August Offensive. These matters would have dramatically hindered the navy's ability to partake in offensive warfare should the army have succeeded in advancing across the peninsula. As it stood, the army would not hint at future naval actions; rather, this was perceived as the responsibility of the navy alone. But were Allied naval forces prepared to undertake such action in any case?

Questioning the Viability of a Naval Offensive

A lack of interservice cooperation was not the only reason why there was no offensive naval plan for the August Offensive. Documentary evidence suggests two more possible reasons, both of which relate to de Robeck's mindset. The first was de Robeck's reservations about the navy's ability to succeed should it launch offensive operations in August. As has been noted, he was worried about the health and suitability of his fleet. His doubts concerning the navy's ability to get through the Narrows mirrored those of his predecessor, Admiral Sackville Carden, who developed the original offensive naval plans of February and March.[116] The second, and more likely reason, however, was that de Robeck did not believe that the army had any hope of securing its objectives. It is clear that he opposed another naval only attempt and refused to contemplate sailing through the Narrows until the army controlled the Gallipoli Peninsula, thus securing his passage and lines of communication into the Sea of Marmara.[117] For de Robeck, combined operations would not be possible *until* the army held up its end of the deal. Yet he was not confident in the ability of Hamilton's land forces to deliver—and for good reason. Everything thus far had proven that the army was not capable of achieving its objectives. In doubting the MEF's capabilities, de Robeck was not alone. His staff also believed that the army's plans for August possessed defects "which mitigated against the chances of success."[118]

Vice-Admiral de Robeck was by no means a passive or timid character. To the contrary, he was "a fearless man," who had "a reputation for being a thruster," and who had shown his willingness to prosecute offensive warfare if he believed success was possible (as shown by his involvement at the Dardanelles in February and March).[119] Nor was he against the concept of offensive naval action. Indeed, he realized the importance of renewing the naval attack against the Ottoman forts, and thus maintaining pressure on the enemy, but the failure of 18 March had convinced him that it would be futile for the navy to consider such an attack until the peninsula was securely in Allied hands.[120] This had been his (and the Admiralty's) opinion since the decision was taken on 22 March to land an army on the peninsula.[121] It had also been the opinion of the CID in 1906, which, in its study of the possibility of a joint naval and military attack on the Dardanelles, concluded that "unaided action by the Fleet, bearing in mind the risks involved, is much to be deprecated."[122] This attitude was clear to all those in the theater. Lieutenant-Colonel Hankey, for example, informed Prime Minister Asquith two days before the August Offensive began that "the naval people . . . are very unwilling to attempt a new attack on the forts until the enemy is sufficiently driven back to enable them to anchor up the Straits and register systematically on the forts, exactly as the shore guns do."[123]

Vice-Admiral de Robeck's position was staunchly supported (in the first instance) by Admiral Fisher; his successor, Admiral Jackson; and the other sea lords at the Admiralty.[124] Even de Robeck's negative response to their query (on 19 August) of whether the battleships could be used in a more productive manner drew unmitigated support from the Admiralty. Notwithstanding his statement that "to attack the Narrows now with battleships would be a grave error as the chance of getting even a small squadron past Chanak [was] very remote," and that it was regretful "but in the light of past experience [and] present knowledge, it is the only possible conclusion," the Admiralty reaffirmed its support for de Robeck, informing him that it had the "fullest confidence in your judgment."[125] That said, de Robeck later admitted that he would have obeyed orders, if issued, whether or not he agreed with them.[126] That they were not issued at any time throughout the campaign is evidence that the senior naval officers consistently concurred with his position. Supporting land operations remained the only option.[127]

There were, of course, those who differed in their views, but they represented a minority (even if the most vocal) of the naval opinion in the theater.[128] The most notable opponent was de Robeck's ever-optimistic chief of staff, Roger Keyes. Like Churchill, Keyes was in favor of a renewal of the naval offensive.[129] His campaigning in this regard, though, did not begin until *after* the failure of the August Offensive. Keyes first hinted to his wife on 12 August that he had a plan, and four days later wrote, "I am sure my gallant lionhearted admiral will see it clearly soon."[130] The following day, 17 August, Keyes submitted an appreciation to de Robeck outlining his views, which were supported by Commander Lionel Lambart—who was initially the chief staff officer to the SNO at Anzac Cove but who was attached to de Robeck's staff for the August Offensive—and Captain William Godfrey, de Robeck's war staff officer.[131] The crux of their argument was that, as proven by the failure of the August Offensive, the army could not succeed. The time for a combined offensive had passed, and a resumption of the naval-only offensive against the Narrows "was the only solution."[132] Rear-Admiral Wemyss, who had initially opposed single naval action, now also felt that the MEF's land forces would never succeed and supported Keyes's scheme.[133] Wemyss informed Keyes: "A naval attack on our objective is the only way now to avert a winter campaign whose greatest achievement can only be stale mate [sic] at the cost of much wastage. The presence of but a small number of ships on the other side of the Narrows would so alter the situation in our favour that it would surely be worth the loss of an equal number of ships."[134]

Keyes's proposed plan of attack resembled that of 18 March, but he and his supporters were confident that an attack along these lines held greater prospects of success after August than it had in March. They had faith in the improved RNAS and the minesweeping flotilla—the first of which, as we have seen, was not efficient, and the second, at their own admittance, still required training.[135] Their primary argument, however, was that a renewed attack would "probably" surprise the enemy, whom had "possibly" removed some of the guns that had hindered earlier minesweeping operations in February and March.[136] Not surprisingly, de Robeck was unconvinced and asked Keyes how exactly a new attack would surprise the enemy. The vice-admiral also noted that in his opinion the Ottomans had acquired additional guns.[137] This did not discourage Keyes, who persisted (unsuccessfully) in his efforts to persuade de Robeck for the next two months.[138]

Despite his own personal and continuing reservations about the Keyes plan, and although supported by other senior naval officers, including Arthur Limpus, admiral superintendent in Malta, who knew the Dardanelles better than any other Allied commander; Admiral John Jellicoe, commander in chief of the Grand Fleet and the foremost British naval commander at the time; and the French officers in the Dardanelles, de Robeck had enough respect for Keyes that he allowed him to return to London and put his proposal directly to the Admiralty.[139] Exhausted from months of stress and insomnia, de Robeck also asked Keyes to pass on de Robeck's request to the Admiralty for a brief rest from duties if no significant naval action was planned for the immediate future.[140] He also gave Keyes a personal letter for the first lord of the admiralty that outlined de Robeck's opposition to Keyes's proposal. While he hoped that "every consideration will be given to the proposals," de Robeck noted, "I differ profoundly from him [i.e., Keyes] as to the chances of success of the scheme—as I do not think it would achieve the object we desire." For de Robeck, "the only possible solution is the absolute destruction step by step of the forts and defences of the Dardanelles and this can only be done with the assistance of the army."[141] He also informed the Admiralty (through Keyes) that if Keyes's proposal was accepted, they should send someone—who was confident of success—to replace de Robeck.[142]

After much discussion the Admiralty confirmed de Robeck's position. Keyes's plan was considered doubtful and losses certain. The Admiralty was prepared, if the army agreed, to partake in a combined operation—but Lieutenant-General Sir Charles Monro, who replaced Hamilton as GOC of the MEF when the latter was removed from command in October, refused to commit the MEF to another offensive. Keyes later commented that neither department was prepared to take responsibility for a renewed attempt, or shoulder the burden of another failure: "The Admiralty wished to make the War Office responsible, and the War Office wished to make the Admiralty responsible—there was no one to give a decision or an order."[143]

The failure of Keyes's post-August proposal for naval offensive action is further evidence of the consistent support for de Robeck's persistent stance, particularly among the naval experts. Contrary to Keyes, who lived by the maxim that "attack was the best defence," and whose judgment it has been said was often blurred by his aggression, de Robeck remained calm and objectively analyzed the situation.[144] He was not passive, but rather a realist, who understood that the navy could not succeed—especially if the army did not control the Gallipoli Peninsula.[145] That de Robeck appreciated the situation correctly, commanded with conviction, and stuck to his principles deserves much credit. Another man may have buckled under the pressure and unwillingly committed the navy to something beyond its capabilities.

From another perspective, however, de Robeck has a case to answer. Should the MEF have succeeded in achieving its objectives and crossing the peninsula, it would have been very difficult for naval forces to act without any real preplanning and forethought. The *Manual of Combined Naval and Military Operations* had stressed this issue, stating, "Owing to the difficulty of transmitting orders when at sea, and also to allow sufficient time for completion of necessary arrangements, naval orders . . . should, whenever possible, be drawn up and issued before an expedition puts to sea."[146]

The manual also stated that plans should be framed for subsequent operations, therefore instilling a basic idea of what would be expected. These should remain flexible to adapt to circumstances as they arose, but still, the existence of a plan, however flexible, was a requirement and *not* an option.[147] This never happened at Gallipoli with regard to the August Offensive. It was a significant omission as well as a doctrinal mistake. This was realized in the theater shortly after the failure of the August Offensive, with Godfrey suggesting that a memorandum explaining the outline of any future attack be sent to the captains of the fleet, and Keyes suggesting to de Robeck that "in order to be prepared for any eventuality, a plan of action should be drawn up now and the organization of an efficient force proceeded with at once." Keyes continued, "I venture to submit that the plan for co-operating with the army in the forthcoming operations should include a detailed plan of action for forcing the Straits. . . . In the event of Admiralty approval I would suggest that this plan should be confidentially issued to the commanding officers of the ships which will take part in order that they may be thoroughly prepared in good time for what may be required of them."[148]

Yet these suggestions were not made until offensive action was proposed *after* the failure of the August Offensive—there were no such preparations for the initial attack or subsequent operations during the offensive. The important point is that even if the decision not to force the Narrows in conjunction with the land offensive in August was valid, it does not explain why the naval staff neglected its duty of planning for naval action, which would commence after the army had succeeded in its three phases. By overlooking this need, had the offensive been successful, the naval staff would have introduced an element of delay that, as had been shown in February and March, would inevitably allow the Ottomans to improve their defensive measures and greatly hinder subsequent operations. Success in the fourth phase of the August Offensive would be unlikely, to say the least, without this naval planning and forethought. The final word with this regard should go to the "Mitchell Report," which concluded: "The principal lessons to be learnt from a study of the Naval [a]ttack on the Dardanelles [d]efences would appear to be that it is essential that operations of this nature should be based on a previously well considered estimate of the sea, land and air forces necessary to obtain the results desired, and the manner in which they can be most profitably employed either separately or in conjunction. . . . Any departure from these principles discount the full value of sea power and tends to produce failure."[149]

Neither Willing nor Able

The importance of the navy to an operational study of the Allies' capabilities to achieve their August Offensive objectives is clear. Without offensive naval action during the fourth phase of operations, the August Offensive could not succeed—yet no such plans or preparations were ever made. Without naval preplanning or forethought, and without a willingness by de Robeck to undertake an active role in operations, the August Offensive could *only* fail. This is not to put sole or undeserved blame on Vice-Admiral de Robeck for the failure of the offensive. He was a realist who understood the difficulties of the task set and who maintained his convictions in the face of persistent efforts to the contrary. Even had de Robeck wanted to attack the Narrows, he was limited by an inability to coordinate his intentions with those of General Hamilton and by the fact that the navy would have to wait for the army to complete its three phases—something that never eventuated. Willingness aside, there are serious questions as to the navy's capability to conduct offensive operations in August 1915. To a very substantial degree it was struggling to simply cope with its supporting role. Colonel Hans Kannengiesser, GOC Ottoman 9th Division, certainly felt that the Allied naval forces at Gallipoli were not capable of fighting and supporting the army ashore.[150] Vice-Admiral de Robeck too had significant reservations, stressing to the Admiralty less than three weeks before the August Offensive that, if more naval personnel were not made available, "a day will arrive when the Navy will fail to fulfil its obligations owing to shortage of men and possibly endanger the success of the Military operations."[151]

This chapter, like those preceding it, aimed to test the long held belief that the August Offensive was a "near run thing." It is clear, however, that the EMS was unwilling, unprepared, and unable to partake in combined offensive warfare in August 1915. From this perspective alone, the August Offensive did not, and could not, approach anything that resembled a "near success." The stress placed upon the navy was clearly a burden upon its shoulders, and one that manifested itself in the supply and transport of men, munitions, and materiel to the Gallipoli Peninsula.

CHAPTER 5

LINES OF COMMUNICATION

The importance of logistics in war is axiomatic. Yet military supply involves far more than types and quantities of various stores. Underpinning the logistic process, or "the practical art of moving armies and keeping them supplied," are the crucial, yet complex, administrative systems comprising the acquisition, transportation, and allocation of the services and resources necessary for victory.[1] While logistic supremacy does not in itself equate to success, it is clear that supplies, and supply lines, however masked they may be by the flash of guns or the mayhem of battle, can and often do have a direct impact on the success or failure of military operations.[2] The potential of an offensive to succeed, especially a prolonged one like the August Offensive, therefore in many ways rests upon the logistic and administrative systems that support it. Without the essentials—food, water, ammunition, and materiel—troops cannot fight, at least at their full capacity, for prolonged periods.[3] Any assessment of the operational level of war, and whether an offensive such as that launched by the Allies in August 1915 could succeed is not complete without an examination of the logistic capabilities of the attacking force.

Given the importance and complexity of logistics in the Dardanelles, this is the first of two chapters dealing with the logistics of the August Offensive. This chapter is concerned with the administrative process of supplying the MEF, particularly the organization and difficulties faced on the lines of communication (L-of-C); the process of getting supplies, stores, and men to the high-water mark (just off the beaches); and the administrative relationships between and within the services.[4] Attention is paid to the situation at the MEF's intermediate base at Mudros Harbour (Lemnos Island), especially the question of whether the processes and administration were effective enough to allow for the timely delivery of supplies to the peninsula. As such, in many ways this chapter is the first part of an analysis of the MEF's logistic framework and is a crucial foundation for the chapter following, which focuses on the disembarkation and distribution of these items ashore and the logistic aspects of evacuating the wounded.

Due to incomplete and unavailable record keeping, neither this nor the following chapter attempts to quantify what was exactly sent to or landed on the Gallipoli Peninsula. Rather, the emphasis is on the capability of the L-of-C to transport men, stores, and supplies from the United Kingdom to the Gallipoli Peninsula, with a particular focus on the four fundamental components of military logistics: supply, transport, facilities, and personnel.[5] Such an analysis will enable conclusions to be drawn as to whether Hamilton's plan for August was logistically feasible, and whether the supply arrangements were sufficient to enable success.

The "Pull" System

The MEF's L-of-C differed greatly from that employed on the Western Front, where the BEF was backed by a sympathetic civilian population; preexisting and established supply routes in the form of road and rail networks; and a short sea passage between the UK and the Continent. With such a foundation, the maintenance of the BEF—even with all of its difficulties—was essentially assured. At Gallipoli, however, the Allies had none of these elements.[6] Indeed, the quartermaster general (QMG) at the War Office, Major-General John Cowans, described the Dardanelles logistic system as "abnormal and peculiar."[7]

Further contrasting the two fronts was the process by which stores and supplies were requested, acquired, and then delivered. At Gallipoli, the MEF employed what can be described as a pull-type logistics system, whereby units submitted daily requests to GHQ, outlining what items they believed would be required in the immediate future. GHQ then forwarded these on to the War Office in London. It was therefore the responsibility of the MEF to inform the War Office of its needs with regard to men, supplies, and stores (therefore "pulling" their requirements), rather than having them "pushed" from home. This was an inefficient method of operating. The BEF abandoned this process in July 1915, and introduced a push system in its place, which saw the BEF automatically forwarded—or pushed—a divisional pack containing its average daily

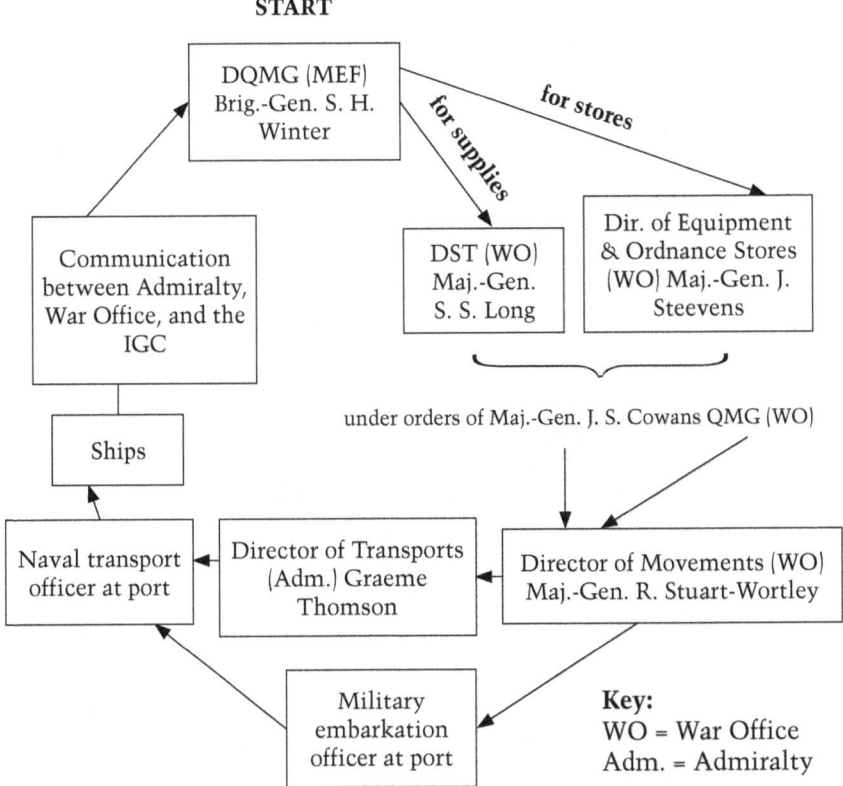

Request, Acquisition, and Disembarkation Cycle

requirements. This measure greatly reduced the amount of red tape and administrative time lapse experienced by the BEF.[8]

The pull system in the Dardanelles allowed Hamilton's headquarters to request items specific to the war it was fighting and to respond to the particular needs of the campaign. But it also resulted in substantial problems. The delay caused by the sheer distance of Gallipoli from the UK meant that by the time many of the items requested actually arrived in the theater, they were often no longer required.[9] This process was also fraught with administrative difficulties. General Hamilton, for example, often made personal requests for men and munitions to Secretary of State for War Lord Kitchener, thereby bypassing the official channel. Requests, rather, should have been made through Hamilton's staff officers (see figure).

The existence of parallel official and unofficial channels caused both confusion and delay. Indeed, Major-General Cowans complained to Lieutenant-General Edward Altham, the MEF's inspector general of communications (IGC), immediately before the August Offensive that there was still confusion as to who was responsible for requesting items, informing him that "it is impossible to deal with demands unless they all come through one recognized channel."[10]

Acquisition and Disembarkation

Once informed of what was required in the Mediterranean theater by Hamilton's administrative staff, it was the duty of the War Office to acquire these items. According to Colonel George MacMunn, who was sent to the Dardanelles in July as Altham's assistant quartermaster general (AQMG), the lack of organization, forethought, and preparations at the War Office, where arrangements were not made until a request was received, meant that further delay inevitably ensued.[11] After the War Office acquisition was complete—whether in men, supplies, or stores—arrangements then began for the transportation of these items to their ports of embarkation. Responsibility thus transferred to Major-General Richard Stuart-Wortley, director of movements at the War Office, who was responsible for all military movements within the UK. An essential element of Stuart-Wortley's role was communication with the Admiralty. It was he who informed the director of transports at the Admiralty, Graeme Thomson (a civil servant with no rank), of what the War Office wanted sent to the MEF. Thomson then allotted the requisite transports and was responsible for loading them and dispatching them overseas.[12]

Upon arriving at the port of embarkation, the War Office logistic trains were met by a military embarkation officer, who allotted the troops, supplies, and stores to various transports.[13] A naval transport officer, acting under orders from Thomson then took control and superintended the actual loading of the transports.[14] The principle was to embark units whole, rather than splitting them up, and to place various types of supplies and stores in separate ships.[15] This process, however, was not always possible, and caused some serious complaints. The director of supplies and transport (DST), Brigadier-General Frederick Koe, for example, expressed his dissatisfaction

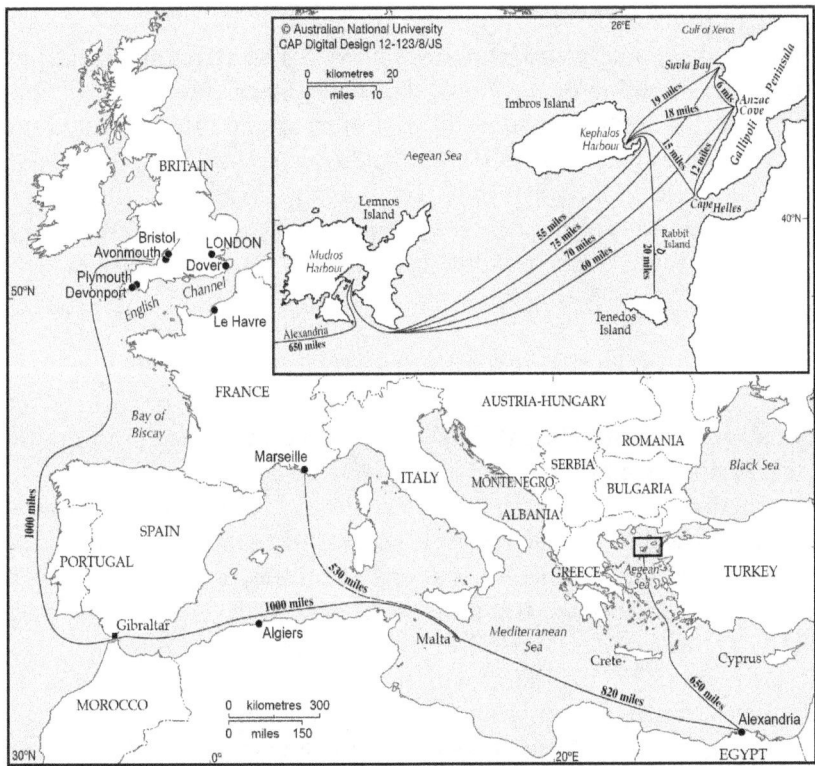

Map 5. Allied lines of communication

less than a week before the August Offensive with how the supply ships bound for Gallipoli were loaded in the United Kingdom.[16] Maurice Hankey echoed Koe's concerns. On 4 August, Hankey informed Prime Minster Asquith that, while the situation was improving, "supplies are sent from England in bulk, but are required here [i.e., at the Dardanelles] in rations." Rather than being carefully loaded to arrive with their cargoes ready to dispatch in a form and in the order in which they were required in the theater, Hankey explained, ships sent from the United Kingdom were being loaded in a hurry, with items merely being pushed on board.[17] Further delay at the front, where such stores were needed, was the net result.

This issue aside, once loaded, the naval transports were ready for the sea voyage to the theater. The War Office was at this stage responsible for informing the MEF of what was being sent out, but the liability for the safe "provision, despatch and control of sea transport" lay solely with the Royal Navy.[18] The Mercantile Marine, under the direction of the Naval Transport Department, undertook the majority of the transportation, protected and often manned by the navy throughout the passage.[19] Additional delay was often experienced due to a lack of transports available in the UK, but more often it was caused by a lack of torpedo-boat destroyers to act as escorts for these transports during their voyage to Gallipoli.[20]

Voyage to the Theater

The L-of-C for the Dardanelles commenced at either Avonmouth (near Bristol), which the War Office preferred because of its good railway facilities, or Devonport (near Plymouth), which the Admiralty preferred because it was 150 miles closer to "safe water" than the former.[21] On rare occasions, and only in times of great urgency, a dual L-of-C was opened and items were sent from the BEF's reserves at the French port of Marseilles, thus shortening the voyage by up to 2,100 miles.[22] This route, which required diplomatic permission from the French, was only used in exceptional circumstances.[23]

It was along the former route (from the UK), with a distance of nearly 3,500 miles, that most men, animals, guns, vehicles, stores, and supplies destined for the MEF were transported.[24] Such a long L-of-C, which General Sir Ian Hamilton described as the "biggest and most difficult Line of Communication ... the world has probably seen since the day of Xerxes," far exceeded the one hundred miles of the Ottoman L-of-C from Constantinople to the trenches at Gallipoli.[25] As such, the British logistic effort demanded a large fleet of colliers, transport ships, store ships, and escorts.[26] At such a distance, where the voyage from the first request to the eventual arrival on the Gallipoli Peninsula took between five and six weeks, there was a persistent shortage of stores and supplies.[27] Hamilton realized the complications caused by this supply arrangement, as did Major-General Gerald Ellison, who was appointed deputy IGC after arriving at the Dardanelles in late July.[28] Ellison contended that the difficulties of supplying the MEF along this complicated route "were beyond description or possibility of exaggeration." The complexities of the journey were further and perpetually heightened by the weather, delays at the various ports of call, or threats posed by hostile submarines.[29]

After leaving the home ports, the transports destined for Gallipoli traveled in a southwesterly direction into the Bay of Biscay, which they followed around Portugal until they reached their first port of call, one thousand miles from their point of departure, the British naval base at Gibraltar. The convoys then continued in an easterly direction along the coast of Algeria and Tunis for a further one thousand miles until they reached the Mediterranean island of Malta. Here, they received further sailing orders from Rear-Admiral Arthur Limpus, admiral superintendent, Malta, before continuing their easterly voyage for another 820 miles through the Mediterranean Sea to the MEF's main supply base at Alexandria. After repacking their cargoes they then traveled 650 miles in a northwesterly direction, through the narrow channels of the Aegean Sea, until they reached the MEF's intermediate base at Mudros Harbour, where they were temporarily sheltered from enemy submarines.[30] Supervision of this final leg, from Alexandria to Mudros, and the safety of British transports in these vulnerable waters, was the responsibility of the French naval commander in chief (Mediterranean), Vice-Admiral Boué de Lapeyrère, whom Hamilton described as "no use at all."[31] Thus, the Mercantile Marine supply ships destined for Gallipoli came under French command, despite the French having nothing to do with British supplies and transport in any other regard.

The U-boat Threat

From the moment they left the UK until they arrived at Mudros, the MEF's supply convoys, carrying a vast range of goods, were vulnerable to attack from German U-boats. This was particularly the case at the mouth of the English Channel and during the latter voyage from Alexandria to Mudros, where the narrow channels of the Aegean Sea were favorable avenues for enemy submarines launched from the Austro-Hungarian base at Pola (Pula).[32] The conclusion of the Mitchell Committee, though, which was convened to look into the naval aspects of the Dardanelles campaign and discern the lessons to be learned from its failure, was that, despite adding "to the already difficult problem of maintaining the supply of the Army," the presence of enemy submarines had no significant effect on Allied operations.[33] Such a conclusion, however, ignored the impact that their threat (whether existential or perceived) had on the morale and confidence of the Allied command.

The fear of enemy submarines was very real and had a tangible influence on the decision-making process. The Ottomans realized this and on 26 June threw a proclamation into the Allies' trenches reminding them that the MEF was entirely dependent on vulnerable sea transport for food, water, and every other kind of war material and that "soon all supplies will be entirely cut off from your landed force" by German submarines, thus exposing the MEF's troops "to perdition by starvation and thirst."[34] Such threats did not fall on deaf ears, and surely stimulated Vice-Admiral de Robeck's existing concerns. The sinking of HMS *Triumph* and HMS *Majestic* in May 1915 seemed to confirm de Robeck's anxieties about the impact that hostile submarines could have on both his fleet and the supply service.[35] Since then, there had been a substantial redefinition of the role of the fleet, and an even more dramatic reorganization of the L-of-C.

Immediate steps were taken to transform Mudros into an intermediate base—thus providing a location safe from submarines, closer to the peninsula. Transports were instructed to proceed from Alexandria to Mudros (rather than directly to the peninsula), and they were barred from proceeding beyond the safety of its harbor.[36] As a rule, no vessel over 500 tons was permitted to approach the beaches—a limit that was increased for the August Offensive to 1,500 tons due to a lack of available lighters.[37] The issue played on de Robeck's mind to such an extent that in early July he proposed that the L-of-C be further altered so that troop transports be sent directly from Malta to Mudros—bypassing Alexandria—thus reducing their exposure to submarines by seven hundred miles.[38] The Admiralty agreed with the proposal: "Not only would this course greatly decrease the danger of submarine attack, but it would also have the advantage of rendering the transports available for further service sooner than would otherwise be the case."[39] The new route—which applied to troops but not supplies—was approved but did not take effect until mid-August, and was therefore too late to have an impact on the August Offensive. Vice-Admiral de Robeck's fear, however, led to an alteration in the L-of-C organization and further slowed the supply and transport process.

August was the quietest month for enemy submarine action throughout the Gallipoli Campaign; de Robeck did not know this and believed that his vessels remained at constant risk of being torpedoed. In this regard neither de Robeck, nor any other British commander in the theater, had the benefit of hindsight. All that could be relied upon were intelligence reports, two of which arrived from Salonica and Malta in early August informing de Robeck that enemy submarines had been sighted in the area.[40] These reports reaffirmed de Robeck's suspicions. In fact, the Turko-German submarine war was far from over; indeed, it was on the increase. At 8:15 A.M. on 13 August (two days before the Allies' new route direct from Malta to Mudros came into effect) the German submarine *UB14*—which had been ordered to attack Allied shipping on the route between Alexandria and Mudros—fired on the troopship HMT *Royal Edward*, which was traveling without an escort, sinking it within five minutes.[41] A nearby hospital ship collected 630 survivors, but the damage was felt, with 994 men, who were meant for the 29th Division, the Royal Army Medical Corps, and stevedore duties at Mudros, lost to the sea.[42]

As a consequence of the *Royal Edward* incident, the course from Alexandria to Mudros was changed the following day, with transports ordered to take a more westerly route through the Aegean.[43] The threat was underscored again on 14 August when another German submarine, *UB8*, missed with a torpedo shot at HMS *Manica* off Suvla Bay, followed by a similarly unsuccessful attack four days later on HMS *Hector*.[44] The impact was immediate. Vice-Admiral de Robeck was so concerned for the safety of his ships that he instantly ordered all transports at Suvla (with the exception of two supply ships) to return to Mudros. Despite the problems that this caused to IX Corps' ammunition supply, de Robeck was not prepared to run the risk of losing any more cargo or vessels, and instructed Lieutenant-General Stopford that in the future his headquarters would be required to foresee their wants at least two days ahead and to provide sufficient working parties to enable the timely clearing of lighters.[45] In addition, although August was the quietest month for the enemy's submarines, September was the busiest.[46] Such an increased presence of hostile submarines would undoubtedly have played a large role if the Allied offensive had proceeded into its second, third, and fourth phases—particularly with the increased shipping that such Allied successes would inevitably have demanded.

The principle impact of the enemy submarines was therefore not the tonnage of supplies sunk, but the fear it inspired and the subsequent delay it caused to the entire supply process. The risk posed by submarines had a profound impact on the speed of delivering supplies to the peninsula and no doubt seeded many of the logistic problems faced at Alexandria and Mudros. Prior to the advent of the submarine menace, transports went directly from Alexandria to the advanced bases at Helles and Anzac. Once Mudros began being used it added another stop—a particularly lengthy one—to the logistic chain. In this context, it is prudent to now examine the logistic process from the point of disembarkation and some of the difficulties faced at the MEF's bases at Alexandria, Mudros, and Kephalos.[47]

The Base at Alexandria

For the majority of troops and supplies bound for Gallipoli, the established port of Alexandria (Port Said was also occasionally used)—the MEF's main base during the Gallipoli Campaign—was but a temporary stopover on their voyage. Troops, such as those of the new formations sent out for the August Offensive, were dispersed across twelve nearby camps, while they waited for the majority of guns, animals, and vehicles to be disembarked.[48] As horses (and vehicles) were not required in large numbers on the peninsula, and because the MEF could not take any more at either Lemnos or Imbros, the majority of the MEF's animals were retained in Egypt, much to the despair of Lieutenant-General John Maxwell, GOC of the Force in Egypt, who pleaded with Lord Kitchener to stop sending horses because they could not be accommodated.[49] With Alexandria's wharves, piers, jetties, railway lines, and cranes for unloading large ships, Hamilton's CGS, Major-General Braithwaite, described the port as having "everything one wants in reason."[50]

Being both a port for the forces in Egypt as well as for the MEF meant that Alexandria was under dual administrative control. The base commandant, Brigadier-General Charles McGrigor, who reported directly to the MEF's IGC, commanded the MEF's base at Alexandria.[51] The port itself, however, fell under Lieutenant-General Maxwell's command. This posed some problems for Hamilton's headquarters, which was often at odds with Maxwell about the relative importance of the Dardanelles theater. Prior to the August Offensive, Braithwaite made a point of informing Major-General Cowans that, while McGrigor did good work in running the base, he was often placed in a "difficult situation" by Maxwell who, through his personal relationship with Lord Kitchener, tried to control everything in Alexandria.[52]

Aside from such administrative issues in Egypt, which did not seriously affect supply to the peninsula, the primary problem associated with using Alexandria as a supply base for the MEF was the additional distance its deviation (from the route Malta–Gallipoli) added to Hamilton's L-of-C.[53] In spite of the route changes that occurred as a result of the enemy submarine presence, almost all shipping from the UK was still sent first to Alexandria.[54] As a consequence of the problems with loading in the UK, and because the intermediate base at Mudros lacked adequate transhipment facilities, most ships that arrived at Alexandria had to be disembarked, re-sorted, repacked (into ration sizes rather than bulk), and then reloaded onto the same ships before being forwarded to Mudros.[55] Such practice invariably delayed the overall logistic process. Given the state of Mudros, however, the holdup was perhaps a blessing in disguise.

Intermediate Base, Mudros Harbour

As noted, after the advent of the submarine menace in May, transports were prohibited from approaching the Gallipoli Peninsula to offload their cargoes due to the fear that these big ships would be overly vulnerable while waiting offshore to be unloaded.[56] Rather, they were to proceed to Mudros Harbour and transfer their goods into smaller craft, which would then make the fifty-, seventy-, or seventy-five-mile voyage to Helles, Anzac, or Suvla Bay (in August) respectively.[57] The reasoning behind the decision to tranship all items was that the Allied command did not think the enemy's submarines would consider small craft worthwhile targets, therefore guaranteeing a continuation (in small packets) of supply to the peninsula.[58] And while the facilities for such movements existed at Alexandria, it was feared that too many small craft would be lost during the long voyage to the peninsula if sent directly rather than from Mudros.[59] Lemnos Island, therefore, became the key intermediate logistics base for the MEF. Suggestions were made among the MEF's administrative staff to bypass Alexandria completely and to make Mudros the main base. The idea was never entertained, however, due to the difficulties faced in transforming the harbor into a workable port.[60]

The choice of Mudros as the intermediate base was controversial. To legally facilitate its use, the British treated it as Ottoman territory rather than an island of neutral Greece, as it actually was.[61] Control of the civil administration of the island fell under Rear-Admiral Rosslyn Wemyss, the SNO at Mudros, who also acted as governor of Lemnos, but control of the base came under the personal command of the IGC (Major-General Alexander Wallace until he was replaced by Lieutenant-General Altham in July).[62] Despite its close proximity to the peninsula and its relative protection from the weather (heavy gales being the exception) and, more importantly, its protection against submarines—the harbor itself being protected by light guns, searchlights, submarines, patrols, and two antisubmarine nets—Mudros Harbour proved to be the source of the greatest delay and confusion on the L-of-C from the UK to the Gallipoli Peninsula.[63]

Mudros was simply not prepared for its new function and was, according to the MEF's director of works, Brigadier-General Alain Joly de Lotbiniére, "anything but an ideal base."[64] Initially, the harbor had none of the facilities required of a functioning port, and the situation had barely improved by the August Offensive.[65] Lieutenant-General Altham, who arrived at Mudros on 22 July to take over the post of IGC—with the task of restructuring the L-of-C—immediately informed the War Office that Mudros was in a state of "appalling confusion."[66] He later expanded on this, describing it as "a magnificent natural anchorage, but totally undeveloped in the matter of piers, landing places, storehouses, buildings, etc."[67] Colonel MacMunn, who arrived with Altham as his AQMG, described the chaotic state of the harbor in similar terms. It was congested with ships, many waiting to be unloaded, but there were no jetties, no facilities, no port labor, no shore commandants, and no provost marshals. Moreover, there were not enough small craft for handling stores and men of any increased proportion. Furthermore, there were no roads on the island; water supply was poor (indeed, this was this factor that had turned Hamilton off using Mudros as a base for the initial landings in April, and was a particular anxiety of Lieutenant-General Altham); there were minimal engineer stores; and local transport was insufficient.[68]

Mudros was thus in great need of improvement, and even though attempts were made to make it ready for the August Offensive, these were insufficient, according to MacMunn.[69] A proper reorganization and improvement required time; and according to the superintending transport officer (STO) at Mudros, Captain Henry Simpson, at least six months were needed to get Mudros to the necessary state.[70] Given the importance of Mudros, above any other logistic hub, to the supply of the MEF, attention will now turn to those elements noted by Altham and MacMunn and their impact on the supply process for the August Offensive.

Congestion in Mudros Harbour

Congestion was always a problem at Mudros, particularly in the lead-up to the August Offensive. In mid-July, when preparations for the offensive were under way, there could be as many as two hundred deepwater ships, and countless small craft crowded into the harbor, either taking refuge, awaiting their voyage to the peninsula, or waiting to have their cargoes transhipped (or to be loaded).[71] By 1 August, numbers had increased to such an extent that the king's harbour master doubted whether he could accommodate them all.[72] Indeed, Lieutenant-Colonel Rettie, the CO of the 59th Bde., RFA, who on 4 August was with his unit at Mudros, described the harbor as "a most interesting sight at this time, crammed as it was with all sorts of vessels . . . amongst which was a wooden bogus battleship."[73] In such cramped conditions, collisions were not uncommon. Indeed, the refrigerator ship SS *Pfalz* was damaged in a crash on 18 July as it commenced its return journey to Alexandria to collect supplies.[74] Losses like this could hardly be afforded, and as it eventuated—and as further evidence of the difficulty of organizing a L-of-C so far from home—a replacement was not found for SS *Pfalz*, the only refrigerator ship in the theater, until 27 August, thus depriving the attacking ground force of frozen meat throughout the August Offensive.[75]

Overcrowding at Mudros also affected the ability to communicate within the harbor. Upon his return to Mudros on 30 July, Major-General Frederick Shaw, the GOC of the 13th Division, commented, "The ship came alongside the *Aragon* and received a peremptory order to go alongside the hospital ship *Icuros* and discharge some wounded, no mention was made of the whereabouts of such a ship, so we had to cruise about asking everyone where she was: at last after half-an-hour's search she was found and her name was not *Icuros* but *Ituros* and she was not a hospital ship at all."[76] In another example, a loaded lighter was unable to berth alongside its

132 CLIMAX AT GALLIPOLI

ship on 1 August because this ship was wedged between two other large ships.⁷⁷ Communication with the island was also constantly interrupted as anchors destroyed cables.⁷⁸ In addition to the congestion in the harbor, the island itself was also crowded with units of IX Corps awaiting the landing at Suvla, with troops having a brief rest from the peninsula, and with the hospitals based ashore.⁷⁹

Congestion in Mudros Harbour was largely the result of disorganization, unpreparedness, and a lack of resources. The congestion was compounded by a dearth of knowledge of what items ships contained upon their arrival. Most vessels arrived without a manifest of goods contained aboard, thus making it difficult to locate specific items, or to prioritize which ships should be unloaded first. A telling example of this was the case of ten thousand friction tubes, which were at Mudros but which could not be found, thus rendering ten thousand desperately needed shells useless for the August Offensive.⁸⁰ Once items were finally located, the process of getting to them and then unloading them was often just as problematic. During his rounds of the store ships in the lead-up to the offensive, Maurice Hankey noted that picks and shovels were urgently needed, and, while there was ample supply aboard one ship, these were covered by a mass of mining timber and were therefore difficult to extricate. Similarly, the dispatch of the 40th Field Butchery to Helles was delayed because of the difficulty in disentangling their equipment "owing to the absurd manner in which it was stowed" on SS *Cawdor Castle*. Such problems led Hankey to conclude that "the marvel is not that there are occasional shortages of various materials, but that these are not endemic."⁸¹

Transhipping at Mudros

Such problems in Mudros Harbour combined to impede the transhipping process, thus delaying the turnaround of transports and supply ships, which after offloading their cargoes were meant to return to either Alexandria or the UK to restock their depleted hulls. Delay was inevitable given the inherent difficulty of the process.⁸² The bulky cargoes could not be cleared until a berth became available alongside one of five floating depots in Mudros Harbour, which were used in place of depots ashore because of a lack of facilities to handle and then store the cargoes on the island.⁸³ The retention of these floating depots, which were themselves merely converted store ships, did not appeal to the Admiralty or the naval authorities in the theater, who felt that it was too expensive to have such ships sit inactive, and who felt that they should be returned to the UK to collect more reinforcements and stores.[84]

Admiralty dissatisfaction aside, after a ship found a berth at Mudros there was then the slow process of transferring cargoes, which frequently entailed removing small quantities from numerous ships, rather than fully clearing one ship.[85] Items were then stockpiled on board the floating depots, and, when required, transferred to smaller craft. Space was required for this task, little of which was available on either the depot ships or in the hull of the transport alongside.[86] If anything urgent was required from a transport or supply ship, a party was sent into its hull to search for the item—another time-consuming process.[87] As more ships arrived the delay only increased, and it was not uncommon for ships to remain unemptied in Mudros Harbour for weeks on end, or to be sent away before being cleared, much to the annoyance of the Transport Department at the Admiralty.[88]

This particular problem came to a head in the days leading up to the August Offensive when there were not enough ships at Alexandria to take reinforcements to the peninsula, due to their being held up at Mudros.[89] Captain Simpson, who was responsible directly to the Admiralty for the timely dispatch of these transports back to the UK, reminded Lieutenant-General Altham that the transports should be unloaded promptly upon arrival at Mudros, thus freeing them up for further work. He also stated that the situation was difficult enough without the Mudros holdups, because twenty-five ships that should have been returned home to collect reinforcements and stores were instead retained in the theater as temporary ambulance carriers.[90]

Apart from holding back transports for further duty, problems at Mudros also delayed the transportation of much-needed stores to the peninsula. A telling example of this was the case of a 15-inch howitzer, the largest caliber field gun in the theater, which remained on SS *Baron Jedburgh* for nearly four months, thus keeping the ship from duties elsewhere. After numerous representations from the Admiralty to the army to remove the gun, the decision was eventually made to return the ship—with the howitzer still aboard—back to France![91] The situation did not improve throughout August, and Simpson was still complaining bitterly in mid-September about continuing delays in unloading the ships at Mudros.[92]

There is no doubt that the delay in transhipment at Mudros could have been reduced if the harbor had been better prepared and equipped with deepwater piers. While some problems would have invariably existed, Brigadier-General de Lotbiniére believed that it would have been much easier to get to those items located at the bottom of the ships, in a more timely manner, if there had been proper piers.[93] The importance of constructing deepwater piers on both the eastern and western sides of Mudros Harbour was actually mentioned as early as 30 June 1915 by Brigadier-General Winter, deputy quartermaster general (DQMG); yet discussions were still under way as to the type and positioning of these piers at the commencement of the August Offensive.[94] In any case, given the time required to construct new piers, work would have had to commence as early as March to be ready for the August Offensive.[95] Thus, in August 1915 there was only one pier at Mudros. "Australian Pier," as it was known, was made of mud and stone and was located on the eastern side of the harbor. It had a depth of only seven feet and was therefore unsuitable for large transport ships to go alongside. Appeals were made by Brigadier-General Winter in late June to extend the pier into deeper water, but, given the overall shallowness of the harbor, it would have required an extension of up to 350 yards, and then the elongated pier could have only been used during calm weather. In time though, a deepwater pier, with a depth of seventy feet, was constructed on the west side of the harbor, but this was not even contemplated until 24 September, well after the failure of the August Offensive, and not until concerns about the impact that bad weather could have on supply to the peninsula became too widely felt to continue to ignore.[96] The absence of piers (and facilities such as cranes) at Mudros had a profound impact on the timely functioning of the L-of-C.[97] Subsequent delay during the transhipping process foiled the timely arrival of much-needed supplies at the Gallipoli Peninsula. This was especially the case during August when Mudros was at its busiest trying to supply the largest offensive of the campaign.

A Shortage of Labor

Port facilities were not the only problem at Mudros. Delays were further compounded by the lack of available labor—most notably to load and unload cargoes. Despite there being a labor surplus above the war establishment of 71 officers and 230 other ranks on the L-of-C at the end of July 1915—with an effective strength of 536 officers and 8,621 other ranks—this was only because the establishment was itself deficient.[98] It took no account of the size and scale of the MEF's L-of-C, and was based on a force operating from a single base rather than from a number of bases.[99] Even with the addition of Greek and Egyptian laborers—the former being "very expensive, and not too efficient" and the latter relatively cheap and satisfactory—plus an order that all bakers and butchers not presently working in their trade were to train in loading pack mules, the MEF's L-of-C always suffered from a lack of manpower.[100]

The labor problem was acute during the August Offensive. Numbers were so short at Mudros that despite a deficiency in the war establishment of base troops on the peninsula, IX Corps was stripped of its fortress companies for work on the L-of-C.[101] By 5 August—the day before the offensive—the labor situation was so dire that Lieutenant-General Altham requested that an entire infantry battalion of the 53rd Division (army reserve) be allotted to him for fatigue work. Altham's request was approved by GHQ on 11 August but was retracted three days later upon opposition from IX Corps, to whom 53rd Division was by then attached and who desperately needed the troops.[102] General Headquarters MEF acknowledged the serious labor problems faced on the L-of-C, where soldiers who should have been fighting, and even Ottoman prisoners of war, were doing stevedore work. Hamilton's staff subsequently requested that the War Office send out two extra battalions, no matter how poorly they were trained, for fatigue duty on the L-of-C.[103] These, however, did not arrive in time to improve the logistic situation in August.

A Shortage of Small Craft

Aside from inadequate manpower, the MEF's L-of-C also suffered from a lack of small craft during August 1915. An insufficient number of motor launches hindered communications between ships, and between ship and shore, while a shortage of lighters adversely affected transhipping. Requests were continually made for the former, but their availability in the UK, combined with the difficulty of transporting them to the theater—where they were towed behind ships and as such were vulnerable to being lost in strong gales and high seas—meant that they were never forthcoming in sufficient numbers.[104] There were only eight motor launches available for Altham's staff at the commencement of the August Offensive, and of the fourteen requested by GHQ for use during the offensive only three had left the UK by 17 August.[105] This caused perpetual and considerable problems for the organization of the L-of-C. Lieutenant-Colonel Thomas Kearns, the AQMG of IX Corps, for example, stated that "the paucity of boats and lighters made things somewhat inconvenient as one had the greatest difficulty in getting to ships as they arrived" at Mudros.[106] Ellison, who by now had been promoted from deputy IGC to DQMG, agreed, noting that on account of the shortage of small vessels it was very difficult to get about in Mudros Harbour during the lead-up and commencement of the offensive.[107] While agreeing that more craft were required, Rear-Admiral Wemyss believed that the difficulties were not as grave as many claimed and were largely caused because military personnel were used to walking between locations when desired, rather than having to wait for craft, as was the naval way.[108] Wemyss's perspective was, of course, skewed by self-interest and the preservation of his professional reputation. It was clear at the time, as it is today, that the number of motor launches was not sufficient to enable timely communication and organization at Mudros, and elsewhere on the L-of-C, during the August Offensive.

The shortage of lighters for supply and transport purposes was equally acute. By August, Vice-Admiral de Robeck had recalled the majority of small craft and lighters from the L-of-C for use with the Suvla landing, while most of the remaining steam pinnaces and lighters were being used to fit out the ambulance carriers for medical evacuation.[109] According to Lieutenant-General Altham, this shortage had a direct impact upon the speed at which the cargoes of ships could be transhipped at the peninsula.[110] The shortage also caused concerns on Lemnos Island itself, where the quantity of supplies ashore for the troops awaiting the offensive was diminishing without being replenished.[111] Hamilton was concerned about what impact this shortage may have on the August Offensive, and warned Lord

Kitchener in July that "a deficiency in shipping and small craft might seriously hamper our operations."[112] The Admiralty realized the gravity of the situation and sent out Vice-Admiral Douglas Gamble (who had been head of the British Naval Mission to Constantinople, 1909–1910, and was now a member of the Admiralty's War Staff) "for a short visit to ascertain in detail the requirements of the Army in small vessels for [the] forthcoming operations."[113] Gamble, however, did not arrive until 22 July and only remained for a week: too late and too short a visit to influence or have an impact upon the August Offensive.[114] Like the motor launches, additional lighters were forthcoming prior to August but never in the necessary numbers. The Admiralty informed de Robeck that they were "squeezed dry, as regards small vessels" and that it was difficult to acquire more in the theater, for they were scarce and expensive.[115]

Not everyone thought the small-vessel transport situation was dire. Indeed, de Robeck informed the First Lord of the Admiralty, Arthur Balfour, that "with what we have already here and with what has been sent out to us there should be sufficient craft to meet our requirements." He added, "There has been some misrepresentation to the War Office as to the difficulties of transport. The Navy has always been able to meet any demands that have been made on it by the Army up to the present, and I see no reason that we will not continue to do so."[116] The first point to note in this regard, however, is de Robeck's professional bias. Given that the EMS's role prior to August was predominantly to act as a transport force, it is unlikely that de Robeck would report anything other than his ability to cope. Second, while it was true that supplies were reaching the peninsula, they often did so in vessels that should have been employed in other roles. The vice-admiral's defensive optimism was contrasted by the realism of the secretary of the Dardanelles Committee, Maurice Hankey, who informed Prime Minister Asquith on 4 August that the principle naval transport officer (PNTO), Commodore Richard Phillimore, "has at his disposal barely enough craft for the daily requirements of the Peninsula and islands. For any exceptional move [such as the offensive] he has to apply to the Vice Admiral for additional assistance, and other vessels, mine-sweepers, net-drifters, vessels on anti-submarine patrol . . . or destroyers have to be withdrawn from their legitimate job for the purpose."[117]

Hankey's fears that the MEF's supplies could only be maintained by reducing the fighting efficiency of the naval forces—which, as noted in chapter 4, could be ill-afforded—were proven to be well-founded by subsequent events. On 16 August, Hankey informed Balfour that during the August Offensive, "a great part of the patrols had to be called in, in order that the vessels might be used for transport purposes." Again in contrast to de Robeck's position, Hankey also felt that the shortage of craft was particularly felt at Mudros during these trying days, and described the "scramble for boats" as "at times a veritable pandemonium" owing to the large amount of transhipment necessarily undertaken, and felt that "a great deal more [small craft] will be required" in the future.[118] Despite the problems faced at Mudros in terms of organization and resources, it remained a crucial logistic hub throughout the campaign, particularly during the August Offensive. Lieutenant-General Altham believed that, in spite of its long list of difficulties, Mudros was an indispensable base, necessary because of the enemy submarine presence and valuable because of its close proximity to the peninsula.[119]

Kephalos Harbour

The pressures faced at Mudros Harbour were somewhat relieved by the smaller advanced base at Kephalos Harbour (Imbros Island), which was established and used simultaneously with the Lemnos port. This location faced even more problems than Mudros owing to its poorer facilities and greater exposure to the weather, especially northerly gales.[120] At only fifteen, eighteen, and nineteen miles from Helles, Anzac, and Suvla respectively, Kephalos was much closer to the peninsula than Mudros.[121] It was therefore used as a thoroughfare for small vessels and supply ships traveling from Mudros to the peninsula, which could wait at Kephalos during daylight hours, before proceeding to the beaches with their cargoes at night.[122] A site was selected onshore at Imbros in July for a supply depot, from which supplies could be drawn for the Anzac and Suvla sectors during the August Offensive, but its potential size was still being debated in late August and was therefore of no use.[123]

In reality, Kephalos was little more than an overflow for Mudros. Its prime function was serving as the site of GHQ and as an area where troops from the peninsula could go for a brief rest. Nonetheless, Kephalos was fundamentally important in the preparations for the August Offensive. Commodore Oliver Backhouse, the

CO of the 2nd Brigade, Royal Naval Division, arrived at Kephalos aboard HMS *Renard* on 6 August, and described the harbor as "alive with vessels and shore crammed with troops."[124] These were troops of 11th Division, destined for Suvla, who were accommodated and trained on the island in the lead-up to the offensive.[125] Kephalos Harbour was therefore a staging area rather than a logistic center, and it was in this function that Kephalos served the Allies during the August Offensive.

From the Intermediate to Advanced Bases

Apart from the length of the journey, whether proceeding from Mudros or Kephalos, the voyage to the peninsula was much the same for all small supply craft. After transhipping, small vessels proceeded to the advanced bases on the peninsula, with only those carrying valuable items, such as guns, receiving an escort. The service between these bases and the beaches was undertaken by small supply ships—fifteen of which were permanently allotted to the force—officered and manned by the Royal Naval Reserve, which were, due to the pressures experienced in obtaining sufficient numbers of lighters, permitted to run the risk of encountering submarines.[126] The journey took place under the cover of darkness, thus offering protection from both the submarines and enemy shelling when the supply ships approached and lay off the beaches. Because of the distances involved and the fact that unloading could only be done at night, it was not usually possible to do more than one round trip in twenty-four hours.[127]

Upon arriving off the beaches of the Gallipoli Peninsula, the cargoes of the supply ships had to be transhipped *again* into lighters, so as to be able to go alongside the piers—which, with the exception of the pier extending to the grounded collier *River Clyde* in the French sector at Helles, were all incapable of taking a vessel larger than a motor lighter.[128] Through this process the navy was able to tranship three hundred to four hundred tons daily from large to small vessels at Mudros, and again to lighters on arrival at the beaches. According to Hamilton, however, this could only be done so long as no "untoward circumstances" arose, such as the sinking of lighters or the temporary disablement of ships. Importantly, this "best case" tonnage was insufficient for the August Offensive, which would, according to Hamilton, require an increase to seven hundred to eight hundred tons per day, and a further increase to two thousand tons daily once the MEF advanced across the peninsula to Maidos in accord with the objectives of the offensive.[129] While Hamilton knew that additional lighters were being sent from the UK, he stressed that even more should be sent to allow for wastage, and that demands should be met quickly and "in a generous spirit."[130] As it eventuated, these craft did not arrive in time for the offensive, and the situation was still so problematic by 19 August that Colonel George MacMunn informed the QMG at the War Office that the MEF were still "hopelessly bereft of craft for the front."[131] It was perhaps fortunate for the MEF that the offensive did not progress into its second, third, or fourth phases, as there would surely not have been enough small craft to keep the attackers supplied to the levels necessary.

Naval Administration of the L-of-C

As outlined, the entire L-of-C supply process from the UK to the high-water mark off the peninsula was the responsibility of the navy. The military only took control of goods and distributed them to the various units once they were landed (discussed in chapter 6).[132] This entire system was plagued, however, by even greater administrative difficulties than the serious and systemic organizational and structural L-of-C problems discussed thus far.[133]

The administrative system in operation at the Dardanelles was, like that used on the Western Front, based on the conventions set forth in part two of *FSR*. While flexible and open to adaptation, these arrangements were based on the necessities of previous British military engagements and, as such, were from the outset insufficient for war on the scale of that experienced from 1914 to 1918. The MEF, like the BEF, was therefore administratively unprepared for the war with which it was faced.[134] Hamilton's administrative staff was thus forced to develop its systems in an ad hoc fashion both to meet local demands and to overcome problems as they arose. This type of improvisation worked in the early stages of the war, but as the size of the force increased and the logistic needs became greater, problems began to surface. This was especially the case at the Dardanelles. With the majority of experienced staff officers bound for France at the outbreak of the war, the MEF was, from its inception, seriously short of experienced administrators. Those who were available were hindered by the structural deficiencies of their training, which continually stressed the importance of command over logistics. The result was that when faced with the logistic difficulties of supplying an expeditionary force 3,500 miles from its home base, Hamilton's and de Robeck's staffs struggled to cope.[135] Improvisation was rife, but so was disorganization.

The initial British administrative system at the Dardanelles, based on prewar regulations, did not work. It did not suit the theater, nor did it suit an amphibious campaign. Rather than being specific to the Dardanelles, the early system mirrored that used on the Western Front, which had the advantage of transportation between well-equipped ports and a network of railways and roads. It was not until May 1915, however, with the introduction of the submarine menace, that the ad hoc and stopgap nature of the MEF's logistic arrangements was revealed as deficient. As such, it became necessary to improvise an entirely new system—one developed to suit the theater and the campaign.[136]

Although the administration and command of the L-of-C was a military matter, transportation was a naval concern. Upon arriving at Gibraltar and Malta, transports and supply ships were under the charge of the SNOs, who distributed sailing orders and ensured that the vessels were adequately prepared—with regard to fuel and provisions for the crew—for the next leg of their voyage. When vessels reached Alexandria, and were being repacked, responsibility for issuing further orders fell to the port admiral.[137] Once ships left Alexandria, responsibility transferred to the representative of the Naval Transport Department, Captain Henry Simpson, who, as the STO at Mudros, was responsible for those Mercantile Marine vessels chartered by the Admiralty.[138] It was Simpson's duty to interview the masters of all transports upon their arrival at Mudros and determine what they required, and then to find berths for them to tranship their cargoes.[139]

The lead-up to the August Offensive was a particularly trying time for Simpson. Not only was it his busiest period; it was also a time of great stress, and one that the director of transports at the Admiralty, Graeme Thomson, believed "overwhelmed" him.[140] In addition to trying to introduce some order to the chaotic transhipment process, Simpson was under constant pressure from Thomson to clear the transports and return them to the UK for further work.[141]

Simpson's task was made even more difficult by the fact that until 11 August he was supported by a meager staff of only three officers, and also because Rear-Admiral Wemyss, whose organizational skills usually made "things hum in the port of Mudros," was confined to bed from 4 to 17 August.[142] Neither was Simpson helped by his limited experience in administrative matters, which, according to Lieutenant-Colonel Forster, AA&QMG at Lemnos, significantly and negatively impacted upon the supply system.[143]

Simpson's responsibility for these vessels ceased as soon as the cargoes were placed on the small craft bound for the beaches. At this point responsibility was transferred to another naval officer, the PNTO, Commodore Richard Phillimore. Prior to being appointed PNTO, Phillimore had been captain of HMS *Inflexible*, which was damaged in the naval attack on the Dardanelles of 18 March, and had been the principal beach master at Helles on 25 April.[144] As PNTO, Phillimore's role was to control the transportation arrangements between Mudros, Kephalos, and the Gallipoli Peninsula.[145] Given that the military was entirely dependent on the EMS for its logistic resupply—in that it relied on the navy to transport the goods from the UK to the peninsula—close cooperation between the PNTO and Hamilton's staff was essential.[146] To encourage this, a military officer was attached to Phillimore's staff, and Phillimore was located on the same ship (HMT *Aragon*) as Captain Simpson and Lieutenant-General Altham. This administrative organization was complex. There were no fewer than six individuals (and their respective staffs) in charge of naval transport for the MEF. According to Lieutenant-General Altham, this was too many to allow the system to work effectively. In his opinion, the situation would have been better if control had been vested "in one person's hands," as was the case with the army.[147]

The Role of the Inspector General of Communications

While the military's logistic system was theoretically less complex than the naval model (in that the administration of the L-of-C fell under one individual, the IGC), it was, in fact, no more efficient in practice. The IGC's duties, as defined by *FSR*, included "the selection, appropriation, and allotment of sites and buildings for depots of all kinds, quarters, offices, hospitals, plant and material of every description that may be required for the service of the L-of-C." The IGC was also "responsible for the disposition of all reinforcements, supplies, and stores on the L-of-C, and for sending up to within reach of field units. . . . Similarly he arranges for the evacuation of all that is superfluous." In effect, the IGC coordinated all traffic on the L-of-C.[148] The IGC, more than anyone else, was therefore fundamental to the efficiency of the L-of-C system—especially one with six separate naval personnel responsible for transportation—and as such needed to be an excellent administrator.

Despite commanding the L-of-C, the IGC remained under Hamilton's command and received his instructions through the branch of Hamilton's headquarters concerned (i.e., the General Staff Branch; Adjutant-General's Branch; or Quartermaster-General's Branch). The overall purpose of the position of IGC was, according to Major-General Braithwaite, "to take the burden of the executive work connected with the administrative services off the shoulders of GHQ," particularly the DQMG, whose role it was to inform the War Office in London and the IGC of the MEF's requirements. One issue that arose with having both an IGC and DQMG in the Dardanelles was that *FSR*'s definitions of the various roles were based on the IGC being a long way from the theater and the DQMG being stationed at GHQ, and did not consider the impact that having these two officers in close proximity would have on the conflict of very similar roles.[149]

There was no IGC at the Dardanelles until 7 June, and therefore no one to perform these duties, which were instead left to the DQMG, Brigadier-General Samuel Winter, and the base commandant at Alexandria, Brigadier-General McGrigor.[150] These men unsurprisingly struggled with the increased workload, and the logistic system suffered from a commensurate lack of cohesion and direction. Hamilton realized the impact this was having on the transportation and distribution of stores and equipment, and therefore requested that Major-General Gerald Ellison, who had acted under Hamilton as CGS for four years prior to the war, be sent out from England as IGC.[151] Despite pressing "for the matter as far as I could," Hamilton noted that Ellison could not be spared, and Lord Kitchener insisted instead that Major-General Wallace, who was at that moment a surplus general in Egypt, take up the post.[152] Hamilton protested, but Kitchener was adamant.[153]

Wallace was at an immediate disadvantage upon his arrival at Mudros. He had no staff, and those allotted to his headquarters did not leave the UK until 9 June.[154] He also had no experience with logistic chains or systems. Nonetheless, his first task was to organize Mudros and make it an efficient base—a task that both Hamilton and Braithwaite thought beyond him, and one that Lieutenant-General Maxwell considered "an impossible task" beyond any individual, including "God Almighty Himself."[155] By the end of the month, Wallace's predictable ineffectiveness, combined with Hamilton's growing concern about the L-of-C, resulted in calls for his replacement.[156] Braithwaite later described Wallace as "an apology for an IGC."[157] Hamilton felt that the MEF needed "someone with the biggest administrative brains in the army" to run the L-of-C and informed Major-General Cowans that "I worry just as much over things behind me as I do over the enemy in front of me. What I want is a really big man there [as IGC], and I don't care one D [sic] who he is. A man I mean who, if he saw the real necessity, would wire for a great English contractor and 300 navvies without bothering or referring the matter to anyone. The present man [i.e., Wallace] wouldn't dream of ordering a tooth-pick without consulting General Headquarters."[158]

Despite having made up his mind that Wallace was to go, Hamilton refrained from directly asking for a replacement for fear of upsetting Kitchener. It was not until 6 July that he informed Kitchener, "I am becoming seriously apprehensive about my [L-of-C]. . . . The [IGC] must be a man of energy and ideas" and while Wallace "is probably excellent in his own line . . . he himself . . . doubts his own ability to cope with one of the most complicated situations imaginable."[159] In fact, three weeks after commencing as IGC, Wallace had informed Major-General Winter that, "I feel that the organisation of the Lines of Communication and making it work is such a task that I sometimes doubt myself whether I am equal to it."[160] On 9 July, Hamilton was informed that Lieutenant-General Edward Altham, described in another letter as "one of the most able administrators we have in the Army," was being sent out to replace Wallace.[161]

Altham left England on 15 July and arrived at Mudros a week later.[162] He immediately got to work on studying the administrative position and within twenty-four hours wrote to the quartermaster general at the War Office, informing him that the IGC's staff was out of touch with the L-of-C.[163] Altham also realized that, while the military supply and transport services were running satisfactorily, without closer cooperation between his headquarters and the administrative services at GHQ the L-of-C could not function efficiently.[164] He therefore suggested a major overhaul to the military's administrative structure—less than two weeks before the August Offensive.

On 25 July, Altham presented two alternatives to Hamilton and his staff officers: either responsibility for the L-of-C be given entirely to GHQ, thus ensuring cooperation between the L-of-C and GHQ; or it should be vested solely to the IGC, thus allowing the DAG and DQMG to turn their focus from the L-of-C to administration in the field. This second option would require the directors of the administrative services—on whom the IGC relied for information about stocks and supplies, but over whom he had no command—moving to Mudros to ensure closer contact between GHQ and the IGC.[165] Hamilton approved the second option, and in accord with Altham's wishes, the director of ordnance services and the DST were transferred to Altham's headquarters on HMT *Aragon*.[166] In addition to these changes, Altham was relieved of the responsibility of local work at Mudros. This role was given to Wallace, who was subsequently transferred from his new role as deputy IGC, to GOC Intermediate Base.[167] None of these changes, however, were made in time to have a positive effect on the August Offensive. Wallace's new staff, for example, did not begin arriving until 1 August, thus delaying necessary improvements at Mudros.[168] Likewise, the director of ordnance services, Brigadier-General Robert Jackson, did not arrive at Mudros until 4 August, thus robbing the IGC of valuable information about the ordnance situation for the August Offensive.[169] The DST, Brigadier-General Koe, was still at GHQ in September.[170] These delays led to Colonel MacMunn's conclusion that the "reorganisation was scarcely ready in time for the new landing" at Suvla Bay.[171]

Altham, nonetheless, was a man of experience and action, and under him the L-of-C immediately began to transform. The SNO and governor of Lemnos, Rear-Admiral Wemyss, believed that from the point of Altham's arrival, Mudros "underwent a rapid change for the better," especially in terms of facilities, while Commodore Keyes noted that the navy's "difficulties were greatly lightened" because of the centralization of the military's administration.[172] Others, however, were not so pleased. Major-General Ellison, who acted as Altham's deputy from 28 July to 7 August, before replacing Major-General Winter (invalided with dysentery) as DQMG at GHQ, thought that the administrative changes made under Altham—which shifted control from GHQ to the IGC—were negative moves.[173] By making Altham responsible for the administrative services, Ellison believed that it made Ellison's position at GHQ redundant and entirely dependent upon Altham for information about stocks of stores and supplies. He also believed that it further stretched the already strained relationship between the administrative and general staffs at GHQ. Ellison thought that a more appropriate and efficient system would have been possible if the DQMG retained responsibility for the administrative services in the field, while his deputies should be responsible for those on the L-of-C.[174] Therefore, while there can be little doubt that the efficiency of the L-of-C improved under Altham, it must be stressed that the situation was still far from perfect, even after his arrival—which was too late to have any measurable impact on the first phase of the August Offensive, but which would have improved during subsequent phases had they been launched. The pressure of work on Altham's headquarters was always "exceedingly great," notwithstanding the assistance provided by the arrival of additional staff; in September even de Robeck admitted that, while the situation was improving, the administration of the MEF's resupply was still not perfect.[175]

Interservice Administration

Importantly, for the duration of the Gallipoli Campaign, underscoring the naval and military administrative systems discussed was a strained administrative relationship between the services. Like that between Vice-Admiral de Robeck and General Hamilton, the relationship was cordial on the surface, but frustration and ill feeling ran deep. Both services had different staff systems, and neither really understood or appreciated the other's methods or processes.[176] Captain Simpson summed up the situation well, observing that the two services "simply looked at the problem from different sides."[177] Both, however, thought that theirs was the correct way to proceed. The navy, for instance, complained that the military's demands, particularly with regard to small craft, were unreasonable, and that the majority of problems on the L-of-C were because the military had failed to build proper facilities.[178] Military men, for their part, complained about the navy's poor organization and inability to provide sufficient craft.[179] There were perpetual problems in matching military requirements and expectations with naval capabilities.[180]

Behind-the-scenes bickering was rife, with letters and telegrams regularly sent complaining of the other service's lack of common sense. Rear-Admiral Wemyss, for example, told his wife on 12 August that "we [the navy] labour for ever [sic] and continuously for the Army—of course they couldn't do it without us, but they are not easy people to work with. . . . They certainly are not clever, nor do they make the best of what they have got."[181] Similarly, Commodore Keyes complained in his memoirs that the military "found it difficult to adjust their ideas to the peculiar conditions of amphibious warfare." The traditional divide between the military's administrative and general staff surprised him, especially considering that in the EMS, everything, whether connected with operations or administration, came through Keyes.[182]

Many senior military officers thought the navy's methods just as peculiar. Hamilton, for example, believed that "our charming coadjutors have no business methods whatsoever; keep no copies of their letters or orders, and are, generally speaking, as unbusinesslike as they are brave."[183] Lieutenant-General Altham too recorded that "our different organizations and systems want fitting into each other and at times the Navy system does not seem to us altogether well-adapted to the particular job we are both at now." Despite this, Altham realized that the navy "are doing everything in their power to help us," and therefore did all he could to improve the relationship, upon which the proper working of the L-of-C depended.[184]

Difficulties and Delays

In spite of ongoing changes in the administrative personnel and styles of the MEF, developments to the L-of-C did not occur in time to improve the logistic process for the August Offensive. The combination of a disorganized and incapable administrative system in the lead-up to the offensive, with the inherent difficulties of a seaborne supply and transport system—which had to first acquire items in the UK and then transport them for 3,500 miles through vulnerable waters and numerous bases—compounded the problems faced on the L-of-C and resulted in considerable delay. Supplies and stores were required in a timely fashion, and the failure to deliver items when required meant that by the time they arrived, many items were no longer required or could not be used. Nonetheless, it was true that despite the complexities and problems of the logistic process—both in terms of the physical journey and the administrative system—stores, supplies, and reinforcements did, in the main, successfully arrive at the beachheads during August 1915.[185]

Despite its "abnormal and peculiar" nature, especially when compared to the process of supplying the BEF on the Western Front—which acquired supplies from a number of sources and from a number of routes—there was never a complete breakdown in the main supply to the Gallipoli Peninsula. Irrespective of the difficulties faced by and the great demands placed on the naval forces, they were successful, although with great delays, in meeting the MEF's demands.[186] The system of getting supplies to the peninsula, therefore, functioned, even if ineffectively. Whether this could have been maintained if the August Offensive had progressed into its subsequent phases, however, is another question entirely. In any case the problem was not transporting enough stores to the peninsula; rather, the problem was distributing these to the frontline units. This was a military responsibility.

Lieutenant-General Sir William Birdwood, GOC ANZAC, outside his dug-out. Birdwood's initial objective of strengthening his perimeter grew into a large-scale plan to push across the Gallipoli Peninsula. Australian War Memorial, G00761.

Looking north from Anzac at the foothills of the Sari Bair Ridge. Suvla Bay is in the distance. Attacking from the shore, New Zealanders, Australians, and Indians pushed inland over and through this complex terrain. The country alone was a significant obstacle to mobility. The ground continues to rise, culminating in Chunuk Bair, Hill Q, and Hill 971 (not shown). Australian War Memorial, G00410.

Gunners of the 7th Indian Mountain Artillery Brigade, who, with their obsolete 10-pounder mountain guns, accompanied the advancing columns toward the Sari Bair Ridge. Because of their close proximity to the troops, these mountain batteries were forced to employ crossfire techniques, firing in support of their flanking column rather than their own. Australian War Memorial, C02192.

Mutual understanding, goodwill, and cooperation between the army and navy were a necessity but were unfortunately lacking during the August Offensive. Despite their efforts to work together, both services were hamstrung by a combination of tradition, culture, pride, and personalities. From left to right are Commodore Roger Keyes, chief of staff to Vice-Admiral John de Robeck; Vice-Admiral John de Robeck, commander of the EMS; General Sir Ian Hamilton, GOC of the MEF; and Major-General Walter Braithwaite, chief of the general staff of the MEF. Australian War Memorial, H10350.

Ships anchored in Mudros Harbour (Lemnos Island), with a British airship, known as a "Submarine Scout," flying overhead. Supplies sent from the UK to Gallipoli first went to Alexandria, where they were repacked. They would then proceed to Mudros, where they were placed onto smaller vessels for the journey to the peninsula. Mudros Harbour suffered from a lack of port facilities and congestion and was a source of great delay on the lines of communication. Australian War Memorial, G00464.

Once supplies reached the beaches at Gallipoli, they had to be offloaded onto the piers and manhandled ashore. They were then stockpiled and distributed forward to the troops. In the absence of mechanical transport, mules and men undertook this work. In this picture, two field guns are being brought ashore at Anzac Cove. Note the stacks of stores and the congestion on the beach. Australian War Memorial, C011133.

The troops lived in harsh conditions. Never far from the front lines, they were always within range of the enemy's artillery and sniper fire. Here, Australian soldiers sit in the support trenches on Pope's Hill on 6 August, awaiting the commencement of the August Offensive that afternoon. Australian War Memorial, C02699.

Commencing at 5:30 P.M. on 6 August, the feint attack by the 1st Australian Brigade at Lone Pine raged for four days. The fighting was tough, often relying on fists, bayonets, and bombs (primitive hand grenades). Although it was the only Australian success of the August Offensive, the capture of Lone Pine did little to alter the overall offensive. The dead, who littered the trenches, were often buried where they fell; sometimes the trenches were simply filled in to create mass graves. Australian War Memorial, H00405.

The August Offensive included a new amphibious landing by the British IX Corps at Suvla Bay. The purpose of this landing was to create a safe base that, because of its better beaches, could be used as a logistic hub to supply the offensive as it progressed across the Gallipoli Peninsula. Here, troops unload supplies from the motor lighters, known as "beetles" because of their design, which delivered men, munitions, and supplies to Suvla Bay. Note the animals, wagons, and wheelbarrows used for transporting supplies. Australian War Memorial, A01266.

This photo, taken at Chunuk Bair—the position reached by the New Zealanders on 8 August—shows the Dardanelles in the distance. Note the exposed nature of the crest, the complexity of the terrain, and the protection afforded Ottoman supply columns. If the offensive were to progress into its second, third, and fourth phases, the allies would have to hold this ground as well as the intervening ridges, and push across the waist of the peninsula. Australian War Memorial, G01801.

CHAPTER 6

SUPPLY AND TRANSPORT

Being logistically prepared is an essential component of planning for military operations. British *FSR*, which established the framework for how the Allied system of military supply was supposed to operate in 1915 (at Gallipoli and on the Western Front), instructed its readers that "the mobility of an army depends directly on the efficiency of the organization by which its daily requirements are supplied." "This organization," it explained, "must provide not only for the immediate replacement of deficiencies in personnel, animals, supplies, and material of all kinds, but for the prompt removal of everything that is no longer required at the front, such as sick, wounded, and prisoners."[1] The message contained within this little bloodred pocketbook was not lost on General Hamilton, who later described these elements as the fundamental "wants of an army."[2] But to what degree were efficient, or even adequate, supply and transport systems in place for the August Offensive?

The nature of the terrain of the Gallipoli Peninsula, which was sparsely populated, arid, and not cultivated, meant that everything the MEF required for its war effort, and indeed its very survival, had to be sent by sea. As noted in the previous chapter, the first component of this process—sourcing the items and transporting them to the theater—was largely successful in spite of the difficulties and delays experienced. The second stage, where these items had to be disembarked, stockpiled, and then distributed to the field units, was more complex, more vulnerable to breakdown, and far less successful.

Following the previous chapter's examination of the L-of-C, this chapter focuses on the three-part process of supply and transport in preparation for, and during, the offensive: disembarkation, stockpiling, and the distribution of items to the units. In so doing, the chapter seeks to determine whether the August Offensive was, from a supply and transport viewpoint, a logistically viable operation. To achieve this, numerous aspects specific to the August Offensive are examined, including the process of disembarking items onto the various beaches at Gallipoli; the suitability of these beaches as advanced bases and as localities for stockpiling local reserves; the process of distribution, especially the accessibility and suitability of supply routes and the availability of animals for transport purposes; the availability of specific items during the offensive; and the extent to which medical evacuation impacted battlefield operations.

As noted in chapter 5, due to the unsuitability of the MEF's piers on the Gallipoli Peninsula, which were not deep enough to allow supply vessels alongside, those ships that traveled to the peninsula from Mudros or Kephalos were forced, upon reaching their destination, to lie off the coast and await the arrival of lighters from the shore. Their cargoes were then transferred into the lighters, whose shallow draught allowed them to go alongside the few piers that extended out from the various beaches. Stores were then offloaded and manhandled ashore, where they were stockpiled in field depots and subsequently issued forward to the units. This entire process was done at night to shield the activity from Ottoman observers and to protect fatigue parties from the danger of enemy shelling.[3] In theory, this process was rather straightforward. In practice, however, it was complicated by a combination of poor organization, mismanagement, and the sheer magnitude and difficulty of the task. Before examining this process, however, it is important to understand the particulars of the Allied advanced bases on the Gallipoli Peninsula.

The Advanced Bases

There were three Allied advanced bases on the peninsula at the commencement of the August Offensive: two at Cape Helles and one in the Anzac sector. The French (who supplied themselves), situated on the right flank of the Helles sector, used V Beach and its piers, which extended out to the grounded collier *River Clyde*. The British, having handed over V Beach to the French early in the campaign, relied on W Beach, also known as Lancashire Landing, and its associated piers.[4] The third advanced base was Anzac Cove. This small beach, with its six piers, was the logistic hub of the Anzac sector, and by extension, of the August Offensive. Ordnance and supply depots littered its shores, while various headquarters and dugouts pocked its hillsides. A short jetty extended out from the stretch of sand south of

Anzac Cove, known as Brighton Beach, but given its visibility from the enemy's observation post at Gaba Tepe, it could only be used at night. To the north of Anzac Cove was the aptly named North Beach. While much larger than Anzac Cove, and with more space available inland for stockpiling ordnance and supplies, North Beach and its approaches were vulnerable to sniper and machine-gun fire and were therefore considered too dangerous to use before the gains of the August Offensive secured the area (it was still not safe at the end of August). Construction work began on a pier (Walker's Pier) at North Beach during the offensive, and while it succeeded in reducing some of the congestion in Anzac Cove, it could still only be used at night and its logistic impact was not felt until after the offensive had failed.[5]

A fourth advanced base was established at Suvla Bay during the offensive. Its purpose was twofold: to supply IX Corps and to be used as a base of supply for the subsequent phases of the August Offensive. It will be remembered that there were three beaches at Suvla: A, B, and C. Initially, it was intended to use the first two of these for the disembarkation of troops, while the third, C Beach, was to be used for landing artillery, animals, and supplies.[6] But on the afternoon of 7 August the decision was made to make a small beach, situated to the north of Suvla Bay (later known as New A Beach), the main landing place for stores and supplies in this sector.[7] Prior to August the Ottomans had heavily mined this area as a defensive measure against amphibious landings, and it took much hard work by the Royal Engineers during the offensive, in the removal of over one hundred mines, before New A Beach was considered safe to use.[8]

None of these beaches, irrespective of the sector, were logistically suitable. Those at Helles and Anzac were narrow, with little room for storage, and as such were regularly overcrowded.[9] Commodore Roger Keyes complained of this after the August Offensive failed, noting that "the lack of space for safe storage in the vicinity of the beaches was frequently given as a reason for refusing to accept stores, etc., and for requests to re-embark stores and beasts already landed." Keyes particularly singled out the narrowness of Anzac Cove, believing that "this is still a bar to the accumulation of a large reserve."[10] Those beaches that were large enough, such as North Beach or Suvla, were too vulnerable to Ottoman fire to be described as satisfactory bases. This situation, combined with a constant lack of men for fatigue duty, meant that items could never be landed and stockpiled quickly enough. This, in turn, led to bottlenecks and serious delay in landing supplies in the lead-up and during the August Offensive.

Responsibility on the Beaches

Similar to the problems faced on the L-of-C, the responsibility and distribution of duties on the beaches also suffered from a lack of concise doctrinal regulation. In spite of its section titled "Division of duties between Navy and Army," which attempted to define who was responsible for what, *FSR* was unclear in this regard. Essentially, these regulations, which were not developed for amphibious operations, failed to adequately stipulate the boundaries of responsibility. To make matters worse, the *Manual of Combined Naval and Military Operations*, which *was* written specifically for this type of warfare, merely quoted from *FSR*. Its directions were vague: "In landings and embarkations the navy will have full control of the entire beach up to high-water mark, and of such further positions of the beach and of such piers and wharves as may be necessary to enable them to control the work of embarkation and disembarkation. Within these limits the military officers will carry out all instructions issued by the naval commander, but beyond them the responsibility for the safety and transportation of men, animals, guns, vehicles, and stores on shore will rest with the army."[11]

Further complicating such matters was an inherent contradiction in the regulations. While part 1 ("Operations") of *FSR* (as seen above) stipulated that military officers would "carry out the instructions *issued by* the naval commander [emphasis added]," part 2 ("Organization and Administration") stated that "all details of . . . landings are arranged by the military landing officer *in concert* with [the naval commander] and the base commandant [emphasis added]."[12] Just who was responsible for disembarking the various items, depended, it seems, on what volume of *FSR* one consulted.

In the case of the August Offensive, the division of these types of logistic duties differed between sectors. At Helles and Anzac, where the advanced bases were already established and the staff experienced in the work of embarkation/disembarkation, all work was overseen by the beach commandants: Major James Watson at Helles and Lieutenant-Colonel Frederick Young at Anzac.[13] Being appointed by the IGC, the beach commandant—and by extension the IGC—was responsible for disembarkation and any work on the beaches at Helles and Anzac. Given the amount of work required at the latter, GHQ attached three "special service" officers to the ANZAC "for such duties in connection with the landing as the G.O.C. may direct." With no defined role, however, it was left to Birdwood to employ them as he saw fit. Birdwood was also directed by Hamilton's headquarters to select those officers who were to assist Lieutenant-Colonel Young.[14] The same flexibility was not afforded Birdwood's counterpart at Suvla, Lieutenant-General Stopford, whose officers were chosen for him by GHQ.

While the process of disembarkation was much the same at Suvla as at Anzac and Helles, the task at Suvla was inherently more difficult, especially considering the need to establish a new advanced base with minimal delay, while at the same time landing every single item necessary for IX Corps operations. To further complicate the situation, the arrangements for disembarkation at Suvla contrasted with those at Helles and Anzac, and were considerably more complicated. The principal difference at Suvla was that GHQ, not the IGC, assumed direct control and responsibility for the landing of goods.[15] Rather than learning from the lessons of 25 April and applying the same arrangements in use at Helles and Anzac—which had adapted throughout the campaign to meet the challenges faced in this task—GHQ instead chose to follow the vague guidelines of *FSR* (part 1). As a result, a level of confusion was injected into the process of disembarkation and stockpiling at Suvla that could have been, and indeed was, avoided in the other sectors. This ineffective arrangement continued until 10 August—when a beach commandant was finally appointed—which saw Suvla placed on the same footing as the other advanced bases. The arrangements were again changed in late August, this time putting the landing places and their administrative services solely under the orders of the corps commander.[16]

Even with the appointment of a beach commandant, however, the bounds of responsibility at Suvla remained unclear and confused.[17] In effect, the navy's principal beach master (PBM), Captain Henry Talbot—appointed by Vice-Admiral de Robeck and answerable to him—was responsible for offloading the various cargoes that arrived at the advanced bases and conveying them to the high-water mark (the level reached by the sea at high tide). Equipped with an inventory of all that was to be landed and in what order, Talbot was also charged with selecting the most appropriate locations for the various piers and landing stages.[18]

Once the cargo was disembarked, responsibility for the various items transferred from the PBM to the army's principal military landing officer (PMLO) at Suvla, Colonel William Western.[19] As PMLO, Western was responsible for unloading cargoes, safeguarding supplies, and stockpiling them on the beach. He was also responsible for arranging with the medical authorities for the embarkation of sick and wounded.[20] Western's, and therefore GHQ's, responsibility ceased once the items had been placed where desired. Responsibility then transferred to Brigadier-General Joseph Poett, deputy adjutant and quartermaster general (DA&QMG), IX Corps, who took control and organized for their subsequent distribution.[21]

Throughout this entire process, the division of responsibility at Suvla was blurred.[22] Despite orders clearly stating that the beach parties were under Colonel Western's control, everything on the beach including the beach parties, according to one eyewitness, was under practical command of Captain Talbot.[23] This overlap was primarily caused by the vagueness of the regulations. Aside from reducing effectiveness, this confusion also led to strained relations between the naval and military officers. For all its deficiencies, *FSR* at least realized that this was to be avoided if the disembarkation process was to succeed: "The complicated duties of embarking and landing troops and stores can only be carried out successfully so long as perfect harmony and co-operation exist between the naval and military authorities, and when the staff duties devolving on both services have been carefully organized and adjusted."[24]

Despite reassurances from both services that relations were good, and that they worked well together, the evidence suggests otherwise. The case of Captain Edmund Carver, who replaced Talbot as PBM at A Beach at noon on 8 August (Talbot being required to command a battleship), was a suitable case in point.[25] In spite of being reminded of the importance of cooperation, and warned that he would be removed if he could not work with his army counterpart, Carver often overstepped his mark and demanded more of the military than his authority allowed, much to the irritation of Colonel Western.[26] Rather than confining himself to disembarkation, Carver was unhappy with the military's procedures, particularly what he perceived as a lack of organization and urgency, and therefore concerned himself with everyone and everything on the beach.[27] There were even reports that he ventured as far as two miles inland to interfere. While Carver's intention may have been to improve the situation, his methods were counterproductive.[28] Realizing that Carver's personality was affecting relations with the army, and in turn, having an impact upon the logistic process, de Robeck replaced him on 10 August with Commander Edward Unwin (who had previously commanded the motor lighters used to convey the troops during the Suvla landings).[29] This instance is but one example of the many difficulties experienced during the disembarkation stage of the logistic process.

Problems with Transhipping

The first difficulty faced in getting supplies ashore in August was in relation to a lack of lighters available for transhipment and ferrying items to the piers. Other small craft such as lifeboats and horse boats could be used, but these often leaked and damaged supplies. In any case, these small craft were required to land men, animals, guns, and wagons, and as such could not be spared indefinitely for landing supplies. The lighters, therefore, were the best and only means available of landing supplies.[30] Opinion as to whether there were sufficient lighters for the task was divided. The army believed that there were not, while the navy was adamant that numbers were sufficient and that the problem lay with the military's ability to clear and free them up for additional work.[31] There is evidence to back up both arguments, which again highlights an important lack of cooperation and understanding between the services.

The army's case was clear. It had constantly reported the shortage of lighters and warned of its repercussions, but felt it was being ignored. After requesting more lighters on 20 July, Hamilton's assistant director of supplies, Lieutenant-Colonel Walter Parker, vented his anger in his unit's war diary: "Seems Navy will never take this matter properly in hand—am sick and tired of representing it. Wired [IGC] again about lighters and again represented to DQMG [Brigadier-General Winter] the seriousness of the situation."[32] Parker repeated his concerns the next day: "The position is getting desperate as regards the lack of provision of lighters and tugs by the Royal Navy—and in spite of daily appeals nothing is done." Such anger and frustration was well warranted. The want of lighters had resulted in a paucity of forage on the peninsula—the equivalent of having no fuel for motor lorries on the Western Front.[33] Urgent calls were put to the IGC (who passed them onto the PNTO) for more lighters, but there were no surplus craft to send.[34] The situation was particularly acute in the Anzac sector, where the reserve of forage had run out by 21 July. HMT *Edenmore*, laden with hay, was in fact turned away from Anzac Cove on 22 July because no lighters were available to unload it.[35] The same happened to HMT *Efi* on 1 August.[36] The inability to build up a stockpile meant that it was necessary to land *daily* requirements of forage during the August operations, thus further complicating an overworked supply system.[37]

In the army's opinion the navy was to blame—it had not provided enough lighters to unload and land everything required, thus resulting in a depletion of reserve supplies on the peninsula. Despite constant army warnings, major problems continued to be faced at the commencement of the August Offensive and persisted until well after it had failed. On 10 August, for instance, the DST, Brigadier-General Koe, informed the IGC of the urgent need for more lighters at Anzac, stating that without them "there is not sufficient lighterage or towage available to enable me to send sufficient [supplies] for daily requirements." He also warned that if something was not done to increase the reserve on the peninsula, the Anzac sector would run out of supplies within a week.[38] Koe's concerns became reality three days later when his deputy, Major George Raynell, informed the IGC that, because of the lighter shortage, it had been impossible to land an adequate reserve and the force was now living "from day to day."[39] It was a similar story at Suvla.[40] Koe's concerns reached their zenith on 23 August. After reminding the IGC that the situation had not improved, he warned that unless his demands for additional craft were met the MEF could have a "disaster" on its hands.[41] Another three days passed before the number of lighters available started to match the army's demands.[42] This was not satisfactory. By this time, three weeks had elapsed since the commencement of the August Offensive, and the force was only now starting to land sufficient supplies. The impact was profound.

Evidence also suggests that the naval point of view was not without substance. While admitting that there was an overall lack of lighters, Commodore Keyes observed that by withdrawing vessels from their proper duties—the operational impact of which he failed to discuss—the navy actually delivered more stores to the beaches than what the army could find space for, and more than the MEF's working parties could handle.[43] Put simply, the navy felt that the number of lighters available was irrelevant, as there were not the facilities to allow for the quick disembarkation even if more lighters were present. The first problem was an absence of deepwater piers; the second, a lack of fatigue parties. The navy was right to blame the MEF for this, as both were military responsibilities.

Unlike men, who could jump into the water and wade ashore, supplies—particularly ordnance—had to be landed dry. Indeed, after wading ashore at Suvla during the night of 6 August the 11th Battalion, Manchester Regiment, found that the salt water had put three hundred of its rifles and one machine gun out of action.[44] Piers were therefore essential. As noted, the piers at Helles and Anzac were not capable of allowing anything larger than lighters alongside.[45] This resulted in delay, as it meant that all supplies had to be transhipped again (having previously been transhipped at Mudros) before being landed. But at least some piers existed at Helles and Anzac, unlike at Suvla, where they had to be constructed as soon as practicable.

Responsibility for the construction of piers at Suvla fell to IX Corps' chief engineer, Brigadier-General Painter, and the 68th Field Company, Royal Engineers.[46] Their task was complicated from the beginning. Putting aside the difficulties of working under fire, they were further hindered by a lack of materials, poor communications, and a commander who was "really ill and quite unfit for duty."[47] Upon landing, for example, Painter was forced to allot the 68th Field Company to water duties because a communication mix-up had resulted in their pier-building materials being landed three miles north of where he expected them.[48] By the time he realized the problem and collected his men, Painter, who had been unwell before the landing, "practically fainted" in the arms of Brigadier-General Poett. Painter was subsequently invalided to the UK and replaced by Brigadier-General Edward Bland.[49] As it eventuated, construction of the first pier at Suvla did not begin until the Royal Australian Naval Bridging Train (RANBT) arrived on 8 August—towing with it the pontoons the men had built at Imbros prior to the offensive.[50] Together, the RANBT and 68th Field Company constructed a barrel pier at A Beach on 8 August, followed by a stone pier at A West, and another below Lala Baba.[51] It should be noted that all of these piers had to be built during the offensive—and until this was done the troops at Suvla could not be adequately resupplied.

Fatigues

Aside from the specific problem of building piers at Suvla, in Keyes's opinion the problem of securing enough labor to undertake the difficult and exhausting work of manhandling the supplies and stores from the lighters onto the piers, and thence onto the shore where they were stockpiled for distribution, was the real obstacle to rapid and sufficient disembarkation everywhere during the August Offensive. After the offensive had failed, he concluded that "the lack of working parties was, and is, a constant source of delay."[52] Keyes later contended that this led to a breakdown in the supply system with the MEF being forced to live "a hand to mouth existence."[53] There is much evidence from both services to give credence to this view. Major-General Gerald Ellison, DQMG of the MEF, for example, agreed that "the provision of labour presents great difficulty . . . in respect to beaches for off-loading stores etc.," while Maurice Hankey, secretary of the Dardanelles Committee, reported that the amount of fatigue work required on the beaches had been completely "overlooked" when planning the offensive.[54] There simply were not enough men allotted to this duty. This shortage ignored the *Manual of Combined Naval and Military Operations*, which warned of the need for labor units: "In order that the maximum number of troops may be available for operations ashore," it noted, "it may be advisable to enrol a special corps of labourers for work on the beaches in connection with the landing of stores, supplies, guns and vehicles."[55] Rather than a special corps, the MEF had to rely upon its fighting troops to do the work.

In contrast to the Western Front, or the MEF's island bases for that matter, there was little civil labor available on the Gallipoli Peninsula. That which did exist could not be used in any meaningful sense because laborers refused to work while the beaches were being shelled.[56] The Egyptian Labour Company, which was sent to Suvla during the offensive, had to be returned to Mudros owing to a "shyness" of shellfire, while Greek laborers quickly stopped working when shelling commenced, and often had to be coerced into recommencing. This meant that troops who were desperately needed for the operations, and who were exhausted from a lack of rest, had to be employed instead. Using military labor, however, was far from ideal, for it not only depleted the strength in the trenches but rendered these men—already exhausted from their trench duties—unable to work at a rate that they might otherwise have been able to.[57] Hamilton's headquarters realized this, but the August Offensive had been fought and had failed before anything useful could be done.[58]

In spite of a policy to try and keep the fatigues undertaken by troops to a minimum, the beach parties in the Anzac sector always consisted primarily of fighting troops.[59] Some 250 men of the Army Service Corps assisted the Anzac parties, but this still was not enough to cope with the work of disembarking stores, working the depots, and loading supplies for forwarding onto units.[60] A further 378 reserves were sent to Anzac from Suvla for fatigues, but this did little except deplete the numbers available in the Suvla sector.[61] It was not until 17 August that a permanent beach party was available at Anzac—and this was only formed in an ad hoc way by removing a noncommissioned officer and eight men from each battalion.[62] This did not fix the situation; on 31 August the DST reported: "Cannot work supplies ashore fast enough at Anzac owing to lack of labour."[63] After the failure of the offensive, Lieutenant-General Birdwood was of the opinion that his men were too exhausted to undertake fatigues, and furthermore, he could not "spare any" due to the length of line now held by his corps.[64] This itself suggests the scale of difficulties that would have been faced in this regard should the offensive have proceeded beyond its first phase objectives. Just who would have undertaken such fatigue work in subsequent phases is unclear.

It was a similar story at Suvla. Despite being allotted one thousand men of the Royal Naval Division as beach parties, IX Corps was informed that these men could only be used for general beach duties for the first twenty-four hours of operations, after which they would be used specifically and solely for landing mules.[65] In IX Corps too, therefore, there was a reliance on its own troops for fatigue work. Again, however, these men were required for operations. The labor situation at Suvla was so dire that four hundred infantry reinforcements arriving on 12 August were immediately put to work on the beach, rather than proceeding to their units.[66] Another seven hundred laborers were promised on 14 August, but this still was not enough. Two days later Brigadier-General Koe noted that labor was still the most pressing need at Suvla—a claim he repeated on 26 August. Military labor could always be used, but the "men [were] dead beat and available only at uncertain times and for indefinite periods."[67] In other words, combat troops being used on fatigues were exhausted, were difficult to find, and were constantly withdrawn on account of the changing military situation.[68]

Vulnerability of the Beaches

The danger posed by Ottoman artillery was another serious problem for the disembarkation process, and further "complicated the question of landing supplies" during the August Offensive.[69] Each Allied beach—and its occupants—was vulnerable to shellfire at any time of the day. At Helles, both V and W Beaches were an excellent target for the Ottoman artillery on the Asiatic shore. Similarly, the beaches at Anzac—and the ships that lay off them—were within range of most of the Ottoman guns in the area. The beaches at Suvla were more concealed than Anzac, but the ground close to them was visible to the enemy, and all, including ships coming to unload there, were within the range of Ottoman artillery.[70] The war diary of the 40th Depot Unit of Supply clearly highlights the dangers and difficulties faced on the beaches. This unit, which was responsible for transferring supplies from HMT *Edenmore* to the lighters off Suvla Bay, noted that it was under shellfire "almost every day" in August, during which time *Edenmore* was "hit twice."[71] This was a unique problem. The beaches—or advanced bases—at Gallipoli were the equivalent of the railheads of the Western Front. But, unlike the BEF's railheads, the MEF's advanced bases were constantly exposed to artillery fire. Lieutenant-General Altham believed that it was this key difference that made supply at Gallipoli particularly difficult: "It was quite a new problem and the novelty of it was that the lines of communication came right up into the firing zone. Everything had to be landed under fire. . . . In fact at one time they were losing more men on the beaches every day than they did in the trenches."[72] To combat this problem, supplies were predominantly disembarked at night, using the darkness as a screen against Ottoman observation. Though this was partially successful, it was not without complications of its own. In truth, as it eventuated, it was only a lack of Ottoman artillery ammunition that prevented a complete breakdown of Allied supply on the beaches.[73]

The precarious system described thus far was also dependent on favorable weather. Poor conditions could have a grave impact not only on transporting supplies to the peninsula but also in offloading stores onto the beaches.[74] This was especially the case at Helles whenever there was an onshore wind, or at Anzac if there was any swell.[75] In such circumstances the best scenario was a delay; the worst was the loss of a lighter or its cargo. Such was the case on the morning of 24 July when a lighter, laden with valuable engineer stores, including eighteen water tanks and fourteen thousand feet of piping, was sunk owing to a sudden rise in the wind.[76] Fortunately for the Allies, the weather was generally good throughout the August Offensive. But had the offensive proceeded into the second, third, and fourth phases—something requiring time—the attackers would have been gambling against the weather. Indeed, the first serious gales arrived on 8 October—only nine weeks after the commencement of the August Offensive. These gales caused havoc to the piers, washing some away and destroying others, and briefly put a stop to supplies landing at the Gallipoli beaches altogether.[77] The Allies then had only a nine-week window in which to achieve the three subsequent phases without major interruptions to their supplies. After this the weather would have made supplying a large force, especially one now distant from its base and stretched across tenuous terrain, a near impossible task.

Stockpiling

Having examined the disembarkation process and its complexities during the August Offensive, it is now appropriate to focus on the final tier of the Allied supply process at Gallipoli: stockpiling those stores received and their subsequent distribution to frontline units. Once disembarked at the beach, the various supplies were taken to locations chosen by each corps.[78] The DA&QMG, whose role it was to oversee all administrative arrangements in his sector and report his formation's supply requirements to his superior at GHQ (the DQMG), was the senior administrative officer at corps level. In effect, he was responsible for ensuring that there were adequate supplies for his corps, and that there was adequate transport available to distribute these. But his influence was restricted. Brigadier-General Poett, for example, described himself as a mere "spectator" in the planning process. Rather than being involved in the supply and transport arrangements for Suvla Bay, Poett found that this was done entirely by GHQ, which then placed responsibility for executing its plan in the hands of its representative (the PMLO), who was junior in rank to Poett. Indeed, Poett later stated that Lieutenant-General Stopford was not permitted to consult Poett or discuss such supply arrangements with him prior to the offensive, and that he himself did not know of the details of the logistics plan until they were issued to the troops. Thus, while Poett was responsible for supplying his formation, the actual officers who carried out these duties were not under his orders, but those of GHQ. The net result was that Poett felt as though he had no control over the supplies, for which he was ultimately responsible, until they reached him. In this case Poett was also not helped by the fact that when he landed at A Beach on 7 August he was without his staff, including his deputy, who remained with Stopford on board HMS *Jonquil*.[79] It should be noted, however, without undermining Poett's cause for complaint, that the DA&QMG's role was primarily managerial and comprised largely of reporting and coordinating the supply and transport arrangements of his respective divisions.

The substantive arrangements for distributing stores landed at the various beaches to the front line were undertaken by the AA&QMG, who was responsible for the control and supervision of all administrative matters at the divisional level.[80] This officer thus controlled both the A (personnel) and Q (maintenance) functions of his division.[81] Despite these wide-ranging and crucial responsibilities, AA&QMGs were not chosen based on individual knowledge or expertise, but more by way of a rotational system. As a representative of both branches of the administrative staff, each AA&QMG was selected by either the DQMG or DAG at GHQ, who took turns to nominate an officer. As such, the AA&QMG—the person responsible for ensuring that his troops received their supplies—did not necessarily have specific experience in Q work (nor A work for that matter).[82]

A necessary element of the distribution process at Gallipoli (and elsewhere) was the storing and stockpiling of "the wants of an army." This stockpiling not only enabled each divisional AA&QMG to calculate his needs and quickly distribute the required items but also acted as a reserve in case of emergency. Supply depots, field depots, and ammunition dumps littered the shores and gullies of the advanced bases at Gallipoli, and it was from these that the MEF's forward units were supplied. Aside from stocking the MEF's daily requirements, these locations were also filled with reserves. The threat that bad weather could cut off the "lifeblood" of the MEF at any time was at the forefront of GHQ's concerns and preparations.[83] To obviate the risk posed by this prospect, it was necessary to take certain precautions—not least of which was landing surplus items during times of good weather so as to accumulate a stockpile of reserve stores and supplies on the peninsula. The greater the reserve, the better placed the MEF was to meet any challenges. As a benchmark, twenty-four days' worth of stores was considered premium, but the ultimate goal was to gradually increase stocks until there were thirty days' supplies on shore.[84] Amassing and maintaining this level proved to be difficult. To achieve this the MEF was required to disembark quantities over and above those essential for daily consumption—which, prior to the August Offensive, amounted to one hundred tons at Helles and eighty-five at Anzac. These numbers were to increase to 140 tons of rations and at least 30 tons of forage at Anzac alone during the offensive.[85]

Despite its difficulties, the MEF was able to build significant reserves prior to the offensive. By mid-July a reserve of twenty-four days' rations for forty-five thousand men, four days' forage for eight thousand animals, and ten days' fuel existed at Helles. At Anzac there were twenty-three days' rations for twenty-five thousand men, five days' grain and one day of hay for one thousand animals, and two days' fuel.[86] Helles reached its target of thirty days' rations by 23 July—an achievement possible only because of the limited role prescribed to VIII Corps for the forthcoming offensive. The Anzac sector, on the other hand, reached its pinnacle in mid-July, and its reserves were already dwindling by the end of the month. As the reserves grew at Helles, those in the Anzac sector actually fell to fifteen days' rations.[87] The heavy demands placed on the sector were responsible for this. As well as landing its ever-increasing daily requirements and attempting to build a reserve, the Anzac sector was being transformed in preparation for the offensive. Bivouacs were constructed on the slopes of the few available gullies to accommodate reinforcements, and a large assortment of guns, ammunition, and equipment—all of which were required for the offensive—were disembarked.[88] Understandably, the work associated with this transformation had a significant impact on the further accumulation of supply stockpiles. Further, by increasing troop numbers at Anzac—without a proportional increase in surplus supplies—the reserves stockpiled in this sector were now required to fill daily usage.

The depletion of reserves was not helped by an order on 3 August that put a ten-day freeze on supplies being sent to Anzac and stipulated that Birdwood's corps would instead live on the reserve already accumulated. By 13 August the reserve within the Anzac sector had been reduced to nine days, compared with one month at W Beach.[89] During the August Offensive the troops within the Anzac sector were increasingly living day by day.

The accumulation of a reserve at Suvla was also a priority. It was planned to land seven days' supplies and forage for IX Corps "as soon as possible"—amounting to approximately 250 tons.[90] Things did not go to plan. On 7 August, HMT *Edenmore* and HMT *Ikalia*, laden with forage and supplies, lay off Suvla awaiting lighters to discharge their goods. These lighters had still not arrived by the morning of 8 August, and IX Corps' troops were forced to live off their emergency iron rations. A full week passed before there was any accumulation ashore, and the target still eluded the logisticians at Suvla by 21 August.[91]

The absence of a reserve does not necessarily impact the conduct of operations. But it does reduce a force's ability to survive a disaster should something not go to plan. As already discussed at length in previous chapters, such unforeseen problems were likely—especially if the August Offensive became a prolonged operation and gambled with the weather. Without a reserve the MEF would be forced into a hand-to-mouth existence, or worse. The effect that this would have on the conduct of the offensive is beyond question. Without surety that his troops could be maintained, it might be considered irresponsible for a commander to commit his force to any extended operation. Thus, one might contend that in the absence of a sufficient stockpile of reserve supplies, it is unlikely that Hamilton would or could ever have committed the MEF to a protracted fight across the Gallipoli Peninsula.

Nonetheless, it was from these main store depots, located on or near the beaches, that the distribution process began. Each sector had its own peculiarities, but the procedure was fundamentally the same. After imported water—which was crucial for the sustenance of the MEF—was pumped from water lighters to tanks ashore, it was again pumped into reservoirs and storage tanks in the immediate vicinity of the firing lines. Most of this work was done by hand.[92] There was a pumping plant at Anzac Cove to help this process along, but it was unreliable and subject to breakdown, and as such this type of labor was often done manually.⁹³ Ammunition supply worked in a similar manner. Small arms ammunition (SAA) and artillery ammunition was kept in the divisional ammunition columns on the beach.⁹⁴ The brigade ammunition columns, which were usually situated in rear of the trenches, collected the required ammunition directly from the beach.⁹⁵ Like most of the supply work at Gallipoli, the movement of ammunition between these positions was generally done at night.⁹⁶

In preparation for the offensive, water and SAA were pushed forward into locations where replenishing the troops during their attacks would be easier.⁹⁷ For the feint operations planned within the Anzac sector on 6–7 August, these were to be found in the usual localities: Russell's Top, Reserve Gully, Monash Valley, Bridges' Road, White's Valley, Victoria Gully, and Brown's Dip. For the operations against the Sari Bair Ridge, water was stored at No. 2 Outpost, and SAA at this location and in Mule Gully. The units advancing on Sari Bair were also given canvas tanks to carry with them in order to establish water reservoirs as far forward as possible.⁹⁸ These were to be filled as soon as practicable by mules. With regard to ammunition for the Sari Bair attacking force, 1,404 boxes of SAA would be collected and dumped as far forward as possible. Also in preparation for the first phase attack, the requisite ammunition for every artillery piece was placed in close proximity to that gun.⁹⁹

Distribution

Having established the theoretical processes for disembarkation and stockpiling, it is necessary to outline the procedure for the distribution of such stores. The supply and transport process was unique at Gallipoli, especially when compared to that on the Western Front. Owing to the unsuitability of the terrain, the lack of roads, the difficulty in landing them, and the lack of fuel, there was (with the exception of a small amount used at Helles where the terrain was more accommodating) no mechanized transport at Gallipoli.¹⁰⁰ As such, rather than employing supply columns—which were a fundamental element of supply and transport on the Western Front—the MEF had to rely almost solely on the divisional train or troop labor to transport its requirements. This was an unsuitable arrangement, according to *FSR*, as not every unit was allotted a train, and units could scarcely afford to release men from the trenches for fatigue work.[101] It also meant that animals were required to take the place of the three-ton motorized transport vehicles that were standard in British supply columns on the Western Front.[102]

The divisional train at Gallipoli, as instructed in *FSR*, consisted of horses and mules and was separated into baggage and supply sections.[103] It was the divisional train's duty, when requested by the fighting units, to convey baggage, stores, and supplies to them.[104] During the August Offensive, mules were limited solely to the conveyance of food, water, and SAA. Equipment, such as that used by engineers and signallers (picks, shovels, sandbags, and cable), which was usually carried in carts or wagons, was instead carried in barrows or by hand, as was artillery ammunition—the transportation of which remained the responsibility of artillery units.[105] After delivering their loads to positions specified by the units, the mules returned to the beaches to collect further loads.[106]

During the offensive, requests for transport were made through the divisional transport officers, who conveyed these requests to the representative of the DST on the peninsula: Lieutenant-Colonel Oscar Striedinger, assistant director of transport at Anzac, and Major Gerald Badcock, deputy assistant director of transport at Suvla.[107] These officers then allotted transport as they saw fit, whereupon it became the duty of the OC of the divisional train to prioritize this transport and distribute it in accord with the GOC's intentions.[108] If transport was approved, it was the duty of the requesting unit to provide troops for loading and unloading the animals.[109] If a request for transport was denied, all items had to be collected from the beaches and carried to the front lines by the troops themselves—thus further depleting the fighting strength of the unit that had made the original request and increasing the physical strain on troops who could otherwise have been resting. The divisional train formed the backbone of the transport system during the August Offensive. The system, however, was a two-way process of delivery and collection, whereby both men and animals were used to replenish the supplies in the front line.

The Use of Mules

Unlike those on the Western Front, the divisional train at Gallipoli consisted predominantly of mules, with horses reserved for moving artillery. The reason was that mules were generally more suitable than horses for transporting supplies in difficult terrain (because of their shorter legs), required less feed, and remained, in the main, calmer under fire.[110] Due to the difficulty of the terrain, especially at Anzac and Suvla, the mules were largely used as pack animals, where their loads were slung over their backs rather than conveyed in wagons or carts.[111] Through this method a mule could carry, for example, two eight-gallon water bags at a time (or four four-gallon tins in the case of the mules used by the Zion Mule Corps at Cape Helles).[112] At a minimum of a half-a-gallon water ration per man, per day—which was actually half rations—this amounted to enough water for thirty-two men in a single journey. Given the lack of places to store water, and the fact that men were spread out over the peninsula, it was not possible for mules to deliver half a gallon at once to each man, and they therefore had to do multiple and continuous trips between the beach and the front line.[113]

The number of mules allotted to a formation was based on the number of men to be supplied.[114] For the operations at Anzac and Suvla in August, GHQ determined that supply arrangements should be calculated to ensure that mules made a *maximum* of two trips per day.[115] There were 950 mules at Anzac prior to the offensive.[116] By the time the attack commenced, though, these mules, and particularly their drivers, were exhausted. They had worked continuously for weeks, with practically no rest, preparing the Anzac sector for the offensive. The drivers were, according to Captain Heber Alexander of the Indian Mule Cart Train, "done to a turn."[117] It was intended to land an additional 1,836 mules at Anzac and 1,664 at Suvla on 7–8 August—the majority of which belonged to the Indian Mule Cart Train—to further supplement this transport.[118] Intention, however, did not transform into reality. None were landed on 7 August owing to Ottoman shellfire, and only 238 and 303 mules were disembarked the following day at Anzac and Suvla respectively.[119]

Thus, in the early stages of the offensive, the MEF was only able to land *15 percent* of its target transport. Despite the prior realization that it would be difficult to land sufficient transport in the early stages of the offensive, such a deficiency was beyond the capacity of the troops to make good, who now had to carry supplies while at the same time fighting desperately to establish and consolidate their positions. The result was a complete breakdown in the logistic process and, by extension, of offensive operations at Suvla. It also caused a great deal of anxiety at Anzac. Major-General Ellison made his concerns clear to Vice-Admiral de Robeck. Without mules, he stated, there was "no means of transporting food, water, or ammunition."[120] General Hamilton agreed, and warned de Robeck on 8 August that if mules were not landed in sufficient quantities, the MEF could lose the ground it had gained at Sari Bair.[121]

Throughout the most crucial period of the August Offensive (6–10 August), there were 1,742 mules at Anzac (including the 950 already present, plus 792 landed on 8–9 August).[122] Based purely on the optimistic calculations of the ANZAC General Staff—which had mules in the current Anzac sector making five journeys a day (rather than the maximum of two), and the troops of the 1st Australian Division manhandling *all* of their supplies—this represented a deficiency of 208 animals.[123] Indeed, it was only "by working mules incessantly day and night" that water, rations, and ammunition supply did not completely break down in this sector as well during the offensive.[124] This level of pressure on the mules and their drivers could not be maintained for long. During the same period, approximately 768 mules were landed at Suvla.[125] At Suvla (like Anzac) the mules were in constant demand and, according to the Indian Mule Cart Train's war diary, had practically "no rest."[126] There were, therefore, approximately 2,510 mules to cater for the 57,000 troops in the core sectors of Anzac and Suvla during the offensive, or roughly 1 mule for every 23 men.[127] Crude but simple calculations enable a rough determination of whether this was sufficient. With regard to water alone, 1,781 mules were required (calculated on each mule carrying eight gallons twice a day) to supply half rations to each troop at Anzac and Suvla each day.[128] In other words, 71 percent of the *total* mules available would be required for the sole purpose of transporting water.[129] This, however, meant that there were only 729 mules remaining to deliver all ammunition and food for the same number of troops (57,000) during the August Offensive. This was clearly insufficient—not to mention the ever-growing demands and distances that would be part of a successful advance across the peninsula.

The reasons for the MEF's failure to disembark enough mule transport are varied. Landing them was a difficult process—especially in the dark—and could only be done by specially trained personnel. The lack of piers was also a hindrance. Given the urgency of the situation, some work had to be undertaken during daylight hours. In the Anzac sector, this necessitated landing mules at North Beach as anything that entered Anzac Cove in daylight hours drew shellfire. But disembarking at North Beach was, in itself, not an easy proposition. The motor lighters, which carried the mules, came aground in about five feet of water.[130] Making this process more unwieldy was the nature of the lighters themselves. According to the OC of the Indian Mule Cart Train, Lieutenant-Colonel Charles Beville: "Motor lighters were found to be very unmanageable, cumbersome and faulty for the purpose. Although probably suited for the conveyance of troops and stores, for mules and carts they were expensive in time and space was lost in each. Good Horse Boats would have got the work done far quicker in my opinion."[131]

Even more germane was the delay caused by the simultaneous disembarkation of mules with reinforcements, stores, supplies, and guns and horses. Indeed, because of this it was found that only three hundred mules could be landed in total at each sector per day, rather than three hundred from each ship as was expected.[132] This, in turn, frustrated the EMS, which worked with "furious energy" to speed up the process and land more mules, fully realizing they were desperately required to supply the troops. The navy's solution was to pack more mules into the lighters than what they were designed to carry. In one case 127 were seen to emerge from a lighter—considerably more than the 50 it was meant to carry. Once again, the EMS believed that the problems were caused not by its inability to supply the beaches but by the army's failing to move stores (in this case mules) once they arrived.[133]

Numbers aside, the individual pressure placed on the mules and their drivers was intense. If the mules survived the journey to the peninsula—many did not and drowned during the voyage or while being landed—they remained under constant danger of being shelled. A mule convoy was a valuable and vulnerable target to an Ottoman gunner, and losses suffered by this means during the August Offensive were significant. At Anzac alone, where the entire track from Mule Gully to No. 2 Outpost (the route used by all transport moving from Anzac Cove to the units fighting for Sari Bair) was completely exposed to machine-gun fire, 22 men and 259 mules were killed, with a further 155 and 599 respectively wounded throughout August.[134] Similarly, 158 mules were killed, and a further 189 wounded on the exposed plains of Suvla throughout August.[135]

Further hindering the work of the mules was a lack of water and forage to maintain them. The pressure on the mules greatly increased once the hot weather came and the local wells "dried up."[136] Watering the mules was therefore particularly difficult during the summer heat of the August Offensive. At Anzac, the mule drivers initially scraped small holes in the ground to provide for their beasts, but the amount produced by this method was insufficient, and the water quickly became "brackish." The mules in this sector were eventually led to a well south of Brighton Beach, but because of its exposure to the Ottoman observation post at Gaba Tepe, they could only be watered at night.[137] This was problematic, especially considering that the work of transporting supplies and ammunition forward also took place at night.[138]

Watering the mules was also an issue at Suvla. Few mules were watered on 8–9 August because the spring that had been allotted solely for their use was inundated with desperately thirsty men—their own water supply having broken down. In response to warnings that unless water was promptly received the Indian Mule Cart Train could not guarantee that its animals could continue working, its mules were permitted to drink from buckets at A Beach (as there were no troughs).[139] Despite improvements as August progressed, the deputy director of veterinary services reported that the situation was still inadequate at the end of the month and described mule watering arrangements as "very limited."[140]

A Breakdown in Supply

Overall, the difficulties faced during disembarkation, stockpiling, and distribution thus far discussed resulted in a near complete breakdown of the MEF's logistic system during the first phase of the August Offensive. There were some positive reports at a local level—supplies of food and ammunition to the 1st Australian Division were "generally speaking very satisfactory," and "the ammunition supply continued without a hitch throughout the operations" at Suvla—but such positive sentiments were in the minority.[141] Whether the supply and transport systems were perceived as a success or failure could depend on the locality of a unit or the personality of the officer reporting. For example, the description given by Brigadier-General Talbot Hobbs, CRA of the Australian Divisional Artillery, of his ammunition supply as "satisfactory" was in stark contrast to the 1st New Zealand Field Artillery Brigade's complaint the previous day that there was no 18-pounder ammunition available from the supply depot.[142] It should also be noted that optimistic reports were more likely to come from units situated close to the beach, where the distance that the supplies had to be carried was often less than half a mile. Local success or failure aside, it is important to assess these reports from a broader, more strategic perspective. The individual in the best position to do this was the IGC, Lieutenant-General Altham. After analyzing the array of reports received throughout the offensive, Altham informed his chief at the War Office, Major-General Cowans, that the transport system was a shambles, and concluded that as a whole, the supply situation during the August Offensive was "unsatisfactory."[143]

The lack of water for men, let alone the situation for mules during the August Offensive, is a key example of this unsatisfactory situation. Before the offensive both Hamilton and de Robeck voiced their concerns about the MEF's ability to supply the troops with sufficient water, especially those operating from Anzac.[144] A system of pumps and pipes were established to distribute water around the sector, but these were unreliable and broke down on 29 and 31 July, and again on 1 August.[145] Without a workable pump, the reservoir on Plugge's Plateau (capable of holding thirty thousand gallons) could not be filled—which meant that the other storage tanks spread throughout the Anzac sector, which drew their water from this reservoir, were also chronically short.[146] Birdwood was particularly anxious about the availability and supply of water. On 1 August he recorded in his diary, "Wells have dried up and pump is not working." He feared that unless water arrived immediately he would be forced to turn away the reinforcements arriving for the upcoming offensive. Another breakdown the next day prompted him to raise his tone and warn GHQ that if the situation did not improve, not only would he be prevented from accepting more troops, but he would also have to begin a "partial withdrawal." The situation began to improve that night, and while this gave Birdwood some short-term confidence, he realized that the situation was still unsatisfactory.[147] On 5 August, Birdwood informed Major-General Ellison, the deputy IGC, "We are still living from hand to mouth, and have not been able to build up any reserve."[148] The water supply at Anzac remained unsatisfactory throughout August. Indeed, the logistic difficulties in getting water forward were so paramount in Birdwood's mind, and so important from an operational perspective, that he declined Hamilton's offer to deploy the last remaining reserve, the 54th Division, on 9 August, because he did not think he could water the extra men.[149]

The Australian official historian, Charles Bean, was confused as to what impact the lack of water had on the August Offensive. In one instance he wrote that "the supply never fell so short as to hamper operations."[150] In another he noted that the lack of water "seriously affect[ed] the course of operations" on one occasion.[151] Although Bean does not name the specific occasion, there can be little doubt that he was referring to the situation at Chunuk Bair. The want of water in this position did not directly lead to its loss, but that it hampered operations and the fighting ability of the troops located there, cannot be disputed. Supplying the troops at Chunuk Bair and the posts to its rear was, in Hamilton's words, "no child's play."[152] Private Cecil Malthus of the Wellington Battalion went a step further, describing it a "physical impossibility."[153]

All approaches to Chunuk Bair were commanded by Ottoman rifle, machine-gun, and artillery fire, which prevented the delivery of much-needed supplies. On 8 August, for example, the Wellington Battalion, fighting desperately to hold their positions against Ottoman counterattacks at Chunuk Bair, noted that "ammunition and water which were urgently wanted by us could not be brought forward."[154] Indeed, the New Zealanders were living off a quarter gallon of water per day—a mere 25 percent of the minimum requirement as laid down in British manuals.[155] The inability to get sufficient supplies to the New Zealanders was, according to Hamilton, one of the reasons why the 6th Bn., Loyal North Lancashire Regiment replaced them on the night of 9 August.[156]

The water situation only worsened after the loss of Chunuk Bair on 10 August.[157] The approaches to the forward Allied positions became even more dangerous. Enemy snipers took up new positions in the broken country, and greater observation allowed the Ottoman artillery to sweep Allied supply routes with greater accuracy.[158] Birdwood realized that under these circumstances there could be no question of resuming the offensive. The water supply was such a problem "that we [i.e., ANZAC] can only just hold on to our present position."[159] If the water shortage was not the singular reason why the August Offensive failed, it was definitely a significant reason why it was not resumed after 10 August.

The reasons for the breakdown of the water supply system at Anzac during the August Offensive were varied. First, there was no contingency plan for any setback. Birdwood was confident of advancing beyond the Sari Bair Ridge and finding water there. As a result of this optimism, he was reluctant to build a large reserve of water in the newly captured area, a reserve that would soon become redundant should the offensive press forward.[160] Further, there were not enough mules or water receptacles to transport the requisite water to the troops in the forward positions.[161] Ultimately, though, the failure was a direct result of the ambitious nature of the plan for the offensive itself. Birdwood's corps had struggled to supply itself prior to August, when the force and its perimeter were much smaller. The task of maintaining the force while attacking was simply beyond its capabilities.

There was also a complete breakdown in the supply of water at Suvla, which had an even more profound impact on operations than it did at Anzac. While a shortage of water was expected, the situation was so serious that it practically brought operations to a standstill on 7 August and was of more concern to IX Corps headquarters on 8 August than the ongoing operations or the Ottoman defenders.[162] The problem continued to hinder operations throughout the rest of the month. An order to attack Tekke Tepe Ridge at dawn on 13 August, for example, was canceled when it was realized that, if successful, the 54th Division could not be supplied with food and water so far from Suvla's logistic base.[163] In order to ease the logistic strain, it was also decided that same day to reduce the perimeter by withdrawing the force back toward the beaches.[164] Another attack against the Anafarta Spur was canceled in mid-August because Major-General Henry de Beauvoir de Lisle, who temporarily commanded IX Corps after Stopford's removal, believed that "the difficulties of supply and water would be greater than our available transport could carry out."[165] With very little or, at times, no water, Major-General Frederick Shaw, GOC of the 13th Division, thought it extraordinary that the inexperienced troops of IX Corps were able to fight during the day and dig throughout the night.[166] The inexperience of the troops was itself one of the many reasons for the lack of water at Suvla. Driven by nerves, excitement, and pure fear, the previously untried men of IX Corps failed to conserve their water in the face of fierce Ottoman opposition and extreme heat. As a result, supplies ran out quicker than expected. Far outweighing the troops' natural urge to reach for their water bottles, however, was the fact that troops at Suvla were let down by a supply and transport system that failed to maintain them.

Water arrangements for the landing at Suvla were lax. Unlike Anzac, where the natural sources of water were scarce, it was anticipated—from intelligence gained in July—that water for drinking purposes would be found in abundance throughout the Anafarta Valley. All the troops would need to do to secure it was advance. This, however, they soon found was no easy task. In fairness, GHQ made provisions to land 450 tons of fresh water at Suvla during the early hours of 7 August, but this resupply was merely meant to supplement the water that would be found in the Anafarta Valley, and was to be reserved, in the main, to supply the beach parties and animals.[167] These arrangements faltered from the outset. Of the four water lighters expected, only one could be found in the first instance, but it lay two hundred yards offshore. The second, grounded off A Beach, was found only in the afternoon of 7 August. The third did not arrive until 9 August, while the fourth remained in port at Imbros.[168] Despite the delays faced in getting this water ashore, an even more serious collapse occurred when moving the water from the beach to the troops at Suvla.[169]

The first obstacle in this regard was a shortage of receptacles for the conveyance of water, and a complete absence of storage facilities ashore.[170] This remained the case throughout the offensive, and was still an acute problem on 18 August when Vice-Admiral de Robeck informed the Admiralty that there was still "no adequate provision for storing water ashore" at Suvla.[171] Indeed, there was still no reserve of water at Suvla at the end of the month.[172] As noted, these problems were compounded by a lack of mules and men to carry the supplies from the beaches. The transport mules of IX Corps did not commence landing at Suvla until 8 August. Until this time no attempt had been made to supply the troops with water. By 9 August there were 542 mules at Suvla, which were theoretically capable, if used purely for distributing water, to supply half a gallon each to 17,344 men.[173] Thus, even on half rations, and supposing the drivers could find their way in unfamiliar terrain while under fire, there were still not enough mules to transport the daily water requirements of IX Corps, let alone food and ammunition.

The main reason for the failure of the water supply system at Suvla was the confusion as to who was responsible for it. As the historian Tim Travers has noted, "There were an astonishing number of people in charge of different aspects of the Suvla water plan."[174] Hamilton's staff was responsible for the overall scheme, and the director of works was tasked to ensure an adequate supply of tins and receptacles to carry it.[175] Like all other supplies, the navy was responsible for the water's voyage to the peninsula and handed over control to the military at the high-water mark. Once disembarked, the water became the responsibility of the DA&QMG at corps level to coordinate his divisional AA&QMGs, who were themselves responsible for the local storage and distribution of water within their divisional areas.[176] Throughout this entire process, engineers were required to build storage facilities and to sink wells to provide supplementary natural supplies.[177] There were, therefore, no fewer than eight officers involved in the process. That the system broke down is not surprising.

The Logistics of Medical Evacuation

Logistics is a two-way process. In addition to moving supplies forward, a force must also be conscious of the mechanics of medical evacuation—described by the historian and former military officer Julian Thompson, as "an important consideration in logistic planning."[178] It is noteworthy, however, that, although troops might legitimately expect to receive prompt evacuation if wounded, a failure in this regard has little direct bearing on the ability of a force to achieve its short-term objectives.[179] Operations took precedence over casualties. This was the view of the War Office in London: "A proper evacuation of wounded is from a humanitarian point of view essential, but when it clashes with the question of victory or the reverse, there is no wounded soldier who would desire to be given preference at the expense of his fighting comrades."[180] It was also the command view at Gallipoli (although not necessarily shared by the medical authorities). The orders for the night attack on Sari Bair, for example, stipulated that there would be no evacuation of the wounded until advancing columns had passed them by and strictly prohibited troops from falling out to assist casualties.[181]

In planning the medical evacuation for the August Offensive, many improvements were made on the original model that had failed in April—and for which British authorities had received much criticism (not least of which from the Dominions). The first improvement was in the estimation of expected casualties. After much consultation, it was decided to accept the advice of the MEF's director of medical services (DMS), Surgeon-General William Birrell, in his estimate of thirty thousand casualties for August. This was the figure upon which all medical arrangements for the offensive were based.[182] Once this estimate had been established, it was necessary to make sure there were enough beds to accommodate this number of wounded. Medical base facilities were therefore ordered to expand to take more cases if required. Mudros, however, could not take the number expected owing to a chronic lack of water. Instead, the extra beds would have to be made up at Egypt and Malta.[183] At the commencement of the August Offensive, these locations could accommodate eighteen thousand casualties between them: far from the thirty thousand required.[184]

The second improvement was an increase in the number of ships to accommodate and transport the wounded. A total of fifteen hospital ships, nine transports converted into temporary ambulance carriers (known as "black ships" and not covered under the Geneva conventions), and a range of small craft—a force much greater than the six hospital ships available in April—were employed in evacuating 13,800 cases from the peninsula between 6 and 10 August.[185] Like the availability of beds, this increase did not meet the MEF's demands. GHQ's requests for more hospital ships could not be met because of the congestion and shortage of labor at various ports in the UK. Moreover, it was not deemed possible to supply the number of hospital ships requested and also maintain the supply of reinforcements, stores, and supplies. Despite being told that it would take upward of four months to fit them out, the principal hospital transport officer (HTO) at the Dardanelles, Surgeon-General Sir James Porter (who had been the Royal Navy's medical director-general before the war), wrote to the Admiralty on 10 August demanding it: "Hurry out Hospital Ships. Situation becoming acute."[186]

The navy and medical services managed to cope with the heavy casualties inflicted during the offensive in spite of the shortages in beds and hospital ships.[187] This was largely the result of increased consultation and cooperation between the general and administrative staffs (at GHQ). Representatives of each branch met regularly with the DMS and a representative of the IGC's staff throughout July and early August to discuss evacuation and medical arrangements.[188] Furthermore, these staffs worked closely with the navy to ensure that there were craft available to evacuate all serious cases.[189] Undermining all of this good work, however, was a confused and confusing medical hierarchy. Like other administrative arrangements, there were, in the words of the IGC, Lieutenant-General Altham, "too many cooks for this particular job." "Such a plethora of experts," in his opinion, was "unnecessary and embarrassing."[190]

As principal director of medical services (PDMS), Surgeon-General William Babtie exercised general supervision over the medical arrangements for the MEF, Malta, and Egypt.[191] The DMS, Surgeon-General Birrell, was under the orders of Babtie.[192] In July, the Admiralty sent out Surgeon-General Porter as HTO.[193] His role was to supervise the transport of the wounded and organize the flow of hospital ships to and from the peninsula—a task previously undertaken by Birrell and supervised by Babtie.[194] The army representatives, Babtie and Birrell, did not welcome Porter's arrival, especially after he assumed control of the evacuation of the wounded from the beaches.[195] Personality issues aside, the navy believed that Porter's appointment did much to improve the evacuation system.[196]

At the front line of the evacuation process were the regimental stretcher-bearers. Stationed at the trenches, stretcher-bearers were charged with collecting the wounded and applying basic triage before removing casualties to regimental aid posts.[197] This work was difficult and dangerous, and many bearers themselves became casualties. On 8 August alone, for example, 25 percent of the New Zealand Mounted Field Ambulance's bearer division were either killed or wounded.[198] Requests for more stretcher-bearers were made constantly by frontline units throughout the August Offensive, and they were soon in such demand that the caveat of prior training for bearers before being deployed to the front was removed.[199] After assessing and classifying the patient, field ambulances then forwarded the wounded to an advanced dressing station where a medical officer conducted an examination before sending severe cases to a main dressing station, or if they were to be evacuated, directly to a casualty clearing station (CCS)—of which there were nine operating during the August Offensive.[200]

Prior to the offensive, Surgeon-General Babtie anticipated that getting the wounded to the beaches would be one of the major difficulties during the August Offensive. "This will," he wrote, "impose a very great strain on the field ambulances who may require such assistance as is possible from the troops and from the fleet, in the position of bearers."[201] Assistance was not forthcoming. While the numbers of medical personnel were sufficient at the base and on the hospital ships or ambulance carriers, the medical units on the peninsula suffered from a lack of personnel. After receiving a single reinforcement on 9 August—the rest being held in Cairo for work in the hospitals—the CO of No. 1 Australian CCS noted, "My unit is very much under strength and I find it scandalous that reinforcements should be diverted from the[ir] intended use to the detriment of units at the front."[202] He was not alone in this sentiment.[203] A further obstacle to this task was the fact that the routes used when removing the wounded to the beach were the same as those used for supply and transport purposes. They were thus perpetually congested and movement was slow.[204]

From the beach, the navy and GHQ took responsibility for evacuating the wounded off the peninsula. This was generally done during the day so as not to interfere with the disembarkation of men, guns, and stores, which occurred at night, but this was not always possible. On 6 August, for example, no casualties were evacuated before midnight. This caused severe congestion on the beaches—which were intermittently shelled by the Ottomans—and further delayed the landing of supplies. According to the CO of No. 1 Australian CCS, the reason for the failure to evacuate the wounded was that "the facilities provided for the conveyance of wounded from the shore to the Hospital Ships are very inadequate."[205] In this he was referring to the lack of small vessels to transport the wounded from the beach out to the waiting ships. Nonetheless, once they left the peninsula, serious cases were be placed onto the hospital ships, which were best equipped to deal with them, while less serious cases were transferred onto the ambulance carriers and taken to Mudros.[206] Stable or less serious cases were then disembarked into one of the stationary or convalescent hospitals at Lemnos and Imbros Islands.[207] The most serious cases remained on board the hospital ships and traveled to the general hospitals in either Egypt or Malta: a forty-eight-hour and fifty-five-hour journey respectively.[208] In some instances the hospital ships or ambulance carriers would go directly to the UK, often taking with them some less severe cases that may well have been able to return to the front.[209] According to Lieutenant-General Altham, this was "unavoidable," but such cases were minimal, and, in the main, the classification system worked rather smoothly.[210]

Through this system a total of 30,890 troops were evacuated from the peninsula from 6 to 21 August.[211] This was a considerable achievement, especially when compared to the evacuation failures in April. Apart from the first few days of the offensive when the system struggled to come to grips with the situation, the evacuation of casualties during August was an imperfect logistic success. So what impact did such medical arrangements have on the wider logistic process in August?

As noted earlier, the unnecessary suffering of casualties has little impact on the operational proficiency of a force. Apart from the impact that it might have had on the morale of the remaining troops, its influence on the August Offensive was negligible. The majority of those cases that were evacuated remained away from the theater for an extended period receiving treatment and convalescing. Those cases that could return were not numerous enough to make an impact on the operational situation. Rather, what matters was the effect that evacuating these casualties had on the overall logistic processes of supply and transport. Here too, it must be noted, the impact was slight. Apart from slowing down anchorages, and at times congesting the beaches and supply routes, the evacuation of the wounded during the August Offensive was largely carried out during daylight hours and therefore had only a minimal influence on logistic and battlefield operations.

Not Logistically Viable

A lack of lighters, insufficient piers, unsuitable beaches, a chronic shortage of personnel for fatigues and mules for transportation, ineffective cooperation, a disjointed administrative system, the dangers posed by enemy shelling, and the difficulties presented by the complicated terrain combined to produce a logistic system at Gallipoli that faced obstacles at every turn. Even if these difficulties were not present, the sea-based logistic chain beyond the beaches lay vulnerable to the whims of the weather. In spite of the relatively well-considered administrative arrangements, which saw a successful buildup of supplies at Anzac in preparation for the offensive, the realization that certain items would need to be stockpiled does not equate to an efficient supply and transport system. Detailed preparations did not compensate for poor performance. The provision of supplies, particularly water, almost broke down completely during the first phase of the August Offensive—by far the easiest, in terms of logistic maintenance, of the four phases.

CHAPTER 7

THE AUGUST OFFENSIVE

Soldiers of the old army and the new.

Some of you have already won imperishable renown at our first landing or have since built up our foothold upon the peninsula, yard by yard, with deeds of heroism and endurance. Others have arrived just in time to take part in our next great fight against Germany and Turkey, the would-be oppressors of the rest of the human race.

You, veterans, are about to add fresh luster to your arms.

Happen what may so much at least is certain.

As to you, soldiers of the new formations, you are privileged indeed to have the chance vouchsafed you of playing a decisive part in events which may herald the birth of a new and happier world. You stand for the great cause of freedom. In the hour of trial remember this and the faith that is in you will bring you victoriously through.

And so General Hamilton addressed his troops on the eve of the largest offensive of the Gallipoli Campaign. By the time this message was issued, over two months had passed since a flanking maneuver from Anzac had first been mentioned (as discussed in chapter 1). Roads and trenches had been widened and improved, piers had been strengthened, supplies had been stockpiled, bivouacs were constructed to house reinforcements for the ANZAC (and new units arriving from the UK), mining operations were still under way, guns were registered on their targets, and feints had been undertaken to the south of the Anzac sector, the aim of which was to induce a belief among the Ottomans that an attack and landing would occur in this vicinity.[1] Due to the importance of surprise for the impending attack, all preparations had been concealed from the enemy.

Zero Hour

At 2:20 P.M. on 6 August 1915, the heavy artillery of the British VIII Army Corps and the French Corps Expéditionnaire, in conjunction with the Royal Navy, opened fire on the Ottoman positions at Cape Helles. With this, the August Offensive was under way. From 3:15 P.M. until the infantry attack thirty-five minutes later, thirty machine guns added their weight of fire. The Ottomans, themselves preparing for an attack, replied immediately, their fire inflicting numerous British casualties, especially in the support trenches, and damaging the telephone lines that connected the British units with their headquarters.[2] The Allied bombardment had failed to subdue the enemy. Major-General Henry de Beauvoir de Lisle, who commanded the British 29th Division, "was horrified to find the shooting erratic and the volume of fire inadequate."[3] Three battalions of the 88th Brigade (29th Division) commenced their attack at 3:50 P.M. but were almost immediately destroyed by the enemy's rifle and concealed machine-gun fire.[4] This failure did not prevent further attempts. At 9:40 the following morning, the 125th and 127th Brigades (42nd Division) attacked to the right of the previous day's attempt. Again, the attack was a failure. Apart from some minor gains at an area known as the Vineyard, the front line remained where it had been on 5 August.[5] The two attacks resulted in 3,335 British casualties and failed in their objective: to distract the enemy's attention, and prevent them from moving troops and artillery to the larger operations in the north.[6]

Meanwhile, another demonstration was under way during the afternoon of 6 August. A party of 350 Greek troops under the command of two French officers landed at Karachali, inside the Gulf of Xeros.[7] Their aim was to deceive the enemy into believing that an attack would take place at Bulair. The Ottoman cavalry easily repulsed these undisciplined troops, who proved difficult to control and who were too small in number to have any impact.[8] One historian aptly described this demonstration as "pointless," "nearly disastrous," and the "least significant" action of the offensive.[9]

The Battle of Lone Pine

At 4:30 P.M., forty minutes after the British had leapt from their trenches at Cape Helles, the Allies opened an intensive bombardment within the Anzac sector on the enemy's positions at Lone Pine and its neighboring works. The aim of the bombardment was to silence the enemy's artillery and to destroy the wire entanglements and overhead cover that protected the Turkish trenches.[10] In addition to the field artillery, HMS *Bacchante*, searching for enemy camps and artillery positions, directed its fire on the valleys northeast and east of the 400 Plateau. It was supported by several British monitors, which shelled the Ottoman batteries north of Gaba Tepe.[11] Like the demonstration at Helles, the intention of this feint was to deceive the enemy into believing that the main effort would be made south of Anzac at Gaba Tepe.[12] Success at Lone Pine would also give the Allies command of the ground to the south of the Anzac sector, thus offering them a significant advantage for the subsequent phases of the operation.[13] Lieutenant-Colonel Maurice Hankey, who was sent to the Dardanelles in July to report back to London on the situation, recognized the capture of Lone Pine as "absolutely essential to the final consolidation of the new position," while General Hamilton—echoing his operational objectives—saw it as "a distinct step on the way to Maidos."[14] As a sign of Lone Pine's importance to the subsequent phases, the 1st Australian Division was ordered—if it succeeded there before the impact of the main attacks farther north were felt by the enemy—to remain in the vicinity of Lone Pine and not push on across the peninsula. By staying put, according to ANZAC headquarters, "You will thus be in a position to cut off the retreat of the enemy from their trenches higher up the valley . . . and at the same time will be well placed to take immediate advantage of any opportunity of joining hands with the columns from Chunuk Bair when the advance down Gun Ridge commences."[15]

Despite his opposition to an attack against Lone Pine, Major-General Harold Walker, GOC of the 1st Australian Division, and his staff developed a plan that was both thorough and imaginative.[16] An underground firing line had been secretly constructed under no-man's-land. When its ceiling was broken from underneath just before the offensive, and the tunnels therefore opened up, this new firing line aided with the surprise and reduced the distance that the initial wave of attack had to cover by thirty yards. At 5:30 P.M., an hour after the bombardment had commenced, three battalions of the 1st Australian Brigade, led by their company commanders, leapt from their positions opposite Lone Pine and charged toward the enemy's trenches. The initial charge and the hand-to-hand fighting that ensued are examples of some of the most intimate fighting at Gallipoli. The success of the attack, as a demonstration, lay with what measures the enemy would take to defend against it.[17] In this respect, it succeeded.

Brigadier Esat Pasha, GOC of the [Ottoman] Northern Group, convinced that Lone Pine was the decisive attack, ordered all available reserves to the area in support of the 16th Turkish Division. These included the 64th and 25th Regiments (9th Turkish Division) from Kayali Tepe (west of the Kilid Bahr Plateau), the 13th Regiment (5th Turkish Division) from Koja Dere, and the 15th Regiment (5th Turkish Division) from Kurt Dere (inland from Chunuk Bair).[18] As it turned out, only the 13th Regiment was actually employed in the attempts to regain Lone Pine; the other units proceeded northward toward Chunuk Bair. Importantly though, the feint at Lone Pine achieved its objective, if only temporarily, by drawing at least one unit (the 15th Regiment) away from the north. The fierce Ottoman counterattacks at Lone Pine, which lasted until 10 August, drew in the 5th, 7th, and 12th Australian Battalions, and the 5th Battalion, Connaught Rangers (29th Brigade, 10th Division), who were given the task of clearing the quagmire of dead bodies from within the Lone Pine trenches.[19] Major John Gellibrand, deputy assistant adjutant and quartermaster general of the 1st Australian Division, who superintended some of this work, described the smell of dead and decaying bodies at Lone Pine as being similar to a pork leg left out in the sun for five days.[20] The Battle of Lone Pine, which resulted in 2,277 Australian and an estimated 6,000 Ottoman casualties, was the most successful aspect of the offensive.[21] Unlike the feints at Helles and Karachali, it achieved its aim of deceiving the enemy.

Clearing the Foothills of the Sari Bair Ridge

For six weeks preceding the August Offensive, the foothills north of the Anzac sector were subject to a program of bombardment by the fleet.[22] This schedule, it was hoped, would create a routine whereby the enemy would take shelter in their trenches until the firing had ceased. When darkness fell on 6 August, the covering forces, consisting of the NZMR Bde. (which consisted of four mounted rifles regiments) and two battalions of the 40th Brigade (13th Div.), began their task of clearing the foothills below the Sari Bair Ridge to allow the advancing columns to advance toward the summits.[23]

At 9:30 P.M., the Auckland Mounted Rifles Regiment (MR Regt.), having advanced under the cover of the ships' bombardment, successfully attacked Old No. 3 Post; within half an hour the post had been captured, consolidated, and converted into an Allied position and was strongly held by 11:30 P.M. Meanwhile, the Wellington MR Regt. advanced up the deep gully Sazli Beit Dere. After a brief encounter with the enemy, the regiment successfully took control of Destroyer Hill. By 12:30 A.M., 7 August (one hour behind schedule), despite taking the wrong route, the regiment had also captured the Table Top.[24] During this time the Otago MR Regt. had reached a position just short of its objective, Bauchop's Hill, but was held up by enemy fire. At the same time the Canterbury MR Regt. successfully captured Walden Point, before proceeding to Bauchop's Hill to support the Otagos. At 12:45 A.M., 7 August, together the two units charged and captured the position. While this was being done, a party of New Zealand engineers (supported by a Maori contingent) removed barbed-wire entanglements in the Chailak Dere, thus creating an opening for the advancing columns to attack their objectives on the Sari Bair Ridge.[25] By 1:00 A.M. on 7 August, the right covering force, under the command of Brigadier-General Andrew Russell, had achieved its aims.[26] The brigade war diary attributed triumph to the success of the regimental leadership, and corps headquarters noted that the units "carried it through with a determination and vigour which cannot be praised too highly."[27]

Simultaneously, the left covering force (consisting of the headquarters of the 40th Brigade; half of the 72nd Field Company, Royal Engineers; the 4th Battalion, South Wales Borderers; and the 5th Battalion, Wiltshire Regiment) under the command of Brigadier-General Jonas Travers, advanced past Bauchop's Hill and Walden Point until it reached the Aghyl Dere. By 3:00 A.M., 7 August, this force was in possession of Damakjelik Bair, thus protecting the northern flank of the advancing columns and directly assisting the landing at Suvla Bay.[28]

Despite their gains, both the left and right covering forces ran behind schedule, thus reducing the time available for the assaulting columns to reach their objectives.[29] This was problematic, as the timescale allotted was rigid and did not allow for hiccups. They also failed to mop up the enemy, which further delayed the

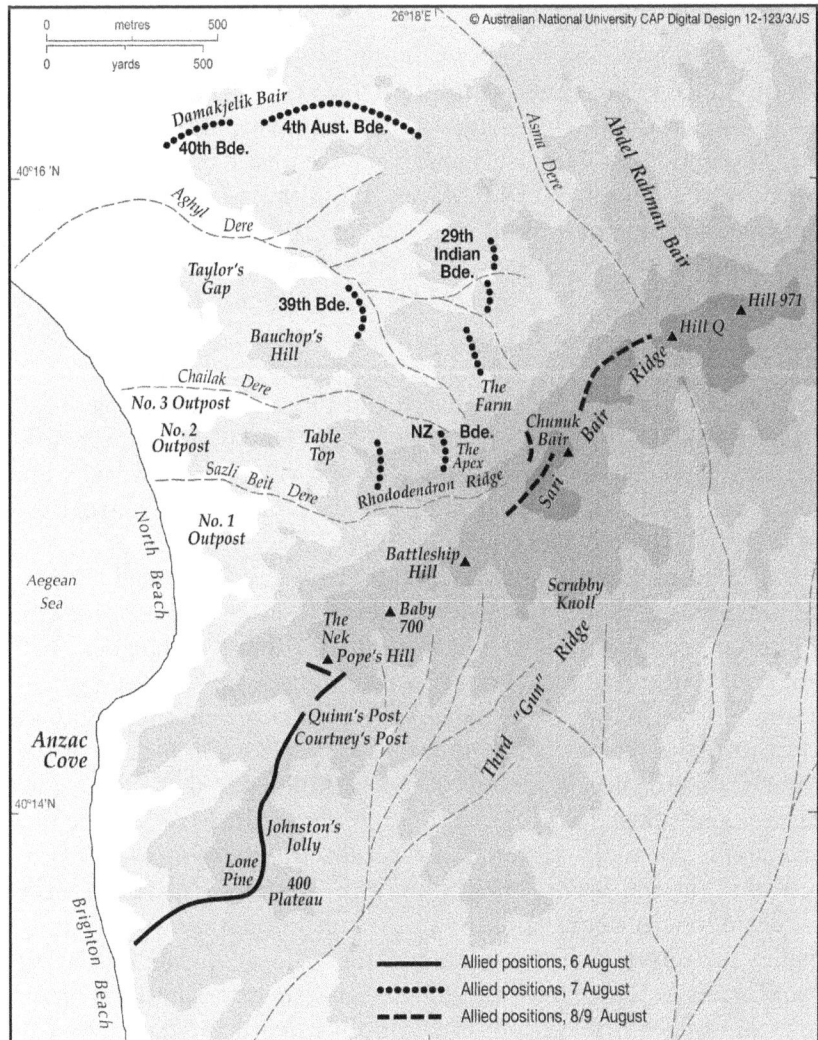

Map 6. The offensive in the Anzac and Sari Bair sectors

advancing columns, who met with unexpected opposition and, in some instances, had to be deployed to help the right covering force defeat pockets of resistance.

The Advance on the Sari Bair Ridge

While the covering forces were executing their objectives, the right assaulting column, which was to take Chunuk Bair, began assembling behind No. 2 Outpost. Lieutenant-General Birdwood was confident of the force's ability to succeed. On the day of the offensive he wrote to the senior naval commander, "We will all be doing our best tonight, and I feel sure my boys will shove through."[30] After an hour's delay, the New Zealand Infantry Brigade commenced its ascent. Two routes were to be used: the Chailak Dere, and the Sazli Beit Dere—both of which should have been cleared by the actions of the covering forces. Those taking the former route (consisting of the Otago Battalion; Wellington Battalion; Auckland Battalion; 1st New Zealand Field Company; and 26th Jacob's Mountain Battery) were further delayed by opposition from Bauchop's Hill, several trenches in the Chailak Dere, and the Table Top.[31]

By 4:30 A.M., 7 August, the right assaulting column had reached its rendezvous point on Rhododendron Ridge.[32] The Canterbury Battalion, commanded by Lieutenant-Colonel John Hughes, had taken the latter route and were nowhere to be seen. Delayed by congestion at No. 2 Outpost, Hughes's unit did not reach the Sazli Beit Dere until 1:00 A.M. (over two hours late).[33] The complexity of the terrain, described by a private of the battalion as "the deepest and most densely wooded of the gullies," combined with the difficulty of marching at night, resulted in the column becoming lost.[34] After retracing the unit's steps, the head of the column realized its mistake and took the correct route; in the confusion, the two rear companies misinterpreted the order and returned to Anzac. Following some brief resistance from the enemy at Destroyer Hill, the remaining half of the battalion continued its advance, meeting up with the Otago Battalion.[35] By 5:30 A.M., 7 August, the New Zealanders were in possession of Rhododendron Ridge and only one thousand yards from their objective, Chunuk Bair.[36]

Like the right assaulting column, the left assaulting column (comprising the 4th Australian Infantry Brigade and 29th Indian Infantry Brigade), commanded by Brigadier-General Herbert Cox, was experiencing similar difficulties. Congestion at Beach Road and No. 2 Outpost caused it to delay the start of its advance. The 4th Australian Bde., tasked with seizing Hill 971, began moving from No. 3 Outpost at 10:30 P.M. To be successful the brigade would have to cover 4.6 miles before daylight, nearly half of which had an average gradient of 1 in 11.5.[37]

Upon commencing its advance, the column immediately came under shrapnel and sniper fire from its right flank.[38] Following its guide, Major Percy Overton of the Canterbury MR Regt., the column turned into Taylor's Gap.[39] Overton had been persuaded by a local guide, against the urgings of the 29th Indian Infantry Brigade's brigade major, that this was a "short-cut" to the Aghyl Dere.[40] This proved to be a poor choice; the column came under increasing fire and, due to the narrowness of the gap, was forced to march single file, thus further slowing its progress. After finally subduing the enemy, the 4th Australian Bde. crossed the Aghyl Dere and formed up on a wheat field. The 13th and 14th Australian Battalions were then ordered to move forward, and by 3:20 A.M., 7 August, they had formed a line, with the 5th Battalion, Wiltshire Regiment on their left flank.[41] Brigadier-General John Monash, the CO of the 4th Australian Bde. and his staff were confused as to their whereabouts and were well short of their objective. Despite the 4th Brigade's failure, its corps commander described the advance as "a magnificent night march through appallingly difficult country."[42]

Following in rear of the 4th Australian Bde. was the 29th Indian Bde. Its objective was for two battalions to assist the 4th Australian Bde. in its attack on Hill 971, and for the remaining two battalions to branch off from the Australians and seize Hill Q. Also behind schedule because of Overton's "short-cut," the brigade did not reach what Overton incorrectly believed to be the fork of the Aghyl Dere where they were to separate until daylight. Here, the 1st Battalion, 5th Gurkha Rifles (1/5th Gurkhas) and 2nd Battalion, 10th Gurkha Rifles (2/10th Gurkhas) were sent up two spurs, both meeting stiff resistance, while the 1st Battalion, 6th Gurkha Rifles (1/6th Gurkhas), followed by the 14th Sikhs, were sent up another spur. By 7:30 A.M. the 1/5th Gurkhas were on a subsidiary spur, with some of the 2/10th Gurkhas, 4th Australian Bde., and 14th Sikhs on their left. The remainder of the 2/10th Gurkhas, the 1/6th Gurkhas, and part of the 1/5th Gurkhas had advanced south and found themselves at the Farm.[43]

Thus, neither attacking column had reached its objective. The New Zealand Infantry Brigade (with some units from the 2/10th Gurkhas) was stationary on Rhododendron Ridge; the 29th Indian Bde. was broken up; and the 4th Australian Bde. was well short of

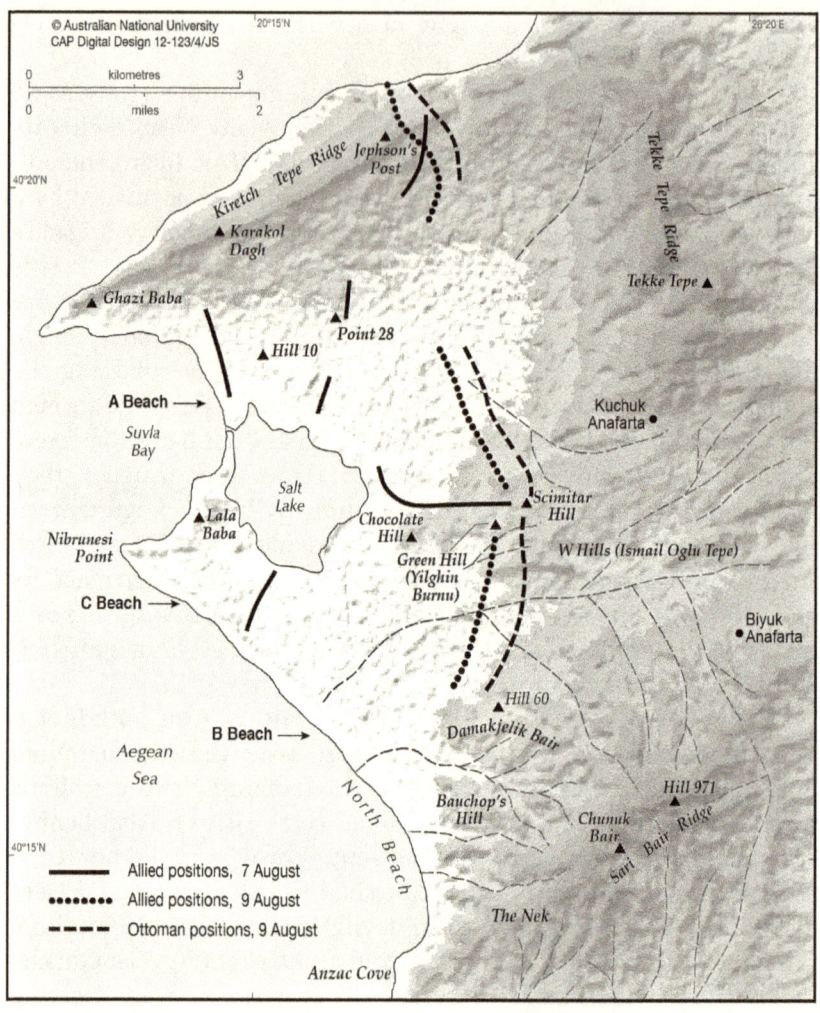

Map 7. The offensive at Suvla Bay

its objective and confused of its locality. Birdwood's prediction that his units would "shove through" during the night was erroneous.

The Landing at Suvla Bay

Shortly before 9:30 P.M. on 6 August, as the New Zealanders were preparing to clear the foothills below the Sari Bair Ridge, the New

Army troops of IX Corps began landing to their north at Suvla Bay. Commanded by the sixty-one-year-old Lieutenant-General Sir Frederick Stopford, who despite having an impressive military career had no previous experience of commanding men in battle, the force was a corps by name only.[44] Four of its infantry brigades had been allotted to the ANZAC as reinforcements, leaving five brigades (twenty thousand men) to capture and secure Suvla Bay, thus creating a safe base that would be used to supply the northern theater of operations as the offensive progressed across the peninsula. Like the landings in April, the landing at Suvla Bay would face the same inherent difficulties as all amphibious landings. There would be no fixed headquarters, communications would be difficult to establish, the infantry would have to establish a beachhead without adequate artillery support, and confusion would reign supreme.[45]

Defending Suvla Bay were three thousand Ottoman troops under the command of a German officer, Major Wilhelm Willmer. Realizing that his force was not large enough to prevent a landing, Willmer focused on how best to delay the enemy and interrupt its advance, thus allowing time for reinforcements to arrive from Bulair. To accomplish this he created defensive localities, whereby his troops would defend their positions, but fall back to the main line of defense on Ismail Oglu Tepe (W Hills) if greatly threatened by the landing force. In addition to this defensive scheme, he had trip wires placed below the water level in Suvla Bay, especially near Lala Baba, and trip wires and contact mines in front of Hill 10 and Yilghin Burnu (Green and Chocolate Hills). This, he hoped, would make up for the lack of sandbags and wire entanglements protecting the Ottoman trenches. In addition to the infantry, Willmer also had eleven field and eight mountain guns.[46]

The initial landing at Suvla was, in fact, successful. Troops of the 33rd and 32nd Brigades disembarked with relative ease and promptly secured Nibrunesi Point. They then headed for Lala Baba. Here, according to the 32nd Brigade's brigade major, the enemy "put up a very stubborn resistance, and kept to their trenches to the bitter end." The 6th Battalion, Yorkshire Regiment, eventually took Lala Baba with bayonets, but lost 15 officers including its commanding officer (killed) and second in command (mortally wounded), as well as 250 other ranks in the process.[47]

The landing of the 34th Brigade, however, was not as successful. Rather than landing at A Beach, the brigade was put ashore half a mile to the south at the Cut. Units became mixed and delay ensued. One unit, the 11th Battalion, Manchester Regiment, proceeded toward Kiretch Tepe Ridge, while the 9th Battalion, Lancashire Fusiliers, proceeded inland toward its first objective. The Lancashires took what they thought was Hill 10 with the bayonet; in reality, they had seized a sand dune, and they soon came under fire from the enemy at the real Hill 10.[48] This was a bonus for Willmer, who considered Hill 10 his weakest position and "practically untenable"; with the Salt Lake dry, there was no obstacle for any advancing troops.[49] Allied confusion and determined Ottoman defense, however, proved otherwise. Adding further confusion and delay, the reinforcements (30th and 31st Brigades, 10th Division) were landed at separate beaches but were unaware of their task. Finally, at 6:30 A.M., 7 August, the 5th Battalion, Dorset Regiment (34th Infantry Brigade), and the 6th Battalion, York and Lancashire Regiment (32nd Infantry Brigade) successfully seized Hill 10.[50] Willmer informed 5th (Ottoman) Army Headquarters that the outposts had been lost, but that the area from Kiretch Tepe Ridge to Yilghin Burnu was "firmly in our hand."[51] Observing from Chunuk Bair, Colonel Hans Kannengiesser, the GOC of the 9th Turkish Division, later described the British at Suvla as "a confused mass of troops like a disturbed ant-heap."[52] It was chaos indeed. Despite partially securing the bay, IX Corps had made no attempt toward Yilghin Burnu or the W Hills. This would come later in the day.

More Feints at Anzac

Throughout the night of 6–7 August, a series of unsuccessful attacks occurred within the Anzac sector. The first was made by the 6th Australian Infantry Battalion from Steele's Post. At half-hour intervals, beginning at 11:00 P.M. and finishing at midnight, mines were detonated under the enemy position opposite Steele's Post, known as German Officers' Trench.[53] The explosions did little except warn the enemy of an impending attack and cause them to bombard Steele's Post, resulting in considerable damage to the Australian trenches and tunnels.[54] This bombardment delayed the Allied attack. At 12:10 A.M., ten minutes after the attack was meant to commence, 2nd Brigade Headquarters, who could not communicate with the 6th Battalion, sent a message to the 8th Battalion ordering them to "tell Bennett to move."⁵⁵ Lieutenant-Colonel Henry Gordon Bennett, CO of the 6th Australian Battalion, had postponed the attack without permission. He "considered it better to get them [i.e., the troops of 6th Battalion] in position first and thus delay the attack rather than launch it with half the men out of position."⁵⁶ The attack commenced at 12:30 A.M., half an hour late, and the expectant enemy immediately opened machine-gun and rifle fire on them. A second attempt was made at 3:15 A.M., but it too was disastrous for the Australians.⁵⁷ Despite the futility of the task, Major-General Walker, GOC of the 1st Australian Division, who has been credited as "not giv[ing] a damn for anyone except his troops" ordered a third attempt.⁵⁸ Birdwood recognized its uselessness and canceled the order.⁵⁹ The failed operation cost the 6th Battalion 145 casualties.⁶⁰

In addition to the action by 6th Battalion, three other attacks were to occur simultaneously at 4:30 A.M., 7 August. The initial aim of these was to clear the way for the second phase of the offensive—the push out from Anzac—to begin. However, due to the delay of the advancing columns farther north below the Sari Bair Ridge, the plan was modified. Corps HQ issued new orders to the units at Quinn's Post, Pope's Hill, and Russell's Top, informing them that their aim was now "to draw off opposition to a further advance" against Sari Bair.⁶¹ The attacks therefore became feints to draw attention away from Sari Bair rather than a direct effort to break out from the Anzac sector.⁶²

The 2nd Australian Light Horse Regiment (ALH Regt.), under the command of Lieutenant-Colonel Robert Stodart, failed to reach the enemy's trenches opposite Quinn's Post. A mine was exploded at 4:30 A.M., and the Australians rushed out from their position. Heavy machine-gun fire was immediately opened on them from both flanks (including German Officers' Trench) and rifle fire from in front. The brigade diary noted that the "first line was mowed down and no-one reached the enemy's trenches." Realizing that no ground could be won in the face of such defense, Stodart canceled further attempts.⁶³

Similarly, at 4:30 A.M. the 1st ALH Regt. commenced its attack from Pope's Hill. The regiment's aim was to capture a portion of the enemy's trenches known as the Chessboard, east of Deadman's Ridge, which had been lost to the Ottomans in early May. Success here would secure the head of Monash Valley, Pope's Hill, and Shrapnel Gully, thus strengthening the Anzac perimeter and improving the safety of Allied supply lines. While successful in taking three trenches, the regiment withdrew after two hours of heavy counterattack by bombing and rifle and machine-gunfire.[64]

The final attack—one that is remembered in Australian history as an example of the futility of war—was that at the Nek. The 8th ALH Regt., commanded by Lieutenant-Colonel Alexander White, and entrenched at Russell's Top, was to attack the enemy at the Nek and thence proceed to Baby 700. The Ottoman defenses at the Nek consisted of deep trenches, protected by belts of barbed wire and interlocking machine-gun fire, and since late July the Ottomans had been "working hard at improving their defences on both sides of The Nek."[65] It was a formidable position. The enemy were subject to a heavy bombardment from 9:25 P.M. to 10:00 P.M., 6 August, followed by a slow fire throughout the night. At 4:00 A.M. on 7 August, the fire increased for twenty-three minutes, at which point it prematurely ceased (it should have continued for another seven minutes).[66] This cessation enabled the Ottomans to return to the firing line and immediately open up "murderous machine gun and rifle fire upon our [the Australian] parapets."[67]

At 4:30 A.M., without any artillery protection, the first line of 150 men from the 8th ALH Regt. emerged from their trenches. They were killed or wounded immediately. They were followed by another line of 150 from the same regiment. The result was the same; the first two lines were practically wiped out at once.[68] Realizing the futility of the attack, Lieutenant-Colonel Noel Brazier, the CO of the 10th ALH Regt., asked for the third line to be canceled; his request was denied by the brigade major, John Antill, who ordered Brazier "to advance at once."[69] The third line (and a portion of the fourth) was launched with similar results. Between them the 8th and 10th ALH Regiments suffered 372 casualties in an area no larger than a tennis court.[70] Despite its failure, Birdwood thought it worthwhile as it pinned the "Turks to the spot," therefore "preventing them from sending reinforcements to the right" (i.e., to Chunuk Bair).[71] Without a converging attack from Chunuk Bair (as was initially planned), however, the attempt could not succeed, and the commanders knew this.[72] Brazier commented, "The attack seemed premature and in view of the heavy machine gun fire, should have been held up, as by demonstrations the Turks would have been held to his position and many valuable lives saved, until the operations on our left had progressed further or the trenches in front were reduced by guns."⁷³

In conjunction with the attack at the Nek, the 8th Battalion, Royal Welch Fusiliers were to advance and seize the enemy's trenches and consolidate the Chessboard. At 5:10 A.M., the battalion received a message that the 2nd ALH Bde. had attacked, and the Fusiliers were accordingly ordered to do likewise. While advancing up the steep sides of Monash Valley, the Fusiliers came under bombing and machine-gun fire from above, the wounded falling down the gully and knocking over those men behind them. An order was then received from Brigadier-General Frederic Hughes, the CO of the 3rd ALH Bde., informing the Fusiliers that the attack at the Nek had failed, and that they were to take immediate cover in the gully.⁷⁴

All of the above attacks failed, both in their initial objective and as feints. Each attack depended on the success of another. The failure to subdue the enemy's machine guns at German Officers' Trench had a direct impact on the operations against Turkish Quinn's and Deadman's Ridge. Similarly, the attack upon the Nek, initially to be supported by an attack from Chunuk Bair (into the rear of the Turkish position at Battleship Hill), was destroyed by an unimpeded enemy who were able to fire freely, and with disastrous consequences; as were the 8th Battalion, Royal Welch Fusiliers, who relied on support from the Nek and their right flank. None of the objectives were gained.

Continuing toward the Sari Bair Ridge: 7 August 1915

With daylight, the surprise that the offensive relied on for success had dissipated. In the Helles sector, the British were cautious not to suffer any more casualties, and the French (on their right flank) had "nothing to report."⁷⁵ While counterattacks continued at Lone Pine, the remainder of the ANZAC was focused on supporting the actions farther north. Units were reorganized and detached to reinforce the assaulting columns, while all artillery not engaged in the actions at Lone Pine was redirected to support the troops below the Sari Bair Ridge. The regiments of the NZMR Bde. spent the day consolidating their positions into a state of defense.⁷⁶ At GHQ, business continued as normal. Captain Orlo Williams, chief cipher officer, noted that on 7 August, "GHQ lived its normal life only a little more electric, the map in Aspinall's tent being spread out and stuck with flags to mark positions."⁷⁷

Having reached Rhododendron Ridge during the previous night, the New Zealand Infantry Brigade was within striking distance of Chunuk Bair. Arriving at 6:00 A.M., 7 August, however, Colonel Kannengiesser was just in time to repel any further Allied advance. Within an hour, the Allies' right assaulting column, which had continued to push forward toward its objective, had been checked and was holding a line from the Apex to the Farm.⁷⁸ Here, only five hundred yards from the crest of Chunuk Bair, the column paused to reorganize and reassess the situation. During this interval the Ottomans, under their German commander, were able to reinforce the crest. By 8:00 A.M., when Kannengiesser was wounded in the chest and evacuated to a hospital, the Ottomans had reinforced Chunuk Bair with two companies of the 72nd (Arab) Regiment (19th Turkish Division) from Battleship Hill, and the 1st Battalion, 14th Regiment.⁷⁹

Realizing the gravity of the situation, Major-General Godley, GOC of the NZ&A Division, sent a message to the New Zealand Infantry Brigade at 9:30 A.M. ordering it to attack Chunuk Bair. It was an hour and a half before the Auckland Battalion and 2/10th Gurkhas were ready to go.⁸⁰ Upon leaving their positions at the Apex, the troops were subjected to heavy rifle and machine-gun fire. The Gurkhas, attempting to avoid the fire, swerved downhill toward the Farm, while the Auckland Battalion pushed on to the Pinnacle.⁸¹ Here, now only three hundred yards from Chunuk Bair, the Auckland Battalion came under heavy enfilade fire from the enemy on its right flank at Battleship Hill.⁸² Shortly after, at 12:30 P.M., the Canterbury Battalion was ordered to support the Auckland Battalion.⁸³ The enemy's fire prevented any further movement, but at 9:45 P.M. orders were received for an attack to be made by the 7th Battalion, Gloucestershire Regiment, and the Wellington Battalion on Chunuk Bair at 4:15 A.M. the following morning.⁸⁴ At 11:30 P.M. GHQ reminded Birdwood that "even if assault [on Chunuk Bair] fails Chief [i.e., Hamilton] relies on your men to dig in where they are, it is vital to retain what we have got and to persevere till we gain the ridge."⁸⁵

Those to the north in the Aghyl Dere fared no better. After its lengthy and confusing night march, the 4th Australian Bde. spent the day largely regrouping and resting on Damakjelik Bair. Opposition during the day was minimal, and apart from some shelling and sniping it was fairly "quiet" for the brigade.[86] Monash was ordered to push on, but this was later canceled because of the exhaustion of his men and their poor physical state.[87] Added to this was the fact that the brigade, division, and GHQ were all still confused about the correct whereabouts of the 4th Australian Bde.[88]

The story was a little more promising for the 29th Indian Bde. Some of its battalions, as has been noted, joined the New Zealanders on Rhododendron Ridge; others dug in at the Farm. The 1/6th Gurkhas, commanded by Major Cecil Allanson pushed on. By 10:00 A.M., they were about halfway to their objective, Hill Q, and had suffered no casualties. However, orders were then received to stop the advance and form an outpost to cover a large body of troops advancing from Anzac. Allanson "was very upset at being told to stop" as his scouts were practically on top of the hill. The unit remained there for the entire day. In 1917, when appearing before the Dardanelles Commission, Allanson stated that he was confident his troops could have taken Hill Q that evening but admitted that he could not have held it.[89] For the rest of 7 August the troops remained stationary and consolidated their positions. They were exhausted from continuous work, and to add to this, they suffered heavy casualties from enemy artillery and rifle fire. At 6:00 P.M. they received orders that the attack would resume at 4:15 the following morning.[90]

Suvla: 7 August 1915

Meanwhile, chaos prevailed at Suvla Bay. Communications were problematic, units mixed and confused, and supplies short. Above all, however, was the issue of command. Lieutenant-General Stopford, at sea on HMS *Jonquil*, was out of touch with his divisional commanders ashore. Further, organization was difficult owing to IX Corps' general and administrative staffs being on separate ships and therefore out of touch with each other.[91]

There was some fighting during the day, but this was rather limited. After capturing Hill 10, the 5th Battalion, Dorset Regiment, and the 4th Battalion, York and Lancashire Regiment, pressed on against the enemy; the latter of these nearly captured a gun but was stopped by friendly fire from its own artillery. The only significant progress of the morning was on the left flank of the sector, where three battalions advanced along Kiretch Tepe Ridge to the point that later became known as Jephson's Post.⁹² Shortly before midday IX Corps reported to GHQ, "We have been able to advance little beyond the edge of the beach."⁹³ Major Willmer, who was still greatly outnumbered by the British, sent a similar report to 5th Ottoman Army Headquarters: "No energetic attacks on the enemy's part have taken place. On the contrary enemy is advancing timidly."⁹⁴ The Allied command, however, was not yet anxious about the lack of progress. Captain Guy Dawnay, who, along with Aspinall, had developed the plan of operations at GHQ, visited Suvla during the day and talked to the staff of 11th Division and "made vehement comment . . . on their inaction." On returning to Imbros, he reported the situation to GHQ "only to gain the impression that I was looked on as unduly impatient."⁹⁵

It was not until the afternoon of 7 August that an attack was launched on one of the principal objectives at Suvla: Chocolate Hill. At 5:15 P.M., all naval and field guns opened fire.⁹⁶ This, however, had no impact on the enemy's artillery, which, according to their commander, "suffered no losses in either personnel or material" and was able to fire on the advancing troops.⁹⁷ After an advance around the northern perimeter of the Salt Lake and much heavy fighting, the 6th Battalion, Lincolnshire Regiment took Chocolate Hill at 9:30 P.M.⁹⁸ At day's end, IX Corps held the ends of the bay, the Salt Lake, Hill 10, Jephson's Post, and Chocolate Hill. No attempt had yet been made on Ismail Oglu Tepe (W Hills).⁹⁹ Throughout the night much work was undertaken to land supplies. Rough seas, however, made the disembarkation more difficult than usual, with one lighter sinking during its voyage and drowning all animals on board.¹⁰⁰

Contrasting Fortunes: Sari Bair, 8 August 1915

The situation was more promising on 8 August. The Australians continued to repulse the enemy's counterattacks at Lone Pine, and the advancing columns resumed their attempts to seize the summits of the Sari Bair Ridge. The navy also played a prominent role; the squadron shelled the slopes of Sari Bair while submarines *E11* and *E14* collaborated in the Sea of Marmara to sink an enemy battleship and a five-thousand-ton supply ship.¹⁰¹

An artillery bombardment of Chunuk Bair commenced at 3:30 A.M., 8 August. The infantry began its advance forty-five minutes later. The Wellington Battalion and a portion of the 7th Battalion, Gloucestershire Regiment, reached the crest of Chunuk Bair without opposition, capturing an Ottoman machine gun section in the process. Heavy fire from their left flank, however, prevented most of the Gloucestershires from reaching the crest. The 8th (Pioneer) Battalion, Welch Regiment, who was in support, also suffered from this fire and deviated to the right.[102] By 6:30 A.M., GHQ had been informed that Chunuk Bair had been captured and was in Allied hands.[103] The position was fiercely contested throughout the day. The Wellington Battalion was subject to heavy rifle, bomb and artillery fire, including some friendly fire from Allied guns, and was eventually bombed out of its position on the crest and forced to dig in on the reverse slope of the ridge.[104] Two squadrons of the Wellington MR Regt. along with the Auckland MR Regt. and the Otago Battalion arrived at dusk to reinforce the position, but, misunderstanding the situation and thinking they were being replaced, the Wellington Battalion and 7th Gloucestershires withdrew whence they were able to be "supplied with plenty of water rations and rum." The MR regiments spent the night holding back the enemy and trying to improve the defenses.[105]

The 8 August also saw the 4th Australian Bde. recommence its attack on Hill 971, via Abdel Rahman Bair. The brigade's plans, however, were still undermined by the fact that it remained confused as to its actual position. Despite this, the initial advance was successful. There was minimal opposition and all seemed to be going well. But upon nearing the Asma Dere, the brigade came under heavy machine-gun fire from the slopes of Abdel Rahman Bair.[106] The divisional commander responsible for the actions against the Sari Bair Ridge later described the incident: "Considerable opposition was immediately met with from well-placed Turkish Machine Guns, and Infantry in position. In spite of every effort, no material progress was made, and on the approach of heavy columns of the enemy, the 4th (Australian) Infantry Brigade, which was then virtually surrounded, was withdrawn to its previous line."[107] In reality, as one historian has put it, the 4th Australian Bde. "had broken and run."[108] Monash's brigade had once again failed to reach its objective, and Monash had failed in his command responsibility by delegating rather than taking command of the attack.[109] The brigade spent the rest of the day withstanding determined counterattacks from the enemy. Meanwhile, the 29th Indian Bde., occupying the

Farm and the spurs to the northeast, spent the day carrying out reconnaissance below Hill Q for the next big attack.[110]

A Day of Rest at Suvla: 8 August 1915

Back at Suvla, the attack on Chocolate Hill during the night of 7 August had significantly dispersed IX Corps.[111] Persuaded by his brigadiers, the GOC of the 11th Division, Major-General Frederick Hammersley, decided that no offensive action would occur on 8 August; rather, the day would be spent resting, consolidating their positions, and organizing supplies. In spite of his decision, there was some fierce fighting throughout the day, with a battalion taking Scimitar Hill, and a continuance of action along the Kiretch Tepe Ridge.

The enemy used the lull on 8 August to prepare defenses and reshuffle units. The 16th Ottoman Army Corps, which had been ordered to march from Bulair to reinforce Willmer's small force at Suvla, had not yet arrived, and there remained a large area from Kiretch Tepe Ridge to Ismail Oglu Tepe that was devoid of any defenders at all.[112] Allied aerial reconnaissance had noticed this, reporting to GHQ that there was no movement in or near the Anafarta villages and that they were open for the taking. GHQ relayed this information onto IX Corps at 10:10 A.M., adding that they "hope [with] this indication you will be able to gain [an] early footing on ... Anafarta Ridge, very important." The Ottomans were relishing in the quiet, but anticipated that hostile attacks would be made that evening. Major Cecil Aspinall, from GHQ, who had drawn up the initial plan for operations at Suvla, arrived in Suvla Bay on board HMS *Jonquil* at noon. After discussing the situation, he wired Hammersley, the senior divisional commander ashore, and ordered him to push forward. Aspinall then proceeded ashore to personally stress the need for action and informed GHQ that "golden opportunities are being lost."[113] Hamilton was also anxious about the situation and prepared to visit Suvla. Getting there, though, posed some problems.

At 10:35 A.M., Hamilton was informed that HMS *Arno* was not available to take him from GHQ to Suvla but that a trawler was fully at his disposal. Despite this, Hamilton continued to ask for *Arno* throughout the day.[114] These unnecessary requests by Hamilton, particularly when a trawler was waiting for him, meant that his arrival at Suvla was delayed until 5:30 P.M.[115] After a brief discussion with Aspinall and Vice-Admiral de Robeck on board HMS *Triad*, Hamilton visited Stopford on HMS *Jonquil*. After discussing the situation, Hamilton proceeded ashore (accompanied by Aspinall and the naval chief of staff, Commodore Roger Keyes; Stopford remained on HMS *Jonquil*) to impress his desire for immediate action upon Hammersley.[116] Hamilton remained on the peninsula for a short time before returning to HMS *Triad* for dinner.[117] Hammersley then altered his plan of attack. Rather than attacking Anafarta Ridge at 5:00 A.M. the following morning, Hamilton had ordered him to commence the attack immediately. The result was not favorable, and Hamilton has been criticized for getting involved and issuing orders directly to a divisional commander (rather than through the corps commander as would be expected).

Due to the dispersion of the 11th Division, it took six and half hours for Hammersley's orders to reach all units concerned. The leading battalion on Scimitar Hill, which had been captured earlier on 8 August, withdrew to concentrate for the attack—a position it would not regain throughout the remainder of the campaign. Further, the advance did not begin until 4:00 A.M., at which time the troops came under heavy fire from the Ottoman reinforcements (the 9th and 12th divisions of 16th Corps)—recently arrived from Bulair—who attacked over the summit of Tekke Tepe and from Biyuk Anafarta.[118] This attack effectively ended any chance of an Allied advance at Suvla.

A Temporary Presence on Hill Q: 9 August 1915

Realizing that the 4th Australian Bde. could not get to Hill 971, Major-General Godley turned his attention to the area between Battleship Hill and Hill Q. The New Zealanders would concentrate on the area from Chunuk Bair to Battleship Hill; the 1/6th Gurkhas and 6th Battalion, South Lancashire Regiment, on the area from Hill Q to Chunuk Bair. A third column of five battalions (6th Battalion, Loyal North Lancashire Regiment; 6th Battalion, East Lancashire Regiment; 5th Battalion, Wiltshire Regiment; 10th Battalion, Hampshire Regiment; and 6th Battalion, Royal Irish Rifles), under the command of Brigadier-General Anthony Baldwin, the CO of the 38th Brigade, would advance between the two.[119] At 4:00 A.M.,

9 August, half an hour before the bombardment was to commence, the Ottomans attacked at Chunuk Bair, thereby ruling the New Zealanders out of the attack. The fighting continued all day.[120]

Nonetheless, at 5:23 A.M., 9 August, the 1/6th Gurkhas and 6th Battalion, South Lancashire Regiment, began their attack. They reached the summit between Chunuk Bair and Hill Q with ease and fired on the retreating enemy.[121] At Allanson's own admittance, it was a "mighty fluke" that they "struck the point at which we were supposed to get."[122] Shortly after, though, they were subject to friendly fire, which, combined with enfilading fire from the enemy to the north, forced Allanson and his men to retreat.[123] Meanwhile, Baldwin's column took an obscure and congested route and became lost. It finally arrived at 8:00 A.M., by which time any advance was impossible. The third attempt at Sari Bair had failed.[124] Furthermore, aerial reconnaissance now showed that the enemy were massing behind Chunuk Bair.[125]

The Loss of Chunuk Bair: An Ottoman Victory

By the early hours of 10 August, all New Zealand troops had been withdrawn from Chunuk Bair and replaced by British troops of the 6th Battalion, Loyal North Lancashire Regiment, and the 5th Battalion, Wiltshire Regiment.[126] At 4:30 A.M., 10 August, the Ottomans launched their counterattack to retake Chunuk Bair.[127] In total, about five thousand troops from the 23rd and 24th Regiments (8th Turkish Division) and the 26th Regiment (13th Turkish Division), led by Colonel Mustafa Kemal (later Atatürk, founding president of the Republic of Turkey) charged over the crest, "shoulder to shoulder" in "7 or 8 lines" and drove the Allies off the Sari Bair Ridge.[128] The defenders were "completely overwhelmed" in what the brigade major of the New Zealand Infantry Brigade described as "a fine counter stroke unflinchingly delivered."[129]

The MEF's positions at Chunuk Bair and the Pinnacle were overrun; Ottoman momentum was only haltered by accurate close-range fire from New Zealand machine guns at the Apex.[130] To the north, the counterattacking Ottomans poured down the slope toward the Farm. Some Allied troops were able to retreat, but the majority were killed.[131] After discussing the situation with Major-Generals Godley and Shaw, Lieutenant-General Birdwood informed GHQ

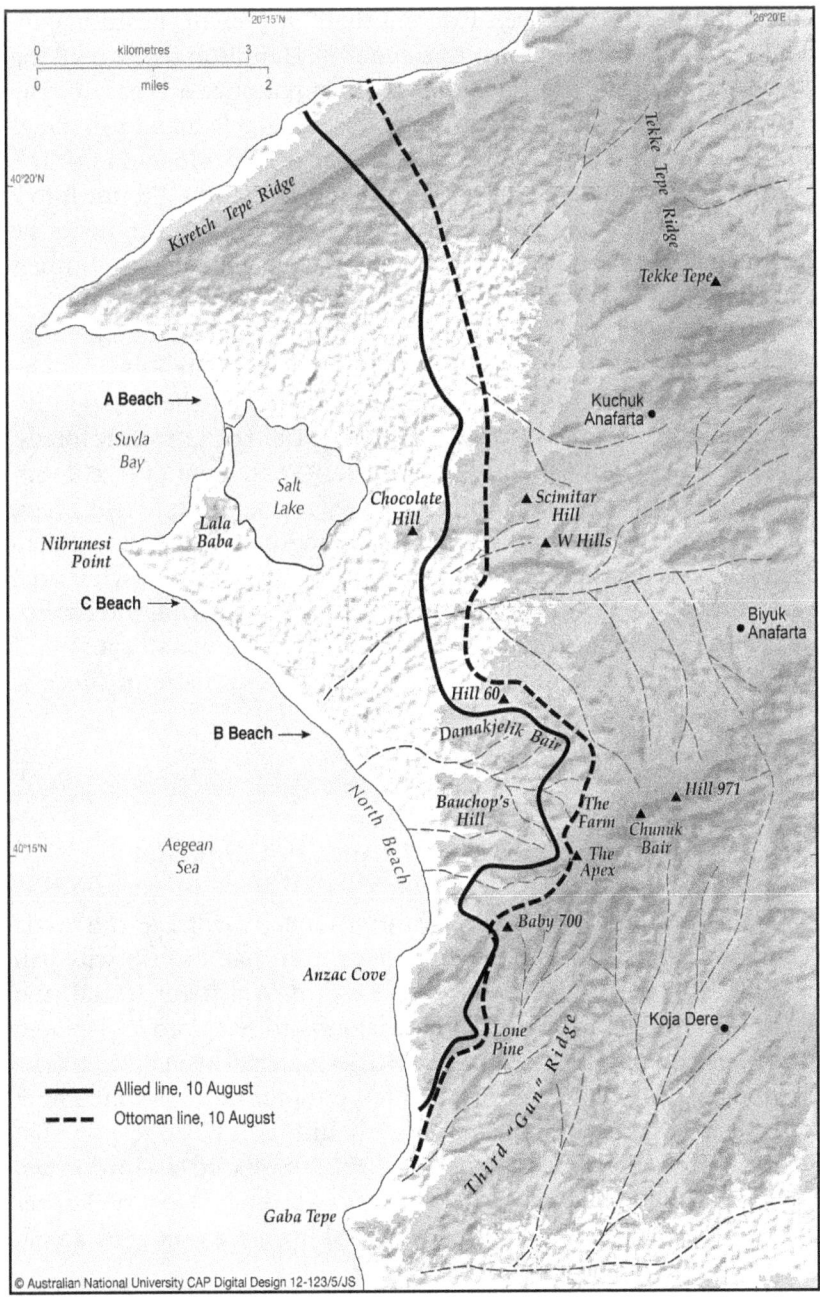

Map 8. Positions after Ottoman victory

that Chunuk Bair had been lost and that "at present, position cannot be retaken, though it must be done."[132] Hamilton replied, saying he was sorry for the loss but stressed the importance of regaining the position. He then asked what troops were available for a fresh counterattack, to which Birdwood replied that it was impossible to tell as "troops very done and disorganized."[133] Hamilton did not know how to regain the lost ground, but in a letter to Lord Kitchener he acknowledged that it must: "We've got to do it somehow or another, and do it we will yet with the help of Providence!"[134]

The remainder of 10 August was spent reorganizing and consolidating the positions now held below the Sari Bair Ridge.[135] The success of the Ottoman counterattack had ended the struggle for possession of the ridges.[136] The commander of the Ottoman forces, Marshal Liman von Sanders, later wrote, "Possession of this dominant mountain was thus definitely secured for the Turks."[137] In effect, the Ottoman success marked the end of the August Offensive. It had been a failure for the MEF. Both Hamilton and Birdwood attempted to downplay the failure (and casualties) by highlighting the casualties inflicted on the enemy, prisoners taken, and guns captured.[138] And despite the failure Hamilton remained optimistic of success: "Next time," he wrote, "we will get them."[139]

A Change in Focus, a Change in Command

After the failure at Sari Bair, Hamilton's focus turned to the Suvla sector. Aerial reconnaissance convinced him that success was still possible. He allotted the force reserve—53rd (Welsh Territorial) and 54th (East Anglian Territorial) Divisions—to Stopford.[140] Isolated attacks continued around Scimitar Hill (which had been given up the previous night) and Kiretch Tepe Ridge, but preparations were under way for a large attack (although with limited objectives) against Scimitar Hill, the W Hills, and Hill 60.[141] Stopford was informed that this attack should commence at dawn on 12 August. Rather than holding a continuous line, the attacking force was to establish redoubts to provide mutual support.[142]

Before the attack could commence, the 54th Division was required to undertake a preliminary operation and clear any parties of the enemy found near the village of Kuchuk Anafarta.[143] This took longer than expected, and during the process the 53rd Division, which was not involved in the fight, showed that it was incapable of any stoic defense and, according to corps headquarters, "at any moment may bolt."[144] The DAG of MEF reminded Stopford that cowardice was not acceptable: "Any case of cowardice [in] 53rd Division should be tried by court martial at once[.] Publish stringent orders to this Division that penalty for cowardice is death[.] Do not mince matters[.] You have under circumstances described by you power to confirm and carry out extreme penalty under rule procedure one twenty two[.] At the same time try and hearten Division by telling them reinforcements are on their way."[145]

Convinced that his units were not fit to undertake an advance at the present moment (an attitude that was shared by both Hammersley and Major-General The Honourable John Lindley, GOC of the 53rd Division), Stopford canceled the attack. GHQ intervened though, and decided that the attack would take place the following day.[146] Major-General Walter Braithwaite, the CGS of the MEF, then visited Stopford to discuss the situation. After hearing Stopford's concerns, Braithwaite agreed to postpone the attack.[147] Meanwhile, correspondence flowed between Lord Kitchener and Hamilton about the issue of command. On 14 August, Kitchener asked, "Have you any competent Generals to replace Stopford[,] Mahon and Hammersley—Should you consider it necessary to do so[?] I think from your report Stopford should come home[.] If any Generals fail do not hesitate to act promptly[.] This is a young man's war and we must have Commanding Officers that will take full advantage of opportunities that do not often occur[.] I will send you any Generals I have available."[148]

Hamilton's response was dispatched within three hours: "Stopford . . . is not in my opinion capable of pulling the 9th Corps together again[.] The matter is urgent and the one man on the spot who could do so is de Lisle[.] Unfortunately Mahon is senior to de Lisle but I would ask Mahon to accept the position for I could not put him into command of the corps at present though as divisional general he has done better than others. . . . What Major Generals have you available to replace others in 9th Corps if found necessary[?] A good brigadier from France with temporary rank would meet the case if no good Major Generals available."[149] On the back of this correspondence, Braithwaite informed Stopford that he was being replaced and asked him "to be good enough to hand over to

Lieutenant-General de Lisle" and then "proceed to England."[150] Before leaving, Stopford ordered an attack be made at Kiretch Tepe Ridge on 15 August. The force (consisting of the 30th and 31st Brigades) succeeded in gaining half a mile of ground but lost it the following day when reinforcements from the 5th Turkish Division pushed the brigades back to their original line.[151]

While the attack was under way, Hamilton was informed that Lieutenant-General Sir Julian Byng was being sent out from France to command IX Corps, with Major-Generals Edward Fanshawe and Frederick Maude to command the 11th and 13th Divisions respectively.[152] Despite Hamilton's efforts, Mahon refused to waive his seniority and serve under de Lisle, and instead resigned his post and left the peninsula. Lieutenant-General de Lisle, who Birdwood described as "a real thruster," arrived at Suvla from Helles on 16 August and immediately began reorganizing his force.[153] He later wrote that his "arrival at the H.Q. of the IX Corps was one of the most trying events of my career, and I knew that the difficulties of the situation would increase."[154] There were now twenty thousand Ottoman troops opposing IX Corps at Suvla with a further eight thousand in reserve near Anafarta.[155]

Although "not favourably impressed" with what he saw during his reconnaissance on 16–17 August, de Lisle realized the importance of launching an attack at Suvla before the enemy did: something he did not think IX Corps could successfully defend against. He therefore made what he later described as "an unfavourable report" suggesting that the 29th Division be brought from Helles (which it was) and an attack be made on 21 August.[156] In addition to this division, the 2nd Mounted Division (of five thousand unmounted troops) was sent from Egypt.[157] Due to Hamilton's concerns that an attack that encompassed taking Anafarta Ridge was "trying to do too much," the plans were reconstructed and a more limited objective was chosen.[158]

At 3:00 P.M., 21 August, after an hour's bombardment, which Lieutenant-Colonel William Rettie, the CO of the 59th Brigade, RFA, described as "rather futile" and "probably only advertised the fact that we were about to do something," the 29th and 11th Divisions commenced their attack against Scimitar Hill and the W Hills respectively.[159] Following this, a multinational combined force (made of portions from the 2/10th Gurkhas; 1/5th Gurkhas; 5th Bn., Connaught Rangers; NZMR Bde.; 4th Australian Bde; and

10th Bn., Hampshire Regt.) attacked toward Hill 60.[160] Isolated attacks continued until 23 August but eventually failed, primarily due to the failure of the artillery to assist the infantry.[161] Looking back on the failure of these operations, de Lisle wrote, "If anyone was to blame it must be myself for reporting that an attack on the 21st had chances of success."[162]

Further attempts were made to strengthen the area between the Anzac and Suvla sectors from 27 to 29 August, but despite some gains at Hill 60 the enemy still held onto its summit.[163] The Ottoman General Staff concluded that these attacks "had no effect except the shedding of blood."[164] With this, the climax at Gallipoli ended; the gains amounting to what Godley described as "five hundred acres of bad grazing ground."[165] These gains, Birdwood added, were of no real value without occupation of the crests.[166] The Allies had suffered 45,000 casualties throughout the month (killed, wounded, missing); 21,500 of these from 6 to 10 August.[167] In comparison to casualty figures in the great battles of the First World War, the numbers for the battle of Sari Bair (as a percentage of available infantry) are comparable to those for the first day of the Somme on 1 July 1916: both represent around 33 percent.[168]

CHAPTER 8

SUBSEQUENT PHASES

History tells us that the August Offensive failed. But history also teaches us that the offensive "nearly succeeded" and would have done so with some luck. Apart from ignoring the role that the Ottomans played in this—and that it was indeed their victory—this view also ignores the fact that the capture and retention of the Sari Bair Ridge was merely the first of four phases in Hamilton's operational plan. Thus far this book has focused on the difficulties and limitations faced prior to and during the first phase of the offensive. Given that "success" lay in a protracted fight across the peninsula, and to test further the "near success" hypothesis, it is also necessary to analyze what would have been required—and what difficulties would have been encountered—had the offensive progressed beyond Sari Bair.

This chapter examines the key aspects already discussed throughout the book—mobility, fire support, naval operations, and logistics—as they pertain to the second, third, and fourth phases of the offensive. Each had to succeed before the next could commence, and success could not be claimed until all had been achieved. This is not an exercise in counterfactual history. It is based on a thorough understanding of how offensive warfare was fought in 1915, but more importantly, on sound (and generally conservative) and informed assessments of the plans, processes, difficulties, and limitations that would have to be overcome should the MEF wish to achieve its operational objectives. Such an approach is the only means by which one can analyze the MEF's capabilities, and the only way to test the "near success" view.

Holding Sari Bair Ridge

Beyond the specific difficulties of the terrain at Sari Bair and Suvla Bay discussed in chapter 2, the very geography of the objectives set for the first phase tended to work against Birdwood's tactical plan. Could the Sari Bair Ridge actually be taken and held? That the Allies were defeated at Chunuk Bair should be evidence enough. This proof, however, is not recognized by those who adhere to the "near success" view. Indeed, General Hamilton was not disheartened by the defeat and actually stated that "two more such defeats, measured in mere acreage, will give us the Narrows."[1] To the contrary, two more such failures would have resulted in the decimation of his force.

Before the subsequent phases of the offensive could begin, it would be necessary to seize, consolidate, and hold the *entire* Sari Bair Ridge.[2] Chunuk Bair was but one portion of this ridge, and Hamilton's statement that "Chunuk Bair will do: with that, we win" was wrong.[3] The successful Ottoman counterattack against this position on 10 August proved that if the entire ridge were not held the enemy could concentrate their assaults on one area and overwhelm the Allied defenders.[4] Without flank protection, Chunuk Bair would continue to be enfiladed from both Hill Q and Battleship Hill.[5] Major-General Godley recognized this prior to the offensive, but also noted that any attempt to seize the whole of the Sari Bair Ridge would be "hampered by the narrowness of the ridge itself."[6] Surely, if the first phase of operations in August was beyond the capabilities of the Allied force (as was proven), then there was no real chance of the MEF progressing any farther across the peninsula. Hamilton acknowledged this in September, when he admitted that after the casualties suffered throughout August there simply were not enough troops to both hold the line and push forward.[7]

Let us assume, however, that Hamilton's (physically depleted) troops were up to the task, that command and control did not falter, that communications could be upheld, and that no body of troops got lost. Let us then assume that, even with the element of surprise now lacking, the entire Sari Bair Ridge was taken. This would only be the first step of an increasingly difficult task. Birdwood expected that the enemy would counterattack in force to regain the ridge, and that defending against this would be difficult.[8] The ridge was barren and therefore offered little protection from Ottoman fire. Furthermore, once the Allies proceeded beyond the ridge—something they would have to do quickly to avoid water shortages—and onto its eastern slopes, they would have come under direct observation and fire from Ottoman troops and artillery at Achi Baba. While the deep valleys on either side of Sari Bair may have offered some protection, a large force would still be required to hold the crest, and would therefore be continually vulnerable to the enemy's artillery fire.[9]

Had the Allies been able to hold on throughout this period—and it must be reaffirmed that they never went close to getting this far—the terrain in front of them would have continued to act as a significant barrier against maneuver and mobility. Troops would have been required to advance in a southeasterly direction down the Sari Bair Ridge and to successfully defeat the strongly held enemy defensive works at Battleship Hill. Cecil Malthus, a private in the Wellington Battalion, recognized the difficulty of such a task, noting that many more men and much more time would be required for such an action.[10] There were, however, not enough of either. As the historian Tim Travers correctly stated, even if all of this could have been achieved, "there would still be much fighting before reaching the Straits."[11]

Numbers for an Advance

When Lieutenant-General Birdwood told his troops that their task would not be complete once the enemy had been driven off the Sari Bair Ridge, he was referring to the breakout from the Anzac sector and the subsequent push across the peninsula to Maidos (see map 3). To achieve this breakout, the force in the Anzac sector, in conjunction with that now positioned along the Sari Bair Ridge, would first have to push forward to Third "Gun" Ridge. This would result in an increased outer perimeter (Hill 971–Gaba Tepe) of 8,600 yards, and an inner line (the "old" Anzac perimeter) of 3,000 yards. Assuming that Birdwood's force had only lost 25 percent of its strength in its attempts to seize Sari Bair (a conservative figure when compared to actual losses, and ignoring issues such as the troops' physical state and the number of men required for fatigues), his force would then amount to 27,750 rifles. Next, based on the acknowledged minimum requirement of three men required per yard for defense (and not allowing for a reserve), 7,500 men would have been absorbed in defending the 2,500 yards of high ground between Hill 971 and Baby 700.[12] With those required for the defense of the inner line (9,000 men), this would leave 11,250 of Birdwood's initial force available for the second phase breakout. Factoring in the *entire* general reserve

(19,000), the total force available for the subsequent phases of the offensive, if all had run smoothly, would have been 30,250 rifles.[13]

The first task of this force would be to break through the Ottoman positions opposite the Anzac sector. It had already been established in June that the enemy's positions in this vicinity were strong and placed in such a way so as to enfilade any frontal attack made directly from Anzac. Behind the Ottoman front trench systems were further prepared lines, all of which could also bring converging fire on any positions gained by the Allies as they progressed forward.[14] Such a breakthrough would always be difficult, especially one attempted on foot. Rapid rifle fire, some well-positioned machine guns, and shrapnel would make this task more deadly.

In conjunction with this assault, the Allies would also be required to launch an attack against the enemy's stronghold at Gabe Tepe in order to secure their right flank and the approach across the peninsula. Should these attacks be successful, the force would then need to proceed into Legge Valley (out of sight of its fire support) and onto Third Ridge. This would not be an easy march. Notwithstanding the well-entrenched enemy positions that commanded the area, all attacking troops would have to advance an average of one thousand yards over and through deep gullies and spurs.[15] In such mountainous and broken terrain, Clausewitz—who all senior officers had no doubt studied—warned that "movement is slower and more laborious . . . any manoeuver will take more time, and cause the troops to be split up." Furthermore, if units were separated, the maneuver would be harder to control, and mobility more difficult.[16] If this succeeded, a line would now be held from Hill 971 to Gaba Tepe (through Scrubby Knoll, Anderson Knoll, and along Wine Glass Ridge). On earlier calculations, achieving this task would cost 25 percent casualties (another conservative estimate); now the total force available for the third phase would amount to approximately 22,700 rifles.

This new extended line would have to be consolidated and, if the defensive ratio requirement previously used is applied, defended by 18,300 rifles. Managing this consolidation and maintaining momentum would be a difficult task.[17] It was from this new position on Third Ridge that the capabilities of the attacking force would be truly tested. Holding such a line would undoubtedly free up many of those holding the inner line, but it would still be important to maintain some defensive capabilities as a contingency precaution.

Working on the assumption that the Anzac sector could be held with a skeleton force of one man per yard (less than the accepted minimum), this would free up 6,000 rifles, bringing the total attacking force for the third phase to 10,400. Reflecting on the ability of his force to actually get this far, Hamilton later wrote: "With such an inexperienced force, would I have been able to keep my grip on the Maidos–Suvla neck? Pondering over the matter now, I gravely doubt it."[18] He went on to consider the impact that this would have had, writing in another letter that it "would have been precursor to something uncomfortable to contemplate."[19] Finally, Hamilton admitted that "fortune had not been too unkind."[20] It is clear that numerically, the MEF was utterly insufficient for the next advance required during the third phase of the offensive—another eight-thousand-yard push to Kilia Liman, the harbor north of Maidos. Nonetheless, to dispel any lingering doubt, it is worth examining the terrain of this area.

Terrain as an Obstacle

Despite being a broad, reasonably flat valley and the narrowest part of the Gallipoli Peninsula, the approach from Gaba Tepe to Kilia Liman was far from easy going. Attacking units, that had successfully taken the second phase objectives, would have to undertake the third phase with practically no further assistance from naval gunfire support.[21] While the roads were of sufficient quality to allow movement, the area was dominated by the Sari Bair Ridge to its north, and the strongly held Ottoman position—the seven-hundred-feet-high Kilid Bahr Plateau, and its offshoot, the Kalkmaz Dagh—to the south.[22] Again, let us note another of Clausewitz's warnings: "No Army is capable of maintaining a position in the valley . . . if it does not command the surrounding heights."[23] Even if the Allies held the Sari Bair Ridge on their left flank, their right flank would have lain open to the enemy on the Kilid Bahr Plateau. Without holding both positions—which there was no plan to do—the task of maintaining their position in the Gaba Tepe–Maidos valley would be a difficult one for the MEF.

Mobility through this area would be inevitably disrupted by the need to dig in for cover. Digging would have been a difficult proposition, especially in a flat valley that offered little protection from enemy observation or fire. Furthermore, the ground in this area was harder than elsewhere on the peninsula, with its mixture of limestone and sandstone. Heavy tools, intensive effort, and considerable time would be required to dig the necessary defensive positions.[24] This would in effect revert the advance back to a form of static warfare. In order to silence the enemy's fire and reintroduce mobility, units would have to be deployed to deal with the Ottomans on the Kilid Bahr Plateau—a position that itself was topographically complex. With a perimeter of ten miles, consisting of a series of precipitous ridges, spurs, and depressions, and being dissected by valleys generally much deeper than those of Sari Bair, it truly was a formidable natural stronghold.[25] In addition, the plateau's northwestern slopes, those overlooking any potential Allied advance in the area, are very steep, and therefore much harder to attack, and even more difficult to maintain communications upon if taken.[26] The Ottoman defenses on the Kilid Bahr Plateau have been described as being as formidable as can be found anywhere in the world, and the plateau even compared to the Rock of Gibraltar.[27] It was, as Sherman Miles, U.S. military attaché to Ankara, wrote, "the citadel of the Turkish defences of the Dardanelles."[28] Indeed, its name translates as "lock of the sea."[29] It is clear that one historian's claim that once Third Ridge was occupied, "it would be easy to make a final thrust across the peninsula" is grossly ignorant of the difficulties posed by the terrain, the Ottoman defenses, and the operational shortcomings that precluded the Allies from undertaking such an action.[30]

There are two more factors which highlight the impact that terrain would have had on the ability of the MEF to achieve the operational objective of the August Offensive. The first was the inability of VIII Corps and Corps Expéditionnaire to push forward from their positions in the Helles sector. The enemy on Achi Baba overlooked the entire area of operations for these two formations. Holding this point was advantageous for the Ottomans as it funneled the Allied force at Cape Helles.[31] Despite striving for this position throughout the entire campaign, the Allies *never* got within two miles of it. And had the Allies reached the summit, they would be no nearer their overall objective. The Kilid Bahr Plateau still obscured any view and approach to the Narrows (see map 1).[32]

A second factor worth considering was that this entire offensive (and the wider Allied campaign) aimed to silence the enemy on the European shore of the Dardanelles. But what about the Asiatic shore—the area that contained the majority of mobile Ottoman howitzers that prevented naval minesweeping operations? Hamilton presumed that once the Gallipoli Peninsula was held, the enemy's defenses on the Asiatic shore would cease to pose a problem.[33] It was presumed that Allied artillery fire from the newly gained positions on the Gallipoli Peninsula would all but silence the Ottomans on the Asiatic shore. Such a presumption, however, itself ignored the terrain on the Asiatic shore—which was more difficult and developed than was acknowledged by the Allies. The mountainous terrain in this region also acted as a perfect screen for hostile artillery.[34] Terrain would have a marked impact even if this, the fourth phase of the offensive, were reached.

Communication Breakdown

Any advance would have relied on establishing and maintaining signals communication across the peninsula—the difficulties of which would have increased the farther the force proceeded from the beach, especially with an ongoing lack of personnel and cables.[35] Unlike on the Western Front, where there was some degree of preexisting communications infrastructure, any advance across the Gallipoli Peninsula would require the construction of an intercommunication system from scratch—linking individual units with their headquarters and their guns and, if cooperation and mobility was to be maintained, with their flanking units. The more the system expanded, the greater it would become in complexity and vulnerability.[36] There was the added difficulty of physically laying the cables. While cable detachments could theoretically keep pace with the advancing columns, in practice they could not. Brigadier-General Monash, CO of the 4th Australian Bde., doubted that the cable runners could keep pace with the advance. So did Arthur Beecroft, a signals officer at Suvla, who noted that it was impossible to keep pace with the infantry while laying lines, especially through unknown country, while keeping silent—and if operating at night, without lights to aid their work.[37] Moreover, even if these lines could be laid, they could not be used until the attacking troops actually stopped advancing.[38]

While visual signaling could be used, this method would be rendered redundant once an attacking Allied force proceeded beyond the Sari Bair Ridge and out of view. Visual communications would be of more value to an advance across the open ground from Gaba Tepe to Maidos, but visual signals were strictly prohibited if the enemy could observe the signals—and in this case the Ottomans on the Kilid Bahr Plateau would overlook the entire area.[39] All signaling tasks would be further compounded by secrecy and the lack of knowledge of the plans on the part of most Allied commanders outside of Hamilton's immediate staff. Indeed, the first lesson learned by the signal service on the Western Front was that intercommunication could not be maintained during mobile warfare *unless* the signal commanders of each formation kept their subordinates constantly informed of their position and any future movements.[40] Without intercommunication, especially lateral communication between attacking units, the ability to conduct a combined and coordinated maneuver would be greatly reduced, if not rendered impossible.

Enemy Action

Had the Allies successfully captured, consolidated, and retained the Sari Bair Ridge, the Ottomans would never have simply capitulated. Birdwood realized this, noting that with the element of surprise thus gone, the enemy would be "sure to endeavour to at once entrench around whatever position we may take up."[41] The Ottomans would be able to utilize their interior lines and quickly move troops to meet an attack.[42] This they did. Although initially outnumbered in various sectors in August, the Ottomans showed that, as was the case in April, they were able to adapt quickly to the situation, mobilize their reinforcements, and move them to where required.[43] In doing so, they were able to call two divisions from Bulair and three from the Asiatic coast. Hamilton did not realize this until after the August Offensive had failed. The situation, he informed Kitchener, had become "a question of who can slog longest and hardest"—this itself was the antithesis of the whole purpose of the August Offensive.[44]

Yet slog it out they would. If forced from one location, the Ottomans would invariably fall back into previously constructed defensive positions, with already established communications. The advantage of not being required to entrench under fire would show itself immediately. Ottoman units would be able to communicate and thus coordinate their defense, and the Allied advance would most likely stall under the difficulties of attacking another well-prepared defensive locality.[45] With defense as the Ottomans' strength, and with their intimate knowledge of the terrain, any push by the MEF across the peninsula would actually play into the hands of the enemy.[46] Moreover, by remaining on the defense the Ottomans would undoubtedly suffer fewer casualties than what they could impose on the Allies. With a force of approximately 110,000 within close proximity of the Gallipoli Peninsula, the Allied-to-Ottoman ratio was effectively equal.[47] The Allies therefore were far from the 3:1 ratio generally accepted as the minimum required for offensive operations. The difficulties of the terrain already discussed further increased the ratio required by the Allies.[48] While numerical superiority is not the only factor in determining whether a battle succeeds, it is, according to Clausewitz, "of vital importance," especially where the terrain favors the defenders.[49] In addition to those troops in the immediate vicinity, the Ottomans could still call upon reinforcements from various parts of their empire. Indeed, by the end of July 1915 only *half* of the 250,818-strong Ottoman 5th Army (that assigned to the Dardanelles) was on the Gallipoli Peninsula.[50] Birdwood commented that it felt as if the Ottomans had an "endless supply of men."[51] While the Allies had committed all available troops to the August Offensive, the defenders were only at half strength and could increase numbers as required.

It is also noteworthy that by August 1915 the Ottomans were fully geared toward war at the Dardanelles, whereas the Allied focus was inevitably, and understandably, on the Western Front. For the Ottomans, Gallipoli was the vital and primary front. The Allies were aware of this and had received intelligence in June that their enemy would sacrifice everything for the defense of Constantinople.[52] In truth, it was the Ottomans, not the Allies, who were well placed for victory during the August Offensive. As Birdwood later admitted to the Dardanelles Commission, the Ottomans were simply "too strong" to be defeated.[53]

Fire Support during the Subsequent Phases

Having shown that success, in terms of mobility alone, was beyond the capabilities of the Allies in August 1915, one could rest here. But, to further test the "near success" view, it is imperative to examine the role that the field artillery could provide during the subsequent phases. Had the offensive progressed this far, Allied artillery would have been required to play a much greater role than that already undertaken and to spearhead the advance across the peninsula. The question is: would this have been possible?

As noted in chapter 3, artillery was regarded as an accessory during the first phase of the offensive, and the artillery commanders had been omitted from the planning process. The role of the artillery would have changed during the second phase of the operations. Rather than merely supporting the infantry, Allied artillery would have had to take a lead role in attempting to cut Ottoman supply routes (land and sea), thus enabling the infantry and field artillery to advance across the peninsula for the third phase. This was the basic reasoning behind the selection of the Sari Bair Ridge as an objective in the first place. Hamilton aimed to use the ridge as an artillery platform to observe and shell Maidos, Kilid Bahr, and Krithia, thus starving the enemy and leading to its capitulation. He wrote, "As soon as we can haul up our big guns we should command, and be able to search, all the ground between the Aegean and the Dardanelles."[54] Birdwood agreed, but, influenced by the opinions of key naval personnel such as Rear-Admiral Cecil Thursby, commander of the British Adriatic Squadron, and Commodore Roger Keyes, chief of staff of the EMS, he also envisaged the ridge as providing an advantageous observation station from which to direct naval fire across the peninsula.[55] On 19 August, Birdwood described the importance of Sari Bair to Kitchener: "not only for our own heavy guns, but as a spotting position from which I had hoped to be able to put all the ships' heavy guns onto the forts and any shipping passing the Dardanelles, which I trusted would have completely cut off the Turks on Kilid Bahr from all supplies etc."[56]

It was imperative that with such a key role in the second phase, plans be developed in accord with the artillery's needs and capabilities. But this did not occur. In the discussions preceding the offensive, the divisional artillery commanders had barely mentioned what might be required of the artillery for the subsequent phases. Lieutenant-Colonel Johnston, CRA of the NZ&A Div. Artillery, for example, informed the Dardanelles Commission in 1917 that, while it was the intention of the higher command to advance from Gaba Tepe to Maidos, he was too occupied with his own task at Anzac to go into details of the subsequent phases. Indeed, he did not anticipate moving his guns "until we had driven the Turks off [the] Kilid Bahr [Plateau]," and, rather than shelling Maidos, he thought it more prudent to shell the Ottomans as they retreated.[57] Again, a damning lack of communication between the general staff and artillery commanders is apparent. Without prior discussion and artillery arrangements, however, all the momentum of a successful first phase would be lost, thus giving the enemy more time to organize for a defense against subsequent phases of the offensive.

In any case, had the infantry succeeded in seizing and consolidating the Sari Bair Ridge without adequate fire support (which of course they did not), much work would be required before the next component of the offensive could begin. New artillery positions would have to be located and emplacements constructed, preferably below the summit of Sari Bair, thus preventing direct Ottoman observation of their positions. Existing roads would have to be improved, and new ones constructed to enable the artillery to be moved into these new positions.[58] Contact would have to be maintained throughout the relocation of the guns, so as to ensure the protection of the infantry—but with this would come all the problems of maintaining communications already discussed.[59] The process of moving the guns was also time consuming, especially in complex terrain such as that in the Anzac and Sari Bair sectors. This task was made even more difficult by the lack of horses and wagons with which to move the guns and their ammunition forward.[60] Then the time-consuming and complex process of target registration would begin. The various Allied guns would have to attempt to locate the Ottomans' guns, the majority of which would still remain concealed by Third Ridge. Time would be of the essence here, but as the BEF's experience at Neuve Chapelle proved, rushing artillery fire without adequate preregistration risked disaster for the infantry.[61] With speed as the essence for success during the push across the peninsula, artillery arrangements would no doubt have been rushed.

Getting the Guns into Position

The second phase objectives were all well and good in theory, but in reality the task of actually getting the guns into position for this stage of the offensive would have been extremely difficult, if not impossible. Had the summit of the Sari Bair Ridge been gained by the infantry, the task of continuing fire support would have largely been left to the field artillery, as any naval fire would be useless owing to the low trajectory of its guns, which could not drop shells over the ridges and into the valleys beyond.[62] But it is questionable whether field guns could have been hauled into position on Sari Bair; after all, it was a difficult enough process getting the guns into position at Anzac and Suvla.[63] The only guns that could be easily manhandled into position were the 10-pounder mountain guns. These were designed for maneuverability, and each gun could be dismantled and carried by three mules. However, as mentioned in chapter 3, these guns were largely unreliable and would have added little to the Allied firepower, especially due to their limited range and lack of ammunition (with only fifty rounds remaining on the L-of-C by 14 August).[64]

What about the 18-pounders? When asked whether he thought it possible to place his 18-pounder field guns on the Sari Bair Ridge, Lieutenant-Colonel Johnston replied that, while possible, it would be difficult, requiring at least one thousand men to physically drag each gun into position.[65] With limited personnel available for the actual fighting, and even greater limitations on numbers available for fatigues, it is difficult to envisage this number ever being allotted to a single fatigue duty. Any attempt would also take a considerable amount of time—an element in short supply to the MEF during the offensive. Even had men been allotted to such tasks, the range of the 18-pounders was not sufficient enough to enable them to hit their targets.

The real difficulty, though, would have been in moving the heavy artillery. The Mk. I 60-pounder and carriage, weighing 4.5 tons, was cumbersome and difficult to move.[66] Indeed, it was deemed too difficult during the offensive to move even the four 60-pounders of the 10th Heavy Battery along the (flat) beach from Anzac to Suvla.[67] The problem of placing a 60-pounder gun on Sari Bair can be further appreciated by comparing the terrain in this vicinity with that at Suvla. On 22–23 August it took a fatigue party of 150 men to move two 60-pounders of the 15th Heavy Battery a distance of approximately six hundred yards. With an average incline of 9.6 percent, and a maximum nearly double that, the task was too steep and too difficult for the horses.[68] In comparison, the route from North Beach (at Anzac) to Chunuk Bair (via the Sazli Beit Dere), a distance nearly *four times* greater than that taken at Suvla, had an average incline of

12.5 percent, which increased at times to 77 percent.⁶⁹ Similar difficulties would be experienced moving the single 4.7-inch naval gun of the Heavy Battery (Australian Divisional Artillery), which weighed a little less than the 60-pounder at 3.8 tons.⁷⁰ It is safe to conclude that it would have been impossible to move these guns to where they were needed, in accordance with the time frame required, and therefore, the MEF could not have proceeded beyond its first phase objectives. This is a clear indication of the basic fallacy of the "near success" claim. The offensive never reached this stage, but, had it done so, no more could have been accomplished due to the sheer difficulty in getting the artillery into place.

Cutting Supplies

Let us assume that by some miracle the MEF were able to place its heavy artillery on the Sari Bair Ridge. By doing so we can assess the claim made by the Australian official historian, Charles Bean, that, at the very least, the Allied occupation of Sari Bair would "render [the enemy's] position so precarious as almost to compel its withdrawal."⁷¹ Would this have been the case? Could the Allied artillery, with the limitations already highlighted, have cut the Ottoman land and sea communications, thus starving the Ottomans to surrender? The answers to such questions may be inferred by comparing operational maps with the resource capabilities of the MEF, yet it was something that does not appear to have been considered by Hamilton or his planners. This is astonishing and beyond comprehension given that the following calculations are based on the 1:20,000 operational maps used during the offensive (see appendix 3).

Maidos, the operational objective of the August Offensive, and the harbor to its north, Kilia Liman, were within maximum range of *only one* gun available at Anzac (the 4.7-inch naval gun). If one includes the unreliable 60-pounders of the 10th Heavy Battery, which were destined for Suvla Bay, the figure increases to five pieces available. Fire directed on these locations, even in significant quantities, however, could not completely cut Ottoman seaborne supplies. As ANZAC HQ realized, this feat could not be accomplished until both Ak Bashi Liman and Kilid Bahr, which were the primary Ottoman harbors on the peninsula, were also destroyed.⁷² Further, Kilid Bahr—the far more important target—was outside the maximum range of *all* Allied guns available on the peninsula. In addition, even had the Allies succeeded in advancing two miles from Helles to Achi Baba (with their guns), Kilid Bahr and the Narrows would still have remained outside their range. Kilid Bahr would not have come into Allied artillery range until the MEF had advanced and occupied the southern portion of Third Ridge (known as Wine Glass Ridge), which would have required traversing difficult country and overcoming significant Ottoman resistance in the area. In addition, despite being within range, the Kilid Bahr Plateau cast a shadow over Kilid Bahr (township and harbor), thus shielding it from observation and artillery fire. These positions were, however, within range of the ships' guns, but, as was proven throughout the campaign, even with observation, naval gunfire was largely inaccurate and ineffective.

It is evident, therefore, that the plan to sever Ottoman sea communications with artillery fire was based more on wishful thinking rather than reality. Hamilton's claim that both Maidos and Kilid Bahr could be shelled from Sari Bair is proof that he did not fully grasp the enormity of the task he had set, nor the difficulties that would inevitably be encountered.[73] Should it be possible (an unlikely event) to drag the guns into position on the Sari Bair Ridge (or on the 400 Plateau for that matter), Kilid Bahr was beyond range while Maidos could only be shelled by a small number of guns, all of which were unreliable and difficult to maneuver.[74] Why Hamilton's staff failed to realize this is perplexing, especially when all that was required was a map, a ruler, and a range table. Such an oversight is further evidence of the inability of those responsible for planning the August Offensive to properly assess the task at hand, particularly the limitation of fire support, and cannot be excused.

Another objective of the second phase—the incapacitation of Ottoman land traffic beyond Sari Bair—would have proven equally problematic. With a significant portion of Ottoman roads within range of the Allied guns (on Sari Bair), it would have been theoretically possible to cut the Ottoman overland supply routes with artillery fire. Such theory, though, once again ignores practical reality. The key supply junctions of Koja Dere and Boghali, which were crucial to the supply of the Ottoman forces opposing Anzac, were within effective range of the 400 Plateau throughout the entire campaign. Despite this, the Allies *never* significantly hindered Ottoman supplies and transport in this area. So too, the combination of Allied

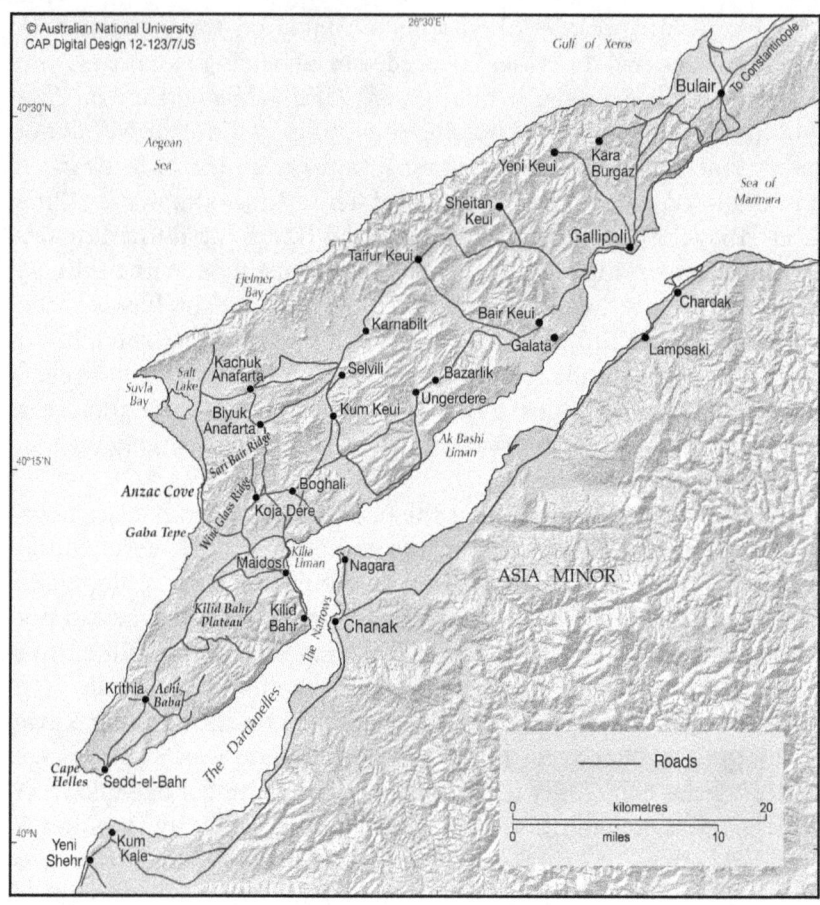

Map 9. Ottoman lines of communication

submarines, aircraft, and destroyers failed to stop Ottoman traffic on these routes throughout the campaign. That this situation might suddenly change with the possession of Sari Bair would have been most unlikely.

Moreover, the Ottoman land routes in question, which ran from Constantinople, were primarily used for troop movements, with the majority of supplies traveling by sea.[75] In addition to the roads on the Gallipoli Peninsula were two roads suitable for wheeled traffic along the Asiatic shore of the Dardanelles.[76] The roads were unpaved and could be repaired easily if damaged by Allied shellfire. The nature of Ottoman road transport, which consisted of mules, donkeys, camels, two- and four-wheeled carts drawn by mules and ponies, and larger carts drawn by bullocks and buffaloes, made it versatile, and it could be diverted from roads if required. To combat the Allied aerial observation superiority, Ottoman transport columns were also separated into small sections of five carts and twenty pack animals, and kept a distance of one mile from each other. They were further ordered to halt and take cover whenever an Allied airplane was sighted, and they normally marched at night to combat Allied observation.[77] Hamilton's staff and the experts in London were all aware of this. Maurice Hankey, the secretary of the Dardanelles Committee, for example, informed the First Lord of the Admiralty, Arthur Balfour, the day before the August Offensive began that: "Judging by the country I have seen, the ground is so dry at this time of year that, except in rocky or bushy districts, carts can go anywhere, and draught transport by horses and mules can go by any track."[78] Furthermore, Ottoman supply routes were often concealed behind ridges and beneath trees and were therefore secure against Allied artillery observation.[79] Indeed, by the time of the August Offensive, the Allies were still not clear as to exactly what routes the Ottomans were using. On 2 August, Balfour wrote to Lord Curzon, a fellow member of the Dardanelles Committee, that, while the Allies knew of the main road from Keshan to Gallipoli, he "rather suspect[s] that the Turks keep more inland by a new road of which we have heard rumours."[80]

The task of cutting land transport routes for Allied artillery, therefore, was particularly difficult. The farther north one traveled up Sari Bair, to make use of the heights for observation, the farther one moved away from the targets.[81] And even if the Allies could direct an accurate and heavy fire on the Ottoman supply routes, this would not necessarily prevent the transportation of supplies. Throughout the entire campaign, for instance, the Ottomans fired on Allied logistic routes, but, by developing protective countermeasures and new methods to meet the challenge, the Allies kept supplies moving.[82] There is little doubt that the Ottomans would do the same.

Furthermore, the land route was but one supply route available to the Ottomans. As was evident in the Balkan Wars, even with their land communications severed at Bulair, the Ottomans were still able to maintain adequate supplies by using the Sea of Marmara.[83] In addition to the sea route from Constantinople, there was also the option of transporting stores, supplies, and men from Asia Minor via Chanak.[84] The wider point is that even had the Allied artillery been able to overcome all of the difficulties mentioned, the possibility of starving out the enemy through artillery fire was an illusion. Lieutenant-Colonel Johnston could not have been more correct when he acknowledged that the scheme of cutting off the enemy south of Maidos and preventing seaborne supplies was beyond the means of the Allied artillery.[85] Even had the offensive advanced this far, it could go no further. Success, therefore, was a distant fantasy, and far from the near success so often claimed by participants and historians.

Mobile Artillery

Again adopting the flexibility of assumption, it is now prudent to examine the artillery capabilities of the MEF should it have reached the third phase of the August Offensive. This phase would have required the Allied artillery to advance across the peninsula in support of the infantry, with the object of severing Ottoman traffic from the Asiatic shore and knocking out the forts that guarded the Dardanelles.[86] While the terrain between Gaba Tepe and Maidos was favorable for the movement of guns, the entire route would be vulnerable to Ottoman fire from the Kilid Bahr Plateau.[87] Allied guns would have been prime targets for the Ottoman artillery—there were at least fourteen known Ottoman artillery pieces in the immediate vicinity.[88] All the while, the Allied guns would not be able to retaliate. Added to this was the timely and cumbersome process of actually moving an artillery piece, which could not maneuver with anything like the speed and agility of an infantry unit. Mobility was limited by a reliance on animals and men, rather than mechanized vehicles, to transport the pieces (and ammunition) over unmetalled roads.[89] The limited number of horses on the peninsula available to move the guns, as well as the physical vulnerability of animals and the difficulty of replacing them should they become casualties, further complicated this task.

In addition to these dangers, Allied artillery would again also be limited by the lack of time available for preparation and registration. Lieutenant-General Hunter-Weston, who had commanded VIII Corps at Helles until he was invalided in July, had warned GHQ in March that without "long and careful preparations and the expenditure of an enormous amount of High Explosive Gun ammunition," an advance of this nature would stall and develop into "a second Crimea."[90] As previously discussed, momentum, technology, experience, and the desire for the breakthrough offensive denied time for adequate registration, while a lack of ammunition, especially high-explosive shells, prevented mass concentrations of artillery firepower at Gallipoli. Also, throughout the entire third phase the artillery would not have been able to rely to any significant extent upon the naval guns, which could have little effect on the concealed Ottoman guns on this flank. It can therefore be concluded that unless *all* Ottoman resistance had been quashed beforehand, this phase would in all likelihood have faltered due to the vulnerability of the guns as they advanced across the open ground between Gaba Tepe and Maidos. Success was, in fact, a long way off. For the offensive to be declared as nearing a successful completion, the artillery, in conjunction with the infantry and navy, was required to destroy the forts and silence the enemy's mobile artillery that protected the minefields.

A Breakdown in Fire Support

Aside from being beyond the means of the infantry, the August Offensive was also beyond the capabilities of the MEF's artillery. The artillery neither succeeded during the offensive nor could hope to succeed during the subsequent phases. The plan, conceived and developed without respect to artillery abilities and limitations, was too ambitious for the insufficient, unreliable, and often obsolete guns available for the August Offensive. The lack of artillery plans fated the offensive for failure. Without such a plan Allied gunners would face numerous difficulties, particularly in the application of unobserved fire and the preregistration of selected targets. These factors would combine to negate the ability of the artillery to adopt an offensive rather than a mere supporting role, at a time when the infantry advance was reliant on accurate artillery fire support. Should the offensive have proceeded across the peninsula, it is clear that much work would be required within each sector to enable the forward movement of the guns. It would have been a difficult enough process to move the field artillery pieces into their new positions, let alone the to carry out the unfeasible task of heaving the heavy artillery onto the Sari Bair Ridge. Should all of this have been accomplished, the key targets would have still been beyond the range of the majority of the available guns, which themselves proved unreliable. The Ottoman overland routes could be shelled, but this task would be confounded by ammunition unavailability, fire inaccuracy, observation difficulties, and problems with interservice communication. Nonetheless, had this been successful, the highly vulnerable guns would then be required to advance across the peninsula to aid the navy in its attempt at silencing the forts that skirted the Narrows—an unlikely proposition.

The Obstacles of a Naval Offensive

Let us temporarily ignore the fact that there was no plan for offensive naval action in August, and assume that the navy would indeed have made an attempt had the first three phases been completed successfully. Such an exercise enables a consideration of what would have been required of the naval forces during the fourth phase of operations as well as an analysis of its capability of achieving its objective—and the overall operational objective of the August Offensive.

Apart from the tasks of supply, transport, fire support, submarine patrols, and blockades discussed previously, the Allied fleet would have had to make another 18 March–type attempt to force a passage through the Narrows if the August Offensive were to succeed. Before this could be done, Vice-Admiral de Robeck's force would first have had to sweep the minefields, silence the forts and minefield batteries, and destroy the Ottoman torpedo tubes that lined the Narrows.[91] As proven by the naval failures in February and March, it is clear that attempting a passage through the Narrows in August would invariably have been a long and difficult process.

The Admiralty realized the difficulty and expected any attempt to "be a slow, long job."[92] Consequently, the prolonged land offensive would invariably have been followed by a prolonged naval operation. As this effort unfolded, the fleet would have been increasingly susceptible to the presence of German U-boats—which, as seen by the sinking of HMT *Royal Edward* (13 August) and the attacks on HMS *Manica* (14 August) and HMS *Hector* (18 August), were active in mid-August. A drawn-out fourth phase naval offensive in August would be made even more difficult by the fact that there were fewer battleships than previously available, and the strength of the Ottoman defenses had, in fact, increased. In reality, de Robeck's task in August would have been *more* difficult than it had been during the EMS's unsuccessful attempts earlier in the year.

The Ottoman minefields were the first obstacle to the fleet, and would have had to be cleared before any warships could attempt a passage into the Sea of Marmara. These ten lines of contact mines, which were protected by a combination of submarine nets, mobile and static howitzer and field gun batteries and forts, and an interlocking network of searchlights, were, in Hamilton's opinion, the "real defence of Constantinople."[93] With the mines spaced forty-four to fifty-five yards apart, the chance of getting through the unswept minefields unharmed into the Sea of Marmara was calculated at one in one hundred.[94] The first step in clearing these mines would have been to silence the eighty-seven guns of the Ottoman minefield batteries; but these were protected by the forts (although, to be fair, these should have been destroyed by the infantry and field artillery prior to the commencement of naval operations), which were in turn protected by the mobile howitzers—which could not be located.[95] Due to the dangers and difficulties of sweeping the minefields during daylight hours, in March this had been undertaken at night. However, by August, night operations were regularly picked up by the Ottoman searchlights, which proved extraordinarily difficult to put out of action.[96] Clearing the minefields, therefore, would be no easy process. Rear-Admiral Mark Kerr, chief of the British naval mission to Greece and commander in chief of the Greek navy, was of the strong opinion that the Ottoman minefields could not be swept. In a letter to the historian, John North, he noted: "Minesweeping is a slow operation. . . . The Dardanelles mine-fields were several miles long, and to sweep a passage through would have been a very long and slow job if there were no batteries, and with batteries firing at them, it was an absolute impossibility."[97] Indeed, it proved a long and difficult process for the Allies to clear the mines after the Armistice—and this was with the aid of the Ottomans—and not in the face of hostile fire.[98]

While the sweeping force was stronger (in terms of size, speed, and quality) in August than it had been in March, the force was still untrained. It would therefore have required time (that it did not have) to become familiar with the process of sweeping mines in a confined area while under fire. As the August sweeping force was never used to sweep the minefields, it is not possible to know whether it overcame the difficulties of the system employed in

February and March.[99] The balance of evidence therefore suggests that the Admiralty's support of de Robeck was a wise choice. What can be said with surety, however, was that even if the minefields could be cleared, this would have been but the first stage of an increasingly difficult naval operation.

In addition to the fixed minefields, there were up to eighty-six floating mines in the Dardanelles by 5 August 1915. While these did not cause any Allied casualties, the EMS was particularly unnerved by their presence, fearing that there was little defense against them.[100] The EMS, and de Robeck in particular, was also conscious of the danger that Ottoman torpedo tubes posed to the sweeping force.[101] This fear was largely unwarranted, with only three tubes actually existing at Kilid Bahr; but the naval command did not know this at the time.[102]

Hostile Shores

The next task required of the fleet, if the August Offensive were to succeed, would be to silence the mobile howitzers and mortars that lined both the European and Asiatic shores of the Dardanelles. This task, however, would be extremely difficult because the guns were hidden in the folds of the terrain and could quickly alter their position if located.[103] Commander Isham Gibson, a gunnery officer on HMS *Albion* (and later a beach master at Suvla during the August Offensive) on 18 March admitted that "we fired at the [mobile] batteries to try and silence them but the country is so ideal for concealed batteries in the scrub and gullies everywhere we didn't do much good I'm afraid."[104] While figures are not specific for August 1915, data from March 1915 suggests there were at least thirty-six Ottoman howitzers and twenty-four mortars in these gullies.[105] The primary function of these concealed batteries was to protect the Ottoman forts by keeping the Allied ships moving, at distance, thus reducing the accuracy of the ships' fire. Indeed, the attacks on the coastal defenses in February and March failed largely because the Allied ships could not locate the mobile howitzers and were therefore unable to anchor to stabilize firing.[106]

Nevertheless, presuming that by this stage of operations the army would have already silenced the forts, the question is what impact these concealed mobile guns would then have on the Allied fleet. Opinion differed in this regard. Keyes felt that they were "a greatly exaggerated menace" as he considered their fire to be "most inaccurate" and that they could cause only minimal damage. Keyes also felt that "the odds against moving ships being hit were very considerable."[107] Vice-Admiral de Robeck disagreed, and felt that they could not be silenced (at least, not by the navy) and could pose a real danger to Allied vessels attempting to pass the Narrows.[108] The wider point is that, even if the concealed guns did not hit the Allied warships, they would no doubt pose a problem for merchant shipping, which was to be used to supply the fleet once it began operating in the Sea of Marmara.[109]

Again, presuming that the MEF controlled the Gallipoli Peninsula and the forts on the European shore, would this have been sufficient to enable the fleet to operate safely inside the Straits? What about the Asiatic forts? These, like their European counterparts, were a fundamental element of the Ottoman defenses and were a significant obstacle to the progress of any naval operation. Allied intelligence from late August suggested that the entire Asiatic coast from Nagara to south of Kum Kale was "carefully fortified" and that "most of the damage inflicted on the forts by our ships [in February and March] has been repaired."[110] Vice-Admiral de Robeck realized the importance of silencing the Asiatic forts but also considered his force incapable of doing this. Like those on the European shore, he believed the Asiatic forts could only be silenced by land troops.[111] Yet, in General Hamilton's opinion, holding the Gallipoli Peninsula was enough.[112]

The problem was that, apart from Hamilton's brief and isolated mention in June of his reserve divisions possibly being employed on the Asiatic shore—there was no real intention to land troops on this coast.[113] Without troops to destroy the guns of these forts (never mind the difficulty of landing such troops, supplying them, and supporting them with artillery fire, and the actual task of the troops' fighting their way along the Asiatic coast), the Allied fleet would have had to attempt the task on its own. But the warships were incapable of permanently silencing the Ottoman forts—especially when protected by concealed howitzers, which, even in the case represented above, would still remain on the Asiatic shore.[114] The forts could only have been permanently put out of action by a direct hit—the chances of which were estimated at less than 2.25 percent.[115] Without silencing the forts, de Robeck's fleet, if it had attempted to proceed up the Dardanelles, would have been an easy target for the guns of the Asiatic forts.[116] Ignoring the Asiatic defenses could only result in failure, but it seems that ignorance of them was an inherent part of the August plans.

If the EMS had somehow been successful in all of its fourth phase offensive operations—and, as noted, this is an extremely dubious proposition—the question then becomes one of the overall strategic potential of the August Offensive. While it is not the purpose of this book to enter into the vigorous strategic debates about the Gallipoli Campaign, it is necessary to note that opinion even within the navy was divided. In this regard, Vice-Admiral de Robeck—knowing that success would mean a fight against the Turko-German fleet in the Sea of Marmara, and fearful that the Straits would be closed behind his ships—was not confident in the navy's ability to achieve is broad strategic objective. In this context, it is unsurprising that he was unwilling to risk the fleet for an operation in August in which he had little faith.[117] It is also noteworthy that in view of the tenacious Ottoman resistance displayed thus far, de Robeck believed that even if the navy had succeeded, "it did not appear that the arrival of the British Fleet off Constantinople would have the desired effect, namely, of a revolution."[118] Even the first lord of the admiralty, who was a staunch supporter of the campaign, was not convinced that operational victory would lead to strategic success.[119]

Unsurprisingly, Churchill, Keyes, and Vice-Admiral Oliver (chief of the naval staff at the Admiralty) all opposed this view, rather believing that if the fleet succeeded in getting into the Sea of Marmara the Ottomans would have been unable to continue the war.[120] What was expected of the fleet at this point is unclear: plans were not discussed and instructions were never issued.[121] As the Ottoman General Staff noted, "It is impossible to estimate the situation which would have arisen if the British Fleet had forced their way past the forts, past the minefields, and entered the Marmara."[122] The battle would be far from complete, and victory by no means guaranteed, even had all phases of the August Offensive been completed successfully.

Keeping the Force Fed and Watered

Perhaps the most important factor to consider in assessing the MEF's capabilities for prolonged offensive operations is logistics. Could an adequate and timely flow of items have been sustained for a prolonged period, thus maintaining the MEF as it advanced across the peninsula in accord with the operational objectives of the August Offensive? What were the likely logistic complications that would have been faced during the subsequent phases of the offensive? In investigating these issues, the chapter pays particular attention to the real intention of Suvla Bay as a logistic hub, and what, if anything, Suvla could ever have added to the MEF's logistic capabilities.

The manpower strength of the MEF in August was almost double that of April 1915.[123] There were, therefore twice as many mouths to feed, ammunition to supply, and men to water in August than experienced in the previous largest Allied offensive at Gallipoli. As outlined in chapters 5 and 6, the supply and transport system was incapable of supplying these men with all their needs during the August Offensive, where the advance made was, at its farthest, three thousand yards from the beach.[124] The supply routes for the second phase, had it been attempted and had it succeeded, would have been roughly equal to this distance, but rather than delivering supplies to a similar front line, the supply and transport system would have been required to supplement a perimeter almost three times larger than that previously supplied (at Anzac alone).[125]

If the third phase of the August Offensive had been pushed to its conclusion, the distance of the supply routes between Gaba Tepe and Maidos alone would have been in the vicinity of 4.6 miles. Until such time that the fourth phase succeeded, and the navy were able to safely enter the Straits and disembark supplies there, all supplies would have had to be transported from one side of the peninsula to the other. When compared to the farthest point reached during the *failed* first phase of the offensive, this represented a 168 percent increase in the distance that supplies would have had to move. This increase alone is a clear indication that the pressures and expectations placed on the supply and transport system would have become increasingly difficult should the August Offensive wish to achieve its overall operational objective. Such a system could not cope with the first phase of the attack, and it could never have dealt with the distances involved in the subsequent phases.

Distance was not the only obstacle that the supply and transport system would have had to overcome if the August Offensive had been pushed to a successful conclusion. Just like the troops who would do the fighting, the logistic system would have had to operate through tough terrain and under constant enemy pressure. Supply convoys, especially those traveling across the open ground between Gaba Tepe and Maidos, would have had little protection against the Ottoman artillery that would have inevitably focused on them. Furthermore, it is important to remember that there were not enough troops available to fight their way across the peninsula, let alone man a greatly extended L-of-C. As was found years later at Normandy, switching from short to long supply routes brought with it a range of new administrative challenges.[126] The various administrative staffs involved in the August Offensive had failed to successfully overcome the difficulties faced during the first phase of operations, where a large proportion of the fighting could still be described as static warfare. Any advance across the peninsula, especially a rapid one like that envisaged, would have reintroduced mobility to the battlefield. Given that the administrative demands of mobile warfare were invariably more complex than those experienced when the battle was static, the subsequent phases would likely have been well beyond the administrative abilities of the MEF. Lord Kitchener himself recognized this, and doubted whether a functional L-of-C could be maintained across the peninsula. In a letter to Prime Minister Asquith, he noted that obtaining proper L-of-C "is the main difficulty in carrying out successful operations on the Peninsula."[127]

Kitchener was right to be concerned. Contrary to the beliefs of the DST, Brigadier-General Koe, there was never enough transport to distribute the requisite stores and supplies across the peninsula.[128] GHQ had considered the need for more transport, realizing that if the offensive proceeded beyond the Sari Bair Ridge a large proportion of the force would be stationed some distance from the established logistic bases.[129] As a result, Hamilton asked the naval forces to move five thousand to seven thousand horses from Alexandria to Mudros, which he intended to land on the peninsula once all reinforcing troops had been disembarked. These, he hoped, would allow the force to be "sufficiently mobile to carry the operations to a conclusion."[130] These intentions did not translate into actions. In any case, unless the supply of water and forage had been exponentially improved, these horses simply could not have been accommodated on the peninsula.[131] The task was therefore left to the insufficient number of mules.

By 27 August there were 2,344 mules at Suvla and 2,106 at Anzac.[132] There were another 1,685 mules available at Mudros, but, given the lack of space and forage or water for them ashore and given that it would take three weeks' continuous work to land them, all bar 100 were eventually returned to Alexandria.[133] It would have been the duty of these 4,450 mules to support any advance across the peninsula, while at the same time supplying those troops who still garrisoned the old sectors. Unlike the first phase, however, these mules could not have been expected to do multiple journeys given that a return trip to Maidos would amount to over nine miles. At this time the force at Suvla and Anzac numbered approximately seventy-six thousand (not accounting for casualties).[134] Based on earlier calculations of half water rations and considering that mules could only make one journey a day, 4,750 mules would have been required to transport the basic water requirements of a force this size during the subsequent phases. Thus, the MEF would have been three hundred mules short of the *minimum* number required for the *sole* purpose of transporting water, not to mention other supplies. Unless more animals arrived and rations were reduced, the work of the mules would exponentially rise.[135]

Putting the mules aside, any increase in the length of the L-of-C on the peninsula would have had a dramatic impact on the mule drivers and supply personnel. At the end of August, Major Frederick Francis, OC of No. 4 Company, 1st Australian Divisional Train, noted, "My Supply details are commencing to feel the strain badly of over 4 months hard work under most trying circumstances." Since landing in April, 45 percent of his personnel had been sent away sick, and none had yet returned.[136] The responsibility of getting supplies to the fighting troops during the push across the peninsula, however, would have continued to fall upon the shoulders of these exhausted and depleted units.

Suvla Bay as a Logistic Hub

Thus far the analysis put forth has not considered the role that Suvla would have played in supplying the advance across the peninsula. As noted in chapter 1, the primary purpose of landing an Allied force at Suvla Bay was to create a safe base that could be used to supply the MEF as it progressed beyond Sari Bair.[137] It is important to remember that the August Offensive failed, in an operational sense, on the slopes of Sari Bair Ridge, and not the plains of Suvla.

While operations at Suvla were a fiasco, this must be viewed within its proper context. Being created as a logistic hub for the subsequent phases, Suvla could not provide much assistance *until* the first phase of the offensive had succeeded at Sari Bair. That the ANZAC failed to achieve its objectives should be attributed to that corps, not to Stopford and IX Corps, as has traditionally been the case. In this light, the failure of IX Corps to obtain the heights surrounding Suvla Bay is inconsequential and nothing more than an embarrassment to the British Army. It was not a cause of the failure of the August Offensive. The real usefulness of Suvla must be understood in terms of what it potentially could have offered to the offensive as a whole, rather than as an illustration of the poor performance of IX Corps.

Due to a lack of information detailing precisely how Suvla was to be used, and what routes supplies would take from there during any forward movement, the only practical point of analysis is the overall suitability of Suvla as a logistic hub. It should be noted at the outset that Suvla was situated on the broadest part of the Gallipoli Peninsula and, as such, was a long way from Maidos. If the decision had been made to send supplies through the Anafarta Gap and thence southeast to Maidos, not only would the transport from Suvla have had to overcome difficult, if not impassable terrain, but a large force would have been required *just* to hold the L-of-C.[138] If, however, Suvla were to be used as a large depot, whereby supplies would be sent on to the Anzac sector—presumably a tramline would link the two—it must be assessed in these terms.[139]

The principal reason why Suvla was originally selected as a logistic hub for August was because of its beaches. During the planning of the offensive, there were grave concerns that as the offensive progressed across the peninsula the weather could turn, thus rendering Anzac Cove unsuitable for landing and stockpiling stores. Suvla, it was felt, would offer better protection from this eventuality than Anzac Cove, and therefore would remove lingering anxieties about a broken supply chain.[140] But how suitable was Suvla for the purpose?

In terms of the increased space for the storage of supplies, Suvla far exceeded Anzac.[141] In fact, the very possession of Suvla improved the storage facilities at Anzac because it removed the Ottoman observation post on this flank, which in turn opened up the use of North Beach. In overall terms, however, as an advanced base Suvla was little better than Anzac. While it was found that during northerly winds supplies could be landed almost anywhere in Suvla Bay, or on the stretch of coast between Nibrunesi Point and Anzac Cove, such was not the case during southerly winds.[142] In addition, from a naval perspective, the approach to Suvla Bay was so difficult when a southwesterly wind blew that it was estimated that at least twenty ships would need to be sunk as a breakwater to provide sufficient shelter inside the bay.[143] During poor weather, therefore, Suvla Bay shared many of the vulnerabilities of Anzac, and as such could no more guarantee a continual flow of supplies than the Anzac beachhead during unfavorable weather.

This vulnerability of Suvla Bay leads to the important question of whether the August Offensive, in all its planned phases, was ever logistically viable. While nothing in war is certain, that the answer is anything but no, is highly improbable. A system that could not cope with the demands of the first phase of operations surely could not have coped with the increased physical and administrative demands that would have been inevitable had the offensive proceeded into its second, third, and fourth phases. Logistics then, is but one more piece to the puzzle, and another thorn in the side of the "near success" myth. Had the supply and transport system been up to the task, there still would have been all of the other difficulties of planning, mobility, fire support, and naval inactivity to overcome before the August Offensive could even stand a chance of success.

Conclusion

This book set out to reevaluate the August Offensive at Gallipoli in 1915. In particular, it sought to analyze whether the MEF was ever capable of achieving the far-reaching objectives it had set for itself. Closely associated with this central purpose was the secondary aim of testing the time-honored and historically accepted idea that the August Offensive was a "near success" and could have, or indeed would have, succeeded if only the Allies had been luckier or had been able to push just a little bit further. Such issues and questions have been investigated by focusing primarily on the operational level of war and by examining issues such as planning, command, mobility, fire support, interservice cooperation, and logistics. This approach, based overwhelmingly on archival and primary source research, not only has allowed this book to avoid much of the nationalistic rhetoric that so often pervades narratives of the August Offensive but also has opened the way for the first detailed and objective account of the real military limitations and operational potential of the August Offensive.

The August Offensive was a complete and utter failure. The Dardanelles Commission, which examined how and why the campaign went wrong, realized this and labeled the offensive "a severe disappointment to the Government and the country."[1] This book has gone further and demonstrated that contrary to the long-standing historiographical interpretation, the MEF did not approach anything that even resembled success during August 1915, *nor could it*. The offensive was, in fact, as good as doomed from the start.

The four-phase Allied plan for the August Offensive, which evolved from a local operation to a large-scale offensive like those attempted on the Western Front at the same time, was always far too ambitious for a force of its size, especially one fighting in unfavorable terrain, struggling with limited resources, and battling a determined and capable enemy. Furthermore, there was no contingency plan in case of any setback, and those who formulated the plan invested too much in the potential of maneuver in an age of modern industrialized positional warfare. As the first phase highlighted, the MEF was not even close to being sufficiently mobile to achieve its objectives. The troops were sick, exhausted, and too few in number; the intercommunication system, overworked and inefficient; and the terrain, too complex to allow for a coordinated movement. These problems would only have worsened had the MEF attempted to advance across the peninsula in accord with the operational objectives of the offensive. Casualties, sickness, and the need to defend an expanding perimeter would have further depleted the number of troops available for subsequent pushes.

Nor was Allied field artillery capable of supporting the infantry to the levels necessary for success. The number of guns and ammunition was insufficient for the task, and those at hand were too often obsolete or unreliable. Moreover, in the absence of an artillery plan for the subsequent phases—and the difficulties of observation and of moving the guns into positions that could cover an infantry advance toward Maidos—had the third phase been attempted, the troops would soon have outrun their land-based artillery support. Naval gunfire support was available but offered little more than a boost to morale in terrain that was distinctly unfavorable for flat-trajectory fire. This limited naval support would also have fallen away if the offensive had progressed into its subsequent phases, whence the EMS would have been required for offensive operations: a role it was not willing or ready to undertake, and one that General Hamilton was reluctant to impose on his naval counterpart, Vice-Admiral John de Robeck. Without offensive naval action during the fourth phase, however, the August Offensive could not hope to succeed. Further hindering the complex multiphase operation was a confused and inefficient logistic system. Administration on the L-of-C was disjointed and led to serious delays in the movement of supplies to the peninsula. Even more crucial, however, was the almost complete breakdown of the supply and transport system from the beaches inland during the offensive—again a task whose difficulty would inevitably have compounded during a prolonged offensive across the peninsula.

As noted in the introduction, the failure of any of those aspects mentioned above creates difficulties and can singularly cause defeat. This book has shown that there were major failures in *all* of these areas. The August Offensive was not a viable operation of war. The

MEF was not capable of achieving its objectives. Success was a distant dream. It is with some hope that this reevaluation of the August Offensive will help quash the "near success" myth once and for all, or at the very least will demonstrate to future authors that the August Offensive was a complex, multiphase, multinational operation, and should be analyzed as such.

Perhaps even more important, however, than debunking well-entrenched misinterpretations about the August Offensive is the significance of considering the offensive within the wider context of British military doctrine and offensive warfare in the early years of the First World War. In this sense, the August Offensive represents a useful case study that provides further evidence of the flawed approach to offensive warfare (both Allied and Central Powers) in 1915: one based on outdated methods when a fresh approach was required, and one that was not yet ready to accept the realities of attrition.

It was never the intention of the author to apportion blame for the failure of the August Offensive, but rather to analyze the MEF's potential, or physical ability, to succeed, and thereby help rectify the contemporary historical misunderstanding surrounding the offensive. To criticize the commanders for attempting such a large-scale maneuver would be both anachronistic and undertaken with the benefit of hindsight. What is important, however, is to understand the crucial question of why Hamilton, and to a lesser extent Birdwood, chose to embark on such an ambitious venture in August 1915. The answer is essentially one of education and institutionalization: it is what their entire military careers had taught them to do.[2]

Five new divisions being sent to Gallipoli from the UK in July 1915 presented Hamilton with another opportunity, after months of stalemate, for the type of decisive victory and the return to a war of movement that he and his ilk considered to be the fundamental nature of war. It is difficult to imagine Hamilton or anyone else, in this context, taking any other action. In addition, when compared to similar approaches being taken on the Western Front at that time, it is difficult to criticize Hamilton for his attempt. This was war and risks had to be taken. What cannot be forgiven, though, is Hamilton's (and his staff's) lack of forethought and inability to undertake an appropriate risk analysis. He should have realized, for example, that there were not enough troops for the subsequent phases of his plan, and that his prime objective during these phases were outside the maximum range of most of his guns. Such observations made throughout this book are drawn from the same data and maps available to Hamilton at the time, and therefore ought to have been clear to his staff prior to the offensive. But again, such errors were not limited solely to the August Offensive, or indeed to the MEF in the first two years of the First World War.

The August Offensive, like the Battles of Neuve Chapelle and Loos on the Western Front, is further evidence of the inherent weakness in the British approach to warfare in 1915: a year of failed offensives marred by "confusion and catastrophe."[3] All three are clear examples of the unsuccessful implementation of prewar British doctrine, and the failure to adapt to the still unfamiliar and unwelcome conditions of modern war. Similarly, all three show quite clearly that the British (including the Dominions)—whether on the Western Front or at Gallipoli—lacked the operational experience to achieve such ambitious plans at this stage of the war.[4] These examples also proved that in situations of positional stalemate, battles with limited goals were more likely to succeed than those with far-reaching objectives.[5] These lessons were by no means limited to the British. Indeed, while all four German and three French attempts (of a considerable scale) to break the opposing lines on the Western Front—in the six months before June 1915—met with some initial success, a British Cabinet document noted that all had "gradually petered out owing to exhaustion of men or of ammunition" and none "had any material effect upon the general situation."[6] They had all aimed for too much. It appears that this information was either not passed onto the MEF or, if it was, did not make much of an impression.

The battles of 1915 need to be examined in this light. Like those on the Western Front, the August Offensive represents the very beginning of the development of a new Allied way of fighting in the First World War—the lessons of which eventually led to success in 1918. By approaching the entire Gallipoli Campaign, or indeed other 1915 battles for that matter, from the same operational framework used in this book, it may be possible to gain a better understanding of the British offensive model of 1915. From this, future historians may draw further conclusions as to what extent the lessons learned informed the learning process that eventually led to Allied victory in the First World War. In this context, the objectives, conclusions, and methods of this book might well serve as a practical basis for further research.

Appendix I

MEF Order of Battle, 6 August 1915

GHQ
Commander in Chief: Gen. Sir Ian Hamilton*

VIII CORPS
GOC: Maj.-Gen. W. Douglas*
29th Div.   Maj.-Gen. H. de B. de Lisle*
   86th Bde.   Brig.-Gen. O. C. Wolley-Dod*
      2/Royal Fusiliers
      1/Royal Munster Fusiliers
      1/Lancashire Fusiliers
      1/Royal Dublin Fusiliers
   87th Bde.   Lt.-Col. C. H. T. Lucas*
      2/South Wales Borderers
      1/Royal Inniskilling Fusiliers
      1/King's Own Scottish Borderers
      1/Border Regt.
   88th Bde.   Brig.-Gen. D. E. Cayley*
      4/Worcestershire Regt.
      1/Essex Regt.
      2/Hampshire Regt.
      1/5th Royal Scots
42nd (East Lancashire) Div.   Brig.-Gen. W. R. Marshall*
   125th Bde.   Brig.-Gen. H. C. Frith
      1/5th Lancashire Fusiliers
      1/6th Lancashire Fusiliers
      1/7th Lancashire Fusiliers
      1/8th Lancashire Fusiliers
   126th Bde.   Brig.-Gen. Viscount Hampden*
      1/4th East Lancashire Regt.
      1/5th East Lancashire Regt.
      1/9th Manchester Regt.
      1/10th Manchester Regt.

*Served in South Africa, 1899–1902

127th Bde.   Brig.-Gen. Hon. H. E. Lawrence*
    1/5th Manchester Regt.
    1/6th Manchester Regt.
    1/7th Manchester Regt.
    1/8th Manchester Regt.

52nd (Lowland) Div.   Maj.-Gen. G. C. A. Egerton
   155th Bde.   Brig.-Gen. J. F. Erskine*
      1/4th Royal Scots Fusiliers
      1/5th Royal Scots Fusiliers
      1/4th King's Own Scottish Borderers
      1/5th King's Own Scottish Borderers
   156th Bde.   Brig.-Gen. H. G. Casson*
      1/4th Royal Scots
      1/7th Royal Scots
      1/7th Scottish Rifles
      1/8th Scottish Rifles
   157th Bde.   Brig.-Gen. P. W. Hendry*
      1/5th Highland Light Infantry
      1/6th Highland Light Infantry
      1/7th Highland Light Infantry
      1/5th Argyll and Southerland Highlanders

Royal Naval Div.   Maj.-Gen. A. Paris*
   1st Bde.   Brig.-Gen. D. Mercer
      Drake Bn.
      Nelson Bn.
      Hawke Bn.
      Hood Bn.
   2nd Bde.   Brig.-Gen. C. N. Trotman
      No. 1 Bn. Royal Marine Light Infantry
      No. 2 Bn. Royal Marine Light Infantry
      Howe Bn.
      Anson Bn.

IX CORPS
GOC: Lt.-Gen. Hon. Sir F. W. Stopford*
10th (Irish) Div.   Lt.-Gen. Sir B. T. Mahon*

---

*Served in South Africa, 1899–1902

29th Bde. Brig.-Gen. R. J. Cooper*
    10/Hampshire Regt.
    6/Royal Irish Rifles
    5/Connaught Rangers
    6/Leinster Regt.
30th Bde. Brig.-Gen. L. L. Nicol*
    6/Royal Munster Fusiliers
    7/Royal Munster Fusiliers
    6/Royal Dublin Fusiliers
    7/Royal Dublin Fusiliers
31st Bde. Brig.-Gen. F. F. Hill*
    5/Royal Inniskilling Fusiliers
    6/Royal Inniskilling Fusiliers
    5/Royal Irish Fusiliers
    6/Royal Irish Fusiliers

11th (Northern) Div. Maj.-Gen. F. Hammersley*
    32nd Bde. Brig.-Gen. H. Haggard*
        9/West Yorks Regt.
        6/Yorkshire Regt.
        8/West Riding Regt.
        6/York and Lancaster Regt.
    33rd Bde. Brig.-Gen. R. P. Maxwell
        6/Lincolnshire Regt.
        6/The Border Regt.
        7/South Staffordshire Regt.
        9/Sherwood Foresters
    34th Bde. Brig.-Gen. W. H. Sitwell*
        8/Northumberland Fusiliers
        9/Lancashire Fusiliers
        5/Dorsetshire Regt.
        11/Manchester Regt.

13th (Western) Div. Maj.-Gen. F. C. Shaw
    38th Bde. Brig.-Gen. A. H. Baldwin*
        6/King's Own
        6/East Lancashire Regt.
        6/South Lancashire Regt.
        6/Loyal North Lancashire Regt.

*Served in South Africa, 1899–1902

39th Bde.   Brig.-Gen. W. de S. Cayley*
    9/Royal Warwickshire Regt.
    7/Gloucestershire Regt.
    9/Worcestershire Regt.
    7/North Staffordshire Regt.
40th Bde.   Brig.-Gen. J. H. du B. Travers*
    4/South Wales Borderers
    8/Royal Welch Fusiliers
    8/Cheshire Regt.
    5/Wiltshire Regt.

ANZAC
GOC: Lt.-Gen. Sir W. R. Birdwood*
1st Australian Div.   Maj.-Gen. H. B. Walker*
    1st Australian Bde.   Col. N. M. Smythe*
        1st Bn.
        2nd Bn.
        3rd Bn.
        4th Bn.
    2nd Australian Bde.   Col. J. K. Forsyth
        5th Bn.
        6th Bn.
        7th Bn.
        8th Bn.
    3rd Australian Bde.   Brig.-Gen. E. G. Sinclair Maclagan*
        9th Bn.
        10th Bn.
        11th Bn.
        12th Bn.
NZ&A Div.   Maj.-Gen. Sir A. J. Godley*
    New Zealand Bde.   Brig.-Gen. F. E. Johnson*
        Auckland Bn.
        Canterbury Bn.
        Otago Bn.
        Wellington Bn.

*Served in South Africa, 1899–1902

    4th Australian Bde.   Brig.-Gen. J. Monash
        13th Bn.
        14th Bn.
        15th Bn.
        16th Bn.
    NZMR Bde.   Brig.-Gen. A. H. Russell
        Auckland Mounted Rifles Regt.
        Canterbury Mounted Rifles Regt.
        Wellington Mounted Rifles Regt.
        Otago Mounted Rifles Regt.
    1st ALH Bde.   Brig.-Gen. H. G. Chauvel*
        1st Light Horse Regt.
        2nd Light Horse Regt.
        3rd Light Horse Regt.
Corps Troops
    2nd ALH Bde.   Brig.-Gen. G. de L. Ryrie*
        5th Light Horse Regt.
        6th Light Horse Regt.
        7th Light Horse Regt.
    3rd ALH Bde.   Brig.-Gen. F. G. Hughes
        8th Light Horse Regt.
        9th Light Horse Regt.
        10th Light Horse Regt.
Attached
    29th Indian Bde.   Maj.-Gen. H. V. Cox*
        14th Sikhs
        1/5th Gurkha Rifles
        1/6th Gurkha Rifles
        2/10th Gurkha Rifles

CORPS EXPEDITIONNAIRE D'ORIENT
Commander: Gen. Bailloud

1st Div.   Gen. Brulard
    1st Metropolitan Bde.
        175th Regt.
        1st Regt. de marche d'Afrique
        Foreign Legion Bn. (2 companies)

*Served in South Africa, 1899–1902

2nd Colonial Bde.
    4th Colonial Regt.
    6th Colonial Regt.
3rd Metropolitan Bde.
    176th Regt.
    2nd Regt. de marche d'Afrique
4th Colonial Bde.
    7th Colonial Regt.
    8th Colonial Regt.

RESERVE
53rd (Welsh) Div.   Maj.-Gen. Hon. J. E. Lindley*
    158th Bde.   Brig.-Gen. E. A. Cowans*
        1/5th Royal Welch Fusiliers
        1/6th Royal Welch Fusiliers
        1/7th Royal Welch Fusiliers
        1/1st Herefordshire Fusiliers
    159th Bde.   Brig.-Gen. F. C. Lloyd*
        1/4th Cheshire Regt.
        1/7th Cheshire Regt.
        1/4th Welch Regt.
        1/5th Welch Regt.
    160th Bde.   Brig.-Gen. J. J. F. Hume*
        2/4th Queen's (Royal West Surrey Regt.)
        1/4th Royal Sussex Regt.
        2/4th Royal West Kent Regt.
        2/10th Middlesex Regt.
54th (East Anglian) Div.   Maj.-Gen. F. S. Inglefield*
    161st Bde.   Brig.-Gen. F. F. W. Daniell*
        1/4th Essex Regt.
        1/5th Essex Regt.
        1/6th Essex Regt.
        1/7th Essex Regt.
    162nd Bde.   Brig.-Gen. C. de Winton*
        1/5th Bedfordshire Regt.
        1/4th Northamptonshire Regt.
        1/10th London Regt.
        1/11th London Regt.

*Served in South Africa, 1899–1902

163rd Bde.   Brig.-Gen. C. M. Brunker*
    1/4th Norfolk Regt.
    1/5th Norfolk Regt.
    1/5th Suffolk Regt.
    1/8th Hampshire Regt.

*Served in South Africa, 1899–1902

Appendix 2

Artillery Available for the Offensive

Unit	Weapon type	Number	Remarks
Helles			
460th (How.) Bde. RFA (29th Div.)	4.5-inch howitzer	4	
15th Bde. RHA (B, L, Y Batteries) (29th Div.)	18-pounder	12	
17th Bde. RFA (13th, 26th, 92nd Batteries) (29th Div.)	18-pounder	12	
147th Bde. RFA (10th, 97th, 368th Batteries) (29th Div.)	18-pounder	12	
90th Heavy Battery RGA (29th Div.)	60-pounder	4	
14th Siege Battery RGA (29th Div.)	6-inch howitzer	4	
1/1st East Lancashire Bde. RFA (5th, 6th Batteries) (42nd Div.)	15-pounder BLC gun	8	
1/3rd East Lancashire Bde. RFA (18th, 19th, 20th Batteries) (42nd Div.)	15-pounder BLC gun	12	
1/4th East Lancashire (How.) Bde. RFA (1st and 2nd Cumberland (How.) Batteries) (42nd Div.)	5-inch BL howitzer	8	
1/2nd Lowland Bde. RFA (1/1st and 1/2nd Ayrshire, 1/1st Kirkcudbrightshire Batteries) (52nd Div.)	18-pounder	12	
66th Bde. RFA (A, B, C, D Batteries) (13th Div.)	18-pounder	16	
1st Bde. Aust. FA (1st, 2nd, 3rd Batteries) (1st Aust. Div.)	18-pounder	12	

APPENDIX 2

Unit	Weapon type	Number	Remarks
6th Battery, 2nd Bde. Aust. FA (1st Aust. Div.)	18-pounder	4	Returned to Anzac, 19 August
3rd Battery, NZ Artillery Bde. (NZ&A Div.)	18-pounder	4	Returned to Anzac, 18 August
91st Heavy Battery RGA	60-pounder	4	
Attached naval guns	12-pounder naval guns	4	
Helles total		**132**	

Anzac

Unit	Weapon type	Number	Remarks
2nd Aust. FAB (4th, 5th Batteries)	18-pounder	8	
3rd Aust. FAB (7th, 8th, 9th Batteries)	18-pounder	12	
1st NZ FA Battery	18-pounder	4	
2nd NZ FA Battery	18-pounder	4	
NZ (How.) Battery	4.5-inch howitzer	4	
7th Indian Mountain Artillery Bde. (21st and 26th Batteries)	10-pounder mountain gun	12	
69th (How.) Bde. RFA (A, B, C, D Batteries) (13th Div.)	5-inch howitzer	16	Attached to ANZAC to make up for ANZAC batteries at Helles
1/4th Lowland (How.) Bde. RFA (1/4th, 1/5th City of Glasgow Batteries) (52nd Div.)	5-inch howitzer	8	Sent to Suvla on 19 August
Heavy Battery (Aust. Div.)	4.7-inch gun 6-inch howitzer	1 2	
Additional with NZ&A Div.	6-inch howitzer	1	
Anzac total		**72**	

ARTILLERY AVAILABLE FOR THE OFFENSIVE

Unit	Weapon type	Number	Remarks
Landed at Anzac for transferral to Suvla			
10th Heavy Battery RGA	60-pounder	4	Remained at Anzac, as there was not enough room at Suvla
58th Bde. RFA (A, B, C, D Batteries) (11th Div.)	18-pounder	16	Arrived at Suvla 11/12 August
Total landed for transfer		**20**	
Suvla			
59th Bde. RFA (A, B, C, D Batteries) (11th Div.)	18-pounder	16	"A" Battery arrived 7 August, but other batteries did not arrive until the afternoon of 8 August
60th Bde. RFA (A, B, C, D Batteries) (11th Div.)	18-pounder	16	Remained at Alexandria. Did not arrive at Suvla until 25 October
4th Highland Mountain Artillery Bde. RGA (Argyllshire Battery, Ross and Cromarty Battery)	10-pounder	8	
15th Heavy Battery RGA	60-pounder	4	Arrived at Suvla on 10 August
54th Bde. RFA (A, B, C, D Batteries) (10th Div.)	18-pounder	16	Not sent to Suvla
55th Bde. RFA (A, B, C, D Batteries) (10th Div.)	18-pounder	16	Did not arrive at Suvla until 10 September

Unit	Weapon type	Number	Remarks
56th Bde. RFA (A, B, C, D Batteries) (10th Div.)	18-pounder	16	Did not arrive on the Peninsula until 23 August and were sent direct to Helles
57th (How.) Bde. RFA (A and D Batteries)	4.5-inch howitzer	8	"A" Battery arrived 16 August; "D" Battery, 17 August. Rest of Brigade remained at Mudros. This unit was sent to replace those batteries that had been returned to Anzac
Suvla total		**100**	
GRAND TOTAL		**324**	

Note: Aust. = Australian; BL = breech-loading; FA = Field Artillery; How. = Howitzer; NZ = New Zealand; RGA = Royal Garrison Artillery; RHA = Royal Horse Artillery.

APPENDIX 3

Range/Distance

RANGE

Gun type	Maximum range (yards)
On the peninsula	
60-pounder BL gun (Mk. I)	12,300
4.7-inch QF gun	10,000
4.5-inch QF howitzer	7,300
6-inch howitzer	7,000
18-pounder QF gun (Mk. I)	6,525
15-pounder BLC gun	6,000
10-pounder mountain gun	6,000
12-pounder QF naval landing gun	5,100
5-inch howitzer	4,800
In theater but not on the peninsula	
6-inch BL gun (Mk VII)	13,700
15-inch howitzer	10,795
9.2-inch howitzer	10,060

DISTANCE

From	To	Distance (yards)*
400 Plateau (western edge, as gun could not be placed on the summit)	Mal Tepe (summit)	6,025
	Boghali (western edge of village)	6,560
	Koja Dere (western edge of village)	3,610
	Kilia Liman (the middle of the harbor)	7,655
	Maidos (outskirts of village)	8,530
	Kilid Bahr (to the fort)	13,450
Scrubby Knoll (western slope of Third Ridge)	Mal Tepe (summit)	4,595
	Boghali (western edge of village)	5,075
	Koja Dere (western edge of village)	2,190

260 APPENDIX 3

From	To	Distance (yards)*
	Kilia Liman (the middle of the harbor)	5,650
	Maidos (outskirts of village)	7,875
	Kilid Bahr (to the fort)	13,015
Point 87 (Wine Glass Ridge)	Mal Tepe (summit)	5,360
	Boghali (western edge of village)	6,560
	Koja Dere (western edge of village)	3,720
	Kilia Liman (the middle of the harbor)	6,190
	Maidos (outskirts of village)	6,780
	Kilid Bahr (to the fort)	11,480
Chunuk Bair (Southwestern slope, heading toward Battleship Hill	Mal Tepe (summit)	5,030
	Boghali (western edge of village)	5,140
	Koja Dere (western edge of village)	2,845
	Kilia Liman (the middle of the harbor)	7,435
	Maidos (outskirts of village)	8,965
	Kilid Bahr (to the fort)	14,105
	Ak Bashi Liman (the middle of the harbor)	11,590
Hill 971 (Southwest of summit, toward Hill Q)	Mal Tepe (summit)	4,810
	Boghali (western edge of village)	4,595
	Koja Dere (western edge of village)	3,280
	Kilia Liman (the middle of the harbor)	7,700
	Maidos (outskirts of village)	9,405
	Kilid Bahr (to the fort)	14,655
	Ak Bashi Liman (the middle of the harbor)	10,720
Mal Tepe (summit)	Kilid Bahr (to the fort)	9,840
Achi Baba	Kilid Bahr (to the fort)	13,450
Maidos (southern proximity of town)	Kilid Bahr (to the fort)	4,375

Note: BL = breech-loading; QF = quick-firing.
*Distances calculated based on the Gallipoli 1:20,000 scale map.

Notes

Abbreviations Used in the Notes

ADM	Admiralty records
AWM	Australian War Memorial
BL	British Library, London
CAB	Cabinet records
CAC	Churchill Archives Centre, Churchill College, Cambridge
DADS	Deputy Assistant Director of Supplies
DAS	Director of Army Signals
FSR	*Field Service Regulations*
GS	General Staff
IWM	Imperial War Museum, London
IWCRO	Isle of Wight County Record Office, United Kingdom
LHCMA	Liddell Hart Centre for Military Archives, King's College, University of London
NAM	National Army Museum, United Kingdom
NMM	National Maritime Museum, United Kingdom
RA	Royal Artillery
TNA	The National Archives, United Kingdom
WD	war diary
WO	War Office records

Preface

1. A list of books examining the campaign from the Ottoman perspective can be seen in the bibliography. By far the best source is E. J. Erickson, *Gallipoli: The Ottoman Campaign* (Barnsley: Pen and Sword Military, 2010).

Introduction

1. For more on the role of maneuver in offensive warfare during the early stages of the First World War, see D. E. Showalter, "Manoeuvre Warfare: The Eastern and Western Fronts, 1914–1915," in *The Oxford Illustrated History of the First World War*, ed. H. Strachan (Oxford: Oxford University Press, 1998), 39–53.
2. The most recent attempt to force a way through the Dardanelles was the Duckworth expedition in 1807.
3. R. Prior, *Gallipoli: The End of the Myth* (Sydney: University of New South Wales Press, 2009), 13.
4. R. R. James, *Gallipoli* (Sydney: Angus and Robertson, 1965), 28–34.
5. "The Dardanelles," memo, 2 May 1915, Robertson Papers, LHCMA, Series ROBERTSON, item 3/2/3.

6. J. S. Corbett, *Naval Operations*, vol. 2, *From the Battle of the Falklands to the Entry of Italy into the War in May 1915* (London: Longmans, Green, 1929), 140–56.
7. Ibid., 157–95.
8. The ships consisted of the French battleship *Bouvet*, HMS *Irresistible*, and HMS *Ocean* (all sunk); HMS *Inflexible* (damaged by a mine); and the French battleships *Gaulois* and *Suffren* (both damaged by gunfire). The events of 18 March were seen as a great success for the Ottoman Empire. Corbett, *Naval Operations*, 2:213–23; C. F., Aspinall-Oglander, *Military Operations*, vol. 1, *Inception of the Campaign to May 1915* (London: Heinemann, 1929), 94–98.
9. James, *Gallipoli*, 64–67.
10. J. Lee, "Sir Ian Hamilton, Walter Braithwaite and the Dardanelles," *Journal of the Centre for First World War Studies* 1, no. 1 (July 2004): 40.
11. Throughout the book, "ANZAC" refers to the military formation (Australian and New Zealand Army Corps), whereas "Anzac" refers to the sector in which the ANZAC operated.
12. "Instructions for GOC A&NZ Army Corps," Braithwaite to Birdwood, memo, 13 April 1915, GS WD, GHQ MEF, AWM, Series AWM 4, item 1/4/1 pt. 2.
13. When the 29th Div. HQ first arrived in Egypt, Hamilton's chief cipher officer, Captain Orlo Williams, noted that Hunter-Weston, whom he described as "a vivacious loud voiced man with lots to say," had a reputation as being a "thruster." Diary entry, 30 March 1915, Papers of Dr. O. C. Williams, IWM, item 69/78/1.
14. The 29th Div. consisted of a combination of "regular" units, which, on the outbreak of war, returned to the UK from various garrisons throughout the British Empire. For the 29th Div.'s objectives, see "Force Order No. 1," 13 April 1915, GS WD, GHQ MEF, AWM 4, 1/4/1 pt. 2.
15. C. E. W. Bean, *The Official History of Australia in the War of 1914–1918*, vol. 1, *The Story of Anzac from the Outbreak of War to the End of the First Phase of the Gallipoli Campaign, May 4, 1915* (Sydney: Angus and Robertson, 1921), 575, 602.
16. The figure of 3,000 is taken from Erickson, *Gallipoli: The Ottoman Campaign*, 109.
17. C. E. W. Bean, *The Official History of Australia in the War of 1914–1918*, vol. 2, *The Story of Anzac from 4 May, 1915, to the Evacuation of the Gallipoli Peninsula* (Sydney: Angus and Robertson, 1924), 7–43; Aspinall-Oglander, *Military Operations*, 1:333–47; C. Pugsley, *Gallipoli: The New Zealand Story* (Auckland: Hodder and Stoughton, 1984), 192–207.
18. H. Strachan, *The First World War: A New Illustrated History* (Sydney: Simon and Schuster, 2003), 113.
19. While "bite and hold," the act of taking a part of the enemy's line and holding it against counterattack, was not part of British parlance at this time, the tactics used by Hunter-Weston at Helles are an example of

those later used by Sir Henry Rawlinson on the Western Front. See Prior, *Gallipoli*, 154–59.
20. Hamilton to de Robeck, letter, 5 August 1915, de Robeck Papers, CAC, Series DRBK, item 4/77.
21. Bean, *Official History*, 2:649; the subtitle of Bean's chapters on the fighting at Chunuk Bair (chapters 24 and 25) was "The Climax in Gallipoli." Similarly, John North described the offensive as "the climax of Gallipoli" in J. North, *Gallipoli: The Fading Vision* (London: Faber and Faber, 1966), 104.
22. P. A. Pedersen, "General Sir John Monash: Corps Commander on the Western Front," in *The Commanders: Australian Military Leadership in the Twentieth Century*, ed. D. M. Horner (Sydney: George Allen and Unwin, 1984), 94; H. Kannengiesser, *The Campaign in Gallipoli* (London: Hutchinson, 1927), 227.
23. The most notable of the First World War mythologies is the "lions led by donkeys" myth. The key proponent of this myth was A. Clark, *The Donkeys* (New York: Award Books, 1965). For a critique of this myth, see G. D. Sheffield, *Forgotten Victory: The First World War: Myths and Realities* (London: Review, 2002), xvii.
24. For a critique of the myths surrounding the August Offensive, see R. Crawley, "The Myths of August at Gallipoli," in *Zombie Myths of Australian Military History*, ed. C. Stockings (Sydney: University of New South Wales Press, 2010), 50–69.
25. Hamilton to Wigram, letter, 10 August 1915, Hamilton Papers, LHCMA, HAMILTON 7/1/9.
26. Minutes of the Dardanelles Committee, 19 August 1915, TNA, Series CAB 22/2 (emphasis original).
27. For a list of individuals and references to their statements, see R. Crawley, "'Our Second Great [Mis]adventure': A Critical Re-evaluation of the August Offensive, Gallipoli, 1915" (PhD thesis, University of New South Wales, Australian Defence Force Academy, 2010), 18–19.
28. A. Clark, *History's Children: History Wars in the Classroom* (Sydney: University of New South Wales Press, 2008), 57.
29. J. Ross, *The Myth of the Digger: The Australian Soldier in Two World Wars* (Sydney: Hale and Iremonger, 1985), 12–13.
30. J. Macleod, *Reconsidering Gallipoli* (Manchester, UK: Manchester University Press, 2004), 80–85, 92–93; R. Prior, "The Suvla Bay Tea-Party: A Reassessment," *Journal of the Australian War Memorial* 7 (October 1985): 25.
31. "Appreciation by the General Staff (War Office) of the landing at Suvla Bay," 21 September 1915, Aspinall-Oglander Papers, IWCRO, item OG/AO/G/14.
32. Lt.-Gen. Sir A. Murray, "Landing at Suvla Bay, 6th August 1915,", 20 September 1915, Aspinall-Oglander Papers, IWCRO, OG/AO/G/14.
33. There are many notable and important contributions to the study of the Gallipoli Campaign, but none have deconstructed the August Offensive at the operational level of war. Examples of important reevaluations

include P. A. Pedersen, *Monash as Military Commander* (Carlton: Melbourne University Press, 1985); Prior, "The Suvla Bay Tea-Party"; J. D. Millar, "A Study in the limitations of Command: General Sir William Birdwood and the A.I.F., 1914–1918" (PhD thesis, University College, University of New South Wales, Australian Defence Force Academy, 1993); T. Travers, "Command and Leadership Styles in the British Army: The 1915 Gallipoli Model," *Journal of Contemporary History* 29, no. 3 (July 1994), 403–42; T. Travers, *Gallipoli 1915* (Stroud, UK: Tempus, 2003); Macleod, *Reconsidering Gallipoli*; P. Chasseaud and P. Doyle, *Grasping Gallipoli: Terrain, Maps and Failure at the Dardanelles, 1915* (Kent, UK: Spellmount, 2005); E. A. Cohen and J. Gooch, *Military Misfortunes: The Anatomy of Failure in War* (New York: Free Press, 2006); Prior, *Gallipoli*; and Erickson, *Gallipoli: The Ottoman Campaign*.

34. The concept of the "operational level of war" was introduced to distinguish between larger and smaller unit operations. In effect, it replaced the strategic level, and the term "strategy" was elevated to encompass what was referred to previously as "grand strategy." For more on this, see J. I. Alger, *Definitions and Doctrine of the Military Art: Past and Present* (Wayne, N.J.: Avery Publishing Group, 1985), 4–6; D. Moran, "Operational Level of War," in *The Oxford Companion to Military History*, ed. R. Holmes (Oxford: Oxford University Press, 2003), 672, 676; and J. J. G. Mackenzie and B. H. Reid, eds., *The British Army and the Operational Level of War* (London: Tri-Service Press, 1989).
35. I. M. Brown, *British Logistics on the Western Front 1914–1919* (Westport, Conn.: Praeger, 1998), 12.
36. In accord with how the term was used at the time, "combined operations" is used throughout this book to refer to operations involving both the army and navy. Today, these are known as "joint operations," with "combined operations" being taken to mean multinational or coalition warfare.

1. Planning

1. "Instructions for GOC ANZAC," 30 July 1915, GS WD, GHQ MEF, AWM 4, 1/4/4 pt. 2.
2. The Army Council was the committee, consisting of seven members (four military, three civilian), responsible for the direction of the British Army. T. Coates, ed., *Lord Kitchener and Winston Churchill: The Dardanelles Commission, Part I, 1914–15* (London: Stationary Office, 2000), 43–44.
3. Evidence of Sir Reginald Brade to the Dardanelles Commission, 12 October 1916, TNA, CAB 19/33, 234.
4. Coates, *Lord Kitchener and Winston Churchill*, 44–46.
5. Evidence of Lieutenant-General Sir James Wolfe Murray to the Dardanelles Commission, 10 October 1916, TNA, CAB 19/33, 166.
6. E. Spiers, "Gallipoli," in *The First World War and British Military History*, ed. B. Bond (Oxford: Clarendon Press, 1991), 167.

7. Evidence of The Right Hon. Viscount Haldane of Cloan to the Dardanelles Commission, 18 October 1916, TNA, CAB 19/33, 263.
8. James, *Gallipoli*, 217.
9. Evidence of Sir (William) Graham Greene to the Dardanelles Commission, 10 October 1916, TNA, CAB 19/33, 185.
10. Evidence of Admiral Frederick C. T. Tudor to the Dardanelles Commission, 10 October 1916, TNA, CAB 19/33, 178–81; evidence of Commodore Cecil F. Lambert to the Dardanelles Commission, 10 October 1915, TNA, CAB 19/33, 184.
11. Evidence of Commodore Charles Martin de Bartolomé to the Dardanelles Commission, 5 October 1916, TNA, CAB 19/33, 124.
12. Evidence of Acting Vice-Admiral Sir Henry F. Oliver to the Dardanelles Commission, 5 October 1916, TNA, CAB 19/33, 130.
13. Evidence of Commodore C. F. Lambert to the Dardanelles Commission, 13 October 1916, TNA, CAB 19/33, 238; evidence of Acting Vice-Admiral Sir Henry F. Oliver to the Dardanelles Commission, 5 October 1916, TNA, CAB 19/33, 130.
14. Evidence of Lieutenant Colonel Sir Maurice Hankey to the Dardanelles Commission, 19 September 1916, TNA, CAB 19/33, 25.
15. Coates, *Lord Kitchener and Winston Churchill*, 171; Spiers, "Gallipoli," 176.
16. Evidence of Lieutenant-Colonel Sir Maurice Hankey to the Dardanelles Commission, 19 September 1916, TNA, CAB 19/33, 14–15.
17. Ibid., 26; evidence of Lieutenant-General Sir James Wolfe Murray to the Dardanelles Commission, 10 October 1916, TNA, CAB 19/33, 167; J. A. Fisher, *Memories* (London: Hodder and Stroughton, 1919), 61.
18. Evidence of Lieutenant-Colonel Sir Maurice Hankey to the Dardanelles Commission, 19 September 1916, TNA, CAB 19/33, 26.
19. "The Dardanelles," memo, 2 May 1915, Robertson Papers, LHCMA, ROBERTSON 3/2/3, 1.
20. Notes of War Council meeting, 14 May 1915, LHCMA, MISC 35, 4–6.
21. Bean, *Official History*, 2:433.
22. Corbett, *Naval Operations*, 2:410.
23. M. P. A. Hankey, *The Supreme Command: 1914–1918* (London: Allen and Unwin, 1961), 1:335–37.
24. Hamilton to Churchill, letter, 26 May 1915, Hamilton Papers, LHCMA, HAMILTON 7/1/1.
25. Conclusions of a meeting of the Dardanelles Committee, 7 June 1915, TNA, CAB 22/2. "New Army" or "Kitchener's Army" refers to those units created as a result of Lord Kitchener's appeal for volunteers in August 1914.
26. C. F. Aspinall-Oglander, *Military Operations*, vol. 2, *May 1915 to the Evacuation* (London: Heinemann, 1932), 56–59.
27. Hankey, *The Supreme Command*, 1:340.
28. E. J. Erickson, *Ordered to Die: A History of the Ottoman Army in the First World War* (London: Greenwood Press, 2001), 90; James, *Gallipoli*, 216–17.

29. C. R. Ballard, *Kitchener* (London: Newness, 1936), 246.
30. Report, Asquith to King George V, 19 June 1915, LHCMA, MISC 35.
31. Churchill to Kitchener, letter, 15 June 1915, TNA, CAB 17/132.
32. General J. Joffre, "Object and conditions of combined offensive action," 16 April 1915, TNA, WO 33/717, 2.
33. Chasseaud and Doyle, *Grasping Gallipoli*, xiv.
34. Evidence of Captain William Reginald Hall to the Dardanelles Commission, 24 October 1916, TNA, CAB 19/33, 280.
35. Chasseaud and Doyle, *Grasping Gallipoli*, xiv.
36. Ibid., 122–23; Mackenzie, *Gallipoli Memories* (Melbourne: Cassell, 1929), 47; Great Britain War Office, *Field Service Regulations* (hereafter *FSR*), pt. 1, *Operations* (1909; repr., London: H.M. Stationary Office, 1914), 119.
37. Chasseaud and Doyle, *Grasping Gallipoli*, xiii.
38. *FSR*, 1:120–21.
39. P. Collier, "The Impact on Topographic Mapping of Developments in Land and Air Survey: 1900–1939," in *Cartography and Geographic Information Science* 29, no. 3 (2002): 160–62; Chasseaud and Doyle, *Grasping Gallipoli*, 131.
40. Admiralty, *Report of the Committee Appointed to Investigate the Attacks Delivered on and the Enemy Defences of the Dardanelles Straits: 1919* (London: H.M. Stationary Office, 1921), 500 (hereafter "Mitchell Report").
41. Samson to Hamilton, letter, July 1919, Hamilton Papers, LHCMA, HAMILTON 13/97.
42. C. Clark, "Naval Aviation at Gallipoli," in *Sea Power Ashore and in the Air*, ed. D. Stevens and J. Reeve (Ultimo, Australia: Halstead Press, 2007), 77.
43. Evidence of Brigadier-General Hamilton Lester Reed to the Dardanelles Commission, 27 February 1917, TNA, CAB 19/33, 1025–39.
44. James, *Gallipoli*, 248.
45. Aspinall-Oglander, *Military Operations*, 2:144.
46. "Mitchell Report," 500.
47. Great Britain War Office, *Manual of Combined Naval and Military Operations* (London: H.M. Stationary Office, 1913), 16; Chasseaud and Doyle, *Grasping Gallipoli*, 102–103.
48. *FSR*, 1:120–25.
49. Interpreters attached to the British Med. Expedy. Force," memo, 28 July 1915, HQ IX Corps WD, TNA, WO 95/4276.
50. GHQ to GOC IX Corps, memo, 4 July 1915, HQ IX Corps WD, TNA, WO 95/4276.
51. General Routine Orders by General Sir Ian Hamilton, 23 July 1915; "Notes regarding examination of Turkish prisoners and documents," n.d., both in HQ IX Corps WD, TNA, WO 95/4276.
52. GHQ to GOC IX Corps, memo, 4 July 1915, HQ IX Corps WD, TNA, WO 95/4276.
53. "Intelligence Bulletin," 9 August 1915, HQ ANZAC Intelligence WD, AWM 4, 1/27/6 pt. 1; "Notes regarding examination of Turkish prisoners and documents," n.d., HQ IX Corps WD, TNA, WO 95/4276.

54. "Prisoners captured," n.d., HQ ANZAC Intelligence WD, AWM 4, 1/27/6 pt. 1.
55. "Intelligence Bulletin," 16 August 1915, HQ ANZAC Intelligence WD, AWM 4, 1/27/6 pt. 3.
56. "Notes regarding examination of Turkish prisoners and documents," n.d., HQ IX Corps WD, TNA, WO 95/4276.
57. GHQ to GOC IX Corps, memo, 4 July 1915, HQ IX Corps WD, TNA, WO 95/4276.
58. "Notes regarding examination of Turkish prisoners and documents," n.d., HQ IX Corps WD, TNA, WO 95/4276.
59. "Special Force Order," memo, 17 July 1915, HQ ANZAC Intelligence WD, AWM 4, 1/27/5 pt. 2.
60. Diary entry, 6 July 1915, HQ VIII Corps WD, TNA, WO 95/4273.
61. Diary entry, 13 August 1915, Private war diary of Major-General G. Egerton, TNA, CAB 45/249, 88.
62. Keyes to de Robeck, letter, 17 August 1915, de Robeck Papers, CAC, DRBK 4/78, 3.
63. Hamilton to Kitchener, telegram, 23 June 1915, Hamilton Papers, LHCMA, HAMILTON 7/4/8.
64. James, *Gallipoli*, 218; N. Steel, *The Battlefields of Gallipoli: Then and Now* (London: Leo Cooper, 1990), 149.
65. T. Travers, "The Offensive and the Problem of Innovation in British Military Thought 1870–1915," *Journal of Contemporary History* 13, no. 3 (July 1978): 540.
66. *FSR*, 1:131.
67. Travers, "The Offensive and the Problem of Innovation," 540–41.
68. A. A. Wiest, *Haig: The Evolution of a Commander* (Washington, D.C.: Potomac Books, 2005), 47.
69. P. Griffith, *Battle Tactics of the Western Front: The British Army's Art of Attack, 1916–18* (London: Yale University Press, 2000), 50–53.
70. Alger, *Definitions and Doctrine*, 3.
71. Travers, *Gallipoli 1915*, 228.
72. C. Bellamy, "Manoeuvre Warfare," in Holmes, *Oxford Companion*, 541; Joffre, "Object and conditions of combined offensive action," 16 April 1915, TNA, WO 33/717, 2.
73. Griffith, *Battle Tactics of the Western Front*, 160.
74. Hamilton to French, letter, 17 June 1915, Hamilton Papers, LHCMA, HAMILTON 7/1/2.
75. I. S. M. Hamilton, *Gallipoli Diary* (London: Edward Arnold, 1920), 2:5.
76. Travers, *Gallipoli 1915*, 222.
77. Travers, "The Offensive and the Problem of Innovation," 542.
78. Hamilton to Bean, letter, 22 September 1922, Hamilton Papers, LHCMA, HAMILTON 13/12.
79. Thursby to Birdwood, letter, 3 May 1915, Thursby Papers, NMM, item THY/8/13.
80. Godley to HQ ANZAC, telegram, 2 May 1915, HQ ANZAC WD, AMW4, 1/25/2 pt. 2; diary entry, 4 May 1915, HQ ANZAC WD, AWM 4, 1/25/2 pt. 1.

81. "Information by a Greek Miller of Taifur Keui," 13 May 1915, HQ ANZAC Intelligence WD, AWM 4, 1/27/3 pt. 1.
82. Birdwood to Hamilton, letter, 13 May 1915, Birdwood Papers, AWM 3DRL/3376, 11/16.
83. Ibid.
84. Noted on Birdwood to Hamilton, letter, 13 May 1915, GS WD, GHQ MEF, AWM 4, 1/4/2 pt. 3.
85. Birdwood to Hamilton, letter, 13 May 1915, Birdwood Papers, AWM 3DRL/3376, 11/16.
86. Crawford and Cooke, eds., *No Better Death: The Great War Diaries and Letters of William G. Malone* (Auckland: Reed Books, 2005), 190; Pugsley, *Gallipoli: The New Zealand Story*, 219–20.
87. Hamilton to Skeen, letter, 5 July 1929, Hamilton Papers, LHCMA, HAMILTON 13/101; Pedersen, *The Anzacs: Gallipoli to the Western Front* (Camberwell, Australia: Viking, 2007), 84.
88. "Report of reconnaisance [sic]," Overton to OC Canterbury Mounted Rifles, 15 May 1915, HQ ANZAC Intelligence WD, AWM 4, 1/27/3 pt. 1; Pugsley, *Gallipoli: The New Zealand Story*, 218–20; Steel, *The Battlefields of Gallipoli*, 149.
89. Birdwood to Hamilton, letter, 16 May 1915, Birdwood Papers, AWM 3DRL/3376, 11/5; Birdwood to Hamilton, letter, 18 May 1915, GS WD, GHQ MEF, AWM 4, 1/4/2 pt. 4.
90. Birdwood to Hamilton, letter, 16 May 1915, Birdwood Papers, AWM 3DRL/3376, 11/5.
91. Noted on Birdwood to Hamilton, letter, 16 May 1915, GS WD, GHQ MEF, AWM 4, 1/4/2 pt. 4.
92. "Intelligence Bulletin," 21 May 1915, HQ ANZAC Intelligence WD, AWM 4, 1/27/3 pt. 2.
93. Reconnaissance patrols were sent out on 17 and 27 May to find additional routes to the Sari Bair Ridge. Routes were found, but the patrols also came across small parties of the enemy. Overton reported that the enemy posts in the Aghyl Dere were only occupied at night. See diary entries, 17 and 28 May 1915, NZMR Bde. WD, AWM 4, 35/1/1; and Pugsley, *Gallipoli: The New Zealand Story*, 220. A raid was also launched on Nibrunesi Point on 25 May. No enemy was encountered, but the patrol managed to cut and remove an Ottoman telephone cable and destroy an observation station. See diary entry, 25 May 1915, HQ ANZAC WD, AWM 4, 1/25/2 pt. 1; and diary entry, 24 May 1915, NZMR Bde. WD, AWM 4, 35/1/1. Birdwood personally carried out reconnaissance from on board the minesweeper *Newmarket* on 25 May. See W. R. Birdwood, *Khaki and Gown* (London: Ward, Lock, 1941), 266–67.
94. Bean, *Official History*, 2:197.
95. Aspinall to Birdwood, telegram, 17 May 1915; Braithwaite to Birdwood, telegram, 28 May 1915, both in GS WD, GHQ MEF, AWM 4, 1/4/2 pt. 4; Dawnay to unknown (an individual at the War Office), letter, 1 September 1915, Dawnay Papers, IWM, 69/21/6. Note: Apinall's name was not hyphenated to Aspinall-Oglander until 1927.

96. Bean, *Official History*, 2:188.
97. Birdwood to GHQ, memo, 30 May 1915, Birdwood Papers, AWM 3DRL/3376, 11/16.
98. "Note on proposed advance," 7 June 1915, HQ ANZAC WD, AWM 4, 1/25/3 pt. 3.
99. "Notes on further operations by Australian & New Zealand Army Corps," memo, ca. early June 1915; "Note on proposed advance," 7 June 1915; "Appreciation of the situation at Anzac," 8 June 1915, all in HQ ANZAC WD, AWM 4, 1/25/3 pt. 3.
100. Kitchener to Hamilton, telegram, 7 June 1915, Hamilton Papers, LHCMA, HAMILTON 7/4/8; Hamilton, *Gallipoli Diary*, 1:283.
101. Hamilton to Kitchener, telegram, 8 June 1915, Hamilton Papers, LHCMA, HAMILTON 7/4/8.
102. War Office to Hamilton, telegram, 9 June 1915, Hamilton Papers, LHCMA, HAMILTON 7/2/3.
103. Hamilton to War Office, telegram, 10 June 1915; Kitchener to Hamilton, telegram, 15 June 1915, both in Hamilton Papers, LHCMA, HAMILTON 7/2/3; Hamilton to Kitchener, telegram, 15 June 1915, Hamilton Papers, LHCMA, HAMILTON 7/2/4.
104. Hamilton to War Office, telegram, 16 June 1915, Hamilton Papers, LHCMA, HAMILTON 7/4/8.
105. Hamilton to French, letter, 17 June 1915, Hamilton Papers, LHCMA, HAMILTON 7/1/2.
106. Hamilton, *Gallipoli*, 2:288.
107. Birdwood to Kitchener, letter, 9 June 1915, Kitchener Papers, TNA, PRO 30/57/62.
108. Minutes of Dardanelles Committee meeting, 12 June 1915, TNA, CAB 22/2.
109. Balfour to de Robeck, letter, 14 June 1915, de Robeck Papers, CAC, DRBK 4/69.
110. Hamilton, *Gallipoli Diary*, 2:289–91.
111. Minutes of Dardanelles Committee meeting, 17 June 1915, TNA, CAB 22/2.
112. Diary entry, 17 June 1915, Williams Papers, IWM, 69/78/1.
113. Fitzgerald (Kitchener's Personal Military Secretary) to Braithwaite, letter, 19 June 1915, Hamilton Papers, LHCMA, HAMILTON 7/4/16.
114. Quoted in F. Glen, *Bowler of Gallipoli: Witness to the Anzac Legend* (Loftus, Australia: Australian Military History Publications, 2004), 91.
115. Pugsley, *Gallipoli: The New Zealand Story*, 268–69.
116. Diary entry, 22 June 1915, Williams Papers, IWM, 69/78/1.
117. Hamilton to Kitchener, telegram, 23 June 1915, Hamilton Papers, LHCMA, HAMILTON 7/4/8.
118. Diary entry, 23 June 1915, Williams Papers, IWM, 69/78/1.
119. Godley, "Discussion on plan of attack on Ridge 971," 23 June 1915, HQ ANZAC WD, AWM 4, 1/25/3 pt. 3.
120. Braithwaite to Birdwood, letter, 25 June 1915, GS WD, GHQ MEF, AWM 4, 1/4/3 pt. 3.

121. Diary entry, 26 June 1915, Williams Papers, IWM, 69/78/1.
122. Birdwood to Fitzgerald, letter, 27 June 1915, Birdwood Papers, AWM 3DRL/3376, 11/5; Birdwood to Kitchener, letter, 29 June 1915, Kitchener Papers, TNA, PRO 30/57/62.
123. Diary entry, 28 June 1915, Williams Papers, IWM, 69/78/1.
124. Hamilton to Kitchener, telegram, 29 June 1915, Hamilton Papers, LHCMA, HAMILTON 7/4/8.
125. "Proposals for using reinforcements," Birdwood to GHQ MEF, memo, 1 July 1915, HQ ANZAC WD, AWM 4, 1/25/4 pt. 3.
126. Ibid.
127. "General information on the subject of the issue of maps to the Mediterranean Expeditionary Force," memo, 26 July 1915, HQ IX Corps WD, TNA, WO 95/4276.
128. Kitchener to Hamilton, telegram, 5 July 1915, Hamilton Papers, LHCMA, HAMILTON 7/4/8.
129. Hamilton to Kitchener, telegram, 5 July 1915, Hamilton Papers, LHCMA, HAMILTON 7/4/8.
130. Birdwood to de Robeck, letter, 8 July 1915, de Robeck Papers, CAC, DRBK 4/42.
131. Birdwood to GHQ MEF, memo, 10 July 1915, HQ ANZAC WD, AWM 4, 1/25/4 pt. 3.
132. Ibid.
133. Skeen to NZ&A Div., memo, HQ ANZAC WD, AWM 4, 1/25/4 pt. 4.
134. Diary entry, 16 July 1915, NZ Infantry Bde. WD, AWM 4, 35/17/6.
135. "Intelligence Note," 16 July 1915, HQ ANZAC Intelligence WD, AWM 4, 1/27/5 pt. 2.
136. "Administrative Memorandum No. 26," 17 July 1915, Gellibrand Papers, AWM 3DRL/1473, 95.
137. Braithwaite to Stopford, memo, 10 July 1915, GS WD, GHQ MEF, AWM 4, 1/4/4 pt. 3.
138. Hamilton to de Robeck, telegram, 17 July 1915, GS WD, GHQ MEF, AWM 4, 1/4/4 pt. 2.
139. Diary entry, 20 July 1915, Intelligence WD, GHQ MEF, AWM 4, 1/5/4.
140. Hamilton to Kitchener, letter, 21 July 1915, Kitchener Papers, TNA, PRO 30/57/62.
141. Braithwaite to Stopford, memo, 22 July 1915, GS WD, GHQ MEF, AWM 4, 1/4/4 pt. 2.
142. Diary entry, 25 July 1915, Birdwood Papers, AWM 3DRL/3376, 1/1.
143. "Instructions for G.O.C. 9th Army Corps," Braithwaite to Stopford, memo, 29 July 1915, GS WD, GHQ MEF, AWM 4, 1/4/4 pt. 2.
144. Prior, "The Suvla Bay Tea-Party," 26–27.
145. "Instructions for G.O.C. 9th Army Corps," Braithwaite to Stopford, memo, 29 July 1915, GS WD, GHQ MEF, AWM 4, 1/4/4 pt. 2.
146. Stopford to GHQ, memo, 31 July 1915, HQ IX Corps WD, TNA, WO 95/4276.
147. "Instructions for G.O.C. A& N.Z. Army Corps," Braithwaite to Birdwood, memo, 30 July 1915, GS WD, GHQ MEF, AWM 4, 1/4/4 pt. 2.

148. Kitchener to Hamilton, telegram, 28 July 1915, Hamilton Papers, LHCMA, HAMILTON 7/4/8.
149. James, *Gallipoli*, 273.
150. *FSR*, 1:27.
151. Quoted in S. Sandler, review of *Supplying War: Logistics from Wallenstein to Patton*, by M. van Creveld, *American Historical Review* 83, no. 4 (October 1978): 970.
152. *FSR*, 1:29.
153. Braithwaite to Stopford, telegram, 29 July 1915, GS WD, GHQ MEF, AWM 4, 1/4/4 pt. 2.
154. "Instructions for the attack on H12 and H12A," n.d., HQ VIII Corps WD, TNA, WO 95/4273.
155. S. Miles, "Notes on the Dardanelles Campaign of 1915," pt. 4, *Coast Artillery Journal* 62, no. 3 (March 1925): 207; Hankey to Asquith, letter, 12 August 1915, TNA, CAB 17/123, 23; Travers, *Gallipoli 1915*, 147–49.
156. Hamilton, *Gallipoli Diary*, 1:331.
157. Hankey to Asquith, letter, 12 August 1915, TNA, CAB 17/123, 2, 23.
158. Hamilton's dispatch, 11 December 1915, Hamilton Papers, LHCMA, HAMILTON 7/8/23, 25.
159. "Instructions issued to commanders in accordance with Divisional Order No. 11," n.d., NZ Infantry Bde. WD, AWM 4, 35/17/7.
160. Birdwood's message to ANZAC, 5 August 1915, HQ ANZAC WD, AWM 4, 1/25/5 pt. 3.
161. "Instructions issued to commanders in accordance with Divisional Order No. 11," n.d., NZ Infantry Bde. WD, AWM 4, 35/17/7.
162. "Instructions for Major-General Sir Alex. [sic] Godley," n.d., HQ ANZAC WD, AWM 4, 1/25/5 pt. 3.
163. "Operation Order No. 11," 5 August 1915, NZ Infantry Bde. WD, AWM 4, 35/17/7.
164. "Army Corps Order No. 16," 3 August 1915, HQ ANZAC WD, AWM 4, 1/25/5 pt. 3; "Operation Order No. 11," 5 August 1915, NZ Infantry Bde. WD, AWM 4, 35/17/7.
165. "Instructions for G.O.C. Australian Division," 4 August 1915, HQ ANZAC WD, AWM 4, 1/25/5 pt. 3.
166. Hamilton, *Gallipoli Diary*, 1:360–61.
167. Diary entry, 1–5 August 1915, DDMS WD, VIII Corps, AWM 4, 26/10/5.
168. Keyes to de Robeck, letter, 17 August 1915, de Robeck Papers, CAC, DRBK 4/78, 1.
169. "Instructions for G.O.C. A&N.Z. Army Corps," 30 July 1915, GS WD, GHQ MEF, AWM 4, 1/4/4 pt. 2; the operational objective of the offensive was repeated in "Army Corps Order No. 16," 3 August 1915, HQ ANZAC WD, AWM 4, 1/25/5 pt. 3; and Hamilton's dispatch, 11 December 1915, Hamilton Papers, LHCMA, HAMILTON 7/8/23, 4.
170. "Appreciation" by Lieutenant-Colonel C. F. Aspinall, 20 August 1915, GS WD, GHQ MEF, AWM 4, 1/4/4 pt. 3; diary entry, 13 June 1915,

Williams Papers, IWM, 69/78/1, 100; Hankey to Asquith, letter, 12 August 1915, TNA, CAB 17/123, 23.
171. J. F. Williams, *Anzacs, the Media and the Great War* (Sydney: University of New South Wales Press, 1999), 68.
172. "1st Army Operation Order No. 9," 8 March 1915, HQ IV Corps WD, TNA, WO 95/708.
173. "GHQ Operation Order OA 721," 8 March 1915, 1st Army WD, TNA, WO 95/154.
174. "Operation Order No. 11," 8 March 1915, 8th Div. WD, TNA, WO 95/1671; R. Prior and T. Wilson, *Command on the Western Front: The Military Career of Sir Henry Rawlinson, 1914–1918* (South Yorkshire: Pen and Sword, 2004), 35.
175. Birdwood, *Khaki and Gown*, 274.

2. Mobility

1. Bellamy, "Manoeuvre Warfare," 541.
2. T. J. Granville-Chapman, "The Importance of Surprise: A Reappraisal," in *The British Army and the Operational Level of War*, ed. J. J. G. Mackenzie and B. H. Reid (London: Tri-Service Press, 1989), 55.
3. Joffre, "Object and conditions of combined offensive action," 16 April 1915, TNA, WO 33/717, 2.
4. Braithwaite to IGC, memo, 14 July 1915, Aspinall-Oglander Papers, IWCRO, OG/AO/G/13.
5. James, *Gallipoli*, 247.
6. Hamilton, *Gallipoli Diary*, 1:329.
7. Hamilton to Birdwood, telegram, 11 July 1915, HQ ANZAC WD, AWM 4, 1/25/4 pt. 4.
8. Birdwood to Braithwaite, telegram, 12 July 1915, GS WD, GHQ MEF, AWM 4, 1/4/4 pt. 3.
9. "Statement by Lt-General The Hon. Sir F. Stopford respecting the operations of the 9th Army Corps at Suvla Bay August 6th to 15th 1915," 29 August 1915, TNA, WO 138/40.
10. Hamilton to Kitchener, telegram, 23 July 1915, Hamilton Papers, LHCMA, HAMILTON 7/4/8.
11. L. von Sanders, *Five Years in Turkey* (Annapolis, Md.: United States Naval Institute, 1927), 79–80.
12. "Independent [Ottoman] Cavalry Brigade Order No. 885," 27 July 1915, HQ ANZAC Intelligence WD, AWM 4, 1/27/6 pt. 2.
13. "Intelligence Summary," 7 August 1915; "Intelligence Bulletin," 8 August 1915, both in HQ ANZAC Intelligence WD, AWM 4, 1/27/6 pt. 1.
14. Monash's address delivered to officers and noncommissioned officers of the 4th Australian Bde., 6 August 1915, Monash Papers, AWM 3DRL/2136, 3/20, 1–7.
15. Diary entry, 6 August 1915, Backhouse Papers, IWM, 86/31/1.
16. Arthur Beecroft to Aspinall-Oglander, letter, 9 February 1931, TNA, CAB 45/241.

17. "Attached to IX Corps Operation Order No. 1," memo, 3 August 1915, HQ IX Corps WD, TNA, WO 95/4276.
18. "Instructions issues to commanders in accordance with Divisional Order No. 11," 5 August 1915, NZ Infantry Bde. WD, AWM 4, 35/17/7.
19. Pedersen, *Monash as Military Commander*, 96–98.
20. G. D. Sheffield, "Command, Leadership and the Anglo-American Experience," in *Leadership and Command: The Anglo-American Military Experience since 1861*, ed. G. D. Sheffield (London: Brassey's, 1997), 4; Granville-Chapman, "The Importance of Surprise: A Reappraisal," 66.
21. Circular memo, 2 August 1915, HQ ANZAC WD, AWM 4, 1/25/5 pt. 3.
22. R. Glover, "War and Civilian Historians," *Journal of the History of Ideas* 18, no. 1 (January 1957), 87.
23. Travers, "Command and Leadership Styles in the British Army," 434.
24. Sheffield, *Forgotten Victory*, 121.
25. J. M. Bourne, "British Generals in the First World War," in Sheffield, *Leadership and Command*, 101.
26. Sheffield, "Command, Leadership and the Anglo-American Experience," 5.
27. Hamilton to Kitchener, telegram, 29 July 1915, Hamilton Papers, LHCMA, HAMILTON 7/4/8.
28. "State of the Mediterranean Expeditionary Force according to returns prepared by General Headquarters, 3rd Echelon, Mediterranean Expeditionary Force," 31 July 1915, TNA, WO 162/69.
29. "Fighting strength of ANZAC," 5 August 1915, HQ ANZAC WD, AWM 4, 1/25/5 pt. 6.
30. "Report on operations at Anzac, 6–10 August 1915," Birdwood to GHQ, 4 September 1915, Hamilton Papers, LHCMA, HAMILTON 7/2/45.
31. "Distribution of divisions," 3 August 1915, TNA, WO 159/4.
32. "Details of comparison between original Expeditionary Force and present total Military Forces," 28 September 1915, TNA, WO 159/4.
33. CIGS to GHQ MEF, telegram, 22 June 1915, Hamilton Papers, LHCMA, HAMILTON 7/4/8.
34. James, *Gallipoli*, 250; T. Coates, ed., *Defeat at Gallipoli: The Dardanelles Commission, Part II, 1915–16* (London: Stationary Office, 2000), 286.
35. CIGS to GHQ MEF, telegram, 22 June 1915, Hamilton Papers, LHCMA, HAMILTON 7/4/8.
36. "Statement by Lt-General The Hon. Sir F. Stopford respecting the operations of the 9th Army Corps at Suvla Bay August 6th to 15th 1915," 29 August 1915, TNA, WO 138/40.
37. "Force Order No. 25," 2 August 1915, GS WD, GHQ MEF, AWM 4, 1/4/5 pt. 2.
38. "Notes of a meeting of the Dardanelles Committee," 5 July 1915, TNA, CAB 22/2.
39. Evidence of Lieutenant-Colonel T. H. B. Forster to the Dardanelles Commission, 29 January 1917, TNA, CAB 19/33, 745.

40. Kitchener to Hamilton, telegram, 28 July 1915, Hamilton Papers, LHCMA, HAMILTON 7/4/8.
41. Diary entry, 29 July 1915, Williams Papers, IWM, 69/78/1.
42. Maxwell to Kitchener, telegram, 30 July 1915, GS WD, GHQ MEF, AWM 4, 1/4/4 pt. 3.
43. Hamilton to Kitchener, telegram, 29 June 1915, Hamilton Papers, LHCMA, HAMILTON 7/4/8.
44. A. John, "Lost Opportunity: An Operational Level Analysis of the August Offensive of the Gallipoli Campaign 1915," *Australian Army Journal* (2002): 12.
45. IX Corps to GHQ, telegram, 13 August 1915, HQ IX Corps WD, TNA, WO 95/4276.
46. Millar, "A Study in the Limitations of Command," 85.
47. Pugsley, *Gallipoli: The New Zealand Story*, 272.
48. Bean, *Official History*, 2:265.
49. James, *Gallipoli*, 222.
50. Bean, *Official History*, 2:367.
51. Total ANZAC losses for 1–4 August 1915 were 887, made up of 6 killed, 145 wounded, and 736 sick. HQ ANZAC WD, AWM 4, 1/25/5 pt. 1.
52. Crawford and Cooke, *No Better Death*, 292.
53. Quoted in Bean, *Official History*, 2:377.
54. Monash to Aspinall-Oglander, letter, 22 September 1915, TNA, CAB 45/243.
55. Birdwood to Hamilton, letter, 29 July 1915, Hamilton Papers, LHCMA, HAMILTON 7/1/16.
56. Birdwood to Ellison, letter, 5 August 1915, Ellison Papers, NAM, item 8704/35/216.
57. Birdwood, *Khaki and Gown*, 269–70.
58. Hamilton, *Gallipoli Diary*, 2:51.
59. James, *Gallipoli*, 251–52, 257.
60. Beecroft to Aspinall-Oglander, letter, 9 February 1931, Aspinall-Oglander Papers, IWCRO, OG/AO/G/48.
61. Quoted in P. Liddle, *Men of Gallipoli: The Dardanelles and Gallipoli Experience August 1914 to January 1916* (Devon, UK: David and Charles, 1988), 211.
62. "Report on Operations at Anzac, 6–10 August 1915," memo, 4 September 1915, Hamilton Papers, LHCMA, HAMILTON 7/2/45.
63. CID, "The Dardanelles: Memorandum on the Situation, August 30, 1915," Hamilton Papers, LHCMA, HAMILTON 7/4/33.
64. Evidence of Major-General E. M. Woodward to the Dardanelles Commission, 24 January 1917, TNA, CAB 19/33, 645–46.
65. "Narrative of operations by Major-General J. H. Poett (DA&QMG IX Corps)," n.d., TNA, CAB 45/244.
66. DAG GHQ to IX Corps, letter, 13 July 1915, DQMG WD, TNA, WO 95/4266.
67. Aspinall-Oglander, *Military Operations*, 2:356.
68. Hamilton to de Robeck, telegram, 10 October 1915, de Robeck Papers, CAC, DRBK 4/27.

69. MacMunn to Cowans, letter, 11 August 1915, TNA, WO 107/44.
70. *FSR*, 1:22.
71. "Circular Memorandum," 30 July 1915, HQ IX Corps WD, TNA, WO 95/4276.
72. H. C. B. Wemyss, "Account of Signals—Gallipoli," TNA, WO 106/704, 5.
73. "Summary of 1–5 August," DDMS WD, VIII Corps, AWM 4, 26/10/5.
74. R. E. Priestley, *The Signal Service in the European War of 1914–1918 (France)* (London: W. and J. Mackay, 1921), v.
75. "Operation Order No. 2," 5 August 1915, NZMR Bde. WD, AWM 4, 35/1/4 pt. 1.
76. Communication between the NZ&A Div. and 13th Div. was the exception to this rule: "Instructions regarding inter-communication," n.d., HQ ANZAC WD, AWM 4, 1/25/5 pt. 3.
77. "Narrative of Signal Work (GHQ to IX Corps) for Operations 6–7 August, 1915," DAS WD, GHQ MEF, AWM 6/123. "Notes on signal arrangements decided on by DAS and officers of GHQ in consultation with representative of the RN," memo, 30 July 1915; "Notes on inter-communication for impending operations," memo, 28 July 1915, both in GS WD, GHQ MEF, AWM 4, 1/4/4 pt. 2. Wemyss, "Account of Signals—Gallipoli," TNA, WO 106/704, 6.
78. "Signal organization for combined operations," Wemyss Papers, CAC, WMYS 3/1.
79. Travers, *Gallipoli 1915*, 145.
80. "Statement by Lt-General The Hon. Sir F. Stopford respecting the operations of the 9th Army Corps at Suvla Bay August 6th to 15th 1915," 29 August 1915, TNA, WO 138/40.
81. "Narrative of Signal Work (GHQ to IX Corps) for Operations 6–7 August, 1915," DAS WD, GHQ MEF, AWM 6/123.
82. Evidence of Brigadier-General H. L. Reed to the Dardanelles Commission, 27 February 1917, TNA, CAB 19/33.
83. "Statement by Lt-General The Hon. Sir F. Stopford respecting the operations of the 9th Army Corps at Suvla Bay August 6th to 15th 1915," 29 August 1915, TNA, WO 138/40.
84. Evidence of Brigadier-General H. L. Reed to the Dardanelles Commission, 27 February 1917, TNA, CAB 19/33.
85. "Statement by Lt-General The Hon. Sir F. Stopford respecting the operations of the 9th Army Corps at Suvla Bay August 6th to 15th 1915," 29 August 1915, TNA, WO 138/40.
86. "Narrative of Signal Work (GHQ to IX Corps) for Operations 6–7 August, 1915," DAS WD, GHQ MEF, AWM 6/123.
87. Diary entries, 8–9 August 1915, DAS WD, GHQ MEF, AWM 6/123.
88. Priestley, *The Signal Service*, vii.
89. Diary entries, 6 and 28 August 1915, NZ&A Div. Signal Company WD, AWM 4, 35/15/3.
90. Diary entries, 9, 10, 12, 17, and 20 August 1915, NZ&A Div. Signal Company WD, AWM 4, 35/15/3.

91. Diary entry, 9 August 1915, DAS WD, GHQ MEF, AWM 6/123.
92. "Organization Orders for the troops in Anzac," 3 August 1915, HQ ANZAC WD, AWM 4 1/25/5 pt. 3.
93. "Report on the Operations against the Sari Bair position, 6th–10th August 1915," Godley to Skeen, 16 August 1915, HQ ANZAC WD, AWM 4 1/25/5 pt. 5, 22.
94. Godley to Birdwood, letter, 27 February 1917, Birdwood Papers, AWM 3DRL/3376 item 11/4.
95. *FSR*, 1:23.
96. Godley to Birdwood, letter, 27 February 1917, Birdwood Papers, AWM 3DRL/3376, 11/4.
97. Evidence of Lieutenant-Colonel C. J. L. Allanson to the Dardanelles Commission, 19 January 1917, TNA, CAB 19/33.
98. F. Waite, *The New Zealanders at Gallipoli* (Auckland: Whitcombe and Tombs, 1921), 221–23.
99. P. Doyle and M. R. Bennett, "Military Geography: The Influence of Terrain in the Outcome of the Gallipoli Campaign, 1915" *Geographical Journal* 165, no. 1 (March 1999): 17.
100. Erickson, *Ordered to Die*, 91.
101. H. W. Nevinson, *The Dardanelles Campaign* (London: Nisbet, 1918), 252.
102. Hamilton quoted in Steel, *The Battlefields of Gallipoli*, 155; Shaw quote from diary entry, 4 August 1915, Shaw Papers, IWM, 76/106/1.
103. "Short account of doings of the Australians and New Zealanders sent in for telegraphing to the S[ecretary] of S[tate] for War," 11 August 1915, HQ ANZAC WD, AWM 4, 1/25/5 pt. 4.
104. Godley to Hamilton, letter, 20 May 1925, Hamilton Papers, LHCMA, HAMILTON 13/46.
105. Birdwood to wife, letter, 4 August 1915, Birdwood Papers, AWM 3DRL/3376, 8/2.
106. Ibid.
107. "Organization Orders for the troops in Anzac," 3 August 1915, HQ ANZAC WD, AWM 4, 1/25/5 pt. 3.
108. Evidence of Lieutenant-Colonel C. F. Aspinall to the Dardanelles Committee, 29 January 1917, TNA, CAB 19/33.
109. Evidence of Brigadier-General H. L. Reed to the Dardanelles Committee, Tuesday 27 February 1917, TNA, CAB 19/33.
110. N. Steel and P. Hart, *Defeat at Gallipoli* (London: Pan Books, 2002), 257–58.
111. "Appreciation of the situation in the Dardanelles according to information received up to 25 March 1915, the date of leaving Malta," 30 March 1915, Hamilton Papers, LHCMA, HAMILTON 7/4/15.
112. E. J. Erickson, *Ottoman Army Effectiveness in World War I: A Comparative Study* (London: Routledge, 2007), 62–63; "Extracts from Diary of a Turkish Officer found in trenches by Australian Division, 6 August 1915," Intelligence Bulletin, 17 August 1915, Hamilton Papers, LHCMA, HAMILTON 7/6/72.

113. Cohen and Gooch, *Military Misfortunes*, 134–36; evidence of Brigadier-General H. L. Reed to the Dardanelles Commission, 27 February 1917, TNA, CAB 19/33; E. J. Erickson, "Strength against Weakness: Ottoman Military Effectiveness at Gallipoli, 1915," *Journal of Military History* 65, no. 4 (October 2001): 983–85.
114. Hamilton, *Gallipoli Diary*, 2:304.
115. Ibid., 312.
116. Hamilton to Churchill, letter, 18 June 1915, Hamilton Papers, LHCMA, HAMILTON 7/1/1.
117. Hamilton to Kitchener, telegram, 23 June 1915; Hamilton to Kitchener, telegram, 31 July 1915, both in Hamilton Papers, LHCMA, HAMILTON 7/4/8.
118. Birdwood's message to ANZAC, 5 August 1915, Birdwood Papers, AWM 3DRL/3376, 11/15.
119. Cabinet paper, "The offensive under present conditions," 19 June 1915, Bonar Law Papers, Parliamentary Archives, House of Lords Record Office, BL/56/IE.
120. Griffith, *Battle Tactics of the Western Front*, 49.

3. Fire Support

1. I. Hogg, *Allied Artillery of World War One* (Wiltshire, UK: Crowood Press, 1998), 7.
2. Travers, "The Offensive and the Problem of Innovation," 539.
3. *FSR*, 1:15.
4. S. Bidwell and D. Graham, *Fire-Power: British Army Weapons and Theories of War, 1904–1945* (Barnsley: Pen and Sword, 2004), 61, 72; Griffith, *Battle Tactics of the Western Front*, 135.
5. Bidwell and Graham, *Fire-Power*, 4.
6. Ibid., 3.
7. It must be noted that gas was not used at Gallipoli, despite being available to both sides. This was primarily because of the difficulty and unpredictability of employing gas in windy conditions such as those experienced in the Dardanelles. Another reason was that Gallipoli was viewed, especially by General Sir Ian Hamilton, as a "gentleman's war," where the use of gas was considered barbaric and inhumane. Diary entry, 4 August 1915, GS WD, GHQ MEF, AWM 4, 1/4/5 pt. 1.
8. Diary entries, 1–5 August 1915, CRA VIII Corps WD, TNA, WO 95/4275.
9. "Attack on the 'H' trenches by 29th Division VIIIth Corps on August 6th 1915: Report on the co-operation of the VIIIth Corps Artillery," n.d., CRA VIII Corps WD, TNA, WO 95/4275; Braithwaite to GOC VIII Corps, telegram, 29 July 1915, GS WD, GHQ MEF, AWM 4, 1/4/4 pt. 2; diary entry, 6 August 1915, 29th Div. WD, TNA, WO 95/4305.
10. Diary entry, 6 August 1915, 66th Bde. RFA WD, TNA, WO 95/4301.
11. "Attack on the 'H' trenches by 29th Division VIIIth Corps on August 6th 1915: Report on the co-operation of the VIIIth Corps Artillery," n.d., CRA VIII Corps WD, TNA, WO 95/4275.

12. "Narrative of operations, 6–9 August 1915," 1st Australian Div. Artillery WD, AWM 4, 13/10/12 pt. 1; "Appendix 'A': Action of Artillery in support of forthcoming operations," n.d., HQ ANZAC WD, AWM 4, 1/25/5 pt. 3; diary entry, 6 August 1915, 2nd Australian FAB WD, AWM 4, 13/30/9.
13. "Operation Order No. 1," 3 August 1915, 1st Australian Div. Artillery WD, AWM 4, 13/10/12 pt. 1.
14. "Short account of doings of the Australians and New Zealanders sent in for telegraphing to the S[ecretary] of S[tate] for War," 11 August 1915, HQ ANZAC WD, AWM 4, 1/25/5 pt. 4; "Report on the Operations against the Sari Bair position, 6th–10th August 1915," Godley to Skeen, memo, 16 August 1915, HQ ANZAC WD, AWM 4, 1/25/5 pt. 5.
15. "Notes on further operations by Australian & New Zealand Army Corps," ca. June 1915, HQ ANZAC WD, AWM 4, 1/25/3 pt. 3.
16. "Narrative of operations, 6–9 August 1915," 1st Australian Div. Artillery WD, AWM 4, 13/10/12 pt. 1.
17. "Notes on further operations by Australian & New Zealand Army Corps," ca. June 1915, HQ ANZAC WD, AWM 4, 1/25/3 pt. 3.
18. "Narrative of operations, 6–9 August 1915," 1st Australian Div. Artillery WD, AWM 4, 13/10/12 pt. 1; diary entries, 6 and 9–11 August 1915, Heavy Battery WD, AWM 4, 13/63/2.
19. Four 18-pounders, four 4.5-inch howitzers, and twelve 5-inch howitzers supported the actions at Lone Pine.
20. Diary entry, 10 August 1915, Hobbs Papers, AWM PR82/153, 1/3.
21. Diary entries, 6–7 August 1915, 5th Battery, 2nd Australian FAB WD, AWM 4, 13/67/5.
22. Travers, *Gallipoli 1915*, 120.
23. Evidence of Brigadier-General G. N. Johnston to the Dardanelles Commission, 2 May 1917, TNA, CAB 19/33, 1395.
24. "Notes on further operations by Australian & New Zealand Army Corps," ca. June 1915, HQ ANZAC WD, AWM 4, 1/25/3 pt. 3.
25. R. Keyes, *The Naval Memoirs of Admiral of the Fleet Sir Roger Keyes: The Narrow Seas to the Dardanelles, 1910–1915* (London: Thornton Butterworth, 1934), 384.
26. Evidence of Brigadier-General G. N. Johnston to the Dardanelles Commission, 2 May 1917, TNA, CAB 19/33, 1396.
27. Ibid., 1395.
28. Diary entries, 6–7 and 12 August 1915, 7th IMA Bde. WD, AWM 6/183.
29. "Narrative of operations, 6–9 August 1915," 1st Australian Div. Artillery WD, AWM 4, 13/10/12 pt. 1.
30. Evidence of Brigadier-General G. N. Johnston to the Dardanelles Commission, 2 May 1917, TNA, CAB 19/33, 1395.
31. Hamilton to Callwell, letter, 13 September 1915, Hamilton Papers, LHCMA, HAMILTON 7/3/3.
32. Report, Captain Ian Smith (General Staff), n.d., GS WD, GHQ MEF, AWM 4, 1/4/5 pt. 3.
33. "Report on operations," 8 August 1915, HQ IX Corps, WD TNA, WO 95/4276.

34. Diary entry, 7 August 1915, CRA 11th Div. WD, TNA, WO 95/4298.
35. Unpublished manuscript, Rettie Papers, IWM, 89/9/1, 21; Rettie to Aspinall-Oglander, letter, 16 July 1929, TNA, CAB 45/244.
36. Diary entry, 9 August 1915, CRA 11th Div. WD, TNA, WO 95/4298.
37. Diary entry, 10 August 1915, CRA 10th Div. WD, TNA, WO 95/4294; diary entries, 11–14 August 1915, CRA 11th Div. WD, TNA, WO 95/4298.
38. "Report on operations," 8 August 1915, HQ IX Corps WD, TNA, WO 95/4276.
39. Willmer to Aspinall-Oglander, letter, 15 January 1930, Aspinall-Oglander Papers, IWCRO, OG/AO/G/44.
40. Travers, *Gallipoli 1915*, 176.
41. Aspinall-Oglander, *Military Operations*, 2:393.
42. "Notes on further operations by Australian & New Zealand Army Corps," ca. June 1915, HQ ANZAC WD, AWM 4, 1/25/3 pt. 3.
43. Evidence of Brigadier-General G. N. Johnston to the Dardanelles Commission, 2 May 1917, TNA, CAB 19/33, 1400.
44. "Extract from private diary of Major-General C. Cunliffe Owen," TNA, CAB 45/246.
45. Evidence of Brigadier-General G. N. Johnston to the Dardanelles Commission, 2 May 1917, TNA, CAB 19/33, 1394–96.
46. "Extract from private diary of Major-General C. Cunliffe Owen," TNA, CAB 45/246.
47. Diary entry, 3 August 1915, 3rd Australian FAB WD, AWM 4, 13/31/13; Hobbs, "Operation Order No. 1," 3 August 1915, 1st Australian Div. Artillery WD, AWM 4, 13/10/12 pt. 1.
48. Diary entry, 4 August 1915, 1st Australian FAB WD, AWM 4, 13/29/2 pt. 1; diary entry, 4 August 1915, Heavy Battery, 1st Australian Div. Artillery WD, AWM 4, 13/63/2.
49. Evidence of Brigadier-General G. N. Johnston to the Dardanelles Commission, 2 May 1917, TNA, CAB 19/33, 1399–1400.
50. Diary entry, 2 August 1915, RA GHQ WD, TNA, WO 95/4267; R. Mallett, "The Interplay between Technology, Tactics and Organisation in the First AIF" (MA thesis, University of New South Wales, 1998), 49.
51. Diary entries, 2 and 17 August 1915, RA GHQ WD, TNA, WO 95/4267.
52. Diary entry, 2 August 1915, RA GHQ WD, TNA, WO 95/4267.
53. Diary entry, 17 August 1915, RA GHQ WD, TNA, WO 95/4267; diary entry, 23 August 1915, CRA VIII Corps WD, TNA, WO 95/4275.
54. "8th Army Corps Order No. 22," 21 August 1915, CRA VIII Corps WD, TNA, WO 95/4275.
55. Diary entry, 13 August 1915, RA GHQ WD, TNA, WO 95/4267.
56. Diary entries, 9, 13, and 23 August 1915, CRA 10th Div. WD, TNA, WO 95/4294.
57. Evidence of Brigadier-General G. N. Johnston to the Dardanelles Commission, 2 May 1917, TNA, CAB 19/33, 1394–96.
58. Rosenthal to Hamilton, letter, 7 October 1919, Hamilton Papers, LHCMA, HAMILTON 7/10/9.

59. "Extract from private diary of Major-General C. Cunliffe Owen," TNA, CAB 45/246.
60. Evidence of Brigadier-General G. N. Johnston to the Dardanelles Commission, 2 May 1917, TNA, CAB 19/33, 1397–1401.
61. Travers, *Gallipoli 1915*, 168 (emphasis added).
62. "Attack on the 'H' trenches by 29th Division VIIIth Corps on August 6th 1915: Report on the co-operation of the VIIIth Corps Artillery," n.d., CRA VIII Corps WD, TNA, WO 95/4275; Braithwaite to GOC VIII Corps, telegram, 29 July 1915, GS WD, GHQ MEF, AWM 4, 1/4/4 pt. 2; "Order of Battle of the Mediterranean Expeditionary Force, July 1915," Hamilton Papers, LHCMA, HAMILTON 7/4/28.
63. Diary entry, 30 July 1915, GS WD, GHQ MEF, AWM 4, 1/4/4 pt. 1; Braithwaite to Shaw, telegram, 30 July 1915, GS WD, GHQ MEF, AWM 4, 1/4/4 pt. 2.
64. Diary entry, 2 August 1915, RA GHQ WD, TNA, WO 95/4267; "Extract from private diary of Major-General C. Cunliffe Owen," TNA, CAB 45/246; Braithwaite to Birdwood, "Instructions for GOC A&NZ Army Corps," telegram, 30 July 1915, GS WD, GHQ MEF, AWM 4, 1/4/4 pt. 2.
65. British divisional artillery establishment was three field artillery brigades (each with three batteries of six guns), one howitzer brigade (consisting of three batteries of six howitzers), and one four-gun heavy battery. Bean, *Official History*, 1:57–58.
66. There were eight "British" infantry divisions available for the offensive. These included the 29th Division; 42nd (East Lancashire) Division; 52nd (Lowland) Division; Australian Division; New Zealand and Australian Division; 10th Division; 11th Division; and 13th Division. There was also the 29th Indian Infantry Brigade; two French divisions; the Royal Naval Division; and as a force reserve the 53rd (Welsh) and 54th (East Anglian) Divisions.
67. D. Clarke, *British Artillery 1914–19: Field Army Artillery* (Oxford: Osprey, 2004), 9.
68. This calculation is based on the four-gun battery equation of 52 pieces per division. Not including the French divisions (but inclusive of the 18 French guns/howitzers), the active forces at Helles numbered approximately three divisions (29th Div.; 42nd Div.; 52nd Div.). The artillery establishment at Helles, therefore should have equated to 156 pieces (52 × 3). With a total of 150 pieces, Helles was effectively at establishment.
69. This calculation is based on fifty-two pieces per division. There were 1.66 divisions at Suvla (11th Div.; 10th Div. [less one brigade at Anzac]). Thus, there should have been eighty-six pieces allotted to Suvla (52 × 1.66). With forty-eight pieces at Suvla (inclusive of those landed at Anzac but destined for Suvla), there was a deficiency of thirty-eight pieces (44.2 percent).
70. Similarly, this calculation is based on 52 pieces per division. There were 3.66 divisions at Anzac (Australian Div.; NZ&A Div.; 13th Div.; 29th Indian Infantry Bde.; 29th Infantry Bde. [10th Div.]). Thus, there

should have been 190 pieces available at Anzac (52 × 3.66). With only 72 pieces, Anzac had a deficiency of 118 pieces (62.1 percent).
71. "Replies to questions put by Australian Official Historian [to Turkish General Staff] on fighting in Gallipoli," TNA, CAB 45/236, 5.
72. This is calculated on there being 8.33 divisions (the .33 representing a single brigade)—3.66 of which were at Anzac (three divisions and two brigades), 3 at Helles (three divisions), and 1.66 at Suvla (11th Div. and two brigades of the 10th Div.).
73. Prior and Wilson, *Command on the Western Front*, 23, 34.
74. While the battle at Neuve Chapelle did not involve all four divisions, the surplus in artillery establishment has been calculated based on the assumption that all four divisions were available to be employed at some point during the offensive. The four divisions were the 7th and 8th Divisions (IV Corps, under the command of Lieutenant-General Henry Rawlinson) and the Lahore and Meerut Divisions (Indian Corps, under the command of Lieutenant-General Sir J. Willcocks). Prior and Wilson, *Command on the Western Front*, 21–22, 44–57; J. B. A. Bailey, *Field Artillery and Firepower* (Oxford: Military Press, 1989), 131.
75. Prior and Wilson, *Command on the Western Front*, 33; Bidwell and Graham, *Fire-power*, 73.
76. H. Rawlinson, "Remarks on VIIIth Division Scheme," HQ IV Corps WD, Jan.–Feb. 1915, TNA, WO 95/707, quoted in Prior and Wilson, *Command on the Western Front*, 25; Griffith, *Battle Tactics of the Western Front*, 150–51.
77. Bailey, *Field Artillery and Firepower*, 131.
78. Prior and Wilson, *Command on the Western Front*, 29, 61–63.
79. While previous figures have excluded the French (because they were not utilized for the August Offensive), this calculation must consider the entire Ottoman front at Helles. This frontage was approximately six thousand yards. The ratio at Loos was one gun per twenty-three yards. Bailey, *Field Artillery and Firepower*, 132.
80. This calculation is based on the conservative estimate of an eight-thousand-yard front.
81. There were only twenty-four Allied pieces at Suvla Bay during the first three days of the August Offensive. This was later increased to forty-eight. The Allied positions at Suvla were encircled by approximately twenty thousand yards of high ground, all of which could be used by the enemy for defensive purposes.
82. "Details of comparison between original Expeditionary Force and present total Military Forces," 28 September 1915, TNA, WO 159/4.
83. Great Britain War Office, *Statistics of the Military Effort of the British Empire during the Great War 1914–1920* (1922; repr., Dallington, UK: Naval and Military Press, 1999), 163–64.
84. Ibid., 210; GHQ MEF to War Office, telegram, 4 August 1915, Hamilton Papers, LHCMA, HAMILTON 7/4/8.
85. Brown, *British Logistics on the Western Front*, 90.
86. "Proportion of shrapnel and H.E. issued during week 31st July, 1915," memo, TNA, WO 161/23; "Notes by Lieutenant-Colonel Charles

Rosenthal, Commanding 3rd Australian Field Artillery Brigade, 1st Australian Division, relating to Artillery at ANZAC from 25th April to 25th August, 1915," Hamilton Papers, LHCMA, HAMILTON 7/10/9; Skeen to Aspinall-Oglander, letter, 28 October 1930, TNA, CAB 45/244.

87. The battery fired 826 rounds in May; 1,530 in June; 1,486 in July; and 4,381 in August. Diary entry, 31 August 1915, 9th Battery WD, AWM 4, 13/71/7.
88. "Secretary's notes of a meeting of the Dardanelles Committee," 25 June 1915, TNA, CAB 22/2; War Office to GHQ MEF, telegram, 14 July 1915, Hamilton Papers, LHCMA, HAMILTON 7/4/8; Hamilton to Churchill, letter, n.d., Churchill Papers, CAC, CHAR 2/74/28.
89. Wilson to Bonar Law, letter, 24 July 1915, Bonar Law Papers, Parliamentary Archives, BL/51/1/34.
90. I. M. Brown, "Growing Pains: Supplying the British Expeditionary Force, 1914–1915," in *Battles Near and Far: A Century of Overseas Deployment*, ed. P. Dennis and J. Grey (Canberra: Army History Unit, 2005), 37–38.
91. D. French, "The Military Background to the "Shell Crisis" of May 1915," *Journal of Strategic Studies* 2, no. 2 (1979): 203.
92. "Ammunition situation as regards action at Helles between 09/07/15 and 04/08/15," GS WD, GHQ MEF, AWM 4, 1/4/4 pt. 3; diary entries, 31 July and 9 August 1915, CRA VIII Corps WD, TNA, WO 95/4275; diary entry, 4 August 1915, 2nd Australian FAB WD, AWM 4, 13/30/9.
93. Evidence of Brigadier-General G. N. Johnston to the Dardanelles Commission, 2 May 1917, TNA, CAB 19/33, 1394.
94. Hobbs to GOC 1st Australian Div., telegram, 20 June 1915, HQ ANZAC WD, AWM 4, 1/25/3 pt. 4; "Notes by Brigadier-General Simpson Baikie on the Artillery at Cape Helles in the Dardanelles Expedition," n.d., Hamilton Papers, LHCMA, HAMILTON 7/10/5.
95. Griffith, *Battle Tactics of the Western Front*, 138, 142.
96. Diary entry, 2 August 1915, 3rd Australian FAB WD, AWM 4, 13/31/13; "Notes by Lieutenant-Colonel Charles Rosenthal, Commanding 3rd Australian Field Artillery Brigade, 1st Australian Division, relating to Artillery at ANZAC from 25th April to 25th August, 1915," Hamilton Papers, LHCMA, HAMILTON 7/10/9.
97. Diary entry, 31 July 1915, CRA VIII Corps WD, TNA, WO 95/4275.
98. While not necessarily representative of the ammunition expended on all fronts throughout the August Offensive, comprehensive data is not available for Anzac/Sari Bair or Suvla.
99. Diary entries, 1–31 August 1915, CRA VIII Corps WD, TNA, WO 95/4275.
100. Diary entries, 1–31 August 1915, 9th Battery WD, AWM 4, 13/71/7.
101. Diary entries, 1–31 August 1915, CRA VIII Corps WD, TNA, WO 95/4275.
102. Diary entries, 1–31 August 1915, 9th Battery WD, AWM 4, 13/71/7.
103. Diary entry, 7 August 1915, GS WD, GHQ MEF, AWM 4, 1/4/5 pt. 1; diary entry, 7 August 1915, HQ VIII Corps WD, TNA, WO 95/4273.

104. "Notes by Brigadier-General Simpson Baikie on the Artillery at Cape Helles in the Dardanelles Expedition," n.d., Hamilton Papers, LHCMA, HAMILTON 7/10/5.
105. Diary entry, 11 August 1915, GS WD, GHQ MEF, AWM 4, 1/4/5 pt. 1.
106. GHQ MEF to War Office, telegram, 14 August 1915, Hamilton Papers, LHCMA, HAMILTON 7/4/8.
107. Diary entry, 14 August 1915, DDOS WD, TNA, WO 95/4268.
108. Davies to Braithwaite, memo, 11 August 1915, HQ VIII Corps WD, TNA, WO 95/4273.
109. "Situation in the Aegean: Appreciation by Captain Dawnay, General Staff, Mediterranean Expeditionary Force," September 1915, Dawnay Papers, IWM, 69/21/6.
110. "Notes by Brigadier-General Simpson Baikie on the Artillery at Cape Helles in the Dardanelles Expedition," n.d., Hamilton Papers, LHCMA, HAMILTON 7/10/5; Hogg, *Allied Artillery of World War One*, 9–10.
111. "Notes on 10 pdr [pounder] B. L. [breech-loading] Gun," Fuller to General Staff, memo, 6 September 1915, RA GHQ WD, TNA, WO 95/4267; diary entries, 6–10 and 31 August 1915, 7th IIMA Bde. WD, AWM 6/183.
112. "Notes by Brigadier-General Simpson-Baikie on the Artillery at Cape Helles in the Dardanelles Expedition," n.d., Hamilton Papers, LHCMA, HAMILTON 7/10/5.
113. Hunter to COO *Minnetonka*, telegram, 12 July 1915, RA GHQ WD, TNA, WO 95/4267; diary entry, 23 August 1915, 15th Heavy Battery WD, AWM 6/100.
114. Diary entry, 12 July 1915, RA GHQ WD, TNA, WO 95/4267; "Notes by Brigadier-General Simpson Baikie on the Artillery at Cape Helles in the Dardanelles Expedition," n.d., Hamilton Papers, LHCMA, HAMILTON 7/10/5.
115. Shipman (IOM, MEF) to DDOS, memo, 23 August 1915, RA GHQ WD, TNA, WO 95/4267.
116. Diary entry, 21 August 1915, 15th Heavy Battery WD, AWM 6/100.
117. Hunter to DDOS Imbros, telegram, 14 August 1915, RA GHQ WD, TNA, WO 95/4267.
118. Davies to Braithwaite, telegram, 14 August 1915, CRA VIII Corps WD, TNA, WO 95/4275.
119. Hogg, *Allied Artillery of World War One*, 19–24; Hunter to COO *Minnetonka*, telegram, 12 July 1915, RA GHQ WD, TNA, WO 95/4267.
120. "Notes by Brigadier-General Simpson-Baikie on the Artillery at Cape Helles in the Dardanelles Expedition," n.d., Hamilton Papers, LHCMA, HAMILTON 7/10/5; Hogg, *Allied Artillery of World War One*, 27–29.
121. "Notes by Brigadier-General Simpson-Baikie on the Artillery at Cape Helles in the Dardanelles Expedition," n.d., Hamilton Papers, LHCMA, HAMILTON 7/10/5.

122. Birdwood, *Khaki and Gown*, 241, 267.
123. Diary entry, 16 July 1915, RA GHQ WD, TNA, WO 95/4267.
124. Hunter-Weston to GHQ, telegram, 8 July 1915, CRA VIII Corps WD, TNA, WO 95/4275.
125. Diary entries, 15 and 28 August 1915, RA GHQ WD, TNA, WO 95/4267.
126. Prior and Wilson, *Command on the Western Front*, 40; Hogg, *Allied Artillery of World War One*, 18.
127. "Notes on close shooting by guns and howitzers, registration of targets and calibration," n.d., TNA, WO 33/723, 4.
128. Unpublished manuscript, Rettie Papers, IWM, 81/9/1, 38.
129. "Notes on close shooting by guns and howitzers, registration of targets and calibration," n.d., TNA, WO 33/723, 8.
130. Prior and Wilson, *Command on the Western Front*, 36–37.
131. Bean, *Official History*, 2:64–65.
132. Hogg, *Allied Artillery of World War One*, 15–16.
133. Rettie to Aspinall-Oglander, letter, 16 July 1929, TNA, CAB 45/244, 5–6.
134. Bidwell and Graham, *Fire-Power*, 68.
135. "General Instructions for Artillery in the Advance," memo, 5 August 1915, 1st NZ FAB WD, AWM 4, 35/7/2.
136. Diary entry, 5 August 1915, 3rd Australian FAB WD, AWM 4, 13/31/13; diary entry, 6 August 1915, 1st Australian FAB WD, AWM 4, 13/29/2 pt. 1; diary entry, 7 August 1915, Heavy Battery WD, AWM 4, 16/63/2.
137. Diary entry, 6 August 1915, 8th Battery WD, TNA, WO 95/4338.
138. Diary entries, 6–7 August 1915, 1st NA FAB WD, AWM 4, 35/7/2.
139. Rettie to Aspinall-Oglander, letter, 16 July 1929, TNA, CAB 45/244, 5–6.
140. Travers, *Gallipoli 1915*, 169.
141. Chasseaud and Doyle, *Grasping Gallipoli*, 158–59.
142. Fuller to Braithwaite, "Artillery dispositions, 9th Corps, Suvla," memo, 8 September 1915, RA GHQ WD, TNA, WO 95/4267.
143. "Mitchell Report," 506–507; P. Mead, *The Eye in the Air: History of Air Observation and Reconnaissance for the Army, 1785–1945* (London: H.M. Stationary Office, 1983), 112.
144. Quoted in Hamilton, *Gallipoli Diary*, 2:286.
145. Evidence of Brigadier-General G. N. Johnston to the Dardanelles Commission, 2 May 1917, TNA, CAB 19/33, 1396.
146. Rettie to Aspinall-Oglander, letter, 16 July 1929, TNA, CAB 45/244.
147. Diary entry, 13 August 1915, 15th Heavy Battery WD, AWM 6/100; Travers, *Gallipoli 1915*, 173.
148. Rettie to Aspinall-Oglander, letter, 16 July 1929, TNA, CAB 45/244.
149. Bidwell and Graham, *Fire-Power*, 67; diary entries, 2–3 August 1915, 2nd Australian FAB WD, AWM 4, 13/30/9.
150. [Unidentified officer from] HMS *Talbot*, "Enemy guns on the flanks of ANZAC," 30 July 1915, England Papers, IWM, 76/43/1.
151. Diary, August 1915, 10th Heavy Battery WD, AWM 6/99.

152. Diary entry, 11 August 1915, 1st Australian Div. Artillery WD, AWM 4, 13/10/12 pt. 1; diary entry, 27 July 1915, 2nd Australian FAB WD, AWM 4, 13/30/8; Rettie to Aspinall-Oglander, letter, 16 July 1929, TNA, CAB 45/244.
153. "Sound ranging" and "flash spotting" were used together to pinpoint the location of hostile guns on the Western Front. This was accomplished through the use of microphones, which detected the flight of an enemy shell, and observes, to record the flash from an enemy gun. Griffith, *Battle Tactics of the Western Front*, 200; Hogg, *Allied Artillery of World War One*, 18; Sheffield, *Forgotten Victory*, 142.

4. Combined Operations

1. Throughout this chapter, "joint command" refers to command shared between both the admiral and general. In contemporary use, this term refers to a system whereby one commander is given ultimate command over multiple services.
2. Hankey to Asquith, letter, 28 July 1915, Asquith Papers, New Bodleian Library, MS. Asquith 117, fol. 171.
3. "Programme for Destroyers," memo, 27 July 1915, HQ ANZAC WD, AWM 4, 1/25/4 pt. 6.
4. J. S. Corbett, *Naval Operations*, vol. 3, *May 1915–June 1916* (London: Longmans, Green, 1923), 92.
5. Rear-Admiral Nicholson to CO's HM Ships, memo, 31 July 1915, de Robeck Papers, CAC, DRBK 4/9.
6. A. Moorehead, *Gallipoli* (London: Hamilton, 1956), 240.
7. Keyes, *Naval Memoirs*, 337.
8. H. H. Chrisman, "Naval Operations in the Mediterranean during the Great War, 1914–1918" (PhD diss., Stanford University, 1931), 250.
9. Charles de Bartolomé to de Robeck, telegram, 21 July 1915; de Robeck to de Bartolomé, telegram, 22 July 1915, both in TNA, ADM 137/155.
10. Admiralty to de Robeck, telegram, 7 August 1915, de Robeck Papers, CAC, DRBK 4/51.
11. "Naval force for support of Army," memo, 30 July 1915; de Robeck to EMS, memo, 4 August 1915, both in de Robeck Papers, CAC, DRBK 4/9. "Notes on conference held on 'Triad,'" memo, 2 August 1915; "Naval support to the Army in the forthcoming operations," memo, 3 August 1915, both in Aspinall-Oglander Papers, IWCRO, OG/AO/G/1.
12. "Naval support to the Army in the forthcoming operations," memo, 3 August 1915, Aspinall-Oglander Papers, IWCRO, OG/AO/G/12.
13. See "Appendix 'A': Action of Artillery in Support of forthcoming Operations," n.d.; "Army Corps Order No. 16," 3 August 1915, both in HQ ANZAC WD, AWM 4, 1/25/5 pt. 3; "Operation Order No. 11," 5 August 1915, NZ Infantry Bde. WD, AWM 4, 35/17/7; Mackenzie, *Gallipoli Memories*, 388.
14. De Robeck to Admiralty, telegram, 9 August 1915, TNA, ADM 137/184.

15. De Robeck to Admiralty, telegram, 6 July 1915, TNA, ADM 137/155.
16. De Robeck to Sir Henry Jackson, letter, 15 July 1915, de Robeck Papers, CAC, DRBK 4/70.
17. De Robeck to Balfour, letter, 28 July 1915, de Robeck Papers, CAC, DRBK 4/69; "Particulars of Monitors," memo, 27 September 1915, de Robeck Papers, CAC, DRBK 4/27.
18. De Robeck to Balfour, letter, 28 July 1915, de Robeck Papers, CAC, DRBK 4/69.
19. De Robeck to Admiral Jackson, letter, 25 August 1915, de Robeck Papers, CAC, DRBK 4/70.
20. De Robeck to Balfour, letter, 28 July 1915, de Robeck Papers, CAC, DRBK 4/69.
21. Corbett, *Naval Operations*, 3:89–90; "Mitchell Report," 259–60.
22. Keyes, *Naval Memoirs*, 380.
23. De Robeck to Rear-Admiral Christian, memo, 29 July 1915, de Robeck Papers, CAC, DRBK 4/9.
24. Corbett, *Naval Operations*, 3:93.
25. De Robeck to Admiralty, telegram, 9 August 1915, TNA, ADM 137/184.
26. Keyes, *Naval Memoirs*, 386.
27. Corbett, *Naval Operations*, 3:93.
28. De Robeck to Admiralty, telegram, 9 August 1915, TNA, ADM 137/184.
29. Corbett, *Naval Operations*, 3:94.
30. De Robeck to Rear-Admiral Christian, memo, 29 July 1915, de Robeck Papers, CAC, DRBK 4/9.
31. Keyes, *Naval Memoirs*, 389–91.
32. Hankey to Asquith, letter, 4 August 1915, TNA, CAB 17/123.
33. Simpson-Baikie to wife, letter, 21 July 1915, Simpson-Baikie Papers, LHCMA, SIMPSON-BAIKIE.
34. De Robeck to Godley, letter, n.d., Godley Papers, LHCMA, GODLEY 3/91.
35. Diary entry, 24 July 1915, RA GHQ WD, TNA, WO 95/4267.
36. "Notes on conference held on 'Triad,'" memo, 2 August 1915, Aspinall-Oglander Papers, IWCRO, OG/AO/G/12.
37. "Operation Order No. 1," 3 August 1915, HQ IX Corps WD, TNA, WO 95/4276; diary entry, 8 August 1915, RA GHQ WD, TNA, WO 95/4267.
38. "Statement by Lt-General The Hon. Sir F. Stopford respecting the operations of the 9th Army Corps at Suvla Bay August 6th to 15th 1915," 29 August 1915, TNA, WO 138/40, 15–16.
39. "Naval support to the Army in the forthcoming operations," memo, 3 August, Aspinall-Oglander Papers, IWCRO, OG/AO/G/12.
40. "Mitchell Report," 252, 258.
41. Ship log, HMS *M30*, TNA, ADM 53/50785.
42. De Robeck to Admiralty, telegram, 18 August 1915; de Robeck to Admiralty, telegram, 23 August 1915; Admiral Superintending Malta (based on information from de Robeck) to Admiralty, telegram, 29 August 1915, all in TNA, ADM 137/184.
43. Ibid. (three telegrams).

44. "Report by Captain, HMS 'Talbot,'" 22 September 1915, TNA, ADM 116/1451.
45. Evidence of General Sir Ian Hamilton to the Dardanelles Commission, 17 July 1917, TNA, CAB 19/33, 1546.
46. Travers, *Gallipoli 1915*, 167.
47. Quoted in Keyes, *Naval Memoirs*, 335–36.
48. "Artillery dispositions, 9th Corps, Suvla," memo, 8 September 1915, RA GHQ WD, TNA, WO 95/4267.
49. R. Prior, *Churchill's "World Crisis" as History* (Canberra: Croom Helm, 1983), 150.
50. De Robeck to Admiral Jackson, letter, 25 August 1915, de Robeck Papers, CAC, DRBK 4/70.
51. De Robeck to Admiralty, telegram, 31 August 1915, TNA, ADM 137/184.
52. De Robeck to Admiralty, telegram, 24 July 1915, TNA, ADM 137/155.
53. "Mitchell Report," 388.
54. Travers, *Gallipoli 1915*, 164.
55. Corbett, *Naval Operations*, 3:98.
56. Evidence of Brigadier-General G. N. Johnston to the Dardanelles Commission, 2 May 1917, TNA, CAB 19/33, 1394–96.
57. Ibid.
58. A. J. Marder, *From the Dardanelles to Oran: Studies of the Royal Navy in War and Peace, 1915–1940* (London: Oxford University Press, 1974), 11.
59. Keyes to de Robeck (annotated by de Robeck), letter, 17 August 1915, de Robeck Papers, CAC, DRBK 4/78.
60. "Mitchell Report," 210.
61. "Report by the Captain, HMS *Talbot*," 22 September 1915, TNA, ADM 116/1451; "Report from Colonel F. H. Sykes, R.F.C. on the subject of the RNAS Units and Aerial requirements of the Naval and Military Forces at the Dardanelles," 9 July 1915, TNA, AIR 1/625/17/12, 1.
62. "Kite Balloons for Naval use," Commander in Chief Home Fleets to the Secretary, Admiralty, telegram, 20 August 1915, TNA, AIR 1/636/17/122/138.
63. "Some rough notes on the early development of the Royal Naval Air Service," memo, 30 October 1917, TNA, AIR 1/625/17/1; "Kite Balloons for Naval use," Commander in Chief Home Fleets to the Secretary, Admiralty, telegram, 20 August 1915, TNA, AIR 1/636/17/122/138; No. 1 Kite Balloon Section, "Report of operations," 10 August 1915, TNA, AIR 1/665/17/122/713; report by the Captain, HMS *Lord Nelson*, 2 September 1915, TNA, ADM 116/1451.
64. No. 1 Kite Balloon Section, "Report of operations," 10 August 1915, TNA, AIR 1/665/17/122/713.
65. "Report on attack by torpedo carrying aeroplane," 13 August 1915, TNA, AIR 1, 665/17/122/716; (RNAS) Tenedos to Admiralty, telegram, 21 August 1915, TNA, ADM 137/184.
66. De Robeck to Balfour, letter, 28 July 1915, de Robeck Papers, CAC, DRBK 4/69.

67. "Mitchell Report," 200–202.
68. Boyle, "*E14*—report of proceedings 21st July to 12th August 1915," 14 August 1915; Nasmith, "*E11*—report of proceedings 5th August to 3rd September," 4 September 1915, both in TNA, ADM 137/382.
69. "Questions put to the Ottoman General Staff about the Dardanelles operations and the answers received: second series of questions and answers," n.d., TNA, CAB 45/217.
70. Nasmith, "*E11*—report of proceedings 5th August to 3rd September," 4 September 1915; Stocks, "*E2*—report of proceedings 13th August to 14th September 1915," 16 September 1915, both in TNA, ADM 137/382.
71. R. Wester-Wemyss, *The Navy in the Dardanelles Campaign* (London: Hodder and Stoughton, 1924), 151.
72. Hankey to Balfour, letter, 5 August 1915, TNA, CAB 17/123.
73. "Mitchell Report," 205–207.
74. Keyes, *Naval Memoirs*, 416.
75. "Questions put to the Ottoman General Staff about the Dardanelles operations and the answers received: second series of questions and answers," n.d., TNA, CAB 45/217.
76. P. Halpern, *The Naval War in the Mediterranean, 1914–1918* (London: Allen and Unwin, 1987), 162.
77. Hamilton's dispatch, 11 December 1915, Hamilton Papers, LHCMA, HAMILTON 7/8/23.
78. Balfour to Fisher, letter, 6 June 1915, quoted in J. A. Fisher, *Fear God and Dread Nought: The Correspondence of Admiral of the Fleet Lord Fisher of Kilverstone*, ed. A. J. Marder, vol. 3, *Revolution, Abdication, and Last Years, 1914–1920* (London: Cape, 1959), 255.
79. Keyes to Secretary of the Admiralty, telegram, 27 August 1925, Hamilton Papers, LHCMA, HAMILTON 13/59.
80. Keyes to wife, letter, 5 August 1915, Keyes Papers, BL, Add. 82393.
81. "Orders for Combined Operations," 12 April 1915, Hamilton Papers, LHCMA, HAMILTON 7/4/18.
82. Ibid.
83. De Robeck to Jackson, letter, 15 July 1915, de Robeck Papers, CAC, DRBK 4/70.
84. Keyes to wife, letter, 5 August 1915, Keyes Papers, BL, Add. 82393.
85. Balfour to de Robeck, letter, 11 August 1915, de Robeck Papers, CAC, DRBK 4/14.
86. Balfour to de Robeck, letter, 14 June 1915, de Robeck Papers, CAC, DRBK 4/69.
87. Coates, *Defeat at Gallipoli*, 299.
88. Great Britain War Office, *Manual of Combined Naval and Military Operations*, 9.
89. Keyes to wife, letter, 2 July 1915, Keyes Papers, BL, Add. 82393.
90. Hamilton to Kitchener, letter, 26 July 1915, Hamilton Papers, LHCMA, HAMILTON 7/1/6.
91. G. Penn, *Fisher, Churchill and the Dardanelles* (Barnsley: Leo Cooper, 1999), 8–10, 109.

92. A. J. Marder, "The Influence of History on Sea Power: The Royal Navy and the Lessons of 1914–1918," *Pacific Historical Review* 41, no. 4 (November 1972): 418–19.
93. Evidence of Acting Vice-Admiral Sir Henry F. Oliver to the Dardanelles Commission, 5 October 1916, TNA, CAB 19/33, 130.
94. "The naval memoirs of Admiral J. H. Godfrey," vol. 8, Godfrey Papers, IWM, 74/96/1, 23–24.
95. Gamble to de Robeck, letter, 17 August 1915, de Robeck Papers, CAC, DRBK 4/39.
96. Evidence of Lieutenant-Colonel Sir Maurice Hankey to the Dardanelles Commission, 19 September 1916, TNA, CAB 19/33, 14–15, 25–26.
97. Evidence of Lieutenant-General Sir James Wolfe Murray to the Dardanelles Commission, 10 October 1916, TNA, CAB 19/33, 166.
98. Evidence of The Right Hon. Viscount Haldane of Cloan to the Dardanelles Commission, 18 October 1916, TNA, CAB 19/33, 263.
99. A. J. Marder, *From the Dreadnought to Scapa Flow: The Royal Navy in the Fisher Era, 1904–1919*, vol. 2, *The War Years: To the Eve of Jutland* (London: Oxford University Press, 1966), 297–98; Penn, *Fisher, Churchill and the Dardanelles*, 199–200.
100. Jackson to de Robeck, letter, 13 July 1915; Jackson to de Robeck, letter, 25 August 1915, both in de Robeck Papers, CAC, DRBK 4/30.
101. Corbett, *Naval Operations*, 3:87–88.
102. "The decision to substitute a combined operation for the naval attack," Rayfield Papers, IWM, 69/61/2, 22.
103. M. H. H. Evans, *Amphibious Operations: The Projection of Sea Power Ashore* (Sydney: Brassey's, 1990), 17.
104. S. Miles, "Notes on the Dardanelles Campaign of 1915," pt. 1, *Coast Artillery Journal* 61, no. 6 (December 1924): 515.
105. "The Naval memoirs of Admiral J. H. Godfrey," vol. 8, Godfrey Papers, IWM, 74/96/1, 24.
106. Hamilton, *Gallipoli Diary*, 2:125.
107. E. W. Bush, *Gallipoli* (London: Allen and Unwin, 1975), 229.
108. Hamilton, *Gallipoli Diary*, 2:32.
109. Ibid., 49.
110. Ibid., 124–25.
111. De Robeck to Jackson, letter, 25 August 1915, de Robeck Papers, CAC, DRBK 4/70.
112. Keyes to wife, letter, 2 July 1915, Keyes Papers, BL, Add. 82393.
113. Miles, "Notes on the Dardanelles Campaign of 1915," pt. 1, 514–15.
114. J. Creswell, *Generals and Admirals: The Story of Amphibious Command* (London: Longmans, Green, 1952), 5.
115. Evidence of Rear-Admiral Roger John Brownlow Keyes to the Dardanelles Commission, 15 May 1917, TNA, CAB 19/33, 1481.
116. Evidence of Admiral Sackville H. Carden to the Dardanelles Commission, 6 October 1916, TNA, CAB 19/33, 154.
117. Evidence of Admiral Sir John de Robeck to the Dardanelles Commission, 10 October 1916, TNA, CAB 19/33, 171.

118. "Notes by Keyes for Aspinall-Oglander," n.d., Keyes Papers, BL, Add. 82373, 2.
119. Keyes, *Naval Memoirs*, 438; Marder, *From the Dreadnought to Scapa Flow*, 2:316.
120. "Notes by Keyes for Aspinall-Oglander," n.d., Keyes Papers, BL, Add. 82373, 2.
121. "Secretary's notes of a meeting of a War Council held at 10, Downing Street, May 14, 1915," Miscellaneous Papers, LHCMA, MISC 35, 3.
122. "The Possibility of a Joint Naval and Military Attack upon the Dardanelles," memo, 20 December 1906, Hamilton Papers, LHCMA, HAMILTON 7/4/1.
123. Hankey to Asquith, letter, 4 August 1915, TNA, CAB 17/123.
124. Evidence of Admiral Sir Henry Jackson to the Dardanelles Commission, 6 October 1916, TNA, CAB 19/33, 143; Penn, *Fisher, Churchill and the Dardanelles*, 146–47.
125. De Robeck to Admiralty, telegram, 21 August 1915; Balfour to de Robeck, telegram, 21 August 1915, both in TNA, ADM 137/184.
126. Evidence of Admiral Sir John de Robeck to the Dardanelles Commission, 10 October 1916, TNA, CAB 19/33, 170.
127. Admiralty to de Robeck, telegram, 26 August 1915, TNA, ADM 137/184.
128. Marder, *From the Dreadnought to Scapa Flow*, 2:314.
129. (Renewal of naval attack at the Dardanelles), memo, 21 August 1915, Curzon Papers, BL, F112/160.
130. Keyes to wife, letters, 12 and 16 August 1915, Keyes Papers, BL, Add. 82393.
131. Godfrey to Keyes, letter, 6 June 1917, Keyes Papers, BL, Add. 82385; appreciation, "The position in the Gallipoli Peninsula," Keyes to de Robeck, 17 August 1915, de Robeck Papers, CAC, DRBK 4/78.
132. Keyes to wife, letter, 19 August 1915, Keyes Papers, BL, Add. 82393.
133. Wester-Wemyss, *The Navy in the Dardanelles Campaign*, 176–77.
134. Wemyss to Keyes, letter, ca. 20–30 August 1915, Keyes Papers, BL, Add. 82403.
135. Keyes, *Naval Memoirs*, 435.
136. Appreciation, "The position in the Gallipoli Peninsula," Keyes to de Robeck, 17 August 1915, de Robeck Papers, CAC, DRBK 4/78.
137. Notes on Keyes's appreciation, "The position in the Gallipoli Peninsula," de Robeck Papers, CAC, DRBK 4/78.
138. Marder, *From the Dreadnought to Scapa Flow*, 2:314–15.
139. Halpern, *The Naval War in the Mediterranean*, 49–51; Jellicoe to Hamilton, letter, 9 November 1915, quoted in A. T. Patterson, ed., *The Jellicoe Papers: Selections from the Private and Official Correspondence of Admiral of the Fleet Earl Jellicoe of Scapa* (London: Navy Records Society, 1966), 187; Marder, *From the Dardanelles to Oran*, 23; de Robeck to Balfour, letter, 20 October 1915, de Robeck Papers, CAC, DRBK 4/69.
140. Evidence of Rear-Admiral Roger John Brownlow Keyes to the Dardanelles Commission, 16 May 1917, TNA, CAB 19/33, 1476.

141. De Robeck to Balfour, letter, 20 October 1915, de Robeck Papers, CAC, DRBK 4/69.
142. Keyes, *Naval Memoirs*, 443.
143. Evidence of Rear-Admiral Roger John Brownlow Keyes to the Dardanelles Commission, 16 May 1917, TNA, CAB 19/33, 1475, 1480, 1487; "Mitchell Report," 309.
144. Marder, *From the Dreadnought to Scapa Flow*, 2:14.
145. Prior, *Churchill's "World Crisis" as History*, 277–78.
146. Great Britain War Office, *Manual of Combined Naval and Military Operations*, 20–21.
147. Ibid., 10.
148. Keyes to de Robeck, letter, 23 September 1915, de Robeck Papers, CAC, DRBK 4/78.
149. "Mitchell Report," 388.
150. Kannengiesser, *The Campaign in Gallipoli*, 200.
151. De Robeck to Admiralty, telegram, 21 July 1915, TNA, ADM 137/155.

5. Lines of Communication

1. M. van Creveld, *Supplying War: Logistics from Wallenstein to Patton* (New York: Cambridge University Press, 2004), 1; Alger, *Definitions and Doctrine*, 6.
2. J. Keegan, "Logistics and Supply," in *Military Logistics: A Primer on Operational, Strategic and Support Level Logistics*, ed. M. Coles (Canberra: Australian Defence Studies Centre, 1996), 21.
3. D. Chapman-Huston and O. Rutter, *General Sir John Cowans G.C.B., G.C.M.G.: The Quartermaster-General of the Great War* (London: Hutchinson, 1924), 107.
4. The L-of-C refers to the routes to (and from) the theater, rather than physical lines. M. Kress, *Operational Logistics: The Art and Science of Sustaining Military Operations* (Boston: Kluwer, 2002), 29.
5. J. Sinclair, "Logistics, Principles and Practice," in Coles, *Military Logistics*, 45.
6. E. A. Altham in Chapman-Huston and Rutter, *General Sir John Cowans*, 108.
7. Evidence of Sir John Cowans to the Dardanelles Commission, 30 March 1917, TNA, CAB 19/33, 1330; Cowans was promoted Lieutenant-General in September, 1915.
8. Brown, "Growing Pains," 44.
9. Evidence of Captain H. V. Simpson to the Dardanelles Commission, 2 February 1917, TNA, CAB 19/33, 822.
10. Cowans to Altham, telegram, 24 July 1915, Hamilton Papers, LHCMA, HAMILTON 7/4/8.
11. G. MacMunn, "The Lines of Communication in the Dardanelles," *Army Quarterly* 20, no. 1 (April 1930), 52.
12. Evidence of Graeme Thomson to the Dardanelles Commission, 20 March 1917, TNA, CAB 19/33, 1207; evidence of Major-General The Hon. R. Stuart-Wortley to the Dardanelles Commission, 19 January 1917, TNA, CAB 19/33, 599.

13. Ibid., 605.
14. Evidence of Lieutenant-Colonel H. F. P. Percival to the Dardanelles Commission, 10 January 1917, TNA, CAB 19/33, 461–62.
15. Evidence of Major-General The Hon. R. Stuart-Wortley to the Dardanelles Commission, 19 January 1917, TNA, CAB 19/33, 599; evidence of Graeme Thomson to the Dardanelles Commission, 20 March 1917, TNA, CAB 19/33, 1209.
16. Diary entry, 31 July 1915, DST WD, GHQ MEF, TNA, WO 95/4270.
17. Hankey to Asquith, letter, 4 August 1915, TNA, CAB 17/123, 10.
18. Great Britain War Office, *Manual of Combined Naval and Military Operations*, 8.
19. A. Hurd, *The Merchant Navy* (London: John Murray, 1924), 2:99; "Admiralty Transport Service," n.d., TNA, MT 23/427, T50185/1915.
20. Secretary's notes of a meeting of the Dardanelles Committee, 17 June 1915, TNA, CAB 22/2.
21. Ibid.
22. "The lines of communication: August 1915–January 1916," Rayfield Papers, IWM, 69/61/4.
23. French Naval Attaché, Admiralty, to Marine Paris (French Admiralty), telegram, 23 August 1915, TNA, ADM 137/184.
24. "The lines of communication to 27 May," Rayfield Papers, IWM, 69/61/3, 2.
25. Hamilton to Maxwell, letter, 27 June 1915, Hamilton Papers, LHCMA, HAMILTON 7/1/15.
26. Penn, *Fisher, Churchill and the Dardanelles*, 113.
27. Altham to Hamilton, letter, 7 December 1916, Hamilton Papers, LHCMA, HAMILTON 8/1/2.
28. Braithwaite to Altham, telegram, 28 July 1915, GS WD, GHQ MEF, AWM 4, 1/4/4 pt. 3.
29. G. Ellison, *The Perils of Amateur Strategy* (London: Longmans, Green, 1926), xxii, 92.
30. "The lines of communication: August 1915–January 1916," Rayfield Papers, IWM, 69/61/4; Corbett, *Naval Operations*, 3:80.
31. Hamilton to Maxwell, letter, 8 June 1915, Hamilton Papers, LHCMA, HAMILTON 7/1/15.
32. "Mitchell Report," 212; "The lines of communication: August 1915–January 1916," Rayfield Papers, IWM, 69/61/4.
33. "Mitchell Report," 246.
34. "Proclamation to the Anglo-French Expeditionary Force," 26 June 1915, Intelligence WD, GHQ MEF, AWM 4, 1/5/3.
35. Halpern, *The Naval War in the Mediterranean*, 116.
36. MacMunn, "The Lines of Communication in the Dardanelles," 55–56.
37. Evidence of Brigadier-General A. Joly de Lotbinière to the Dardanelles Commission, 23 January 1917, TNA, CAB 19/33, 626.
38. De Robeck to Admiralty, telegram, 1 July 1915, TNA, ADM 137/155.
39. W. Graham Greene to the Secretary, War Office, telegram, 2 July 1915, TNA, MT 23/454, T17930/1915.

40. Salonica (Knox) to de Robeck, telegram, 1 August 1915; SNO Malta to de Robeck, telegram, 8 August 1915, both in de Robeck Papers, CAC, DRBK 4/51.
41. The same submarine (*UB14*) hit HMT *Southland* on 2 September 1915, which was transporting members of the 2nd Australian Division from Egypt to Mudros.
42. "The lines of communication: August 1915–January 1916," Rayfield Papers, IWM, 69/61/4, 2–4.
43. De Robeck to Admiralty and SNO, Malta, telegram, 14 August 1915, de Robeck Papers, CAC, DRBK 4/51.
44. "Mitchell Report," 266.
45. Diary entry, 18 August 1915, DQMG WD, GHQ MEF, TNA, WO 95/4266.
46. "Mitchell Report," 213.
47. The MEF's L-of-C consisted of different types of bases: the main base, where the bulk of the stores were located; the intermediate base, a temporary staging base; and the advanced bases, the area from which supplies were issued to the field units.
48. Diary entry, 18 July 1915, Base WD, MEF, TNA, WO 95/4269.
49. Maxwell to Kitchener, telegram, 5 July 1915, TNA, MT 23/429, T50684/1915.
50. Braithwaite to Cowans, letter, 22 June 1915, TNA, WO 107/43.
51. "Statement by Lieutenant-General Sir Edward A. Altham," report to the Dardanelles Commission, 10 January 1917, AWM 51/103, 1.
52. Braithwaite to Cowans, letter, 22 June 1915, TNA, WO 107/43.
53. "The lines of communication to 27 May," Rayfield Papers, IWM, 69/61/3, 1.
54. "Mitchell Report," 212.
55. Altham to War Office, telegram, 22 July 1915, Hamilton Papers, LHCMA, HAMILTON 7/4/8; Hankey to Asquith, letter, 4 August 1915, TNA, CAB 17/123, 10.
56. Memo, 26 May 1915, in "Navy Transport Service," n.d., TNA, MT 23/427, T50185/1915.
57. "The lines of communication: August 1915–January 1916," Rayfield Papers, IWM, 69/61/4.
58. Diary entry, 22 July 1915, Ellison Papers, NAM, 8704/35/214, 2.
59. Evidence of Major-General C. McGrigor to the Dardanelles Commission, 5 January 1917, TNA, CAB 19/33, 404.
60. Diary entry, 15 July 1915, DQMG WD, GHQ MEF, TNA, WO 95/4266.
61. De Robeck to Admiralty, telegram, 9 August 1915, TNA, ADM 137/184.
62. "Statement by Lieutenant-General Sir Edward A. Altham," report to the Dardanelles Commission, 10 January 1917, AWM 51/103, 1.
63. "The Dardanelles: Memorandum on the situation, August 30, 1915," Hamilton Papers, LHCMA, HAMILTON 7/4/33; "The lines of communication: intervention of German submarines to July," Rayfield Papers, IWM, 69/61/3, 1.

64. Evidence of Brigadier-General A. Joly de Lotbiniére to the Dardanelles Commission, 23 January 1917, TNA, CAB 19/33, 626.
65. "Account of Signals—Gallipoli" by Major H. C. B. Wemyss, TNA, WO 106/704, 5–6; Coates, *Defeat at Gallipoli*, 66.
66. Altham to War Office, telegram, 22 July 1915, Hamilton Papers, LHCMA, HAMILTON 7/4/8.
67. Quoted in Chapman-Huston and Rutter, *General Sir John Cowans*, 108.
68. MacMunn, "The Lines of Communication in the Dardanelles," 57; evidence of Lieutenant-General Sir E. A. Altham to the Dardanelles Commission, 10 January 1917, TNA, CAB 19/33, 464; diary entry, 27 July 1915, DST WD, GHQ MEF, TNA, WO 95/4269.
69. MacMunn, "The Lines of Communication in the Dardanelles," 58.
70. Evidence of Captain H. V. Simpson to the Dardanelles Commission, 2 February 1917, TNA, CAB 19/33, 822.
71. Simpson to Thomson, letter, 18 July 1915, TNA, MT 23/427, T50185/1915.
72. Simpson to Thomson, letter, 1 August 1915, TNA, MT 23/431, T51236/1915.
73. "Chapter 3—Eastward Bound," Rettie Papers, IWM 81/9/1, 21.
74. Diary entry, 18 July 1915, DST WD, GHQ MEF, TNA, WO 95/4269.
75. Diary entries, 4, 7, 8, 18, and 27 August 1915, DST "Supply Diary," GHQ MEF, TNA, WO 95/4269.
76. Diary entry, 30 July 1915, Shaw Papers, IWM, 76/106/1, 31.
77. Diary entry, 1 August 1915, DADS WD, TNA, WO 95/4270.
78. "Account of Signals—Gallipoli" by Major H. C. B. Wemyss, TNA, WO 106/704, 5–6.
79. Evidence of Captain H. V. Simpson to the Dardanelles Commission, 2 February 1917, TNA, CAB 19/33, 817.
80. Hankey to Asquith, letter, 4 August 1915, TNA, CAB 17/123, 10; Altham to War Office, telegram, 22 July 1915; Altham to War Office, telegram, 29 July 1915, both in Hamilton Papers, LHCMA, HAMILTON 7/4/8.
81. Hankey to Curzon, letter, 26 October 1915, Keyes Papers, BL, Add. 82393; diary entry, 3 August 1915, DADS WD, TNA, WO 95/4270.
82. "Navy Transport Service," memo, n.d., TNA, MT 23/427, T50185/1915.
83. "The lines of communication: intervention of German submarines to July," Rayfield Papers, IWM, 69/61/3, 32–33.
84. Evidence of Captain H. V. Simpson to the Dardanelles Commission, 2 February 1917, TNA, CAB 19/33, 817.
85. Simpson to Thomson, telegram, 18 September 1915, TNA, MT 23/443, T53963/1915.
86. Evidence of Brigadier-General A. Joly de Lotbiniére to the Dardanelles Commission, 23 January 1917, TNA, CAB 19/33, 626.
87. "The lines of communication: intervention of German submarines to July," Rayfield Papers, IWM, 69/61/3, 32.
88. Evidence of Brigadier-General A. Joly de Lotbiniére to the Dardanelles Commission, 23 January 1917, TNA, CAB 19/33, 632–33; Admiralty

to "Transports, Mudros" (PNTO), telegram, 7 October 1915, TNA, MT 23/442, T53773/1915; Fourth Sea Lord to de Robeck, telegram, 25 July 1915, TNA, ADM 137/155; diary entry, 10 August 1915, DST "Supply Diary," GHQ MEF, TNA, WO 95/4269.

89. Thomson to Simpson and Admiral Robinson, telegram, 3 August 1915; Simpson to Admiralty, telegram, 4 August 1915, both in TNA, ADM 137/184.
90. "Statement by Lieutenant-General Sir Edward A. Altham," report to the Dardanelles Commission, 10 January 1917, AWM 51/103, 1; evidence of Captain H. V. Simpson to the Dardanelles Commission, 2 February 1917, TNA, CAB 19/33, 816–17.
91. Simpson to Thomson, letter, 1 August 1915, TNA, MT 23/431, T51236/1915. War Office to GHQ MEF, telegram, 21 August 1915; Hamilton to de Robeck, telegram, 29 August 1915, both in GS WD, GHQ MEF, AWM 4, 1/4/5 pt. 1.
92. Simpson to Thomson, telegram, 18 September 1915, TNA, MT 23/443, T53963/1915.
93. Evidence of Brigadier-General A. Joly de Lotbiniére to the Dardanelles Commission, 23 January 1917, TNA, CAB 19/33, 632–33.
94. Wemyss to Admiralty, telegram, 7 August 1915; Oliver to Wemyss, telegram, 8 August 1915, both in TNA, ADM 137/184.
95. Evidence of Lieutenant-General Sir E. A. Altham to the Dardanelles Commission, 10 January 1917, TNA, CAB 19/33, 466–68.
96. Keyes, "Notes on piers and naval transport," n.d., de Robeck Papers, CAC, DRBK 4/70. Wallace to Winter, telegram, 1 July 1915; report by Brigadier-General Winter (DQMG), 29 June 1915, both in "A" and "Q" Branch WD, HQ L-of-C, TNA, WO 95/4355. Evidence of Brigadier-General A. Joly de Lotbiniére to the Dardanelles Commission, 23 January 1917, TNA, CAB 19/33, 632–33.
97. Evidence of Major-General C. McGrigor to the Dardanelles Commission, 5 January 1917, TNA, CAB 19/33, 403.
98. "State of the Mediterranean Expeditionary Force according to returns prepared by General Headquarters, 3rd Echelon, Mediterranean Expeditionary Force," 31 July 1915, TNA, WO 162/69.
99. DST MEF to War Office, telegram, 11 June 1915, TNA, ADM 137/155; diary entry, 11 July 1915, DST WD, GHQ MEF, TNA, WO 95/4269.
100. Diary entry, 6 July 1915, DDST WD, TNA, WO 95/4270; diary entries, 11 and 15 July 1915, DST WD, GHQ MEF, TNA, WO 95/4269; Maxwell to Hamilton, letter, 16 July 1915, Hamilton Papers, LHCMA, HAMILTON 7/1/14; diary entry, 25 July 1915, "A" and "Q" Branch WD, HQ L-of-C, TNA, WO 95/4355; diary entry, 26 July 1916, DADS WD, TNA, WO 95/4270; Hankey to Asquith, letter, 4 August 1915, TNA, CAB 19/123, 10–11.
101. GHQ to IX Corps, telegram, 20 July 1915, HQ IX Corps WD, TNA, WO 95/4276.
102. Diary entries, 5, 11, and 14 August 1915, GS WD, GHQ MEF, AWM 4, 1/4/5 pt. 1.

103. GHQ MEF to War Office, telegram, 15 August 1915, Hamilton Papers, LHCMA, HAMILTON 7/4/8.
104. Evidence of Lieutenant-General Sir E. A. Altham to the Dardanelles Commission, 10 January 1917, TNA, CAB 19/33, 464, 468–69.
105. Diary entry, 6 August 1915, DST WD, GHQ MEF, TNA, WO 95/4269; DDST (War Office) to Vice-Admiral Sir Douglas Gamble, letter, 17 August 1915, TNA, ADM 137/184.
106. Kearns to Long, letter, 28 July 1915, TNA, WO 107/44.
107. Ellison to Cowans, letter, 26 August 1915, TNA, WO 107/43.
108. Evidence of Vice-Admiral Sir Rosslyn Erskine Wemyss to the Dardanelles Commission, 31 August 1917, TNA, CAB 19/33, 1659–60.
109. Ellison to Cowans, letter, 26 August 1915, TNA, WO 107/43.
110. Evidence of Captain H. V. Simpson to the Dardanelles Commission, 2 February 1917, TNA, CAB 19/33, 817.
111. Diary entries, 1 and 4 August 1915, DADS WD, TNA, WO 95/4270.
112. Hamilton to Kitchener, telegram, 9 July 1915, Hamilton Papers, LHCMA, HAMILTON 7/4/8.
113. Admiralty to de Robeck, telegram, 12 July 1915, TNA, ADM 137/155.
114. De Robeck to Balfour, letter, 28 July 1915, de Robeck Papers, CAC, DRBK 4/69.
115. Jackson to de Robeck, letter, 27 July 1915, de Robeck Papers, CAC, DRBK 4/30; Wemyss to de Robeck, letter, 14 July 1915, de Robeck Papers, CAC, DRBK 4/32; Thursby to Limpus, letter, 15 July 1915, Limpus Papers, NMM, LIM /65.
116. De Robeck to Balfour, letter, 28 July 1915, de Robeck Papers, CAC, DRBK 4/69.
117. Hankey to Asquith, letter, 4 August 1915, TNA, CAB 17/123, 12.
118. Hankey to Balfour, letter, 16 August 1915, Hankey Papers, CAC, HNKY 7/12.
119. Evidence of Lieutenant-General Sir E. A. Altham to the Dardanelles Commission, 10 January 1917, TNA, CAB 19/33, 466.
120. Corbett, *Naval Operations*, 3:82; evidence of Lieutenant-General Sir E. A. Altham to the Dardanelles Commission, 10 January 1917, TNA, CAB 19/33, 466–67; Keyes, "Notes on piers and naval transport," n.d., de Robeck Papers, CAC, DRBK 4/70; diary entry, 23 July 1915, Ellison Papers, NAM, 8704/35/214, 3–4.
121. "The lines of communication: August 1915–January 1916," Rayfield Papers, IWM, 69/61/4.
122. Diary entry, 19 August 1915, DST "Supply Diary," GHQ MEF, TNA, WO 95/4269.
123. Diary entry, 18 July 1915, DST WD, GHQ MEF, TNA, WO 95/4269; diary entries, 19, 21, and 25 August 1915, DST "Supply Diary," GHQ MEF, TNA, WO 95/4269.
124. Diary entry, 6 August 1915, Backhouse Papers, IWM, 86/31/1.
125. Aspinall-Oglander, *Military Operations*, 2:158.
126. "Navy Transport Service," n.d., TNA, MT 23/427, T50185/1915; diary entry, 1 August 1915, DDST WD, TNA, WO 95/4270.

127. "The lines of communication: intervention of German submarines to July," Rayfield Papers, IWM, 69/61/3, 31-32.
128. Hankey to Asquith, letter, 4 August 1915, TNA, CAB 17/123, 11-12; de Robeck to Admiralty, telegram, 25 July 1915, TNA, ADM 137/155.
129. Hamilton to War Office, telegram, 13 July 1915, Hamilton Papers, LHCMA, HAMILTON 7/4/8.
130. Hamilton to War Office, telegram, 9 July 1915, GS WD, GHQ MEF, AWM 4, 1/4/4 pt. 3.
131. MacMunn to Cowans, letter, 19 August 1915, TNA, WO 107/44.
132. Evidence of Rear-Admiral Roger John Brownlow Keyes to the Dardanelles Commission, 15 May 1917, TNA, CAB 19/33, 1448-50.
133. Hankey to Asquith, letter, 4 August 1915, TNA, CAB 17/123, 11-12.
134. Brown, "Growing Pains," 40.
135. Brown, *British Logistics on the Western Front*, 42-44, 17-20, 117-20.
136. "Statement by Lieutenant-General Sir Edward A. Altham," report to the Dardanelles Commission, 10 January 1917, AWM 51/103, 1.
137. Evidence of Lieutenant-General Sir E. A. Altham to the Dardanelles Commission, 10 January 1917, TNA, CAB 19/33, 468.
138. Evidence of Mr. Graeme Thomson to the Dardanelles Commission, 20 March 1917, TNA, CAB 19/33, 1213.
139. "Admiralty Transport Service," n.d., TNA, MT 23/427, T50185/1915.
140. Evidence of Mr. Graeme Thomson to the Dardanelles Commission, 20 March 1917, TNA, CAB 19/33, 1213.
141. Simpson to Thomson, letter, 11 July 1915, TNA, MT 23/427, T50185/1915.
142. Thomson to Simpson, telegram, 11 August 1915, TNA, MT 23/427, T50185/1915; MacMunn, "The Lines of Communication in the Dardanelles," 58; diary, August 1915, Wemyss Papers, CAC, WMYS 12/4.
143. Evidence of Lieutenant-Colonel T. H. B. Forster to the Dardanelles Commission, 29 January 1917, TNA, CAB 19/33, 745.
144. "The lines of communication to 27 May," Rayfield Papers, IWM, 69/61/3, 7.
145. Simpson to Thomson, letter, 11 July 1915, TNA, MT 23/427, T50185/1915.
146. Ellison to Cowans, letter, 20 October 1915, Ellison Papers, NAM, 8704/35/227, 3.
147. Evidence of Lieutenant-General Sir E. A. Altham to the Dardanelles Commission, 10 January 1917, TNA, CAB 19/33, 463, 468.
148. Great Britain War Office, *Field Service Regulations* (hereafter *FSR*), pt. 2, *Organization and Administration* (1909; repr., London: H.M. Stationary Office, 1914), 32-33; Brown, "Growing Pains," 34-35.
149. Braithwaite to Ellison, letter, 13 August 1915, Ellison Papers, NAM, 8704/35/227, 1; evidence of Major-General G. F. Ellison to the Dardanelles Commission, 23 January 1917, TNA, CAB 19/33, 636.
150. Evidence of Major-General C. McGrigor to the Dardanelles Commission, 5 January 1917, TNA, CAB 19/33, 402.

151. Hamilton to War Office, telegram, 25 May 1915, Hamilton Papers, LHCMA, HAMILTON 7/4/8.
152. Hamilton to Ellison, letter, 11 June 1915 Hamilton Papers, LHCMA, HAMILTON 7/1/17.
153. Braithwaite to Cowans, letter, 22 June 1915, TNA, WO 107/43.
154. War Office to GHQ MEF, telegram, 7 June 1915, Hamilton Papers, LHCMA, HAMILTON 7/4/8.
155. Braithwaite to Cowans, letter, 22 June 1915, TNA, WO 107/43; evidence of Lieutenant-General The Right Hon. Sir John Grenfell Maxwell to the Dardanelles Commission, 5 January 1917, TNA, CAB 19/33, 397.
156. Diary entry, 30 June 1915, Williams Papers, IWM, 69/78/1.
157. Braithwaite to Cowans, letter, 27 July 1915, TNA, WO 107/43.
158. Hamilton to Cowans, letter, 2 July 1915, Hamilton Papers, LHCMA, HAMILTON 7/1/7.
159. Hamilton to Kitchener, telegram, 6 July 1915, Hamilton Papers, LHCMA, HAMILTON 7/4/8.
160. "Copy of letter," Wallace to Winter, 28 June 1915, Hamilton Papers, LHCMA, HAMILTON 8/1/66.
161. War Office to GHQ MEF, telegram, 9 July 1915, Hamilton Papers, LHCMA, HAMILTON 7/4/8; Smith-Dorrien to Hamilton, letter, 28 July 1915, Hamilton Papers, LHCMA, HAMILTON 7/1/37.
162. "Statement by Lieutenant-General Sir Edward A. Altham," report to the Dardanelles Commission, 10 January 1917, AWM 51/103, 1.
163. Altham to Cowans, letter, 23 July 1915, TNA, WO 107/43.
164. "Statement by Lieutenant-General Sir Edward A. Altham," report to the Dardanelles Commission, 10 January 1917, AWM 51/103, 2; Altham to Cowans, letter, 27 July 1915, TNA, WO 107/43; Altham to Braithwaite, telegram, 27 July 1915, GS WD, GHQ MEF, AWM 4, 1/4/4 pt. 3.
165. Altham to Braithwaite, telegram, 27 July 1915, GS WD, GHQ MEF, AWM 4, 1/4/4 pt. 3.
166. "Statement by Lieutenant-General Sir Edward A. Altham," report to the Dardanelles Commission, 10 January 1917, AWM 51/103, 2.
167. Altham to Cowans, letter, 27 July 1915, TNA, WO 107/43.
168. Diary entry, 1 August 1915, "A" & "Q" Branch WD, HQ L-of-C, TNA, WO 95/4355.
169. Altham to Cowans, letter, 4 August 1915, TNA, WO 107/43.
170. Ellison to Cowans, letter, 17 September 1915, Ellison Papers, NAM, 8704/35/223, 3.
171. MacMunn, "The Lines of Communication in the Dardanelles," 58.
172. Wester-Wemyss, *The Navy in the Dardanelles Campaign*, 148; evidence of Rear-Admiral Roger John Brownlow Keyes to the Dardanelles Commission, 16 May 1917, TNA, CAB 19/33, 1488.
173. Ellison to Cowans, letter, 20 October 1915, Ellison Papers, NAM, 8704/35/227, 1-2.
174. Ellison to Hamilton, letter, 11 August 1915, Ellison Papers, NAM, 8704/35/220, 1-2.

175. Diary entry, 7 August 1915, "A" & "Q" Branch WD, HQ L-of-C, TNA, WO 95/4355; de Robeck to Jackson, letter, 16 September 1915, de Robeck Papers, CAC, DRBK 4/70.
176. Hankey to Kitchener, letter, 28 July 1915, TNA, CAB 17/123.
177. Evidence of Captain H. V. Simpson to the Dardanelles Commission, 2 February 1917, TNA, CAB 19/33, 818.
178. Simpson to Thomson, letter, 1 August 1915, TNA, MT 23/43`, T51236/1915; de Robeck to Jackson, letter, 15 July 1915, de Robeck Papers, CAC, DRBK 4/70.
179. Kennedy to Kitchener, letter, 9 June 1915, Kitchener Papers, TNA, PRO 30/57/62.
180. Corbett, *Naval Operations*, 3:82.
181. Wemyss to wife, letter, 12 August 1915, Wemyss Papers, CAC, WYMS 7/11/2.
182. Keyes, *Naval Memoirs*, 360, 418–19; Hankey to Balfour, letter, 16 August 1915, Hankey Papers, CAC, HNKY 7/12.
183. Hamilton to Birdwood, letter, 17 June 1915, Hamilton Papers, LHCMA, HAMILTON 7/1/16.
184. Altham to Cowans, letter, 22 August 1915, TNA, WO 107/43; "Statement by Lieutenant-General Sir Edward A. Altham," report to the Dardanelles Commission, 10 January 1917, AWM 51/103, 1.
185. Winter to Hamilton, letter, 1 November 1916, Hamilton Papers, LHCMA, HAMILTON 8/1/66.
186. Evidence of Major-General Sir John Steevens to the Dardanelles Commission, 4 January 1917, TNA, CAB 19/33, 390.

6. Supply and Transport

1. *FSR*, 2:52–53.
2. Hamilton, *Gallipoli Diary*, 2:72.
3. Winter, "Supply," 28 July 1915, appendix, DQMG WD, GHQ MEF, TNA, WO 95/4266; *FSR*, 2:17.
4. Aspinall-Oglander, *Military Operations*, 1:226, 278.
5. Bean, *Official History*, 2:352–54, 831–32.
6. "Appendix to Force Order No. 25," 2 August 1915, GS WD, GHQ MEF, AWM 4, 1/4/5 pt. 2.
7. Painter to Aspinall-Oglander, letter, 28 February 1931, TNA, CAB 45/244; diary entry, 7 August 1915, DA&QMG IX Corps WD, TNA, WO 95/4279.
8. "Narrative of operations by Major-General J. H. Poett," n.d., TNA, CAB 45/244.
9. Doyle and Bennett, "Military Geography," 30.
10. Keyes, "Notes on piers and naval transport," n.d., de Robeck Papers, CAC, DRBK 4/70.
11. *FSR*, 1:69; repeated in Great Britain War Office, *Manual of Combined Naval and Military Operations*, 8–9.
12. *FSR*, 2:36.

13. Diary entry, 4 August 1915, "A" and "Q" Branch WD, HQ L-of-C, TNA, WO 95/4355; diary entry, 5 August 1915, GS WD, GHQ MEF, AWM 4, 1/4/5 pt. 1.
14. These three officers were Major P. R. Bruce, Captain C. R. Higgins, and Captain Sir E. Pauncefort Duncomber. "Appendix to Force Order No. 25," 2 August 1915, GS WD, GHQ MEF, AWM 4, 1/4/5 pt. 2.
15. Despite a memorandum which stated that the PMLO was under the orders of GOC IX Corps, this officer was, in effect, responsible to GHQ. Braithwaite to Western, memo, 4 August 1915, GS WD, GHQ MEF, AWM 4, 1/4/5 pt. 2.
16. "Narrative of operations by Major-General J. H. Poett," n.d., TNA, CAB 45/244; Altham to Cowans, letter, 22 August 1915, TNA, WO 107/43.
17. Diary entry, 11 August 1915, DST "Supply Diary," GHQ MEF, TNA, WO 95/4269.
18. Talbot was assisted by three beach masters, four assistant beach masters, and ten beach lieutenants. "Narrative of operations by Major-General J. H. Poett," n.d., TNA, CAB 45/244; "Appendix to Force Order No. 25," 2 August 1915, GS WD, GHQ MEF, AWM 4, 1/4/5 pt. 2.
19. Western was assisted by three military landing officers and four assistant military landing officers. Aspinall, "Appendix to Force Order No. 25," 2 August 1915, Appendix, GS WD, GHQ MEF, AWM 4, 1/4/5 pt. 2.
20. "Narrative of operations by Major-General J. H. Poett," n.d., TNA, CAB 45/244; evidence of Major-General J. Poett to the Dardanelles Commission, 9 March 1917, TNA, CAB 19/33, 1126–27; "11th Division Operation Order No. 1," 5 August 1915, 11th Div. WD, TNA, WO 95/4297.
21. Evidence of Major-General J. Poett to the Dardanelles Commission, 9 March 1917, TNA, CAB 19/33, 1137.
22. Evidence of Rear-Admiral Roger John Brownlow Keyes to the Dardanelles Commission, 15 May 1917, TNA, CAB 19/33, 1454.
23. Evidence of Major-General J. Poett to the Dardanelles Commission, 9 March 1917, TNA, CAB 19/33, 1137.
24. *FSR*, 1:69.
25. Evidence of Captain E. C. Carver to the Dardanelles Commission, 1 March 1917, TNA, CAB 19/33, 1047–50.
26. Evidence of Rear-Admiral Roger John Brownlow Keyes to the Dardanelles Commission, 15 May 1917, TNA, CAB 19/33, 1446–47.
27. Evidence of Captain E. C. Carver to the Dardanelles Commission, 1 March 1917, TNA, CAB 19/33, 1048.
28. Evidence of Rear-Admiral Roger John Brownlow Keyes to the Dardanelles Commission, 15 May 1917, TNA, CAB 19/33, 1447.
29. "Narrative of operations by Major-General J. H. Poett," n.d., TNA, CAB 45/244.
30. "Mitchell Report," 399.
31. Hankey to Balfour, letter, 16 August 1915, Hankey Papers, CAC, HNKY 7/12.
32. Diary entry, 20 July 1915, DST War Diary, GHQ MEF, TNA, WO 95/4269.

33. Diary entries, 14 and 21 July 1915, DST WD, GHQ MEF, TNA, WO 95/4269; diary entry, 21 July 1915, DQMG WD, GHQ MEF, TNA, WO 95/4266.
34. Ellison to GOC's of Corps', memo, 29 August 1915, DQMG WD, GHQ MEF, TNA, WO 95/4266.
35. Diary entries, 21–22 July 1915, DQMG WD, GHQ MEF, TNA, WO 95/4266.
36. Diary entry, 1 August 1915, DQMG WD, GHQ MEF, TNA, WO 95/4266.
37. Winter to de Robeck, telegram, 2 August 1915, de Robeck Papers, CAC, DRBK 4/51.
38. Diary entry, 10 August 1915, DST "Supply Diary," GHQ MEF, TNA, WO 95/4269; Koe to Altham, letter, 10 August 1915, DST WD, GHQ MEF, TNA, WO 95/4269.
39. Diary entry, 13 August 1915, DADS (Mudros) WD, TNA, WO 95/4270.
40. Diary entry, 16 August 1915, DQMG WD, GHQ MEF, TNA, WO 95/4266.
41. Diary entry, 23 August 1915, DST "Supply Diary," GHQ MEF, TNA, WO 95/4269.
42. Ellison to Cowans, letter, 26 August 1915, TNA, WO 107/43.
43. "Notes on piers and naval transport," n.d., de Robeck Papers, CAC, DRBK 4/70.
44. Travers, *Gallipoli 1915*, 143–44.
45. Koe to Altham, letter, 10 August 1915, DST WD, GHQ MEF, TNA, WO 95/4269.
46. "Operation Order No. 1," 3 August 1915; "11th Division Operation Order No. 1," 5 August 1915, both in 11th Div. WD, TNA, WO 95/4297.
47. "Narrative of operations by Major-General J. H. Poett," n.d., TNA, CAB 45/244.
48. Diary entry, 7 August 1915, 68th Field Company WD, TNA, WO 95/4298; diary entry, 7 August 1915, Commander, Royal Engineers, 11th Div. WD, TNA, WO 95/4298; Painter to Aspinall-Oglander, letter, 28 February 1931, TNA, CAB 45/244.
49. "Narrative of operations by Major-General J. H. Poett," n.d., TNA, CAB 45/244.
50. Diary entries, 4–6 August 1915, 68th Field Company WD, TNA, WO 95/4298; Painter to Aspinall-Oglander, letter, 28 February 1931, TNA, CAB 45/244.
51. "Summary [of August, 1915]," n.d., DA&QMG WD, IX Corps, TNA, WO 95/4279; diary entries, 8–9 August 1915, 68th Field Company WD, TNA, WO 95/4298.
52. "Notes on piers and naval transport" n.d., de Robeck Papers, CAC, DRBK 4/70.
53. Keyes, *Naval Memoirs*, 360.
54. "War Diary Summary for the month of August, 1915," 20 September 1915, DQMG WD, GHQ MEF, TNA, WO 95/4266; Hankey to Asquith, letter, 12 August 1915, TNA, CAB 17/123, 13.

302 NOTES TO PAGES 166-70

55. Great Britain War Office, *Manual of Combined Naval and Military Operations*, 13.
56. Ellison to Cowans, letter, 26 August 1915, TNA, WO 107/43.
57. "War Diary Summary for the month of August, 1915," 20 September 1915, DQMG WD, GHQ MEF, TNA, WO 95/4266.
58. In response to GHQ's requests for pioneer battalions, the War Office decided on 19 August to send out two garrison battalions, which were unfit for duty in the trenches, as working parties. Two battalions, however, was well short of the 4,000–5,000 that Major-General Ellison believed necessary.
59. Diary entry, 4 August 1915, 1st Australian Div. Admin. WD, AWM 4, 1/43/9.
60. Koe to Altham, letter, 10 August 1915, DST WD, GHQ MEF, TNA, WO 95/4269.
61. Diary entries, 12–13 August 1915, HQ ANZAC Admin. WD, AWM 4, 1/28/9.
62. Diary entry, 17 August 1915, 13th Div. Admin. WD, TNA, WO 95/4300.
63. Diary entry, 31 August 1916, DST "Supply Diary," GHQ MEF, TNA, WO 95/4269.
64. "Notes on visit to Anzac, August 29th 1915," memo, DQMG WD, GHQ MEF, TNA, WO 95/4266.
65. Dawnay to Stopford, memo, 1 August 1915, GS WD, GHQ MEF, AWM 4, 1/4/5 pt. 2.
66. Diary entry, 12 August 1915, 13th Div. Admin. WD, TNA, WO 95/4300.
67. Diary entries, 14, 16, and 26 August 1915, DST "Supply Diary," GHQ MEF, TNA, WO 95/4269.
68. Ellison to Cowans, letter, 26 August 1915, TNA, WO 107/43.
69. "Summary," n.d., DA&QMG WD, IX Corps, TNA, WO 95/4279.
70. "Mitchell Report," 215–16.
71. "Summary [August 1915]," 40th Depot Unit of Supply WD, L-of-C MEF, TNA, WO 95/4358.
72. Evidence of Lieutenant-General Sir E. A. Altham to the Dardanelles Commission, 10 January 1917, TNA, CAB 19/33, 463.
73. "Mitchell Report," 217.
74. "Supply," 28 July 1915, DQMG WD, GHQ MEF, TNA, WO 95/4266.
75. Evidence of Major-General W. G. B. Western to the Dardanelles Commission, 30 January 1917, TNA, CAB 19/33, 759.
76. Diary entry, 24 July 1915, DQMG WD, GHQ MEF, TNA, WO 95/4266.
77. Aspinall-Oglander, *Military Operations*, 2:395.
78. "War Diary Summary for the month of August, 1915," 20 September 1915, DQMG WD, GHQ MEF, TNA, WO 95/4266.
79. Evidence of Major-General J. Poett to the Dardanelles Commission, 9 March 1917, TNA, CAB 19/33, 1126, 1131–33; "Narrative of operations by Major-General J. H. Poett," n.d., TNA, CAB 45/244; diary entry, 7 August 1915, DA&QMG WD, IX Corps, TNA, WO 95/4279.
80. "1st Australian Division Distribution of Duties—Administrative Branch," Gellibrand Papers, AWM 3DRL/1473 item 98.

81. R. Lee, "The Australian Staff: The Forgotten Men of the First AIF," in *1918 Defining Victory*, ed. P. Dennis and J. Grey (Canberra: Army History Unit, 1999), 117.
82. Evidence of Major-General Sidney Selden Long to the Dardanelles Commission, 22 March 1917, TNA, CAB 19/33, 1251.
83. The term "lifeblood" is taken from Julian Thompson's seminal study of logistics in war. See J. Thompson, *The Lifeblood of War: Logistics in Armed Conflict* (London: Brassey's, 1991).
84. De Robeck to Balfour, telegram, 17 July 1915, TNA, ADM 137/155.
85. "Supply," 28 July 1915, DQMG WD, GHQ MEF, TNA, WO 95/4266; Koe to Altham, letter, 10 August 1915, DST WD, GHQ MEF, TNA, WO 95/4269.
86. Diary entry, 17 July 1915, DST WD, GHQ MEF, TNA, WO 95/4269.
87. Altham to Cowans, letter, 23 July 1915, TNA, WO 107/43.
88. Birdwood to GHQ MEF, memo, September 1915, HQ ANZAC WD, AWM 4, 1/25/5 pt. 5.
89. Diary entries, 3 and 13–14 August 1915, DST "Supply Diary," GHQ MEF, TNA, WO 95/4269.
90. Hamilton, *Gallipoli Diary*, 2:302; evidence of Major-General J. Poett to the Dardanelles Commission, 9 March 1917, TNA, CAB 19/33, 1126.
91. Troops were ordered to carry two days' "iron rations" and one day's "biscuit and meat." Diary entries, 7–8 and 13 August 1915, DST "Supply Diary," GHQ MEF, TNA, WO 95/4269; "Supply," memo, n.d., DA&QMG WD, IX Corps, TNA, WO 95/4279.
92. Doyle and Bennett, "Military Geography," 33–34; "Water arrangements at Lancashire Landing and other Beaches," memo, 28 July 1915, DQMG WD, GHQ MEF, TNA, WO 95/4266.
93. De Robeck to Admiralty, telegram, 18 August 1915, TNA, ADM 137/184.
94. To further confuse things, there were two types of SAA for the August Offensive, and both were landed together at Anzac. Mark VI ammunition was used by the ANZAC troops, whereas the British used Mark VII. The two types were differentiated by two V-shaped nicks on the ends of the Mark VII lids, thus enabling them to be distinguished by either sight or touch. Further, the Mark VII ammunition was packed in bandoliers rather than packets. "Ammunition," memo, 28 July 1915, DQMG WD, GHQ MEF, TNA, WO 95/4266.
95. "Operation Order No. 9," 5 August 1915, CRA VIII Corps WD, TNA, WO 95/4275.
96. "Ammunition," memo, 28 July 1915, DQMG WD, GHQ MEF, TNA, WO 95/4266.
97. Birdwood to GHQ, memo, 15 July 1915, HQ ANZAC WD, AWM 4, 1/25/4 pt. 5.
98. "Notes on water supply for Anzac offensive on 6th August 1915," n.d., Birdwood Papers, AWM 3DRL/3376, 11/16.
99. Memo, 3 August 1915, HQ ANZAC WD, AWM 4, 1/25/5 pt. 3.

100. H. M. Alexander, *On Two Fronts: Being the Adventures of an Indian Mule Corps in France and Gallipoli* (London: Heinemann, 1917), 204.
101. *FSR*, 2:98–99.
102. V. J. Moharir, *History of the Army Service Corps (1914–1938)* (New Delhi: Sterling, 1982), 108; R. H. Beadon, *The Royal Army Service Corps: A History of Transport and Supply in the British Army* (Cambridge: Cambridge University Press, 1931), 2:158.
103. *FSR*, 1:54–55.
104. *FSR*, 2:98–99.
105. "Organization orders for the troops in Anzac," 3 August 1915, HQ ANZAC WD, AWM 4, 1/25/5 pt. 3; memo, 26 July 1915, 1st Australian Div. Train WD, AWM 4, 25/14/9.
106. Memo, 3 August 1915, HQ ANZAC WD, AWM 4, 1/25/5 pt. 3.
107. Diary entries, 6–10 August 1915, DST "Transport Diary," GHQ MEF, TNA, WO 95/4269.
108. "Administrative Memorandum No. 14," 29 June 1915; "Administrative Memorandum No. 38," 13 August 1915, both in Gellibrand Papers, AWM 3DRL/1473 item 95.
109. "Corps Orders by Lt-Gen Hon. Sir F. W. Stopford," 15 August 1915, DA&QMG WD, IX Corps, TNA, WO 95/4279.
110. S. Galtrey, *The Horse and the War* (London: Country Life, 1918), 50–51.
111. Doyle, and Bennett, "Military Geography," 32; Moharir, *History of the Army Service Corps*, 109–10.
112. Evidence of Lieutenant-Colonel L. R. Beadon to the Dardanelles Commission, 31 August 1917, TNA, CAB 19/33, 1645; DST to DDST, telegram, 25 August 1915, DDST WD, TNA, WO 95/4270; Moharir, *History of the Army Service Corps*, 108–109.
113. Evidence of Lieutenant-Colonel L. R. Beadon to the Dardanelles Commission, 31 August 1917, TNA, CAB 19/33, 1646.
114. Ibid., 1645.
115. "Appendix to Force Order No. 25," 2 August 1915, GS WD, GHQ MEF, AWM 4, 1/4/5 pt. 2.
116. Aspinall to "Heeltool, London," telegram, n.d., Aspinall-Oglander Papers, IWCRO, OG/AO/G/20.
117. Alexander, *On Two Fronts*, 222.
118. During the August Offensive, Nos. 1 and 5 Mule Cart Corps were used at Anzac; Nos. 2 and 4 at Suvla; and No. 3 at Helles. Moharir, *History of the Army Service Corps*, 108; Nos. 1–5 Mule Cart Corps WD, TNA, WO 95/4358; note to Aspinall (origin unknown), 7 November 1915, "Suvla Transport Scheme," Aspinall-Oglander Papers, IWCRO, OG/AO/G/25.
119. "War Diary summary for the month of August, 1915," 20 September 1915, DQMG WD, GHQ MEF, TNA, WO 95/4266; note to Aspinall (origin unknown), 7 November 1915, "Suvla Transport Scheme," Aspinall-Oglander Papers, IWCRO, OG/AO/G/25.
120. Diary entry, 7 August 1915, DQMG WD, GHQ MEF, TNA, WO 95/4266.

121. Diary entry, 8 August 1915, GS WD, GHQ MEF, AWM 4, 1/4/5 pt. 1.
122. "Record of [mule] arrivals," n.d., DST WD, GHQ MEF, TNA, WO 95/4269.
123. The ANZAC General Staff calculated that 1,170 mules were required for the operations at Sari Bair; 680 for local work in the current Anzac sector (calculated on mules making *five* journeys a day); 50 for ammunition; and 50 as a reserve. "Diary of ADT, ANZAC," DST WD, GHQ MEF, TNA, WO 95/4269; memo, 3 August 1915, HQ ANZAC WD, AWM 4, 1/25/5 pt. 3.
124. "Diary of ADT, ANZAC," DST WD, GHQ MEF, TNA, WO 95/4269.
125. As the figures for 10–12 August (inclusive) do not differentiate between what was landed on each day, this calculation is based on the average for this period (i.e., 678 mules over three days) plus those landed on 8–9 August (303 and 239 respectively). While the calculation is an approximation, the average obtained for 10–12 August is similar to those landed on 8–9 August. Note to Aspinall (origin unknown), 7 November 1915, "Suvla Transport Scheme," Aspinall-Oglander Papers, IWCRO, OG/AO/G/25.
126. Diary entries, 8–10 August, Indian Mule Cart Train WD, TNA, WO 95/4358.
127. The figure of 57,000 is based on there being 37,000 at Anzac (including Sari Bair) and 20,000 at Suvla.
128. Calculation is based on 0.5 gallons × 57,000 troops. Result divided by number of mules available (2,510) = 1,781.
129. This figure is calculated on there being no casualties among either mules or troops (through necessity). It also ignored the fact that troops, especially those in the "old" Anzac sector, often collected their own supplies.
130. "Diary of ADT, ANZAC," DST WD, GHQ MEF, TNA, WO 95/4269.
131. Personal diary of Lt.-Col. C. H. Beville, 8 August 1915, Indian Mule Cart Train WD, TNA, WO 95/4358.
132. "War Diary summary for the month of August, 1915," 20 September 1915, DQMG WD, GHQ MEF, TNA, WO 95/4266.
133. Keyes, *Naval Memoirs*, 394.
134. Moharir, *History of the Army Service Corps*, 121.
135. "Return of mules and carts, August 1915," n.d., DA&QMG WD, IX Corps, TNA, WO 95/4279.
136. Moharir, *History of the Army Service Corps*, 116.
137. Alexander, *On Two Fronts*, 168.
138. Moharir, *History of the Army Service Corps*, 113.
139. Diary entries, 8–10 August 1915, Indian Mule Cart Train WD, TNA, WO 95/4358.
140. Diary entry, 26 August 1915, Deputy Director of Veterinary Services, WD, GHQ MEF, TNA, WO 95/4268.
141. Diary entry, 1–9 August 1915, 1st Australian Div. Train WD, AWM 4, 25/14/10; "Narrative of operations by Major-General J. H. Poett," n.d., TNA, CAB 45/244.

142. Diary entry, 11 August 1915, Hobbs Papers, AWM PR82/153, 1/3; diary entry, 10 August 1915, 1st NZ FAB WD, AWM 4, 35/7/2.
143. Altham to Cowans, letter, 22 August 1915, TNA, WO 107/43.
144. De Robeck to Balfour, letter, 28 July 1915, de Robeck Papers, CAC, DRBK 4/69; Birdwood to Hamilton, letter, 16 May 1915, Birdwood Papers, AWM 3DRL/3376, 11/16.
145. Bean, *Official History*, 2:449.
146. "War Diary Summary for the month of August, 1915," 20 September 1915, DQMG WD, GHQ MEF, TNA, WO 95/4266.
147. Diary entries, 1–2 August 1915, GS WD, GHQ MEF, AWM 4, 1/4/5 pt. 1.
148. Birdwood to Ellison, letter, 5 August 1915, Ellison Papers, NAM, 8704/35/216.
149. Aspinall-Oglander, *Military Operations*, 2:303.
150. Bean, *Official History*, 1:574.
151. Ibid., 2:450.
152. Hamilton's dispatch, 11 December 1915, Hamilton Papers, LHCMA, HAMILTON 7/8/23, 23, 26.
153. C. Malthus, *Anzac: A Retrospect* (Christchurch, NZ: Whitcombe and Tombs, 1965), 122.
154. Diary entry, 8 August 1915, Wellington Bn. WD, AWM 4, 35/20/5.
155. Message, Supply Officer NZ Infantry Bde. to Staff Captain NZ Infantry Bde., 9 August 1915, HQ ANZAC WD, AWM 4, 1/25/5 pt. 7.
156. Hamilton's dispatch, 11 December 1915, Hamilton Papers, LHCMA, HAMILTON 7/8/23, 23, 26.
157. The NZ&A Divisional Engineers, for example, described the supply of water to Rhododendron Ridge on 12 August as "very inadequate," and noted that it "became really serious" on 13 August. Diary entries, 12–13 August 1915, NZ&A Div. Engineers WD, AWM 4, 14/12/6.
158. Birdwood to Hamilton, letter, 13 August 1915, Hamilton Papers, LHCMA, HAMILTON 7/1/16.
159. ANZAC to GHQ, telegram, 13 August 1915, GS WD, GHQ MEF, AWM 4, 1/4/5 pt. 3.
160. Evidence of Rear-Admiral Roger John Brownlow Keyes to the Dardanelles Commission, 15 May 1917, TNA, CAB 19/33, 1452.
161. Diary entry, 12 August 1915, DQMG WD, GHQ MEF, TNA, WO 95/4266; "Notes re: Water bags for Anzac," n.d., DST WD, TNA, WO 95/4269.
162. Diary entry, 7 August 1915, Milward Papers, NAM, 6510/143/3; diary entry, 8 August 1915, GS WD, GHQ MEF, AWM 4, 1/4/5 pt. 1.
163. Evidence of General Sir Ian Hamilton to the Dardanelles Commission, 17 July 1917, TNA, CAB 19/33, 1546.
164. "Operation Order No. 3," 10 August 1915, HQ IX Corps WD, TNA, WO 95/4276.
165. De Lisle to GHQ, telegram, 16 August 1915, GS WD, GHQ MEF, AWM 4, 1/4/5 pt. 3.
166. Diary entry, 17 August 1915, Shaw Papers, IWM, 76/106/1, 51.

NOTES TO PAGES 182–84   307

167. "Operation Order No. 1," 3 August 1915, HQ IX Corps WD, TNA, WO 95/4276; "Intelligence note on roads, water supply etc.," memo, 7 July 1915, AWM 25, 1021/55; evidence of Rear-Admiral Roger John Brownlow Keyes to the Dardanelles Commission, 15 May 1917, TNA, CAB 19/33, 1444.
168. Travers, *Gallipoli 1915*, 155.
169. Evidence of Major-General W. G. B. Western to the Dardanelles Commission, 30 January 1917, TNA, CAB 19/33, 759.
170. Coates, *Defeat at Gallipoli*, 222.
171. De Robeck to Admiralty, telegram, 18 August 1915, TNA, ADM 137/184.
172. Diary entry, 27 August 1915, DQMG WD, GHQ MEF, TNA, WO 95/4266.
173. Note to Aspinall (origin unknown), 7 November 1915, "Suvla Transport Scheme," Aspinall-Oglander Papers, IWCRO, OG/AO/G/25.
174. Travers, *Gallipoli 1915*, 154.
175. Evidence of Major-General C. McGrigor to the Dardanelles Commission, 5 January 1917, TNA, CAB 19/33, 404.
176. "Corps Orders by Lt-Gen Hon. Sir J. H. G. Byng," 25 August 1915, DA&QMG WD, IX Corps, TNA, WO 95/4279.
177. Evidence of Major-General C. McGrigor to the Dardanelles Commission, 5 January 1917, TNA, CAB 19/33, 402–404.
178. J. Thompson, "Expeditionary Forces and Expeditionary Warfare: Major Themes and Issues," in *Battles Near and Far: A Century of Overseas Deployment*, ed. P. Dennis and J. Grey (Canberra: Army History Unit, 2005), 10.
179. Altham in Chapman-Huston and Rutter, *General Sir John Cowans*, 107.
180. The Secretary, War Office, to the Secretary, Admiralty, letter, 31 July 1915, TNA, MT 23/427.
181. Memo, 2 August 1915, HQ ANZAC, WD AWM 4, 1/25/5 pt. 3.
182. "Evacuation of Casualties in the August Operations," n.d., Hamilton Papers, LHCMA, HAMILTON 8/1/12.
183. Evidence of Lieutenant-General Sir E. A. Altham to the Dardanelles Commission, 10 January 1917, TNA, CAB 19/33, 464.
184. Diary entry, 5 August 1915, DQMG WD, GHQ MEF, TNA, WO 95/4266.
185. Porter to Admiralty, telegram, 12 August 1915, TNA, MT 23/429; "Hospital ships on Mediterranean Service," memo, 3 August 1915, TNA, MT 23/427.
186. Cowans to GHQ MEF, telegram, 20 July 1915, Hamilton Papers, LHCMA, HAMILTON 7/4/8; evidence of Mr. Graeme Thomson to the Dardanelles Commission, 20 March 1917, TNA, CAB 19/33, 1208–10; Porter to Admiralty, telegram, 10 August 1915, TNA, MT 23/429.
187. Simpson to Thomson, letter, 20 August 1915, TNA, MT 23/434.
188. For example, see diary entries 2, 23, and 26 July, and 2–5 August 1915, DQMG WD, GHQ MEF, TNA, WO 95/4266.

189. Evidence of Major-General G. F. Ellison to the Dardanelles Commission, 23 January 1917, TNA, CAB 19/33, 634.
190. Altham to Cowans, letter, 22 August 1915, TNA, WO 107/43.
191. Coates, *Defeat at Gallipoli*, 250–51.
192. Birrell was replaced in September because he was unsuitable for the role. Hamilton to Keogh, letter, 17 September 1915, Hamilton Papers, LHCMA, HAMILTON 7/2/39.
193. Coates, *Defeat at Gallipoli*, 250–51.
194. Wester-Wemyss, *The Navy in the Dardanelles Campaign*, 148; Coates, *Defeat at Gallipoli*, 250–51.
195. James, *Gallipoli*, 249; diary entries, 29–30 July 1915, DQMG WD, GHQ MEF, TNA, WO 95/4266; Ellison to Cowans, letter, 26 August 1915; and Altham to Cowans, letter, 1 September 1915, both in TNA, WO 107/43.
196. Evidence of Vice-Admiral Sir Rosslyn Erskine Wemyss to the Dardanelles Commission, 31 August 1917, TNA, CAB 19/33, 1660.
197. L. Markovich, "'Linseed Lancers, Body-snatchers, and Other Cheery and Jovial Names': The Role of the Stretcher-Bearer, Gallipoli, 1915" (BA honours thesis, University of Wollongong, 2009), 38.
198. Diary entry, 8 August 1915, NZ Mounted Field Ambulance WD, AWM 4, 35/26/2.
199. Diary entry, 13 August 1915, DMS WD, AWM 4, 26/3/1.
200. "Evacuation of Casualties in the August Offensive," n.d., Hamilton Papers, LHCMA, HAMILTON 8/1/12.
201. Babtie to Hamilton, letter, 27 July 1915, Hamilton Papers, LHCMA, HAMILTON 7/4/29.
202. Diary entry, 9 August 1915, No. 1 Australian CCS WD, AWM 4, 26/62/7 pt. 1.
203. Diary entry, 16 August 1915, DMS WD, AWM 4, 26/3/1.
204. Bean, *Official History*, 2:645.
205. Diary entries, 6 and 13 August 1915, No. 1 Australian CCS WD, AWM 4, 26/62/7 pt. 1.
206. Diary entry, 3 August 1915, DQMG WD, GHQ MEF, TNA, WO 95/4266.
207. "Medical History of the Dardanelles Expedition from 10th March to 20th September, 1915," by Surgeon-General Birrell, Hamilton Papers, LHCMA, HAMILTON 8/1/12.
208. Diary entry, 9 July 1915, PDMS WD, AWM 4, 26/2/2.
209. Simpson to Thomson, letter, 1 August 1915, TNA, MT 23/431.
210. Evidence of Lieutenant-General Sir E. A. Altham to the Dardanelles Commission, 10 January 1917, TNA, CAB 19/33, 467; Ellison to Cowans, letter, 26 August 1915, TNA, WO 107/43.
211. Porter to "Natronglas," Medical, London, telegram, 22 August 1915, TNA, MT 23/434.

7. The August Offensive

Epigraph. "Special Order," 5 August 1915, GS WD, GHQ MEF, AWM 4, 1/4/5 pt. 2.

1. Diary entry, 6 August 1915, HQ ANZAC WD, AWM 4, 1/25/5 pt. 1.
2. Diary entry, 6 August 1915, 29th Div. WD, TNA, WO 95/4305.
3. "My narrative of the Great German War" by Lieutenant-General Sir Beauvoir de Lisle, 27 July 1919, de Lisle Papers, LHCMA, DE LISLE 3, vol. 1, 86.
4. Aspinall-Oglander, *Military Operations*, 2:171–72; diary entry, 6 August 1915, 29th Div. WD, TNA, WO 95/4305.
5. Diary entry, 7 August 1915, 42nd Div. WD, TNA, WO 95/4313.
6. Aspinall-Oglander, *Military Operations*, 2:175–77; Bush, *Gallipoli*, 233; diary entry, 6 August 1915, 29th Div. WD, TNA, WO 95/4305. Churchill disagreed; stating that the Helles feint both gained ground and prevented the enemy from moving north. See Churchill, *The World Crisis* (London: Butterworth, 1923), 2:434. James and Prior oppose this view. See James, *Gallipoli*, 261–62; and Prior, *Gallipoli*, 169.
7. Bean, *Official History*, 2:500.
8. Kannengiesser, *The Campaign in Gallipoli*, 202.
9. Liddle, *Men of Gallipoli*, 202.
10. Bean, *Official History*, 2:499–500.
11. Diary entry, 6 August 1915, HQ ANZAC WD, AWM 4, 1/25/5 pt. 1.
12. "Instructions for G.O.C. Australian Division," 4 August 1915, HQ ANZAC WD, AWM 4, 1/25/5 pt. 3.
13. Lone Pine was not, as Ashmead-Bartlett claimed, "a perfectly useless position." One only needs to visit the area to understand the command it had over the ground to the south and its importance to any advance from Gaba Tepe. See "Ellis Ashmead-Bartlett on Sir Ian Hamilton's Report," *The World* (London), 1 February 1916, 779.
14. Hankey to Asquith, letter, 12 August 1915, TNA, CAB 17/123; Hamilton's dispatch, 11 December 1915, Hamilton Papers, LHCMA, HAMILTON 7/8/23.
15. ANZAC to 1st Australian Div., memo, 5 August 1915, HQ ANZAC WD, AWM 4, 1/25/5 pt. 3.
16. James, *Gallipoli*, 263.
17. Bean, *Official History*, 2:520.
18. Von Sanders, *Five Years in Turkey*, 83; Aspinall-Oglander, *Military Operations*, 2:181; Bean, *Official History*, 2:522–23, 549–50; Kannengiesser, *The Campaign in Gallipoli*, 202–205; Miles, "Notes on the Dardanelles Campaign of 1915," pt. 4, 217.
19. Bean, *Official History*, 2:553.
20. Gellibrand to Walter (his brother), letter, 18 September 1915, Gellibrand Papers, AWM 3DRL/6541 item 2.
21. R. Crawley, "Perspectives of Battle: Lone Pine, August 1915" (BA honours thesis, University of Wollongong, 2006), 27. Kenan Celik gives a higher figure of 7,164 Ottoman casualties in K. Celik, "A Turkish View of the August Offensive" (lecture, Australian War Memorial Conference, Gallipoli: The August Offensive, Canberra, 5 August 2000).
22. Bean, *Official History*, 2:568.

23. "New Zealand Mounted Rifles Operational Order No. 2," 5 August 1915, NZMR Bde. WD, AWM 4, 35/1/4 pt. 1.
24. Bean, *Official History*, 2:568–73; diary entry, 6 August 1915, NZMR Bde. WD, AWM 4, 35/1/4 pt. 1.
25. Diary entry, 6–7 August 1915, HQ ANZAC WD, AWM 4, 1/25/5 pt. 1.
26. Bean, *Official History*, 2:572–77; Nevinson, *The Dardanelles Campaign*, 256–60.
27. Diary entry, 6 August 1915, NZMR Bde. WD, AWM 4, 35/1/4 pt. 1; diary entry, 6–7 August 1915, HQ ANZAC WD, AWM 4, 1/25/5 pt. 1.
28. "Instructions for Major-General Sir Alex. [sic] Godley," (n.d.), HQ ANZAC WD, AWM 4, 1/25/5 pt. 3. "Instructions issued to commanders in accordance with Divisional Order No. 11," 5 August 1915; diary entry, 6 August 1915, both in 13th (Western) Div. WD, TNA, WO 95/4301. "Notes on chapters 18, 20, 26 [of Aspinall-Oglander, *Military Operations: Gallipoli*, vol. 2]," Colonel L. I. G. Morgan Owen (formerly Brigade-Major, 40th Brigade) to Aspinall-Oglander, 1 January 1931, 40th Bde. WD, TNA, WO 95/4303.
29. Pugsley, *Gallipoli: The New Zealand Story*, 278.
30. Birdwood to de Robeck, letter, 6 August 1915, de Robeck Papers, CAC, DRBK 4/42.
31. Diary entry, 6 August 1915, NZ Infantry Bde. WD, AWM 4, 35/17/7.
32. Diary entry, 7 August 1915, NZ Infantry Bde. WD, AWM 4, 35/17/7.
33. Diary entry, 7 August 1915, Canterbury Bn. WD, AWM 4, 35/19/5; Bean, *Official History*, 2:580.
34. Malthus, *Anzac: A Retrospect*, 101–103, 108.
35. Diary entry, 7 August 1915, Canterbury Bn. WD, AWM 4, 35/19/5.
36. Diary entry, 6–7 August 1915, HQ ANZAC WD, AWM 4, 1/25/5 pt. 1.
37. "Notes on operations towards Koja Chemen Tepe (971)," 2 August 1915, Monash Papers, AWM 3DRL/2316, 3/19.
38. Diary entry, 6 August 1915, Cox Papers, AWM 1DRL/0221, 33.
39. Diary entry, 4th Australian Bde. WD, 6 August 1915, AWM 4, 23/4/1 pt. 2.
40. "Notes on chapters 18–20," Colonel G. L. Pepys (formerly Brigade Major, 29th Indian Infantry Brigade) to the Director, Historical Section (Military Branch), 9 January 1931, 29th Indian Bde. WD, TNA, WO 95/4272.
41. Diary entry, 6 August 1915, 4th Australian Bde. WD, AWM 4, 23/4/1 pt. 2.
42. Birdwood, *Khaki and Gown*, 275.
43. Diary entry, 6–7 August 1915, 29th Indian Bde. WD, TNA, WO 95/4272.
44. James, *Gallipoli*, 240.
45. S. Miles, "Notes on the Dardanelles Campaign of 1915," pt. 3, *Coast Artillery Journal* 62, no. 2 (February 1925): 125.
46. Willmer to Aspinall-Oglander, letters, 15 January and 16 February 1930, Aspinall-Oglander Papers, IWCRO, OG/AO/G/44.
47. "Detailed report of the doings of the [32nd] Brigade from the afternoon of Friday August 6th 1915 to the evening of Saturday 21st 1915," WD

of Captain B. W. Shuttleworth (brigade major, 32nd Bde.), Hamilton Papers, LHCMA, HAMILTON 7/2/37.
48. Prior, *Gallipoli*, 195–97.
49. Willmer to Aspinall-Oglander, letter, 15 January 1930, Aspinall-Oglander Papers, IWCRO, OG/AO/G/44.
50. "Narrative of Brig-Gen Sitwell [GOC 34th Brigade]," 14 November 1916, TNA, CAB 45/244, 8.
51. Willmer to Aspinall-Oglander, letter, 15 January 1930, Aspinall-Oglander Papers, IWCRO, OG/AO/G/44.
52. Kannengiesser, *The Campaign in Gallipoli*, 205.
53. Diary entry, 6 August 1915, HQ ANZAC WD, AWM 4, 1/25/5 pt. 1.
54. Diary entry, 6 August 1915, 6th Australian Bn. WD, AWM 4, 23/23/4.
55. Message, 2nd Bde. to 8th Bn., 7 August 1915, 2nd Australian Bde. WD, AWM 4, 23/2/6.
56. Diary entry, 6 August 1915, 6th Australian Bn. WD, AWM 4, 23/23/4.
57. Diary entry, 6 August 1915, HQ ANZAC WD, AWM 4, 1/25/5 pt. 1.
58. James, *Gallipoli*, 242.
59. Travers, *Gallipoli 1915*, 118; P. Stanley, *Quinn's Post, Anzac, Gallipoli* (Crows Nest, Australia: Allen and Unwin, 2005), 136–37.
60. Diary entry, 7 August 1915, 6th Australian Bn. WD, AWM 4, 23/23/4.
61. Diary entry, 6–7 August 1915, HQ ANZAC WD, AWM 4, 1/25/5 pt. 1.
62. Pugsley, *Gallipoli: The New Zealand Story*, 283.
63. "Brigadier-General H. G. Chauvel's narrative of events," n.d., 1st ALH Bde. WD, AWM 4, 10/1/13 pt. 1.
64. Ibid.
65. Skeen to NZ&A Division, telegram, 27 July 1915, HQ ANZAC WD, AWM 4, 1/25/4 pt. 6.
66. There was no mention of a delay at ANZAC HQ; rather they recorded that the artillery stopped at 4:30 A.M. For example, see diary entry, 6 August 1915, HQ ANZAC WD, AWM 4, 1/25/5 pt. 1. Others say the bombardment stopped at 4:23 A.M. See Bean, *Official History*, 2:612; and James, *Gallipoli*, 275. Pugsley states that it ceased at 4:27 A.M.; see Pugsley, *Gallipoli: The New Zealand Story*, 283.
67. "Report on Operations of 10th L.H. Regiment on Russell's Top, Anzac, on morning of 7 August 1915," n.d., Brazier Papers, AWM 1DRL/0147.
68. Diary entry, 6 August 1915, HQ ANZAC WD, AWM 4, 1/25/5 pt. 1.
69. "Report on Operations of 10th L.H. Regiment on Russell's Top, Anzac, on morning of 7 August 1915," n.d., Brazier Papers, AWM 1DRL/0147.
70. Bean, *Official History*, 2:623; A. G. Butler, *Official History of the Australian Army Medical Services in the War of 1914–1918*, vol. 1, *Gallipoli, Palestine and New Guinea* (Melbourne: Australian War Memorial, 1930), 294.
71. Birdwood, *Khaki and Gown*, 275.
72. J. Robertson, *Anzac and Empire: The Tragedy and Glory of Gallipoli* (Port Melbourne, Australia: Hamlyn, 1990), 126; James, *Gallipoli*, 274–75.
73. "Report on Operations of 10th L.H. Regiment on Russell's Top, Anzac, on morning of 7 August 1915," n.d., Brazier Papers, AWM 1DRL/0147.

74. Diary entry, 7 August 1915, 8th Bn., Royal Welch Fusiliers WD, TNA, WO 95/4303; diary entry, 7 August 1915, 13th (Western) Div. WD, TNA, WO 95/4300.
75. Diary entry, 7 August 1915, GS WD, GHQ MEF, AWM 4, 1/4/5 pt. 1.
76. Diary entry, 7 August 1915, NZMR Bde. WD, AWM 4, 35/1/4 pt. 1.
77. Diary entry, 6 August 1915, Williams Papers, IWM, 69/78/1.
78. Diary entry, 6–7 August 1915, HQ ANZAC WD, AWM 4, 1/25/5 pt. 1; diary entry, 7 August 1915, Canterbury Bn. WD, AWM 4, 35/19/5.
79. Pugsley, *Gallipoli: The New Zealand Story*, 285; Kannengiesser, *The Campaign in Gallipoli*, 205–207.
80. Diary entry, 7 August 1915, NZ Infantry Bde. WD, AWM 4, 35/17/7.
81. Bean, *Official History*, 2:639–40.
82. Diary entry, 6–7 August 1915, HQ ANZAC WD, AWM 4, 1/25/5 pt. 1.
83. Diary entry, 7 August 1915, Canterbury Bn. WD, AWM 4, 35/19/5.
84. Diary entry, 7 August 1915, NZ Infantry Bde. WD, AWM 4, 35/17/7.
85. Diary entry, 7 August 1915, GS WD, GHQ MEF, AWM 4, 1/4/5 pt. 1.
86. Messages, 13th and 16th Battalions to Monash, 7 August 1915, Monash Papers, AWM 3DRL/2316 item 3/20.
87. James, *Gallipoli*, 272–73.
88. Diary entry, 7 August 1915, GS WD, GHQ MEF, AWM 4, 1/4/5 pt. 1; diary entry, 7 August 1915, Cox Papers, AWM 1DRL/0221, 33.
89. Evidence of Lieutenant-Colonel C. J. L. Allanson to the Dardanelles Commission, 19 January 1917, TNA, CAB 19/33, 616.
90. Diary entry, 6–7 August 1915, 29th Indian Bde. WD, TNA, WO 95/4272; diary entry, 7 August 1915, Cox Papers, AWM 1DRL/0221, 33.
91. James, *Gallipoli*, 280–81.
92. "Narrative of Brig-Gen Sitwell," 14 November 1916, TNA, CAB 45/244, 8–9.
93. Diary entry, 7 August 1915, GS WD, GHQ MEF, AWM 4, 1/4/5 pt. 1.
94. Willmer to Aspinall-Oglander, letter, 15 January 1930, Aspinall-Oglander Papers, IWCRO, OG/AO/G/44.
95. Comments by G. F. Dawnay on excerpts from W. H. Deedes's diary, Dawnay Papers, IWM, 69/21/5.
96. "Narrative of Brig-Gen Sitwell," 14 November 1916, TNA, CAB 45/244, 12.
97. Willmer to Aspinall-Oglander, letters, 15 January and 12 April 1930, Aspinall-Oglander Papers, IWCRO, OG/AO/G/44.
98. "Narrative of Brig-Gen Sitwell," 14 November 1916, TNA, CAB 45/244, 12–13; "The Suvla Landing: Report by Captain A. C. Croydon, OC 'A' Company, 6th Battalion, Lincolnshire Regiment," 8 October 1930, TNA, CAB 45/228, 1–2; "The 11th Division at Suvla Bay" by Colonel J. D. Coleridge (general staff, 11th Division), n.d., TNA, CAB 45/227, 7.
99. Nevinson, *The Dardanelles Campaign*, 311.
100. Lieutenant-Colonel W. J. K. Rettie to Aspinall-Oglander, letter, 16 July 1929, TNA, CAB 45/244, 3.
101. Diary entry, 8 August 1915, GS WD, GHQ MEF, AWM 4, 1/4/5 pt. 1; diary entry, 8 August 1915, Backhouse Papers, IWM, 86/31/1; "E14

report of proceedings 21st July to 12th August 1915," by Commander E. C. Boyle, 14 August 1915, TNA, ADM 137/382, 9; "E11 report of proceedings 5th August to 3rd September 1915," by Commander M. E. Nasmith, 4 September 1915, TNA, ADM 137/382, 2–3.
102. Diary entry, 8 August 1915, NZ Infantry Bde. WD, AWM 4, 35/17/7.
103. Diary entry, 8 August 1915, GS WD, GHQ MEF, AWM 4, 1/4/5 pt. 1.
104. Diary entry, 8 August 1915, NZ Infantry Bde. WD, AWM 4, 35/17/7.
105. Diary entry, 8 August 1915, NZMR Bde. WD, AWM 4, 35/1/4 pt. 1; diary entries, 8–9 August 1915, Wellington MR Regt WD, AWM 4, 35/5/4; diary entry, 8 August 1915, Auckland MR Regt WD, AWM 4, 35/2/5.
106. Diary entry, 8 August 1915, 15th Australian Bn. WD, AWM 4, 23/32/10.
107. "Report on the Operations against the Sari Bair Position 6th–10th August 1915," by Major-General A. J. Godley, 16 August 1915, NZ&A Division WD, AWM 4, 1/53/5 pt. 2, 14.
108. James, *Gallipoli*, 285.
109. Pedersen, *Monash as Military Commander*, 112–14.
110. "Report on the Operations against the Sari Bair Position 6th–10th August 1915," by Major-General A. J. Godley, 16 August 1915, NZ&A Division WD, AWM 4, 1/53/5 pt. 2, 14.
111. "Narrative of Brig-Gen Sitwell," 14 November 1916, TNA, CAB 45/244, 14.
112. Colonel Sala-ed-din, "Extract from chapter IX Suvla lent by Military Mission to Turkey 1919," 19 December 1919, Hamilton Papers, LHCMA, HAMILTON 7/2/61; Willmer to Aspinall-Oglander, letter, 15 January 1930, Aspinall-Oglander Papers, IWCRO, OG/AO/G/44.
113. Diary entry, 8 August, GS WD, GHQ MEF, AWM 4 1/4/5 pt. 1; Willmer to Aspinall-Oglander, letter, 15 January 1930, Aspinall-Oglander Papers, IWCRO, OG/AO/G/44.
114. There were numerous messages sent between HMS *Arno*, HMS *Exmouth* (Rear Admiral Nicholson), Hamilton, and HMS *Triad* on 8 August 1915. These can be found in Hamilton Papers, LHCMA, HAMILTON 7/2/12.
115. Signal, HMS *Triad* to HMS *Chatham* (de Robeck), 8 August 1915, Hamilton Papers, LHCMA, HAMILTON 7/2/12.
116. Aspinall to Hamilton, letter, 28 October 1915, Hamilton Papers, LHCMA, HAMILTON 7/2/49.
117. Diary entry, 8 August 1915, Hamilton's Staff Diary, Hamilton Papers, LHCMA, HAMILTON 74/9.
118. Prior, *Gallipoli*, 203–204; Travers, *Gallipoli 1915*, 153; Willmer to Aspinall-Oglander, letter, 16 February 1930, Aspinall-Oglander Papers, IWCRO, OG/AO/G/44.
119. Bean, *Official History*, 2:687–88.
120. Diary entry, 9 August 1915, NZMR Bde. WD, AWM 4, 35/1/4 pt. 1; diary entry, 9 August 1915, Auckland MR Regt WD, AWM 4, 35/2/5.
121. Bean, *Official History*, 2:691–95.

122. Allanson to North, letter, 30 April 1935, North Papers, LHCMA, NORTH I/3/23.
123. Prior, *Gallipoli*, 182.
124. Bean, *Official History*, 2:697–98.
125. James, *Gallipoli*, 292.
126. Diary entries, 9–10 August 1915, NZ Infantry Bde. WD, AWM 4, 35/17/7.
127. Diary entry, 10 August 1915, NZ Infantry Bde. WD, AWM 4, 35/17/7.
128. "Replies to questions put by Australian Official Historian on fighting in Gallipoli," n.d., TNA, CAB 45/236, 6.
129. Diary entry, 10 August 1915, NZ Infantry Bde. WD, AWM 4, 35/17/7; "A personal narrative of the battle of Chunuk Bair, August 6th–10th 1915," by Colonel A. C. Temperley, n.d., TNA, CAB 45/234, 14.
130. Diary entry, 10 August 1915, NZ Infantry Bde. WD, AWM 4, 35/17/7.
131. James, *Gallipoli*, 299–301.
132. Diary entry, 10 August 1915, Birdwood Papers, AWM 3DRL/3376 item 1/1; diary entry, 10 August 1915, GS WD, GHQ MEF, AWM 4, 1/4/5 pt. 1.
133. Diary entry, 10 August 1915, GS WD, GHQ MEF, AWM 4, 1/4/5 pt. 1.
134. Hamilton to Kitchener, letter, 11 August 1915, Hamilton Papers, LHCMA, HAMILTON 7/1/6.
135. Diary entry, 10 August 1915, NZ Infantry Bde. WD, AWM 4, 35/17/7.
136. Malthus, *Anzac: A Retrospect*, 122.
137. Von Sanders, *Five Years in Turkey*, 86.
138. Diary entry, 10 August 1915, Birdwood Papers, AWM 3DRL/3376 item 1/1; Hamilton to Maxwell (GOC Egypt), letter, 10 August 1915, Hamilton Papers, LHCMA, HAMILTON 7/1/15.
139. Hamilton, *Gallipoli Diary*, 2:86–87.
140. Hamilton had first offered these troops to Birdwood, but Birdwood declined owing to the difficulty of supplying more troops at Anzac.
141. Prior, *Gallipoli*, 206.
142. Braithwaite to Stopford, telegram, 11 August 1915, GS WD, GHQ MEF, AWM 4, 1/4/5 pt. 2.
143. "54th Division: Report on Operations from 10th August to night 17/18th August," 19 August 1915, 54th Div. WD, TNA, WO 95/4324, 2.
144. IX Corps to GHQ, telegram, 13 August 1915, GS WD, GHQ MEF, AWM 4, 1/4/5 pt. 3.
145. GHQ to IX Corps, telegram, 13 August 1915, GS WD, GHQ MEF, AWM 4, 1/4/5 pt. 3.
146. Braithwaite to Stopford, telegram, 11 August 1915, GS WD, GHQ MEF, AWM 4, 1/4/5 pt. 2; "Notes of an interview which took place on board H.M.S. 'Triad' between 6 and 7 P.M. on the 13th August 1915, between the General Commanding and Sir Frederick Stopford, Commanding 9th Corps," 14 August 1915, Hamilton Papers, LHCMA, HAMILTON 7/2/24.
147. James, *Gallipoli*, 304.

148. Kitchener to Hamilton, telegram, 14 August 1915, Hamilton Papers, LHCMA, HAMILTON 7/2/23.
149. Hamilton to Kitchener, telegram, 14 August 1915, Hamilton Papers, LHCMA, HAMILTON 7/2/23.
150. Braithwaite to Stopford, telegram, 14 August 1915, Hamilton Papers, LHCMA, HAMILTON 7/2/23.
151. Bean, *Official History*, 2:721–22; Willmer to Aspinall-Oglander, letter, 15 January 1930, Aspinall-Oglander Papers, IWCRO, OG/AO/G/44; "Report of operations: 10th Irish Division, 15–16 August 1915," by Brigadier-General F. F. Hill, n.d., Hamilton Papers, LHCMA, HAMILTON 7/2/32.
152. Kitchener to Hamilton, telegram, 15 August 1915, Hamilton Papers, LHCMA, HAMILTON 7/2/23.
153. Birdwood to wife, letter, 18 August 1915, Birdwood Papers, AWM 3DRL/3376 item 8/2.
154. "My narrative of the Great German War," 27 July 1919, de Lisle Papers, LHCMA, DE LISLE 3 (vol. 1), 87–89.
155. Bean, *Official History*, 2:722.
156. "My narrative of the Great German War," 27 July 1919, de Lisle Papers, LHCMA, DE LISLE 3 (vol. 1), 87–89.
157. Bean, *Official History*, 2:723.
158. GHQ to IX Corps, telegram, 19 August 1915; IX Corps to GHQ, telegram, 20 August 1915, both in GS WD, GHQ MEF, AWM 4, 1/4/5 pt. 2.
159. Rettie to Aspinall-Oglander, letter, 16 July 1929, TNA, CAB 45/244, 8.
160. Bean, *Official History*, 2:724–28.
161. Travers, *Gallipoli 1915*, 162.
162. "My narrative of the Great German War," 27 July 1919, de Lisle Papers, LHCMA, DE LISLE 3 (vol. 1), 87–89.
163. Prior, *Gallipoli*, 206.
164. "Replies to questions put by Australian Official Historian on fighting in Gallipoli," n.d., TNA, CAB 45/236, 6.
165. Quoted in Moorehead, *Gallipoli*, 297.
166. Birdwood to Kitchener, letter, 10 August 1915, Birdwood Papers, AWM 3DRL/3376 item 11/6.
167. Figures are approximate. The overall figures are from "Approximate casualties, MEF 1915," Rhodes James Papers, CAC, RHJS 1/2; the figures for the period 6–10 August include the actions at Helles, Anzac, and Suvla, and are taken from Aspinall-Oglander, *Military Operations*, 2:176, 308.
168. Griffith, *Battle Tactics of the Western Front*, 15; Aspinall-Oglander, *Military Operations*, 2:356.

8. Subsequent Phases

1. Hamilton, *Gallipoli Diary*, 2:106.
2. Prior, *Churchill's "World Crisis" as History*, 152.

3. Hamilton, *Gallipoli Diary*, 2:57.
4. Travers, *Gallipoli 1915*, 136.
5. Crawford and Cooke, *No Better Death*, 316.
6. Godley, "Discussion on plan of attack on Ridge 971," 23 June 1915, HQ ANZAC WD, AWM 4, 1/25/3 pt. 3.
7. Hamilton to de Robeck, letter, 3 September 1915, de Robeck Papers, CAC, DRBK 4/77.
8. Birdwood to GHQ, memo, 10 July 1915, HQ ANZAC WD, AWM 4, 1/25/4 pt. 3; Prior, *Churchill's "World Crisis" as History*, 154.
9. Doyle and Bennett, "Military Geography," 18–24.
10. Malthus, *Anzac: A Retrospect*, 118–19.
11. Travers, *Gallipoli 1915*, 130.
12. It was deemed that three men per yard, with half as many men again as Corps Reserve, was the minimum required to maintain Anzac on the defensive. See Skeen to Braithwaite, telegram, 10 July 1915, GS WD, GHQ MEF, AWM 4, 1/4/4 pt. 3; "Notes on further operations by Australian & New Zealand Army Corps," n.d., HQ ANZAC WD, AWM 4, 1/25/3 pt. 3.
13. The forces at Suvla and Helles must be discounted, as they were only in sufficient number for defense.
14. "Appreciation of the situation at Anzac," 8 June 1915, HQ ANZAC WD, AWM 4, 1/25/3 pt. 3.
15. Birdwood to GHQ, memo, 10 July 1915, HQ ANZAC WD, AWM 4, 1/25/4 pt. 3.
16. C. von Clausewitz, *On War* (1976; repr., Princeton: Princeton University Press, 1989), 349.
17. Griffith, *Battle Tactics of the Western Front*, 57.
18. Hamilton to Maxwell, letter, 24 August 1915, Hamilton Papers, LHCMA, HAMILTON 7/1/15.
19. Hamilton to Selbourne, letter, 25 August 1915, Hamilton Papers, LHCMA, HAMILTON 7/1/34.
20. Hamilton to Callwell, letter, 13 September 1915, Hamilton Papers, LHCMA, HAMILTON 7/3/3.
21. "Appreciation of difficulties of landing on the Gallipoli Peninsula by Maj-Gen A. Paris (GOC RND)," 19 March 1915, Hamilton Papers, LHCMA, HAMILTON 7/4/13.
22. "Report on Landing Places at Kaba Tepe (Gallipoli Peninsula) with two roads leading therefrom to Maidos and the Kilid Bahr Plateau," memo, 28 September 1910, TNA, WO 106/1534; S. Miles, "Notes on the Dardanelles Campaign of 1915," pt. 2, *Coast Artillery Journal* 62, no. 1 (January 1925): 23.
23. Von Clausewitz, *On War*, 353–54.
24. Doyle and Bennett, "Military Geography," 19, 23.
25. "Appreciation by Captain C. F Aspinall and Captain G. P. Dawnay," 23 March 1915, Hamilton Papers, LHCMA, HAMILTON 7/4/14.
26. Doyle and Bennett, "Military Geography," 21–23.
27. Ellison, *The Perils of Amateur Strategy*, 1926, xxi, 17.
28. Miles, "Notes on the Dardanelles Campaign of 1915," pt. 2, 24.

29. "Key to Geographical names," memo, 12 June 1915, Gellibrand Papers, AWM 3DRL/1473.
30. Serle, *John Monash: A Biography* (Melbourne: Melbourne University Press in association with Monash University, 1983), 232.
31. Doyle and Bennett, "Military Geography," 24.
32. Godley to Hamilton, letter, 20 May 1925, Hamilton Papers, LHCMA, HAMILTON 13/46.
33. Coates, *Defeat at Gallipoli*, 15–16, 32.
34. "Appreciation by Captain C. F Aspinall and Captain G. P. Dawnay," 23 March 1915, Hamilton Papers, LHCMA, HAMILTON 7/4/14; "Intelligence Bulletin," 5 August 1915, Hamilton Papers, LHCMA, HAMILTON 7/6/61; "Notes of a meeting of the Dardanelles Committee," 24 July 1915, TNA, CAB 22/2.
35. Priestley, *The Signal Service*, viii.
36. D. M. Johnson, "Telegraph," in Holmes, *Oxford Companion*, 904; Priestley, *The Signal Service*, viii; *FSR*, 1:22; Griffith, *Battle Tactics of the Western Front*, 160–70.
37. Monash's address delivered to officers and noncommissioned officers of the 4th Australian Bde., 6 August 1915, Monash Papers, AWM 3DRL/2316, 3/20; Beecroft to Aspinall-Oglander, letter, 9 February 1931, TNA, CAB 45/241, 3.
38. "Cable Detachments," NZ&A Div. Sig Coy WD, AWM 4, 35/15/3.
39. "Instructions regarding inter-communication," n.d., HQ ANZAC WD, AWM 4, 1/25/5 pt. 3.
40. Priestley, *The Signal Service*, 19.
41. Birdwood to GHQ, telegram, 10 July 1915, Birdwood Papers, AWM 3DRL/3376, 11/16.
42. Birdwood to wife, letter, 4 August 1915, Birdwood Papers, AWM 3DRL/3376, 8/2.
43. Erickson, *Ordered to Die*, 75; Travers, *Gallipoli 1915*, 176.
44. Hamilton, *Gallipoli Diary*, 2:117.
45. Sheffield, *Forgotten Victory*, 121.
46. Erickson, "Strength against Weakness," 985; Ellison, *The Perils of Amateur Strategy*, xxi.
47. "Mitchell Report," 248–49.
48. E. Ashmead-Bartlett, *The Uncensored Dardanelles* (London: Hutchinson, 1920), 220.
49. Von Clausewitz, *On War*, 194–97, 351.
50. Erickson, *Ordered to Die*, 90–91; Bean, *Official History*, 2:522.
51. Birdwood to wife, letter, 18 August 1915, Birdwood Papers, AWM 3DRL/3376, 8/2.
52. Diary entry, 21 June 1915, Intelligence WD, GHQ MEF, AWM 4, 1/5/3.
53. Evidence of Sir William Birdwood to the Dardanelles Commission, 6 March 1917, TNA, CAB 19/33, 1084; Travers, *Gallipoli 1915*, 214.
54. Hamilton, *Gallipoli Diary*, 1:330, 361.
55. Thursby to Birdwood, letter, 6 November 1915, Birdwood Papers, AWM 3DRL/3376 item 2/1; evidence of Sir William Birdwood to the vDardanelles Commission, 6 March 1917, TNA, CAB 19/33, 1084.

56. Birdwood to Kitchener, letter, 19 August 1915, Birdwood Papers, AWM 3DRL/3376 item 11/6.
57. Evidence of Brigadier-General G. N. Johnston to the Dardanelles Commission, 2 May 1917, TNA, CAB 19/33, 1397–98.
58. While existing roads were improved prior to the offensive, this work would have to continue throughout the offensive if the guns were to have any chance of being placed on the Sari Bair Ridge. Godley, "Discussion on plan of attack on Ridge 971," 23 June 1915, HQ ANZAC WD, AWM 4, 1/25/3 pt. 3.
59. Evidence of Brigadier-General G. N. Johnston to the Dardanelles Commission, 2 May 1917, TNA, CAB 19/33, 1400.
60. Godley to HQ ANZAC, telegram, 29 July 1915; Wagstaff to Godley, memo, 29 July 1915, both in HQ ANZAC WD, AWM 4, 1/25/4 pt. 6.
61. Prior and Wilson, *Command on the Western Front*, 62.
62. Malthus, *Anzac: A Retrospect*, 118–19.
63. Rettie to Aspinall-Oglander, letter, 16 July 1929, TNA, CAB 45/244, 1.
64. Hogg, *Allied Artillery of World War One*, 31–34, 212.
65. Evidence of Brigadier-General G. N. Johnston to the Dardanelles Commission, 2 May 1917, TNA, CAB 19/33, 1398.
66. Hogg, *Allied Artillery of World War One*, 65–70.
67. Unpublished manuscript, Rettie Papers, IWM, 89/9/1, 36.
68. The guns were moved from below Charak Cheshma to a position below Karakol Dagh, a distance of 600 yards with a change in height of 165 feet. This works out (rise/run) as an average grade of 9.1 percent. This average is based on a direct line, and irrespective of the variance in incline along the route, despite two sections of the route having a greater-than-average incline (a total of 120 yards were at an incline of 18.2 percent). Diary entries, 22–23 August 1915, 15th Heavy Battery WD, AWM 6/100.
69. Presuming that the guns commenced their movement from the beach adjacent to Fishermen's Hut and were to be placed on the southwestern slope of Chunuk Bair, this distance was approximately 1.2 miles. With a starting elevation of zero, and an end elevation of 820 feet, the average incline is 12.5 percent. This average is based on a direct line between the two points, and is irrespective of the variance in incline along the route. There are numerous stages along the route where the grade is approximately 77 percent. This measurement was calculated from the same 1:20,000 maps used during the August Offensive.
70. Hogg, *Allied Artillery of World War One*, 32.
71. Bean, *Official History*, 2:439.
72. "Intelligence Bulletin," 24 August 1915, HQ ANZAC Intelligence WD, AWM 4, 1/27/6 pt. 5.
73. Hamilton, *Gallipoli Diary*, 1:330.
74. "Notes by Brigadier General Simpson-Baikie on the Artillery at Cape Helles in the Dardanelles Expedition," n.d., Hamilton Papers, LHCMA, HAMILTON 7/10/5.

75. De Robeck to Balfour, telegram, 9 June 1915, TNA, ADM 137/154; "Intelligence Summary," 8 August 1915, HQ ANZAC Intelligence WD, AWM 4, 1/27/6 pt. 1; "Mitchell Report," 90.
76. "Intelligence Bulletin," 11 July 1915, HQ ANZAC Intelligence WD, AWM 4, 1/27/5 pt. 2.
77. "Mitchell Report," 206–209.
78. Hankey to Balfour, letter, 5 August 1915, TNA, CAB 17/123. A copy of this was sent to Prime Minister Asquith and can be found in his papers. See Asquith Papers, New Bodleian Library, MS Asquith 28, fol. 66.
79. "Prisoner of War Statement," Hadji Ali (transport officer, II Army Corps, 5th Ottoman Division), 6 May 1915, HQ ANZAC Intelligence WD, AWM 4, 1/27/3 pt. 1; "Intelligence Bulletin," 21 May 1915, HQ ANZAC Intelligence WD, AWM 4, 1/27/3 pt. 2; "Intelligence Bulletin," 11 July 1915, HQ ANZAC Intelligence WD, AWM 4, 1/27/5 pt. 2.
80. Balfour to Curzon, letter, 2 August 1915, Curzon Papers, BL, F112/159.
81. James, *Gallipoli*, 3.
82. "Mitchell Report," 195.
83. Erickson, "Strength against Weakness," 986–89.
84. "Situation in the Aegean: Appreciation by Captain Dawnay, General Staff, Mediterranean Expeditionary Force," September 1915, Dawnay Papers, IWM, 69/21/6, 2.
85. Evidence of Brigadier-General G. N. Johnston to the Dardanelles Commission, 2 May 1917, TNA, CAB 19/33, 1398.
86. Hamilton to War Office, telegram, 13 June 1915, Hamilton Papers, LHCMA, HAMILTON 7/4/8.
87. "Appreciation by Captain C. F. Aspinall and Captain G. P. Dawnay," 23 March 1915, Hamilton Papers, LHCMA, HAMILTON 7/4/14.
88. [Unidentified officer from] HMS *Talbot*, "Enemy guns on the flanks of ANZAC," 30 July 1915, England Papers, IWM, 76/43/1.
89. Sinclair, "Logistics, Principles and Practice," 50.
90. "Appreciation of the situation in the Dardanelles according to information received up to 25 March 1915, the date of leaving Malta," 30 March 1915, Hamilton Papers, LHCMA, HAMILTON 7/4/15.
91. Evidence of Rear-Admiral Roger Brownlow Keyes to the Dardanelles Commission, 15 May 1917, TNA, CAB 19/33, 1469.
92. Evidence of Acting Vice-Admiral Sir Henry F. Oliver to the Dardanelles Commission, 5 October 1916, TNA, CAB 19/33, 135.
93. Hamilton's agreement with the "real defence of Constantinople" statement can be found in a footnote in Miles, "Notes on the Dardanelles Campaign of 1915," pt. 4, 221.
94. Marder, *From the Dardanelles to Oran*, 12.
95. "Mitchell Report," 9.
96. Evidence of Admiral Sackville H. Carden to the Dardanelles Commission, 6 October 1916, TNA, CAB 19/33, 158.

97. Kerr to North, letter, 1 November 1934, North Papers, LHCMA, NORTH I/3/287.
98. Fisher, *Memories*, 84–85.
99. Marder, *From the Dardanelles to Oran*, 27.
100. Ibid., 2–4; "Mitchell Report," 490–91.
101. Keyes to de Robeck (annotated by de Robeck), letter, 17 August 1915, de Robeck Papers, CAC, DRBK 4/78.
102. Miles, "Notes on the Dardanelles Campaign of 1915," pt. 1, 516.
103. "Mitchell Report," 8.
104. Diary entry, 18 March 1915, Gibson Papers, IWM, 87/32/2.
105. "Mitchell Report," 8.
106. W. D. Puleston, *The Dardanelles Expedition: A Condensed Study* (Annapolis, Md.: United States Naval Institute, 1927), 39–40.
107. R. Keyes, "Memories of the Dardanelles Campaign," *Reveille*, 1 December 1937, 33; evidence of Rear-Admiral Roger Brownlow Keyes to the Dardanelles Commission, 16 May 1917, TNA, CAB 19/33, 1468.
108. Evidence of Admiral Sir John de Robeck to the Dardanelles Commission, 10 October 1916, TNA, CAB 19/33, 173.
109. Evidence of Vice-Admiral Sir Henry F. Oliver to the Dardanelles Commission, 5 October 1916, TNA, CAB 19/33, 135.
110. Diary entry, 30 August 1915, Intelligence WD, GHQ MEF, AWM 4, 1/5/5 pt. 1.
111. De Robeck to Balfour, letter, 9 July 1915, de Robeck Papers, CAC, DRBK 4/69.
112. Coates, *Defeat at Gallipoli*, 15–16, 32.
113. Hamilton to Kitchener, telegram, 29 June 1915, Hamilton Papers, LHCMA, HAMILTON 7/4/8.
114. Hankey to Asquith, letter, 4 August 1915, TNA, CAB 17/123.
115. "Mitchell Report," 73–75.
116. Hogg, *Allied Artillery of World War One*, 12.
117. Evidence of Admiral Sir John de Robeck to the Dardanelles Commission, 10 October 1916, TNA, CAB 19/33, 173; de Robeck to Balfour, letter, 20 October 1915, de Robeck Papers, CAC, DRBK 4/69.
118. De Robeck quoted in "Mitchell Report," 224.
119. Balfour to George (Curzon), letter, 2 August 1915, Curzon Papers, BL, F112/159; evidence of The Right Hon. Arthur James Balfour to the Dardanelles Commission, 13 October 1916, TNA, CAB 19/33, 244.
120. R. Keyes, *Amphibious Warfare and Combined Operations* (Cambridge: Cambridge University Press, 1943), 41; (Renewal of naval attack at the Dardanelles), memo, 21 August 1915, Curzon Papers, BL, F112/160; evidence of Acting Vice-Admiral Sir Henry F. Oliver to the Dardanelles Commission, 5 October 1916, TNA, CAB 19/33, 132.
121. "The naval memoirs of Admiral J.H. Godfrey," vol. 2, Godfrey Papers, IWM, 74/96/1, 1–2.
122. "Questions put to the Ottoman General Staff about the Dardanelles operations and the answers received: second series of questions and answers," n.d., TNA, CAB 45/217.

123. In April the MEF consisted of 75,000 rifles. In August, including the reserve divisions, it amounted to some 139,000.
124. This distance, calculated using the maps used by the MEF when planning the offensive, is based on a straight line from Anzac Cove to Chunuk Bair. This calculation does not take into account the actual routes used or the impact that terrain had on the distance traversed.
125. The Anzac perimeter prior to the August Offensive was approximately 1.7 miles. If the second phase of the August Offensive had been successful, the MEF would have held a line from Hill 971 in the north, along Third Ridge, and finishing at Gaba Tepe in the south. This frontage measured approximately 5 miles. These calculations are based on the maps used by the MEF when planning the August Offensive in 1915.
126. D. Graham and S. Bidwell, *Coalitions, Politicians and Generals: Some Aspects of Command in Two World Wars* (London: Brassey's, 1993), 265.
127. Quoted in Coates, *Defeat at Gallipoli*, 185.
128. Diary entry, 12 August 1915, DST "Transport Diary," GHQ MEF, TNA, WO 95/4269.
129. "Statement of Supply Requirements," attached to "Memorandum of impending landing operations," 16 July 1915, DQMG WD, GHQ MEF, TNA, WO 95/4266.
130. Hamilton to de Robeck, telegram, 17 July 1915, GS WD, GHQ MEF, AWM 4, 1/4/4 pt. 2.
131. "Instructions to Major-General H. de Lisle," memo, 15 August 1915, GS WD, GHQ MEF, AWM 4, 1/4/5 pt. 3.
132. Note to Aspinall (origin unknown), 7 November 1915, "Suvla Transport Scheme," Aspinall-Oglander Papers, IWCRO, OG/AO/G/25.
133. Ellison to Altham, memo, 21 August 1915; Ellison to Braithwaite, memo, 21 August 1915, both in DQMG WD, GHQ MEF, TNA, WO 95/4266.
134. Includes the initial 37,000 of Anzac, the 20,000 of Suvla, and the 19,000 of 53rd, 54th, and 2nd Mounted Divisions. It is important to note that the reserve divisions did not bring transport with them.
135. "Personal diary of Lieutenant-Colonel C. H. Beville," 18 August 1915, Indian Mule Cart Train WD, TNA, WO 95/4358.
136. Diary entry, 29–31 August 1915, 1st Australian Div. Train WD, AWM 4, 25/14/10.
137. Braithwaite to Stopford, memo, 22 July 1915, GS WD, GHQ MEF, AWM 4, 1/4/4 pt. 2.
138. Miles, "Notes on the Dardanelles Campaign of 1915," pt. 2, 27.
139. Diary entry, 29 August 1915, Chief Engineer ANZAC WD, TNA, WO 95/4285.
140. "The naval situation—with regard to future landing operations: survey of present situation," memo, 7 June 1915, GS WD, GHQ MEF, AWM 4, 1/4/3 pt. 3.
141. Evidence of Rear-Admiral Roger John Brownlow Keyes to the Dardanelles Commission, 15 May 1917, TNA, CAB 19/33, 1445.

142. Ellison to Hamilton, telegram, 23 August 1915, GS WD, GHQ MEF, AWM 4, 1/4/5 pt. 3.
143. Evidence of Rear-Admiral Roger John Brownlow Keyes to the Dardanelles Commission, 15 May 1917, TNA, CAB 19/33, 1445.

Conclusion

1. Coates, *Defeat at Gallipoli*, 288.
2. Britain's prewar doctrine stressed the importance of a war of movement, where the ultimate objective was to break through and then break out of the enemy's position. This belief, which was exemplified in *FSR*, was based on the experience gained through colonial wars and was still at the forefront of the British approach to military operations when war broke out in August 1914. The commanders of the MEF, like those of the BEF, applied this approach to warfare in 1915, not realizing that war had essentially moved on and that the technology of modern war had rendered this approach useless. For more on the impact of prewar doctrine on the British approach to war in 1914–1915, see B. Bond, *The Victorian Army and the Staff College, 1854–1914* (London: Eyre Methuen, 1972); T. Travers, *The Killing Ground: The British Army, the Western Front and the Emergence of Modern Warfare, 1900–1918* (Sydney: Allen and Unwin, 1987); Travers, "Command and Leadership Styles in the British Army," 403–42; and S. Robbins, *British Generalship on the Western Front 1914–1918: Defeat into Victory* (London: Frank Cass, 2005).
3. D. Todman, *The Great War: Myth and Memory* (London: Hambledon Continuum, 2005), 79.
4. Robbins, *British Generalship on the Western Front*, 21.
5. J. Smyth, *Leadership in Battle, 1914–1918: Commanders in Action* (New York: Hippocrene Books, 1975), 112.
6. Cabinet paper, "The offensive under present conditions," 19 June 1915, Bonar Law Papers, Parliamentary Archives, BL/56/IE.

Bibliography

Archival Sources, Australia

Australian War Memorial, Canberra
   Official Records
      AWM 4 Australian Imperial Force unit war diaries, 1914–18 War.
      AWM 6 Mediterranean Expeditionary Force unit war diaries, 1914–1918 War.
      AWM 11 Australian Imperial Force Administrative Headquarters registry. "A" (Adjutant-General's Branch) medical (subject) files.
      AWM 13 Australian Imperial Force Administrative Headquarters registry. "Q" (Quartermaster-General's Branch) files.
      AWM 16 Australian War Records Section registry files and register of file titles.
      AWM 25 Written records, 1914–18 War.
      AWM 36 Navy records used by A. Jose (includes United Kingdom records).
      AWM 37 Records of 1st Royal Australian Naval Bridging Train and HMNZT *Willochra*.
      AWM 38 Official History, 1914–18 War: Records of C. E. W. Bean, Official Historian.
      AWM 44 Official History, 1914–18 War. Manuscripts.
      AWM 45 Copies of British war diaries and other records, 1914–18 War ("Heyes papers").
      AWM 51 Confidential and security classified records originally maintained by the Australian War Memorial Library.
      AWM 124 Naval historical collection.
      AWM 224 Unit manuscript histories.

   Private Records
      Antill, John Macquarie (Major-General), 3DRL/3607 and 3DRL/6458.
      Birdwood, Lord William (Field Marshal), 3DRL/3376.
      Brazier, Noel Murray (Lieutenant-Colonel), 1DRL/0147.
      Casey, Richard Gardiner (Captain), 3DRL/3267.
      Cox, Sir Herbert Vaughan (General), 1DRL/0221.
      Davidson, William (Major), 1DRL/0235.
      Elliott, Harold Edward "Pompey" (Brigadier-General), 2DRL/0513.
      Foott, Cecil Henry (Brigadier-General), 3DRL/1768.
      Gellibrand, Sir John (Major-General), 3DRL/1473, 3DRL/6405, and 3DRL/6541.
      Hobbs, Sir Joseph John Talbot (General), 3DRL/2600 and PR82/153.

Howell-Price, Owen Glendower (Lieutenant-Colonel), 1DRL/0362.
Howse, Sir Neville (Major-General), 2DRL/1351.
Monash, Sir John (General), 3DRL/2316.
Morshead, Sir Leslie James (Lieutenant-General), 3DRL/2632.
Pearce, Sir George Foster (Minister for Defence), 3DRL/2222.
Rosenthal, Charles (Major-General), PR90/129.

National Archives of Australia, Canberra
  CA 1, Governor-General.
    A11803 Governor General's correspondence relating to the war of 1914–1918.
    A11804 General Correspondence of Governor-General (excluding war files).
  CA 12, Prime Minister's Department.
    A3934 Correspondence files. SC secret and confidential series (old files).
  CA 19, Department of Defence.
    A5954 "The Shedden Collection."
  CA 1720, Australian Archives. Central Office.
    A6006 Folders of copies of Cabinet papers.
  CA 2001, Australian Imperial Force. Base Records Office.
    B2455 First Australian Imperial Force Personnel Dossiers, 1914–1920.

National Library of Australia, Canberra
  MS 986 Letters 1900–1919 (Major-General Sir Grenville de Laune Ryrie).
  MS 1538 Papers of William Morris Hughes.
  MS 1884 Papers of Sir John Monash.
  MS 2823 Papers of Keith Arthur Murdoch.

Archival Sources, UK

The British Library
  Papers of Arthur James Balfour.
  Papers of Field Marshal Sir William Riddell Birdwood.
  Papers of Lord Curzon.
  Papers of Lieutenant-General Sir Aylmer Gould Hunter-Weston.
  Papers of Lieutenant-General Sir Edward Thomas Henry Hutton.
  Papers of Admiral of the Fleet 1st Baron Roger John Brownlow Keyes.

Churchill Archives Centre, University of Cambridge, Cambridge
  Papers of Winston Churchill.
  Papers of Admiral Sir John de Robeck.
  Papers of First Lord Fisher of Kilverstone.
  Papers of Lord Hankey of the Chart (Maurice Hankey).
  Papers of Robert Rhodes James.

Papers of Reginald McKenna.
Papers of Field Marshal Slim.
Papers of Admiral of the Fleet Lord Wester-Wemyss.

Imperial War Museum, London
Ataturk's memoirs of the Anafartalar Battles.
Papers of Admiral Oliver Backhouse.
Papers of Captain E. W. Bush.
Papers of Sir Gerald Clauson.
Papers of Major-General G. P. Dawnay.
Papers of Rear-Admiral H. T. England.
Papers of Rear-Admiral I. W. Gibson.
Papers of Admiral J. H. Godfrey.
Papers of Admiral Sir Richard Phillimore.
Papers of Colonel F. A. Rayfield.
Papers of Lieutenant-Colonel W. J. K. Rettie.
Papers of Air Commodore C. R. Samson.
Papers of Lieutenant-General Sir Frederick Shaw.
Papers of Major-General A. C. Temperley.
Papers of Dr. O. C. Williams.

Isle of Wight County Record Office, Isle of Wight
Papers of Cecil F. Aspinall-Oglander.

Liddell Hart Centre for Military Archives, King's College, London
MISC 35 The Dardanelles 1915: Selection of Cabinet Office papers made for King's College London.
Papers of General Sir (Henry de) Beauvoir de Lisle.
Papers of General Sir Alexander John Godley.
Papers of General Sir Ian Standish Monteith Hamilton.
Papers of Captain Sir Basil Henry Liddell Hart.
Papers of General Hastings Lionel Ismay.
Papers of Major-General Sir Frederick Barton Maurice.
Papers of Major John Francis Allen North.
Papers of Field Marshal Sir William (Robert) Robertson.
Papers of Brigadier-General Sir Hugh Archie Dundas Simpson-Baikie.

The National Archives, Kew
ADM 1 Admiralty and Ministry of Defence. Navy Department. Correspondence and Papers.
ADM 50 Admiralty. Admirals' Journals.
ADM 53 Admiralty and Ministry of Defence. Navy Department. Ships' Logs.
ADM 116 Admiralty. Record Office. Cases.
ADM 137 Admiralty. Historical Section: Records used for Official History, First World War.
ADM 167 Board of Admiralty: Minutes and Memoranda.

ADM 173 Admiralty, and Ministry of Defence, Navy Department. Submarine Logs.
ADM 182 Admiralty: Admiralty Fleet Orders.
ADM 186 Admiralty: Publications.
AIR 1 Air Ministry: Air Historical Branch. Papers (Series I).
CAB 17 Committee of Imperial Defence. Miscellaneous Correspondence and Memoranda.
CAB 19 Special Commissions to Enquire into the Operations of War in Mesopotamia (Hamilton Commission) and in the Dardanelles (Cromer and Pickford Commission). Records.
CAB 22 War Council and successors. Minutes and Papers.
CAB 41 Photographic Copies of Cabinet Letters in the Royal Archives.
CAB 42 War Council and successors. Photographic Copies of Minutes and Papers.
CAB 45 Committee of Imperial Defence. Historical Branch and Cabinet Office. Historical Section. Official War Histories, Correspondence and Papers.
CAB 63 War Cabinet and Cabinet Office. Lord Hankey. Papers.
CAB 103 Cabinet Office and predecessors. Historical Section. Registered Files (HS and other Series).
MT 23 Admiralty, Transport Department. Correspondence and Papers.
PRO 30/57 Horatio Herbert Kitchener, 1st Earl Kitchener of Khartoum. Papers.
WO 32 War Office and successors. Registered Files (General Series).
WO 33 War Office. Reports, Memoranda and Papers (O and A Series).
WO 78 War Office and predecessors. Maps and Plans.
WO 95 War Office. First World War and Army of Occupation War Diaries.
WO 106 War Office. Directorate of Military Operations and Military Intelligence, and predecessors. Correspondence and Papers.
WO 107 Office of the Commander in Chief and War Office. Quartermaster General's Department. Correspondence and Papers.
WO 138 War Office. Personal Files.
WO 153 War Office. War of 1914–1918: Maps and Plans.
WO 154 War Office War Diaries (Supplementary), First World War.
WO 157 War Office. Intelligence Summaries, First World War.
WO 158 War Office. Military Headquarters. Correspondence and Papers, First World War.
WO 159 War Office. Field Marshal Lord Kitchener, Secretary of State for War. Private Office Papers.
WO 161 War Office. Miscellaneous Unregistered Papers, First World War.
WO 162 Commander-in-Chief and War Office. Adjutant General's Department. Papers.
WO 301 War Office. Geographical Section General Staff. War of 1914–1918: Gallipoli Campaign, Dardanelles Commission and Post-War Maps of Turkey.

The National Army Museum, London
  Papers of Lieutenant-General Sir Gerald Ellison.
  Papers of Major-General Sir Clement Arthur Milward.

National Maritime Museum, London
  Papers of Sir Julian Stafford Corbett.
  Papers of Admiral Limpus.
  Papers of Rear-Admiral H. F. Oliver.
  Papers of Captain H. W. Richmond.
  Papers of Admiral Sir Cecil Fiennes Thursby.

New Bodleian Library, University of Oxford, Oxford
  Papers of Herbert Henry Asquith.

Parliamentary Archives, House of Lords Record Office, London
  The Bonar Law Papers.
  The Lloyd George Papers.

Books, Articles, Theses, Papers, and Lectures

Adams, R. J. Q., ed. *The Great War, 1914–18: Essays on the Military, Political and Social History of the First World War*. College Station: Texas A&M University Press, 1990.

Adam-Smith, P. *The Anzacs*. Victoria, Australia: Thomas Nelson, 1978.

Admiralty. *Report of the Committee Appointed to Investigate the Attacks Delivered on and the Enemy Defences of the Dardanelles Straits: 1919*. London: H.M. Stationary Office, 1921.

Alexander, H. M. *On Two Fronts: Being the Adventures of an Indian Mule Corps in France and Gallipoli*. London: William Heinemann, 1917.

Alger, J. I. *Definitions and Doctrine of the Military Art: Past and Present*. Wayne, N.J.: Avery, 1985.

Andrews, E. M. *The Anzac Illusion: Anglo-Australian Relations during World War I*. Cambridge: Cambridge University Press, 1993.

———. "The Media and the Military: Australian War Correspondents and the Appointment of a Corps Commander, 1918—A Case Study." *War and Society* 8, no. 2 (October 1990): 83–103.

Annabell, N. *Official History of the New Zealand Engineers during the Great War, 1914–1919*. Wanganui, NZ: Evans, Cobb and Sharpe, 1927.

Archer, S. K. "Command Crisis: Influence of Command Culture on the Allied Defeat at Suvla Bay." MA thesis, U.S. Army Command and General Staff College, 1998.

Ashmead-Bartlett, E. *The Uncensored Dardanelles*. London: Hutchinson, 1920.

Ashworth, T. *Trench Warfare 1914–1918: The Live and Let live System*. London: MacMillan, 1980.

Aspinall-Oglander, C. F. *Military Operations: Gallipoli*. Vol. 1, *Inception of the Campaign to May 1915*. London: Heinemann, 1929.

———. *Military Operations: Gallipoli*. Vol. 2, *May 1915 to the Evacuation*. London: Heinemann, 1932.

Asquith, H. H. *How Do We Stand To-day? A Speech Delivered by The Right Hon. H. H. Asquith, Prime Minister, in the House of Commons on the 2nd November, 1915*. London: T. F. Unwin, 1915.
Astore, W. J., and D. E. Showalter. *Hindenburg: Icon of German Militarism*. Washington, D.C.: Potomac Books, 2005.
Austin, R. *Gallipoli: An Australian Encyclopedia of the 1915 Dardanelles Campaign*. Rosebud, Australia: Slouch Hat Publications, 2005.
———. "General Sir Ian Hamilton, GCB, GCMG, DSO: A Reassessment of the 'Romantic Warrior.'" *Sabretache* 39 (September 1998): 10–18.
Austin, R., and S. Austin. *The Body Snatchers: The History of the 3rd Australian Field Ambulance 1914–1918*. Rosebud, Australia: Slouch Hat Publications, 1995.
Bailey, J. B. A. "British Artillery in the Great War." In *British Fighting Methods in the Great War*, edited by P. Griffith, 23–49. Ilford, UK: Frank Cass, 1996.
———. *Field Artillery and Firepower*. Oxford: Military Press, 1989.
Ballard, C. R. *Kitchener*. London: Newnes, 1936.
Barnett, C. *The Great War*. London: BBC, 2003.
———. "The Impact of Surprise and Initiative in War." *RUSI Journal* 129, no. 2 (1984): 20–26.
———. *The Swordbearers: Supreme Command in the First World War*. Bloomington: Indiana University Press, 1975.
Bazley, A. W. "Australia's Official History of World War I." *Stand-To* 6, no. 7 (1959): 22–32.
———. "Responsibility for Gallipoli Failure." *Stand-To* 10, no. 2 (March–December 1965): 23–27.
Beadon, R. H. *The Royal Army Service Corps: A History of Transport and Supply in the British Army*. Vol. 2. Cambridge: Cambridge University Press, 1931.
Bean, C. E. W., ed. *The Anzac Book*. Melbourne: Cassell, 1916.
———. *Anzac to Amiens: A Shorter History of the Australian Fighting Services in the First World War*. Canberra: Australian War Memorial, 1968.
———. "The Australian Army: Its Famous Infantry: Part II, Victoria." *Anzac Bulletin* 50, 21 December 1917, 2–4.
———. "The Australian Army: Its Famous Infantry, Tasmanian Battalions." *Anzac Bulletin* 65, 5 April 1918, 4–5.
———. *Gallipoli Mission*. Crows Nest, Australia: ABC Books, 1990.
———. *The Official History of Australia in the War of 1914–1918*. Vol. 1, *The Story of Anzac from the Outbreak of War to the End of the First Phase of the Gallipoli Campaign, May 4, 1915*. Sydney: Angus and Robertson, 1921.
———. *The Official History of Australia in the War of 1914–1918*. Vol. 2, *The Story of Anzac from 4 May, 1915, to the Evacuation of the Gallipoli Peninsula*. Sydney: Angus and Robertson, 1924.
———. "Sidelights of the War on Australian Character." *Royal Australian Historical Society Journal* 13, no. 4 (1927): 209–23.

———. *Two Men I Knew: William Bridges and Brudenell White, Founders of the A.I.F.* Sydney: Angus and Robertson, 1957.
———. "The Writing of the Australian Official History of the Great War—Sources, Methods and Some Conclusions." *Royal Australian Historical Society Journal* 24, No. 2 (1938).
Beaumont, J. "ANZAC Day to VP Day: Arguments and Interpretations." *Journal of the Australian War Memorial* 40 (February 2007).
———, ed. *Australia's War, 1914–1918.* St. Leonards, Australia: Allen and Unwin, 1995.
———. "The State of Australian History of War." *Australian Historical Studies* 34, no. 121 (2003): 165–68.
Beaumont, R. "Assessing Operational Impact: A Problem in Military Analysis." *Military Affairs* 46, no. 3 (October 1982): 132–33.
Beaverbrook, M. A. *Politicians and the War, 1914–1916.* London: Thornton Butterworth, 1928.
Becke, A. F. *Order of Battle Part 4: The Army Council, G.H.Q.s, Armies and Corps, 1914–1918.* London: H.M. Stationary Office, 1944.
Bellamy, C. "Manoeuvre Warfare." In *The Oxford Companion to Military History*, edited by R. Holmes, 541–44. Oxford: Oxford University Press, 2003.
Bennett, J. *Gallipoli.* Sydney: Angus and Robertson, 1981.
Bentley, J. "Champion of Anzac: General Sir Brudenell White, the First Australian Imperial Force and the Emergence of Australian Military Culture, 1914–18." PhD thesis, University of Wollongong, 2003.
Bidwell, S. *Gunners at War: A Tactical Study of the Royal Artillery in the Twentieth Century.* London: Arrow Books, 1972.
Bidwell, S., and D. Graham. *Fire-power: British Army Weapons and Theories of War, 1904–1945.* Barnsley, UK: Pen and Sword, 2004.
Birdwood, W. R. *Khaki and Gown.* London: Ward, Lock, 1941.
Black, N. *The British Naval Staff in the First World War.* Woodbridge, UK: Boydell Press, 2011.
Blair, D. J. *Dinkum Diggers: An Australian Battalion at War.* Carlton, Australia: Melbourne University Press, 2001.
Blake, R., ed. *The Private Papers of Douglas Haig, 1914–1919.* London: Eyre and Spottiswoode, 1952.
Bond, B. *The Victorian Army and the Staff College, 1854–1914.* London: Eyre Methuen, 1972.
Bourne, J. "British Generals in the First World War." In *Leadership and Command: The Anglo-American Military Experience since 1861*, edited by G. D. Sheffield, 93–116. London: Brassey's, 1997.
Boyd, J. A. *Supply Handbook for the Army Service Corps.* London: H.M. Stationary Office, 1895.
Braga, S. *ANZAC Doctor: The Life of Sir Neville Howse, Australia's First V.C.* Sydney: Hale and Iremonger, 2000.
Brenchley, E., and F. Brenchley. *Myth Maker: Ellis Ashmead-Bartlett, the Englishman who sparked Australia's Gallipoli legend.* Queensland: Wiley and Sons, 2005.

Broadbent, H. *The Boys Who Came Home: Recollections of Gallipoli.* Sydney: ABC Books, 2000.
———. *Gallipoli: the Fatal Shore.* Victoria: Penguin, 2009.
Brooks, S. "The New English Cabinet." *North American Review* 202 (July/December 1915): 100–111.
Brown, I. M. *British Logistics on the Western Front, 1914–1919.* Westport, Conn.: Praeger, 1998.
———. "Growing Pains: Supplying the British Expeditionary Force, 1914–1915." In *Battles Near and Far: A Century of Overseas Deployment*, edited by P. Dennis and J. Grey, 33–47. Canberra: Army History Unit, 2005.
Brown, M. *The Imperial War Museum Book of the First World War.* London: Pan Books, 2002.
Burness, P. *The Nek: The Tragic Charge of the Light Horse at Gallipoli.* Kenthurst, Australia: Kangaroo Press, 1996.
Burton, O. E. *The Auckland Regiment: Being an Account of the Doings on Active Service of the First, Second and Third Battalions of the Auckland Regiment.* Auckland: Whitcombe and Tombs, 1922.
———. *The Silent Division: New Zealanders at the Front, 1914–1919.* Sydney: Angus and Robertson, 1935.
Bush, E. W. *Gallipoli.* London: Allen and Unwin, 1975.
Butler, A. G. *Official History of the Australian Army Medical Services in the War of 1914–1918.* Vol. 1, *Gallipoli, Palestine and New Guinea.* Melbourne: Australian War Memorial, 1930.
Byrne, A. E. *Official History of the Otago Regiment, N. Z. E. F., in the Great War, 1914–1918.* Dunedin, NZ: J. Wilkie, 1942.
Byrne, J. R. *New Zealand Artillery in the Field, 1914–1918.* Auckland: Whitcombe and Tombs, 1922.
Cain, F. "A Colonial Army in Ottoman Fields: Australia's involvement in Britain's Gallipoli Debacle." In *The First World War: Middle Eastern Perspectives*, edited by Y. Sheffy and S. Shai, 174–84. Tel Aviv: Tel Aviv University, 2000.
Callwell, C. E. *The Dardanelles.* London: Constable, 1919.
Cameron, D. W. *The August Offensive at Anzac, 1915.* Australian Army Campaign Series. Sydney: Big Sky Publishing, 2011.
———. *The Battle for Lone Pine.* Victoria: Penguin, 2012.
———. *Gallipoli: The Final Battles and Evacuation of Anzac.* Sydney: Big Sky Publishing, 2011.
———. *"Sorry, Lads, but the Order is to Go": The August Offensive, Gallipoli: 1915.* University of New South Wales Press, 2009.
———. *25 April 1915: The Day the Anzac Legend Was Born.* Crows Nest, Australia: Allen and Unwin, 2007.
Carbery, A. D. *The New Zealand Medical Service in the Great War, 1914–1918: Based on Official Documents.* Auckland: Whitcombe and Tombs, 1924.
Carlyon, L. *Gallipoli.* Sydney: Macmillan, 2004.

Carver, M. *The National Army Museum Book of the Turkish Front, 1914–1918: The Campaigns at Gallipoli, in Mesopotamia and in Palestine.* London: Pan Books, in association with the National Army Museum, 2004.

Cassar, G. H. *The French and the Dardanelles: A Study of Failure in the Conduct of War.* London: Allen and Unwin, 1971.

———. "Kitchener at the War Office." In *Facing Armageddon: The First World War Experiences*, edited by H. Cecil and P. H. Liddle, 37–50. London: Leo Cooper, 1996.

———. *Kitchener's War: British Strategy from 1914 to 1916.* Washington, D.C.: Potomac Books, 2004.

Cecil, H., and P. H. Liddle, eds. *Facing Armageddon: The First World War Experiences.* London: Leo Cooper, 1996.

Celik, K. "A Turkish view of the August Offensive." Lecture presented at Australian War Memorial Conference, Gallipoli: The August Offensive, Canberra, 5 August 2000.

Chambers, S. *Suvla: August Offensive.* Barnsley, UK: Pen and Sword, 2011.

Chapman-Huston, D., and O. Rutter. *General Sir John Cowans G.C.B., G.C.M.G.: The Quartermaster-General of the Great War.* London: Hutchinson, 1924.

Chasseaud, P., and P. Doyle. *Grasping Gallipoli: Terrain, Maps and Failure at the Dardanelles, 1915.* Kent, UK: Spellmount, 2005.

Chataway, T. P., and P. Goldenstedt. *History of the 15th Battalion, Australian Imperial Forces: War 1914–1918.* Brisbane: W. Brook, 1948.

Chatterton, E. K. *Dardanelles Dilemma: The Story of the Naval Operations.* London: Rich and Cowan, 1935.

Chickering, R., and S. Förster, eds. *Great War, Total War: Combat Mobilization on the Western Front, 1914–1918.* Cambridge: Cambridge University Press, 2006.

Chrisman, H. H. "Naval Operations in the Mediterranean during the Great War, 1914–1918." PhD diss., Stanford University, 1931.

Churchill, W. *The World Crisis.* Vol. 2. London: Butterworth, 1923.

Clark, A. *The Donkeys.* New York: Award Books, 1965.

Clark, A. *History's Children: History Wars in the Classroom.* Sydney: University of New South Wales Press, 2008.

Clark, C. "Naval Aviation at Gallipoli." In *Sea Power Ashore and in the Air*, edited by D. Stevens and J. Reeve, 77–89. Ultimo, Australia: Halstead Press, 2007.

Clarke, D. *British Artillery 1914–19: Field Army Artillery.* Oxford: Osprey, 2004.

Coates, T., ed. *Defeat at Gallipoli: The Dardanelles Commission, Part II, 1915–16.* London: Stationary Office, 2000.

———, ed. *Lord Kitchener and Winston Churchill: The Dardanelles Commission, Part I, 1914–15.* London: Stationary Office, 2000.

Cohen, E. A., and J. Gooch. *Military Misfortunes: The Anatomy of Failure in War.* New York: Free Press, 2006.

Coles, M., ed. *Military Logistics: A Primer on Operational, Strategic and Support Level Logistics*. Canberra: Australian Defence Studies Centre, 1996.
Collier, P. "The Impact on Topographic Mapping of Developments in Land and Air Survey: 1900–1939." *Cartography and Geographic Information Science* 29, no. 3 (2002): 155–74.
Cook, T. "Canadian Official Historians and the Writing of the World Wars." PhD thesis, University of New South Wales, Australian Defence Force Academy, 2005.
Coombes, D. *The Lionheart: A life of Lieutenant-General Sir Talbot Hobbs*. Loftus: Australian Military History Publications, 2007.
Cooper, B. *The Tenth (Irish) Division in Gallipoli*. Dublin: Irish Academic Press, 1993.
Corbett, J. S. *Naval Operations*. Vol. 2, *From the Battle of the Falklands to the Entry of Italy into the War in May 1915*. London: Longmans, Green, 1929.
———. *Naval Operations*. Vol. 3, *May 1915–June 1916*. London: Longmans, Green, 1923.
———. *Principles of Maritime Strategy*. New York: Dover, 2004.
Corrigan, G. *Loos 1915: The Unwanted Battle*. Gloucestershire: Spellmount, 2006.
Coulthard-Clark, C. D. *No Australian Need Apply: The Troubled Career of Lieutenant- General Gordon Legge*. Sydney: Allen and Unwin, 1988.
Cowan, J. *The Maoris in the Great War: A History of the New Zealand Native Contingent and Pioneer Battalion, Gallipoli, 1915, France and Flanders, 1916–1918*. Auckland: Maori Regimental Committee, 1926.
Crawford, J., ed. *The Devil's Own War: The Diary of Herbert Hart*. Auckland: Exisle, 2009.
Crawford, J., and P. Cooke, eds. *No Better Death: The Great War Diaries and Letters of William G. Malone*. Auckland: Reed Books, 2005.
Crawley, R. "Lone Pine: Worth the Cost?" *Wartime: Official Magazine of the Australian War Memorial* 38 (2007): 14–17.
———. "The Myths of August at Gallipoli." In *Zombie Myths of Australian Military History*, edited by C. Stockings, 50–69. Sydney: University of New South Wales Press, 2010.
———. "'Our Second Great [Mis]adventure': A Critical Re-evaluation of the August Offensive, Gallipoli, 1915." PhD thesis, University of New South Wales, Australian Defence Force Academy, 2010.
———. "Perspectives of Battle: Lone Pine, August 1915." BA honours thesis, University of Wollongong, 2006.
Creighton, O. *With the Twenty-Ninth Division in Gallipoli*. London: Longmans, Green, 1916.
Creswell, J. *Generals and Admirals: The Story of Amphibious Command*. London: Longmans, Green, 1952.
Cunliffe-Owen, C. "Artillery at Anzac in the Gallipoli Campaign." *Journal of the Royal Artillery* 46 (1921).

Cunningham, W. H. "Chunuk Bair Attack: N.Z. Infantry Brigade." *Reveille*, 1 August 1932.
Danisman, H. B., trans. and ed. *Gallipoli 1915: Bloody Ridge (Lone Pine) Diary of Lt. Mehmed Fasih, 5th Imperial Ottoman Army*. Istanbul: Denizler Kitabevi, 2003.
———. *Gallipoli 1915: 27th Ottoman Inf. Regt. vs. ANZACS Based on Account of Lt. Col. Sefik Aker, Commander of 27th Regt*. Istanbul: Denizler Kitabevi, 2007.
Dare, R. Review of *Churchill's "World Crisis" as History*, by Robin Prior. *Historical Studies* 21, no. 84 (1985): 455–56.
Davies, M. J. "Military Intelligence at Gallipoli—'A Leap in the Dark'?" *Australian Defence Force Journal* 92 (January–February 1992): 37–43.
Dean, A., and E. W. Gutteridge. *The Seventh Battalion, A.I.F.: Resume of the Activities of the Seventh Battalion in the Great War, 1914–1918*. Melbourne: W. and K. Purbrick, 1933.
Denham, H. M. *Dardanelles: A Midshipman's Diary*. London: John Murray, 1981.
Dennis, A. L. P. "The Freedom of the Straits." *North American Review* 206, no. 805 (July/December 1922): 721–34.
Dennis, P. "Introduction." *Revue Internationale d'Histoire Militaire* 72 (1990): vii–xxii.
Dennis, P., and J. Grey, eds. *Battles Near and Far: A Century of Overseas Deployment*. Canberra: Army History Unit, 2005.
Dennis, P., Grey, J., Morris, E., Prior, R., and J. Connor, eds. *The Oxford Companion to Australian Military History*. Melbourne: Oxford University Press, 1995.
Denton, K. *Gallipoli Illustrated*. Adelaide, Australia: Rigby, 1981.
Derham, R. *The Silence Ruse: Escape from Gallipoli: A Record and Memories of the Life of General Sir Brudenell White*. Melbourne: Cliffe Books, 1998.
Doyle, A. C. *The British Campaign in France and Flanders, 1915*. London: Hodder and Stroughton, 1917.
Doyle, P. *Gallipoli 1915*. Stroud, UK: Spellmount, 2011.
Doyle, P., and M. R. Bennett. "Military Geography: The Influence of Terrain in the Outcome of the Gallipoli Campaign, 1915." *Geographical Journal* 165, no. 1 (March 1999): 12–36.
Dudley Ward, C. H. *History of the 53rd (Welsh) Division (T.F.) 1914–1918*. Cardiff, UK: Western Mail, 1927.
Edmonds, J. E. *Military Operations: France and Belgium, 1915*. Vol. 2, *Aubers Ridge, Festubert and Loos*. London: Macmillan, 1928.
Edmonds, J. E., and G. C. Wynne. *Military Operations: France and Belgium, 1915*. Vol. 1, *Winter 1914–15. Neuve Chapelle-Ypres, December 1914–May 1915*. London: Macmillan, 1927.
Egremont, M. *Balfour: A Life of Arthur James Balfour*. London: Collins, 1980.
Ekirch, A. A. J. "Military History: A Civilian Caveat." *Military Affairs* 21, no. 2 (Summer 1957): 49–54.

Ellison, G. *The Perils of Amateur Strategy as Exemplified by the Attack on the Dardanelles Fortress in 1915.* London: Longmans, Green, 1926.
Encel, S. "The Study of Militarism in Australia." *Australian and New Zealand Journal of Sociology* 3, no. 1 (April 1967): 2–18.
Erickson, E. J. *Gallipoli and The Middle East, 1914–1918.* London: Amber, 2008.
———. *Gallipoli: The Ottoman Campaign.* Barnsley, UK: Pen and Sword, 2010.
———. "One More Push: Forcing the Dardanelles in March 1915." *Journal of Strategic Studies* 24, no. 3 (September 2001): 158–76.
———. *Ordered To Die: A History of the Ottoman Army in the First World War.* London: Greenwood Press, 2001.
———. *Ottoman Army Effectiveness in World War I: A Comparative Study.* London: Routledge, 2007.
———. "Strength against Weakness: Ottoman Military Effectiveness at Gallipoli, 1915." *Journal of Military History* 65, no. 4 (October 2001): 981–1011.
Etcell, P. M. "Our Daily Bread: The Field Bakery and the Anzac Legend." PhD thesis, Murdoch University, 2004.
Evans, M. *From Legend to Learning: Gallipoli and the Military Revolution of World War I.* Canberra: Land Warfare Studies Centre, 2000.
Evans, M. H. H. *Amphibious Operations: The Projection of Sea Power Ashore.* Brassey's Sea Power 4. Sydney: Brassey's 1990.
Falls, C. *The Art of War: From the Age of Napoleon to the Present Day.* New York: Oxford University Press, 1961.
———. *The Great War: 1914–1918.* New York: Capricorn Books, 1961.
Farndale, M. *History of the Royal Regiment of Artillery: The Forgotten Fronts and the Home Base, 1914–18.* London: Royal Artillery Institution, 1988.
Farrar, L. L., Jr. "The Strategy of the Central Powers, 1914–1917." In *The Oxford Illustrated History of the First World War,* edited by H. Strachan, 26–38. Oxford: Oxford University Press, 1998.
Fay, S. *The War Office at War.* Wakefield, UK: EP Publishing, 1973.
Fayle, C. E. *The War and the Shipping Industry.* Oxford: Oxford University Press, 1927.
Ferguson, D. *The History of the Canterbury Regiment, N.Z.E.F., 1914–1919.* Auckland: Whitcombe and Tombs, 1921.
Fewster, K. "Expression and Suppression: Aspects of Military Censorship in Australia During the Great War." PhD thesis, University of New South Wales, 1980.
———, ed. *Frontline Gallipoli: C.E.W. Bean Diaries from the Trenches.* Sydney: Allen and Unwin, 1983.
Fewster, K., Basarin, V., and H. Basarin. *Gallipoli: The Turkish Story.* Crows Nest, Australia: Allen and Unwin, 2003.
Fisher, J. A. *Memories.* London: Hodder and Stroughton, 1919.
Forbes, A. *A History of the Army Ordnance Services.* Vol. 3. London: Medici Society, 1929.

Fortescue, G. R. *Russia, the Balkans and the Dardanelles.* London: A. Melrose, 1915.
Frame, T. *The Shores of Gallipoli: Naval Dimensions of the Anzac Campaign.* Sydney: Hale and Iremonger, 2000.
Fraser, P. *Lord Esher: A Political Biography.* London: Hart-Davis, MacGibbon, 1973.
French, D. "The Dardanelles, Mecca and Kut: Prestige as a Factor in British Eastern Strategy, 1914–1916." *War and Society* 5, no. 1 (1987): 45–61.
———. "The Meaning of Attrition, 1914–1916." *English Historical Review* 103, no. 407 (1988): 385–405.
———. "The Origins of the Dardanelles Reconsidered." *History* 68 (July 1983): 210–24.
———. "The Strategy of the Entente Powers, 1914–1917." In *The Oxford Illustrated History of the First World War,* edited by H. Strachan, 54–65. Oxford: Oxford University Press, 1998.
French, D., and B. H. Reid, eds. *The British General Staff: Reform and Innovation c. 1890–1939.* London: Frank Cass, 2002.
Frewen, H. M. "Helles, Suvla and Anzac." *Stand-To* 10, no. 3 (January–March 1966): 9–15.
Gall, H. R. *Questions and Answers on "Field Service Regulations Part I (Operations) 1909."* London: H. Rees, 1910.
Galtrey, S. *The Horse and the War.* London: Country Life, 1918.
Gammage, B. *The Broken Years: Australian Soldiers in the Great War.* Ringwood, Australia: Penguin, 1980.
———. "The Crucible: The Establishment of the Anzac Tradition, 1899–1918." In *Australia: Two Centuries of War and Peace,* edited by M. McKernan and M. Browne, 147–66. Canberra: Australian War Memorial in association with Allen and Unwin, 1988.
Gerster, R. *Big-noting: The Heroic Theme in Australian War Writing.* Melbourne: Melbourne University Press, 1992.
Gilbert, M. *Churchill: A Life.* London: Heinemann, 1991.
———. *The Straits of War: Gallipoli Remembered.* Stroud, UK: Sutton, 2000.
———. "Winston Churchill and the Strain of Office, 1914–1915." In *Facing Armageddon: The First World War Experiences,* edited by H. Cecil and P. H. Liddle, 27–36. London: Leo Cooper, 1996.
GLC. "Engineers at Gallipoli—1815." *Royal Engineers Journal,* 111, no. 1 (April 1997): 31–39.
Glen, F. *Bowler of Gallipoli: Witness to the Anzac Legend.* Loftus: Australian Military History Publications, 2004.
Glover, R. "War and Civilian Historians." *Journal of the History of Ideas* 18, no. 1 (January 1957): 84–100.
Godley, A. *Life of an Irish Soldier.* London: John Murray, 1939.
Gooch, J. "Failure to Adapt: The British at Gallipoli, August 1915." In *Military Misfortunes: The Anatomy of Failure in War,* edited by E. A. Cohen and J. Gooch, 133–64. New York: Free Press, 2006.

———. *The Plans of War: The General Staff and British Military Strategy, c. 1900–1916*. London: Routledge and Kegan Paul, 1974.
Gooder, J., and F. W. Speed. "Gallipoli: The Heroic Campaign: The Battle of Koja Chemen Tepe." *Army Quarterly and Defence Journal* 112, no. 1 (January 1982): 62–69.
Gough, B. M. "Maritime Strategy: The Legacies of Mahan and Corbett as Philosophers of Sea Power." *RUSI Journal* 133, no. 4 (Winter 1988): 55–62.
Graco, W. "Some Reasons for the Failure of Gallipoli." *Defence Force Journal* 64 (May–June 1987): 40–42.
Graham, C. A. L. *The History of the Indian Mountain Artillery*. Aldershot, UK: Gale and Polden, 1957.
Graham, D., and S. Bidwell. *Coalitions, Politicians and Generals: Some Aspects of Command in Two World Wars*. London: Brassey's, 1993.
Granville-Chapman, T. J. "The Importance of Surprise: A Reappraisal." In *The British Army and the Operational Level of War*, edited by J. J. G. Mackenzie and B. H. Reid, 51–75. London: Tri-Service Press, 1989.
Great Britain War Office. *Field Service Regulations*. Part 1, *Operations*. 1909. Reprinted with amendments. London: H.M. Stationary Office, 1914.
———. *Field Service Regulations*. Part 2, *Organization and Administration*. 1909. Reprinted with amendments. London: H.M. Stationary Office, 1914.
———. *Manual of Combined Naval and Military Operations*. London: H.M. Stationary Office, 1913.
———. *Statistics of the Military Effort of the British Empire during the Great War, 1914–1920*. 1922. Reprint, Dallington, UK: Naval and Military Press, 1999.
Green, A. *Writing the Great War: Sir James Edmonds and the Official Histories 1915–1948*. London: Frank Cass, 2003.
Greenhalgh, E. *Victory through Coalition: Britain and France during the First World War*. Melbourne: Cambridge University Press, 2005.
Grey, E. *Twenty-five Years, 1892–1916*. Vol. 2. New York: Frederick A. Stokes, 1925.
Grey, J. "Cuckoo in the Nest? Australian Military Historiography: The State of the Field." *History Compass* 6, no. 2 (2008): 455–68.
———. *A Military History of Australia*. Melbourne: Cambridge University Press, 2008.
Grey, J., Dennis, P., and I. McGibbon. "Australia and New Zealand." In *Researching World War I: A Handbook*, edited by R. Higham and D. Showalter, 265–78. Westport, Conn.: Greenwood Press, 2003.
Griffith, P. *Battle Tactics of the Western Front: The British Army's Art of Attack, 1916–18*. London: Yale University Press, 2000.
Guinn, P. *British Strategy and Politics, 1914 to 1918*, Clarendon Press, Oxford, 1965.
Hall, D. D. "Field Artillery of the British Army, 1860–1960 (Part 1)." *Military History Journal* 2, no. 4 (December 1972).

———. "Field Artillery of the British Army, 1860–1960 (Part 2, 1900–1914)." *Military History Journal* 2, no. 5 (June 1973).
———. "Field Artillery of the British Army, 1860–1960 (Part 3, 1914–1960)." *Military History Journal* 2, no. 6 (December 1973).
Halpern, P., ed. *The Keyes Papers: Selections from the Private and Official Correspondence of Admiral of the Fleet Baron Keyes of Zeebrugge*. London: Allen and Unwin for the Navy Records Society, 1972.
———. *The Naval War in the Mediterranean 1914–1918*. London: Allen and Unwin, 1987.
Hamer, R. "D-day in Normandy and Suvla Bay." *Sabretache* 39 (September 1998) 3–9.
Hamilton, I. S. M. *Gallipoli Diary*. 2 vols. London: Edward Arnold, 1920.
———. "Gallipoli: Varying Figures of Enemy Losses: Suvla, ANZAC, Helles." *Listening Post* 13, no. 9 (23 September 1933): 19–21.
———. "Lack of Guns in Gallipoli Campaign." *Reveille* 6, no. 1 (1932): 2–3.
Hamilton, I. S. M., and C. Mackenzie. "Gallipoli—A Retrospect." *Listener*, 29 April 1931, 709–10, 739.
Hamilton, J. *Goodbye Cobber God Bless You: The Fatal Charge of the Light Horse, Gallipoli, August 7th 1915*. Sydney: Pan Macmillan, 2004.
Handel, M. I., ed. *Clausewitz and Modern Strategy*. London: Frank Cass, 1986.
Hankey, M. P. A. *The Supreme Command: 1914–1918*. 2 vols. London: Allen and Unwin, 1961.
Hargrave, J. *The Suvla Bay Landing*. London: Macdonald, 1964.
Harper, G., and C. Richardson, *In the Face of the Enemy: The Complete History of the Victoria Cross and New Zealand*. Auckland: HarperCollins 2007.
Harrison, H. C. "Calibration and Ranging." *Journal of the Royal Artillery* 47, no. 6 (1920): 265–68.
Hart, P. *Gallipoli*. London: Profile Books, 2011.
Harvey, N. K. *From Anzac to the Hindenburg Line: The History of the 9th Battalion, A.I.F.* Brisbane: 9th Battalion A.I.F. Association, 1941.
Haythornthwaite, P. J. *Gallipoli, 1915: Frontal Assault on Turkey*. London: Osprey, 1991.
Head, C. O. *A Glance at Gallipoli*. London: Eyre and Spottiswoode, 1931.
Henniker, A. M. *Transportation on the Western Front, 1914–1918*. London: H.M. Stationary Office, 1937.
Hickey, M. *Gallipoli*. London: John Murray, 1995.
———. "Gallipoli—A British Perspective." *RUSI Journal* 140, no. 6 (December 1995): 47–53.
Higham, R. "Air power in World War I, 1914–1918." In *The War in the Air 1914–1994*, edited by A. Stephens, 23–46. Canberra: Air Power Studies Centre, 1994.
Hill, A. J. "Chauvel and Monash." *Journal of the Royal Australian Historical Society* 53, no. 4 (December 1967): 323–39.
———. "General Sir Harry Chauvel: Australia's First Corps Commander." In *The Commanders: Australian Military Leadership in the*

Twentieth Century, edited by D. M. Horner, 60–84. Sydney: Allen and Unwin, 1984.

Hirst, M. "Narrative in the War Histories of C. E. W. Bean." *Access: History* 2, no. 2 (Summer 1999): 65–76.

Hogarth, D. G. "Geography of the War Theatre in the Near East." *Geographical Journal* 45, no. 6 (June 1915): 457–67.

Hogg, I. *Allied Artillery of World War One*. Wiltshire, UK: Crowood Press, 1998.

———. *A History of Artillery*. Sydney: Hamlyn, 1974.

Holland, A. F. "Short History of the 1st Royal Australian Naval Bridging Train." *Sabretache* 17, no. 3 (April 1976): 206–207.

Holmes, R., ed. *The Oxford Companion to Military History*. Oxford: Oxford University Press, 2003.

Horner, D. M., ed. *The Commanders: Australian Military Leadership in the Twentieth Century*. Sydney: Allen and Unwin, 1984.

———. *The Gunners: A History of Australian Artillery*. St. Leonards, Australia: Allen and Unwin, 1995.

———. "The Influence of the Boer War on Australian Commanders in the First World War." In *The Boer War: Army, Nation and Empire*, edited by P. Dennis and J. Grey, 173–90. Canberra: Army History Unit, 2000.

———. Introduction to *The Commanders: Australian Military Leadership in the Twentieth Century*, edited by D. M. Horner, 1–10. Sydney: Allen and Unwin, 1984.

Howard, M. *The Causes of Wars and Other Essays*. London: Unwin Paperbacks, 1984.

———. "The Forgotten Dimensions of Strategy." *Foreign Affairs* 57, no. 5 (Summer 1979): 975–86.

———. *Studies in War and Peace*. London: Temple Smith, 1970.

Hudson, N. "Trench Mortars in the Great War." *Journal of the Royal Artillery* 47, no. 1 (1920): 17–31.

Hughes, M. "The French Army at Gallipoli." *RUSI Journal* 150, no. 3 (June 2005): 64–67.

Hurd, A. *The Merchant Navy*. Vol. 2. London: John Murray, 1924.

Hurst, J. *Game to the Last: The 11th Australian Infantry Battalion at Gallipoli*. South Melbourne: Oxford University Press, 2005.

Huston, J. A. *The Sinews of War: Army Logistics, 1775–1953*. Washington, D.C.: Office of the Chief of Military History, United States Army, 1966.

Hutchison, G. S. "Machine Guns in Battle." *Army Quarterly* 34, no. 2 (July 1937): 301–310.

Hynes, S. *The Soldier's Tale: Bearing Witness to Modern War*. London: Pimlico, 1998.

Inglis, K. S. "The Anzac Tradition." *Meanjin Quarterly* 20, no. 1 (March 1965): 25–44.

Israel War Veterans League. *Zion in Gallipoli: Record of a Campaign*. Tel Aviv: Israel War Veterans League, 1965.

James, R. R. *Gallipoli*. Sydney: Angus and Robertson, 1965.

———. "Gallipoli Campaign." In *The Oxford Companion to Military History*, edited by R. Holmes, 343–45. Oxford: Oxford University Press, 2003.

———. "Hamilton." In *The War Lords*, edited by M. Carver. Barnsley, UK: Pen and Sword, 2005.

———. "A Visit to Gallipoli, 1962." *Stand-To* 9, no. 2 (1964): 5.

Jauffret, J. C. "Gallipoli: A French Perspective." *Army Quarterly and Defence Journal* 126, no. 4 (October 1996): 466–74.

———. "Gallipoli: A French Perspective—Part 2." *Army Quarterly and Defence Journal* 127, no. 1 (January 1997): 93–101.

John, A. "Lost Opportunity: An Operational Level Analysis of the August Offensive of the Gallipoli Campaign 1915." *Australian Army Journal* (2002): 1–18.

Johnson, D. M. "Telegraph." In *The Oxford Companion to Military History*, edited by R. Holmes, 904. Oxford: Oxford University Press, 2003.

Johnstone, T. "Suvla—A Study of Command and Staff Failures." *Sabretache* 48, no. 1 (March 2007): 13–30.

Jomini, H. *The Art of War*. Westport, Conn.: Greenwood Press, 1971.

Jones, H. A. *The War in the Air: Being the Story of the Part Played in the Great War by the Royal Air Force*. Vol. 2. London: Oxford University Press, 1928.

Jose, A. W. *Official History of Australia in the War of 1914–1918*. Vol. 9, *The Royal Australian Navy 1914–1918*. Sydney: Angus and Robertson, 1928.

Kannengiesser, H. *The Campaign in Gallipoli*. London: Hutchinson, 1927.

Kearney, R. *Silent Voices: The Story of the 10th Battalion AIF in Australia, Egypt, Gallipoli, France and Belgium during the Great War 1914–1918*. Frenchs Forest, Australia: New Holland, 2005.

Kearsey, A. *1915 Campaign in France: The Battles of Aubers Ridge, Festubert and Loos Considered in Relation to the Field Service Regulations*. Aldershot, UK: Gale and Polden, 1929.

———. *Notes and Comments on the Dardanelles Campaign*. Aldershot, UK: Gale and Polden, 1939.

Keegan, J. *Intelligence in War: Knowledge of the Enemy from Napoleon to Al-Queda*. London: Hutchinson, 2003.

———. "Logistics and Supply." In *Military Logistics: A Primer on Operational, Strategic and Support Level Logistics*, edited by M. Coles, 17–29. Canberra: Australian Defence Studies Centre, 1996.

———. *The Mask of Command*. New York: Penguin, 1988.

Kent, D. A. "The Anzac Book and the Anzac Legend: C. E. W. Bean as Editor and Image-Maker." *Historical Studies* 21, no. 84 (April 1985): 376–90.

Keyes, R. *Amphibious Warfare and Combined Operations: Lees Knowles Lectures, 1943*. Cambridge: Cambridge University Press, 1943.

———. *The Fight for Gallipoli*. London: Eyre and Spottiswoode, 1941.

———. "Memories of the Dardanelles Campaign." *Reveille*, 1 December 1937, 6, 30–33.

———. *The Naval Memoirs of Admiral of the Fleet Sir Roger Keyes: The Narrow Seas to the Dardanelles, 1910–1915*. London: Thornton Butterworth, 1934.
King, J. *Gallipoli Diaries: The Anzacs' Own Story Day by Day*. Sydney: Kangaroo Press, 2003.
Kinloch, T. *Echoes of Gallipoli: In the Words of New Zealand's Mounted Riflemen*. Auckland: Exisle, 2005.
———. *That Bloody Death Trap! New Zealand's Mounted Riflemen at Gallipoli*. Auckland: Exisle, 2005.
Kinross, P. *Atatürk: The Rebirth of a Nation*. London: Phoenix, 2001.
Knightley, P. *The First Casualty—From the Crimea to Vietnam: The War Correspondent as Hero, Propagandist, and Myth Maker*. Sydney: Pan Books, 1989.
Kress, M. *Operational Logistics: The Art and Science of Sustaining Military Operations*. Boston: Kluwer, 2002.
Laffin, J. *British Butchers and Bunglers of World War One*. Melbourne: Macmillan, 1988.
———. *Damn the Dardanelles: The Story of Gallipoli*. Lane Cove, Australia: Doubleday, 1980.
Layman, R. D. *Naval Aviation in the First World War: Its impact and Influence*. London: Chatham, 1996.
Lee, J. "Sir Ian Hamilton after the War: A Liberal General Reflects." In *Facing Armageddon: The First World War Experiences*, edited by H. Cecil and P. H. Liddle, 879–90. London: Leo Cooper, 1996.
———. "Sir Ian Hamilton, Walter Braithwaite and the Dardanelles." *Journal of the Centre for First World War Studies* 1, no. 1 (July 2004): 39–64.
———. *A Soldier's Life: General Sir Ian Hamiliton, 1853–1947*. London: Pan Books, 2000.
Lee, R. "The Australian Staff: The Forgotten Men of the First AIF." In *1918 Defining Victory*, edited by P. Dennis and J. Grey, 114–29. Canberra: Army History Unit, 1999.
Liddell Hart, B. H. *History of the First World War*. London: Cassell, 1970.
Liddle, P. *Men of Gallipoli: The Dardanelles and Gallipoli Experience August 1914 to January 1916*. Devon, UK: David and Charles, 1988.
Lindsay, K. "Logistics." In *Australian Centenary History of Defence*. Vol. 6, *Australian Defence: Sources and Statistics*, edited by J. Beaumont, 410–12. Melbourne: Oxford University Press, 2001.
Loughran, H. G. "Hill 60: 4th Brigade Attacks." *Reveille* 6, no. 12 (1 August 1933): 36, 52–53.
Luttwak, E. N. "The Operational Level of War." *International Security* 5, no. 3 (Winter 1980–81): 61–79.
Luvaas, J. "The First British Official Historians." *Military Affairs* 26, no. 2 (Summer 1962): 49–58.
Macdonald, L. *1915: The Death of Innocence*. London: Headline, 1993.
MacFetridge, C. H. T., and J. P. Warren, eds. *Tales of the Mountain Gunners*. Edinburgh: William Blackwood, 1974.

MacGregor, D. "The Use, Misuse, and Non-use of History: The Royal Navy and the Operational Lessons of the First World War." *Journal of Military History* 56, no. 4 (October 1992): 603–15.
Mackay, R. F. *Fisher of Kilverstone*. Oxford: Clarendon Press, 1973.
Mackenzie, C. *Gallipoli Memories*. Melbourne: Cassell, 1929.
Mackenzie, J. J. G., and B. H. Reid, eds. *The British Army and the Operational Level of War*. London: Tri-Service Press, 1989.
Macksey, K. *For Want of a Nail: The Impact on War of Logistics and Communications*, Brassey's, London, 1989.
Macleod, J. "The British Heroic-Romantic Myth of Gallipoli." In *Gallipoli: Making History*, edited by J. Macleod, 73–85. London: Frank Cass, 2004.
———, ed. *Gallipoli: Making History*. London: Frank Cass, 2004.
———. "General Sir Ian Hamilton and the Dardanelles Commission." *War in History* 8, no. 4 (November 2001): 418–41.
———. *Reconsidering Gallipoli*. Manchester: Manchester University Press, 2004.
MacLeod, R. M., and E. K. Andrews. "Scientific Advice in the War at Sea, 1915–1917: The Board of Invention and Research." *Journal of Contemporary History* 6, no. 2 (1971): 3–40.
MacMunn, G. *Behind the Scenes in Many Wars*. London: Murray, 1930.
———. "The Lines of Communication in the Dardanelles." *Army Quarterly* 20, no. 1 (April 1930): 52–63.
Mallett, R. "The Interplay Between Technology, Tactics and Organisation in the First AIF." MA thesis, University of New South Wales, 1999.
Malthus, C. *Anzac: A Retrospect*. Christchurch, NZ: Whitcombe and Tombs, 1965.
Manera, B. "Hill 60: The Last Battle: 29 August 1915." Lecture presented at Australian War Memorial Conference, Gallipoli: The August Offensive, Canberra, 5 August 2000.
Marder, A. J., ed. *Fear God and Dread Nought: The Correspondence of Admiral of the Fleet Lord Fisher of Kilverstone*. Vol. 3, *Revolution, Abdication, and Last Years, 1914–1920*. London: Cape, 1959.
———. *From the Dardanelles to Oran: Studies of the Royal Navy in War and Peace, 1915–1940*. London: Oxford University Press, 1974.
———. *From the Dreadnought to Scapa Flow: The Royal Navy in the Fisher Era, 1904–1919*. Vol. 2, *The War Years: To the Eve of Jutland*. Oxford University Press, London, 1966.
———. "The Influence of History on Sea Power: The Royal Navy and the Lessons of 1914–1918." *Pacific Historical Review* 41, no. 4 (November 1972): 413–43.
Markovich, L. "'Linseed Lancers, Body-snatchers, and Other Cheery and Jovial Names': The Role of the Stretcher-Bearer, Gallipoli, 1915." BA honours thesis, University of Wollongong, 2009.
Marshall, S. L. A. "Suvla Bay." *Military Review* 43, no. 11 (November 1963): 60–68.
Masefield, J. *Gallipoli*. Adelaide, Australia: Rigby, 1978.

McCarthy, D. *Gallipoli to the Somme: The Story of C.E.W. Bean*. Sydney: John Ferguson, 1983.

McCartney, H. "Interpreting Unit Histories: Gallipoli and After." In *Gallipoli: Making History*, edited by J. Macleod, 125–35. London: Frank Cass, 2004.

McCartney, I. *British Submarines of World War I*. Oxford: Osprey Publishing, 2008.

McDougall, I. "Gallipoli: A Gigantic Combined Operation." *Reveille* 25, no. 8 (1 April 1952): 7–9, 28–29.

McGeoch, I. L. M. "Sea Power and the Dardanelles." *RUSI Journal* 101 (February/November 1956): 580–86.

McKernan, M. "Writing about War." In *Australia: Two Centuries of War and Peace*, edited by M. McKernan and M. Browne, 11–21. Canberra: Australian War Memorial in association with Allen and Unwin, 1988.

McKernan, M., and M. Browne, eds. *Australia: Two Centuries of War and Peace*. Canberra: Australian War Memorial in association with Allen and Unwin, 1988.

McMullin, R. *Pompey Elliott*. Melbourne: Scribe, 2002.

McNicoll, R. R. *The Royal Australian Engineers, 1902–1919: Making and Breaking*. Canberra: Royal Australian Engineers Corps Committee, 1979.

McQuilton, J. *Rural Australia and the Great War: From Tarrawingee to Tangambalanga*. Melbourne: Melbourne University Press, 2001.

Mead, P. *The Eye in the Air: History of Air Observation and Reconnaissance for the Army, 1785–1945*. London: H.M. Stationary Office, 1983.

Meldrum, W. "Simple: Table Top Capture." *Volunteers: The Journal of the New Zealand Military Historical Society* 18, no. 1 (June 1992): 15–20.

Miles, S. "Notes on the Dardanelles Campaign of 1915." Pt. 1. *Coast Artillery Journal* 61, no. 6 (December 1924): 506–21.

———. "Notes on the Dardanelles Campaign of 1915." Pt. 2. *Coast Artillery Journal* 62, no. 1 (January 1925): 23–42.

———. "Notes on the Dardanelles Campaign of 1915." Pt. 3. *Coast Artillery Journal* 62, no. 2 (February 1925): 119–43.

———. "Notes on the Dardanelles Campaign of 1915." Pt. 4. *Coast Artillery Journal* 62, no. 3 (March 1925): 207–25.

Millar, J. D. "A Study in the Limitations of Command: General Sir William Birdwood and the A.I.F., 1914–1918." PhD thesis, University of New South Wales, Australian Defence Force Academy, 1993.

Moharir, V. J. *History of the Army Service Corps (1914–1938)*. New Delhi: Sterling, 1982.

Molkentin, M. *Fire in the Sky: The Australian Flying Corps in the First World War*. Crows Nest, Australia: Allen and Unwin, 2010.

Moorehead, A. *Gallipoli*. London: Hamilton, 1956.

Moran, D. "Operational Level of War." In *The Oxford Companion to Military History*, edited by R. Holmes, 672, 676. Oxford: Oxford University Press, 2003.

Mordike, J. *An Army for a Nation: A History of Australian Military Developments 1880–1914*. Sydney: Allen and Unwin, 1992.
Morillo, S., and M. F. Pavkovic. *What Is Military History?* Cambridge: Polity Press, 2006.
Mortlock, M. J. *The Landings at Suvla Bay, 1915: An Analysis of British Failure during the Gallipoli Campaign*. Jefferson, N.C.: McFarland, 2007.
Moyar, M. "The Current State of Military History." *Historical Journal* 50, no. 1 (2007): 225–40.
Murray, J. *Gallipoli 1915*. Bristol, UK: Cerberus, 2004.
Neame, P. *German Strategy in the Great War*. London: Edward Arnold, 1923.
Neiberg, M. S. *Fighting the Great War: A Global History*. London: Harvard University Press, 2005.
Neillands, R. *The Death of Glory: The Western Front, 1915*. London: John Murray, 2007.
Neilson, K. *Strategy and Supply: The Anglo-Russian Alliance, 1914–17*. London: Allen and Unwin, 1984.
Nevinson, H. W. *The Dardanelles Campaign*. London: Nisbet, 1918.
Nicol, C. G. *The Story of Two Campaigns: Official War History of the Auckland Mounted Rifles Regiment, 1914–1918*. Auckland: Wilson and Horton, 1921.
North, J. *Gallipoli: The Fading Vision*. London: Faber and Faber, 1966.
Olson, W. *Gallipoli: The Western Australian Story*. Crawley: University of Western Australia Press, 2006.
O'Neill, R. "Alliances and Intervention: From Gallipoli to the 21st Century." *RUSI Journal* 146, no. 5 (October 2001): 56–61.
Orchard, A. A. "With the Field Guns on Gallipoli (1)." *Reveille* 7, no. 8 (April 1934): 40, 63.
Page, C. *Command in the Royal Naval Division: A Military Biography of Brigadier General A. M. Asquith*. Staplehurst, UK: Spellmount, 1999.
———. "The Royal Naval Division at Gallipoli." In *Sea Power Ashore and in the Air*, edited by D. Stevens and J. Reeve, 68–76. Ultimo, Australia: Halstead Press, 2007.
Palazzo, A. P. "The British Army's Counter-Battery Staff Office and Control of the Enemy in World War I." *Journal of Military History* 63, no. 1 (January 1999): 55–74.
Paton, D. N. *Army Rations: Their Bearing on the Efficiency of the Soldier*. London: H.M. Stationary Office, 1919.
Patterson, A T., ed. *The Jellicoe Papers: Selections from the Private and Official Correspondence of Admiral of the Fleet Earl Jellicoe of Scapa*. London: Navy Records Society, 1966.
Patterson, J. H. *With the Zionists in Gallipoli*. London: Hutchinson, 1916.
Pedersen, P. A. *The Anzacs: Gallipoli to the Western Front*. Camberwell, Australia: Viking, 2007.
———. "General Sir John Monash: Corps Commander on the Western Front." In *The Commanders: Australian Military Leadership in the*

Twentieth Century, edited by D. M. Horner, 85–125. Sydney: Allen and Unwin, 1984.

———. *Images of Gallipoli*. Melbourne: Oxford University Press, 1988.

———. *Monash as Military Commander*. Carlton: Melbourne University Press, 1985.

Penn, G. *Fisher, Churchill and the Dardanelles*. Barnsley: Leo Cooper, 1999.

Perry, R. *Monash: The Outsider Who Won a War: A Biography of Australia's Greatest Military Commander*. Milsons Point, Australia: Random House, 2004.

Perry, W. "Major General John Keatly Forsyth, C.M.G." *Sabretache* 10, no. 1 (July 1967): 1–4.

Priestley, R. E. *The Signal Service in the European War of 1914–1918 (France)*. London: W. and J. Mackay, 1921.

Prior, R. *Churchill's "World Crisis" as History*. Canberra: Croom Helm, 1983.

———. *Gallipoli: The End of the Myth*. Sydney: University of New South Wales Press, 2009.

———. "Maritime Aspects of the Gallipoli Operation." In *Sea Power Ashore and in the Air*, edited by D. Stevens and J. Reeve, 61–67. Ultimo, Australia: Halstead Press, 2007.

———. "The Strategy Behind Gallipoli: Strategic Decision-making in the Dardanelles and Gallipoli." *Strategic Insights* 15 (April 2005): 1–9.

———. "The Suvla Bay Tea-Party: A Reassessment." *Journal of the Australian War Memorial* 7 (October 1985): 25–34.

Prior, R., and T. Wilson. *Command on the Western Front: The Military Career of Sir Henry Rawlinson, 1914–1918*. Barnsley, UK: Pen and Sword, 2004.

———. "Conflict, Technology, and the Impact of Industrialization: The Great War 1914–1918." *Journal of Strategic Studies* 24, no. 3 (September 2001): 128–57.

———. *The First World War*. London: Cassell, 2001.

———. *The Somme*. Sydney: University of New South Wales Press, 2006.

Pugsley, C. *Gallipoli: The New Zealand Story*. Auckland: Hodder and Stoughton, 1984.

———. *On the Fringe of Hell: New Zealanders and Military Discipline in the First World War*. Auckland: Hodder and Stoughton, 1991.

Puleston, W. D. *The Dardanelles Expedition: A Condensed Study*. Annapolis, Md.: United States Naval Institute, 1927.

———. *High Command in the World War*. London: Scribner's, 1934.

Ramsay, D. *"Blinker" Hall: Spymaster*. Gloucestershire: Spellmount, 2010.

Reid, R. *Gallipoli 1915*. Sydney: ABC Books, 2002.

Robbins, S. *British Generalship on the Western Front 1914–1918: Defeat into Victory*. London: Frank Cass, 2005.

Roberts, C. "The Landing at ANZAC: A Reassessment." *Journal of the Australian War Memorial* 22 (1993): 24–34.

Robertson, J. *Anzac and Empire: The Tragedy and Glory of Gallipoli.* Port Melbourne, Australia: Hamlyn, 1990.
Robson, L. L. "The Australian Soldier: Formation of a Stereotype." In *Australia: Two Centuries of War and Peace*, edited by M. McKernan and M. Browne, 313–37. Canberra: Australian War Memorial in association with Allen and Unwin, 1988.
———. *The First A.I.F : A Study of Its Recruitment, 1914–1918.* Melbourne: Melbourne University Press, 1970.
———. "The Origin and Character of the First A.I.F., 1914–1918: Some Statistical Evidence." *Historical Studies* 15 (1973): 737–49.
Rose, L. A. *Power at Sea: The Age of Navalism, 1890–1918.* Vol. 1. Columbia: University of Missouri Press, 2007.
Roskill, S. W., ed. *Churchill and the Admirals.* Barnsley, UK: Pen and Sword, 2004.
———. *Documents Relating to the Naval Air Service.* Vol. 1. London: Navy Records Society, 1969.
———. *Hankey: Man of Secrets.* Vol. 1. London: Collins, 1970.
———. "Some Reasons for Official History." In *Official Histories: Essays and Bibliographies from around the World*, edited by R. Higham, 10–19. Manhattan: Kansas State University Library, 1970.
Ross, J. *The Myth of the Digger: The Australian Soldier in Two World Wars.* Sydney: Hale and Iremonger, 1985.
Rowan-Robinson, H. "The Limited Objective." *Army Quarterly and Defence Journal* 2 (1921): 119–27.
Rudenno, V. *Gallipoli: Attack From The Sea.* Sydney: University of New South Wales Press, 2008.
Samson, C. R. *Fights and Flights.* London: Ernest Benn, 1930.
Sandler, S. Review of *Supplying War: Logistics from Wallenstein to Patton*, by M. van Creveld. *American Historical Review* 83, no. 4 (October 1978): 970.
Sarin, P. *Military Logistics: The Third Dimension.* New Delhi: Manas Publications, 2000.
Scates, B. *Return to Gallipoli: Walking the Battlefields of the Great War.* Melbourne: Cambridge University Press, 2006.
Schuler, P. F. E. *Australia in Arms: A Narrative of the Australasian Imperial Force and Their Achievement at Anzac.* London: T. Fisher Unwin, 1917.
Scott, D. J. *The Naval Campaign in Gallipoli—1915: Lessons Learned.* Maxwell Air Force Base, Ala.: Air War College, 1986.
Scott, E. *Official History of Australia in the War of 1914–1918.* Vol. 9, *Australia during the War.* Sydney: Angus and Robertson, 1937.
Seal, G. *Inventing Anzac: The Digger and National Mythology.* St. Lucia, Australia: University of Queensland Press, 2004.
Sellers, L. *The Hood Battalion: Royal Naval Division, Antwerp, Gallipoli, France, 1914–1918.* London: L. Cooper, 1995.
Serle, G. "The Digger Tradition and Australian Nationalism." *Meanjin* 24, no. 2 (1965): 149–58.

———. *John Monash: A Biography.* Melbourne: Melbourne University Press in association with Monash University, 1983.

Shaw, P. A. "A Brief History of the 10th Light Horse." *Sabretache* 9, no. 2 (October 1966): 39–47.

Sheffield, G. D. "Command, Leadership and the Anglo-American Experience." In *Leadership and Command: The Anglo-American Military Experience since 1861*, edited by G. D. Sheffield, 1–13. London: Brassey's, 1997.

———. *Forgotten Victory: The First World War: Myths and Realities.* London: Review, 2002.

———, ed. *Leadership and Command: The Anglo-American Military Experience since 1861.* London: Brassey's, 1997.

Sheffield, G. D., and D. Todman, eds. *Command and Control on the Western Front: The British Army's Experience 1914–1918.* Chalford: Spellmount, 2007.

Sheffield, G. D., and J. Bourne, eds. *Douglas Haig: War Diaries and Letters, 1914–1918.* London: Weidenfeld and Nicolson, 2005.

Showalter, D. E. "Manoeuvre Warfare: The Eastern and Western Fronts, 1914–1915." In *The Oxford Illustrated History of the First World War*, edited by H. Strachan, 39–53. Oxford: Oxford University Press, 1998.

———. "Mass Warfare and the Impact of Technology." In *Great War, Total War: Combat Mobilization on the Western Front, 1914–1918*, edited by R. Chickering and S. Förster, 73–94. Cambridge: Cambridge University Press, 2006.

Shrader, C. R. "'Maconochie's Stew': Logistical Support of American Forces with the BEF, 1917–18." In *The Great War, 1914–18: Essays on the Military, Political and Social History of the First World War*, edited by R. J. Q. Adams, 101–131. College Station: Texas A&M University Press, 1990.

Simkins, P. *Kitchener's Army: The Raising of New Armies, 1914–1916.* Manchester: Manchester University Press, 1988.

Simpson, A. *Directing Operations: British Corps Command on the Western Front 1914–18.* Gloucestershire: Spellmount, 2006.

Sinclair, J. *Arteries of War: Military Transportation from Alexander the Great to the Falklands—and Beyond.* Shrewsbury, UK: Airlife, 1992.

———. "Logistics, Principles and Practice." In *Military Logistics: A Primer on Operational, Strategic and Support Level Logistics*, edited by M. Coles, 45–59. Canberra: Australian Defence Studies Centre, 1996.

Singleton, J. "Britain's Military Use of Horses, 1914–1918." *Past and Present* 139 (May 1993): 178–203.

Smith, C. J. "Great Britain and the 1914–1915 Straits Agreement with Russia: The British Promise of November 1914." *American Historical Review* 70, no. 4 (1965): 1015–34.

Smith, H. *On Clausewitz: A Study of Military and Political Ideas.* Basingstoke, UK: Palgrave Macmillan, 2005.

Smyth, J. *Leadership in Battle, 1914–1918: Commanders in Action.* New York: Hippocrene Books, 1975.

Southey, R. J. "Gallipoli: Then and Now." *Military History Journal* 1, no. 7 (December 1970).
Spiers, E. "Gallipoli." In *The First World War and British Military History*, edited by B. Bond, 165–88. Oxford: Clarendon Press, 1991.
Stanley, P. "An Entente . . . Most Remarkable? Indians at ANZAC." *Sabretache* 22, no. 2 (April–June 1981): 17–21.
———. *Quinn's Post, Anzac, Gallipoli*. Crows Nest, Australia: Allen and Unwin, 2005.
Steel, N. *The Battlefields of Gallipoli: Then and Now*. London: Leo Cooper, 1990.
———. *Gallipoli*. Barnsley, UK: Leo Cooper, 1999.
Steel, N., and P. Hart. *Defeat at Gallipoli*. London: Pan Books, 2002.
Stockings, C. "The End of Strategy? Not So Fast." *Australian Army Journal* 4, no. 1 (Autumn 2007): 11–31.
Strachan, H. *The First World War: A New Illustrated History*. Sydney: Simon and Schuster, 2003.
———. "From Cabinet War to Total War: The Perspective of Military Doctrine, 1861–1918." In *Great War, Total War: Combat Mobilization on the Western Front, 1914–1918*, edited by R. Chickering and S. Förster, 19–34. Cambridge: Cambridge University Press, 2006.
———, ed. *The Oxford Illustrated History of the First World War*. Oxford: Oxford University Press, 1998.
Strong, P., and S. Marble. *Artillery in the Great War*. Barnsley, UK: Pen and Sword, 2011.
Stuermer, H. *Two War Years in Constantinople: Sketches of German and Young Turkish Ethics and Politics*. London: Hodder and Stroughton, 1917.
Sumida, J. T. "British Naval Operational Logistics, 1914–1918." *Journal of Military History* 57, no. 3 (July 1993): 447–80.
Sun-Tzu. *The Art of War*. Edited and translated by J. Minford. New York: Penguin, 2003.
Swain, R. M. "The Development of a Logistics System for the British Army, 1856–1896." PhD thesis, Duke University, 1975.
Tekşut, I. *Turk Silahe Kuvvetleri Tarihi Osmanli Devri Birinci Dunya Harbinde Türk Harbi Vncu Cilt: Çanakkale Cephesi Harekati (Haziran 1915–Ocak 1916) [Turkish Armed Forces History of the Ottoman State, The Turkish War in the First World War: Gallipoli Front Operations (June 1915–January 1916)]*. Vol. 3. Ankara: Genelkurmay Basimevi, 1980.
Terraine, J. *The Western Front, 1914–1918*. Barnsley, UK: Pen and Sword, 2003.
Thompson, J. "Expeditionary Forces and Expeditionary Warfare: Major Themes and Issues." In *Battles Near and Far: A Century of Overseas Deployment*, edited by P. Dennis and J. Grey, 4–20. Canberra: Army History Unit, 2005.
———. *The Lifeblood of War: Logistics in Armed Conflict*. London: Brassey's, 1991.

———. "Principles: The Disciplines of War." In *Military Logistics: A Primer on Operational, Strategic and Support Level Logistics*, edited by M. Coles, 165–70. Canberra: Australian Defence Studies Centre, 1996.

Thomson, A. *Anzac Memories: Living with the Legend*. Melbourne: Oxford University Press, 1994.

———. "'Steadfast until Death'? C. E. W. Bean and the Representation of Australian Military Manhood." *Australian Historical Studies* 23, no. 93 (October 1989): 462–78.

———. "'The Vilest Libel of the War?': Imperial Politics and the Official Histories of Gallipoli." *Australian Historical Studies* 25, No. 101 (1993): 628–36.

Thorpe, G. C. *Pure Logistics: The Science of War Preparation*. Washington, D.C.: National Defense University Press, 1996.

Till, G. "Brothers in Arms: Navy and Army Cooperation at Gallipoli." In *Facing Armageddon: The First World War Experiences*, edited by H. Cecil and P. H. Liddle, 160–79. London: Leo Cooper, 1996.

Todman, D. *The Great War: Myth and Memory*. London: Hambledon Continuum, 2005.

Travers, T. "Command and Leadership Styles in the British Army: The 1915 Gallipoli Model." *Journal of Contemporary History* 29, no. 3 (July 1994): 403–42.

———. "Gallipoli: Film and the Traditions of Australian History." *Film and History* 14, no. 1 (February 1984): 14–20.

———. *Gallipoli 1915*, Stroud, UK: Tempus, 2003.

———. "The Hidden Army: Structural Problems in the British Officer Corps, 1900–1918." *Journal of Contemporary History* 17, no. 3 (July 1982): 523–44.

———. *How the War Was Won: Command and Technology in the British Army on the Western Front, 1917–1918*. Barnsley, UK: Pen and Sword, 2005.

———. *The Killing Ground: The British Army, the Western Front and the Emergence of Modern Warfare, 1900–1918*. Sydney: Allen and Unwin, 1987.

———. "Learning and Decision-Making on the Western Front, 1915–1916: The British Example." *Canadian Journal of History* 18, no. 1 (April 1983): 87–97.

———. "Limon von Sanders, the Capture of Lieutenant Palmer, and Ottoman Anticipation of the Allied Landings at Gallipoli on April 25, 1915." *Journal of Military History* 65, no. 4 (October 2001): 965–79.

———. "The Offensive and the Problem of Innovation in British Military Thought 1870–1915." *Journal of Contemporary History* 13, no. 3 (July 1978): 531–53.

———. "The Other Side of the Hill." *MHQ: The Quarterly Journal of Military History* 12, no. 3 (Spring 2000): 6–19.

———. "The Ottoman Crisis of May 1915 at Gallipoli." *War in History* 8, no. 1 (January 2001): 72–86.

Travers, T., and B. Celik. "Not One of Them Ever Came Back: What Happened to the 1/5 Norfolk Battalion on 12 August 1915 at Gallipoli." *Journal of Military History* 66, no. 2 (April 2002): 389–406.

Trumpener, U. "Turkey's War." In *The Oxford Illustrated History of the First World War*, edited by H. Strachan, 80–91. Oxford: Oxford University Press, 1998.
Tuncoku, A. M. *Anzaklarin Kaleminden Mehmetçik: Çanakkale 1915*. Ankara: Atatürk Araştirma Merkezi, 1997.
Tyquin, M. *Gallipoli: An Australian Medical Perspective*. Newport, Australia: Big Sky Publishing, 2012.
———. *Gallipoli: The Medical War: The Australian Army Medical Services in the Dardanelles Campaign of 1915*. Kensington: University of New South Wales Press, 1993.
———. "Medical Evacuation During the Gallipoli Campaign—An Australian Perspective." *War and Society* 10, no. 2 (1992): 57–72.
Usborne, C. V. *Smoke on the Horizon: Mediterranean Fighting 1914–1918*. London: Hodder and Stroughton, 1933.
Uyar, M., and E. J. Erickson. *A Military History of the Ottomans: From Osman to Atatürk*. Santa Barbara, Calif.: Praeger Security International, 2009.
Van Creveld, M. *The Art of War: War and Military Thought*. London: Cassell, 2000.
———. *Command in War*. Cambridge, Mass.: Harvard University Press, 1985.
———. *Supplying War: Logistics from Wallenstein to Patton*. New York: Cambridge University Press, 2004.
———. "Thoughts on Military History." *Journal of Contemporary History* 18, no. 4 (October 1983): 549–66.
———. "World War I and the Revolution in Logistics." In *Great War, Total War: Combat Mobilization on the Western Front, 1914–1918*, edited by R. Chickering and S. Förster, 57–72. Cambridge: Cambridge University Press, 2006.
Van Hartesveldt, F. R. *The Dardanelles Campaign, 1915: Historiography and Annotated Bibliography*. Westport, Conn.: Greenwood Press, 1997.
Verney, G. "General Sir Brudenell White: The Staff Officer as Commander." In *The Commanders: Australian Military Leadership in the Twentieth Century*, edited by D. M. Horner, 26–43. Sydney: Allen and Unwin, 1984.
Von Clausewitz, C. *On War*. Edited and translated by M. Howard and P. Paret. 1976. Reprint, Princeton: Princeton University Press, 1989.
Von Sanders, L. *Five Years in Turkey*. Annapolis, Md.: United States Naval Institute, 1927.
Waite, F. *The New Zealanders at Gallipoli*. Auckland: Whitcombe and Tombs, 1921.
Walker, R. *To What End Did They Die? Officers Died at Gallipoli*. Worcester, UK: R. W. Walker Publishing, 1985.
Ward, M. "A Stab in the Front: The British Army's Weapons System on the Western Front, 1918." BA honours thesis, University of Adelaide, 2008.
Watson, M. B. *Sea Logistics: Keeping the Navy Ready Aye Ready*. Ontario: Vanwell, 2004.

Wavell, A. P. *Generals and Generalship: The Lees Knowles Lectures Delivered at Trinity College, Cambridge in 1939*. Harmondsworth, UK: Penguin, 1941.
Wester-Wemyss, R. *The Navy in the Dardanelles Campaign*. London: Hodder and Stoughton, 1924.
White, T. A. *The History of the Thirteenth Battalion, A.I.F.* Sydney: Tyrrell's, 1924.
Wiest, A. A. *Haig: The Evolution of a Commander*. Washington, D.C.: Potomac Books, 2005.
Wilkie, A. H. *Official War History of the Wellington Mounted Rifles Regiment, 1914–1919*. Auckland: Whitcombe and Tombs, 1924.
Williams, J. F. *Anzacs, the Media and the Great War*. Sydney: University of New South Wales Press, 1999.
Williams, P. D. *The Battle of Anzac Ridge: 25 April 1915*. Loftus: Australian Military History Publications, 2007.
Wilson, G. "'Everything on its Belly'—Feeding the First AIF: Problems and Solutions of Australian Army Rationing and Catering in the First World War." *Sabretache* 41 (September 2000): 9–39.
———. "The Relevance of Miscellany Administrative, Support and Logistic Units of the AIF: A Postscript." *Sabretache* 44, no. 4 (December 2003): 21–24.
Wilson, T. *The Myriad Faces of War: Britain and the Great War, 1914–1918*. Cambridge: Polity Press, 1986.
———. "The Significance of the First World War in Modern History." In *The Great War, 1914–18: Essays on the Military, Political and Social History of the First World War*, edited by R. J. Q. Adams, 7–27. College Station: Texas A&M University Press, 1990.
Winter, D. *Making the Legend: The War Writings of C. E. W. Bean*. St. Lucia, Australia: University of Queensland Press, 1992.
———. *25 April 1915: The Inevitable Tragedy*. St. Lucia, Australia: University of Queensland Press, 1994.
Winter, J., Parker, G., and M. R. Habeck, eds. *The Great War and the Twentieth Century*. New Haven, Conn.: Yale University Press, 2000.
Winters, H. A., Galloway, G. E., Reynolds, W. J., and D. W. Rhyne. *Battling the Elements: Weather and Terrain in the Conduct of War*. Baltimore: Johns Hopkins University Press, 1998.
Wragg, D. *A Century of British Naval Aviation, 1909–2009*. Barnsley, UK: Pen and Sword Maritime, 2009.
Wray, C. *Sir James Whiteside McCay: A Turbulent Life*. South Melbourne: Oxford University Press, 2002.
Wray, F. W. "The Fourth Brigade at ANZAC." *Reveille* 6, no. 12 (1 August 1933): 6–7, 62.
Wright, R. M. "Machine-gun Tactics and Organization." *Army Quarterly* 1 (October 1920): 290–313.
Yung, C. D. *Gators of Neptune: Naval Amphibious Planning for the Normandy Invasion*. Annapolis, Md.: Naval Institute Press, 2006.

Index

Main entries and subentries for numbered military units are listed alphabetically. However, when subentries consist solely of numbered military units, the units are listed consecutively.

Abdel Rahman Bair, 205
A Beach, 60, 97, 159, 162, 165, 168, 170, 178, 182
Achi Baba, 6–7, 215, 219, 227
Admiralty, 12–14, 17; and de Robeck, 117, 182, 234; relations with War Office, 17, 108–109; role in logistics, 121–22, 124, 126, 133, 137, 141, 184–85; on role of the navy, 107–108, 111, 113, 115–16, 232; on the strength of the Eastern Mediterranean Squadron, 95
Aerial observation. *See* Royal Naval Air Service
Aghyl Dere, 192, 195, 202, 268n93
Ak Bashi Liman, 226
Alexander, Gavin, 63
Alexander, Heber, 175
Alexandria, 125–29, 131–33, 141, 142–43, 238–39
Allanson, Cecil, 203, 208
Altham, Edward, 122, 130–31, 133, 135–36, 138, 142, 144–47, 168, 179, 185–86
Ammunition supply. *See* Logistics
Anafarta Gap, 36, 38, 182, 240
Anderson Knoll, 43, 217
Antill, John, 200
Anzac Cove, 6, 26, 35, 37, 158–59, 164, 172, 177, 240–41
Anzac sector, 6–7, 262n11; artillery, 69–74, 76–81, 83–84, 87–89, 189–90, 224–27; attacks from, 189–90, 194, 198–201; Braithwaite visits, 31; command in the, 51; communications, 60–63; Hamilton visits, 27, 30; logistics, 41, 128–29, 138, 153, 158–61, 164–65, 167–69, 171–82, 187, 237–41; naval support for, 95, 191; open left flank, 19, 21, 25, 29, 36, 188; push out from, 32–33, 35, 42–43, 45, 47, 55–56; strengthen the sector, 7, 12, 16, 26, 28, 31, 45, 216–18; terrain, 101, 150, 224
Apex. *See* The Apex
Ari Burnu. *See* Anzac Cove
Armistice, 6
Army Council, 12–13
Artillery: accuracy, 10–11, 72, 88–92, 232; ammunition, 32, 82–85, 173–74, 225; at Anzac, 70–71, 73, 77–78, 80–81, 84, 89, 189–90, 281n80; Argyll Battery, 4th Highland Mountain Brigade, 73–74; Australian Divisional Artillery, 71, 73, 178, 226; at Cape Helles, 70, 76–78, 80–81, 83–84, 86, 189, 281n79; command, 76–77; communication, 89–90; comparisons to Western Front, 75, 79–82, 102; counterbattery work, 71, 80, 84, 86, 88, 90–91, 94, 99, 101, 190, 204; difficulty of moving guns, 29, 43, 224–26, 230; during subsequent phases, 70, 222–32, 243; 18-pounder field gun, 70–71, 73–74, 78, 86, 80, 83–84, 86, 88, 179, 225, 278n19; 11th Divisional Artillery, 77; 15-pounder BLC, 78, 86–87; 15th Heavy Battery, 74, 86, 91, 225; 59th Brigade, 73, 77, 88, 131, 212; 1st New Zealand Field Artillery Brigade, 178; 5-inch howitzer, 71, 78, 84,

351

Artillery (continued)
87, 278n19; 4.5-inch howitzer, 71, 78, 83–84, 87–88, 278n19; 4.7-inch naval gun, 71, 78, 226; 4th Highland Mountain Brigade, 73–74, 85; French, 70, 78, 79; gun emplacements, 26, 75, 80, 87–88, 91, 224; New Zealand and Australian Divisional Artillery, 72–73, 102, 223; New Zealand Field Artillery Brigade, 89, 178–79; observation, 5, 10, 75, 89–92, 99, 101–103, 227, 229, 232, 243; Ottoman, 28, 33, 35, 37–39, 64, 71, 74, 80, 86, 90–91, 102, 114, 159, 168–69, 175, 178, 180, 186, 215, 229–31, 234, 238; personnel, 82; planning, 69, 72–77, 92, 223–24, 243; preliminary bombardments, 70–71; quality, 75, 85–87; quantity, 78, 79–82, 97; 7th Indian Mountain Artillery Brigade, 72–73, 85–86, 150, 194; 6-inch howitzer, 71, 78, 84, 88; 60-pounder field gun, 74, 78, 83–84, 86, 88, 225–26, 318n68, 318n69; supporting Sari Bair, 72–73, 86–87, 201, 204; at Suvla Bay, 38, 54, 69, 73–74, 77–78, 80–81, 86–87, 213, 281n81; 10-pounder mountain gun, 72–73, 78, 84–86, 150, 225; 10th Heavy Battery, 74, 225, 236; 3rd Australian Field Artillery Brigade, 77, 82, 84, 89; 21st Kohat Mountain Battery, 72–73; 29th Divisional Artillery, 76, 98; 26th Jacob's Mountain Battery, 72, 194

Ashmead-Bartlett, Ellis, 31, 309n13

Asiatic coast, 6, 33, 43, 48–49, 55, 168, 219–21, 228–30, 234–36

Asma Dere, 205

Aspinall-Oglander, Cecil: as historian, 8–9; as officer, 9, 66, 202, 204, 206–207

Asquith, Herbert, 14–15, 31, 41, 113, 123, 137, 238, 319n78

Atatürk, 208

August Offensive: at Cape Helles, 40, 70, 189, 201, 309n6; evolution of plans, 12, 16, 19, 24–46, 74, 242; expected casualties, 183–84; failure, 8–9, 11, 85, 92, 181, 210, 215, 231, 240, 242–44; first phase, 28, 40–42, 44–45, 56, 58, 72, 81, 84–86, 92, 94, 103, 106, 146, 167, 173, 178, 214–15, 223–24, 226, 237–41, 243; fourth phase, 44, 85, 93, 106–107, 116–17, 127, 140, 156, 169, 214, 220, 232–37, 241, 243; naval planning, 98–99, 106–107, 116–17; operational objective, 10–11, 40–44, 47, 52, 60, 69, 93, 106, 110, 214, 226, 232, 237, 243; preparations, 37, 171, 188; Sari Bair foothills, 28, 30, 150, 191–93, 196; Sari Bair Ridge, 194–96, 201–10, 215; second phase, 41, 43, 50, 56, 59, 66, 70, 80, 85, 89, 103, 127, 140, 156, 169, 190, 199, 214–18, 220–21, 223–24, 226–30, 237–39, 241, 321n125; secrecy, 13, 18–19, 41, 45, 47–50, 73, 76, 221; strategic direction, 12–16, 109; strategic objective, 44, 236; third phase, 43–44, 50, 55–56, 59, 66, 70, 80, 85, 89, 91, 103, 106, 127, 140, 156, 169, 214, 217–24, 226–31, 237–39, 241, 243. *See also* Anzac sector; Cape Helles; Sari Bair Ridge; Suvla Bay

Australian and New Zealand Army Corps. *See* Mediterranean Expeditionary Force corps

Babtie, William, 185

Baby 700, 29–30, 35, 42–43, 56, 71, 200, 216

Backhouse, Oliver, 50, 138

INDEX   353

Badcock, Gerald, 174
Bailloud, Maurice, 48
Baldwin, Anthony, 207–208
Balfour, Arthur, 14–15, 31, 103–105, 107–109, 115, 137–38, 229, 236
Balkans, 4, 17, 229
Barbed wire, 71, 80–81, 192, 200
Bassett, Cyril, 64
Battleship Hill, 27, 29, 37, 42–43, 56, 71, 201–202, 207, 215–16
Bauchop, Arthur, 32
Bauchop's Hill, 27, 192, 194
B Beach, 60, 97, 159, 168
Bean, Charles, 7, 56, 180, 226
Beecroft, Arthur, 50, 57–58, 220
Beetles. *See* Motor lighters
Bennett, Henry Gordon, 199
Beville, Charles, 177
Birdwood, William, 5–6, 45, 149; appeal of maneuver, 23, 244; on artillery, 87; as commander, 52, 56–59, 161, 167, 172, 199–200; confidence, 194, 196; evolution of plans, 25–39, 65; experience, 22–23; and Hamilton, 48, 202; on importance of Sari Bair, 223; on loss of Chunuk Bair, 209–210, 213; on the Nek, 200; on Ottoman capabilities, 67, 215, 221–22; on subsequent phases, 41, 215–16; on water supply, 55, 179–81
Birrell, William, 183–85, 308n192
Biyuk Anafarta, 25, 35, 206–207
Bland, Edward, 165
Board of the Admiralty, 13
Boer War, 22, 27, 51, 87, 247–53
Boghali, 35, 227, 258–59
Bonar Law, Andrew, 8, 32, 82
Boué de Lapeyrère, Augustin, 125
Bowman-Manifold, Michael, 60
Boyle, Algernon, 95
Boyle, Edward, 104
Braithwaite, Walter, 31, 75, 128, 143–44, 211
Brazier, Noel, 200–201
Breakthrough offensive, 10, 24, 44–45, 79, 217, 231, 244, 322n2

Bridges' Road, 173
Brighton Beach, 159, 178
British Expeditionary Force, 3, 16, 44, 82–83, 92, 120–21, 124, 140, 148, 168
British General Staff, 13, 109
Brown's Dip, 173
Bulair, 31–32, 41, 49, 189, 197, 206–207, 221, 229
Bulgaria, 17
Byng, Julian, 30, 212

Callwell, Charles, 13, 17
Cape Helles: artillery, 70, 76–81, 83–84, 86–87, 189, 280n68; communications, 60, 89; feint during August, 40, 69–70, 189–91, 201, 309n6; landings in April, 6–7, 262n19; logistics, 128–29, 132, 138–39, 158–61, 165, 168–69, 171–73, 175; naval support, 95, 98–99; terrain, 219, 227
Carden, Sackville, 112
Carver, Edmund, 162–63
Casualties, 7, 28, 58–59, 71, 168, 177, 183–87, 189, 191, 197, 199–200, 203, 208, 210, 213, 215, 222, 239, 243, 274n51, 309n21, 315n167
C Beach, 60, 97, 159, 168
Chailak Dere, 192, 194
Chanak, 43, 113, 229
Chana Ovasi, 96
Chessboard, 43, 70–71, 199, 201
Chocolate Hill, 35, 38–39, 197, 204, 206
Christian, Arthur, 62, 96
Chunuk Bair, 26–28, 32, 43, 56, 62, 64, 74, 180, 190–91, 194, 198, 200–202, 204–205, 207–10, 215, 225–26
Churchill, Winston, 3, 13–16, 31, 113, 236, 309n6
Combined operations, 5–6, 9, 11, 44, 93–118, 264n36
Command, 10, 151; adaptation, 23, 67; appeal of large-scale

Command (continued)
offensive, 12, 24, 44, 51, 244, 322n2; at Anzac, 26–27, 51, 63; of artillery, 76–77, 223–24; on the beaches, 160–63; at Helles, 6, 31, 51; impact of secrecy upon, 49–50, 221; joint command, 93, 109–12, 160–63; 285n1; of lines of communication, 128–30, 141, 143, 145; naval, 5, 95, 115, 127, 234; operational, 33; Ottoman, 6, 96, 202, 204, 210; prior experience of, 22, 51, 197; relationship, 11, 99, 108–12; at Sari Bair, 205; structure, 50–52, 74–75; at Suvla, 30–31, 38–39; 48, 51, 62, 77, 165, 181, 197, 203, 206–207, 210–13
Committee of Imperial Defence, 4, 58, 113
Communications, 10, 51, 59–64, 69, 71, 77, 89–90, 99, 135, 197, 203, 219–21, 224, 275n76
Constantinople: as Allied strategic objective, 3, 5, 44, 236; defense of, 222; logistic route to Gallipoli, 41, 43, 124, 228–29; political situation, 17
Corbett, Julian, 110
Cowans, John, 120–22, 128, 144, 179
Cowell, Henry, 77
Cox, Herbert, 194
Cunliffe Owen, Charles, 76

Dacre, George, 103
Damakjelik Bair, 27, 192, 202
Dardanelles: allied attempts to force, 3–4; defenses, 4–5, 19, 43–44, 93, 103, 115, 219, 230–31, 233–36; naval action against, 5, 112, 142, 262n8; submarine passages, 19; the Straits, 25–26, 43, 66, 113, 116, 216, 235–37
Dardanelles Campaign: command relationship, 108–12; comparisons with the Western Front, 9–10, 52, 54, 60, 62, 64, 69, 75, 79–83, 101–102, 120–21, 140–41, 148, 157, 164, 166, 168, 173–75, 213, 220–22, 224, 242, 244–45; discussions about evacuation, 14–16; force strength (Allied), 52–54; force strength (Ottoman), 222; impact on Western Front, 16, 30, 82–83; operational objective, 47, 93, 105, 223, 230, 232; origins of, 3–5, 113; strategic objective, 3, 5, 12, 15, 44, 236
Dardanelles Commission, 55, 75, 102, 203, 222–23, 242
Dardanelles Committee, 8, 15–16, 30–33, 49, 54, 109, 229
Davies, Francis, 85
Dawnay, Guy, 85, 204
Deadman's Ridge, 199, 201
De Lisle, Henry de Beauvoir, 181, 189, 211–13
De Lotbiniére, Alain Joly, 130, 134
Denton, John, 26
De Robeck, John, 151, 163; on army affairs, 111, 146; on army capabilities, 112–13; on Bulair proposal, 30–31; concerns about fleet, 95–96; concerns about U-boats, 98, 126–27; on logistics, 179, 182; on naval capabilities, 99, 101, 103, 112, 117–18; on naval offensive, 5, 106–107, 112–18; on Ottoman defenses, 232–35; relationship with Hamilton, 11, 110–12, 243; on strategic potential, 236; on strength of his fleet, 95–96, 136–38; off Suvla Bay, 207
De Rougemont, Cecil, 76
Destroyer Hill, 192, 194
Doctrine, 18–19, 23, 40, 44, 59, 69, 74, 108, 116, 140, 142–43, 157, 160–62, 166, 173–74, 244–45, 322n2. *See also* Breakthrough offensive; *Field Service Regulations*; *Manual of Combined Naval and Military Operations*

Eastern Mediterranean Squadron, 5, 17, 19, 44, 93–99, 102–103, 105–107, 118, 137, 142, 147, 177, 204, 233–34, 236, 243; ammunition expenditure, 99–100; comparison between April and August, 94–95, 106; 1st Squadron, 95, 99; HMS *Albion*, 234; HMS *Arno*, 206, 313n114; HMS *Aster*, 97; HMS *Bacchante*, 190; HMS *Chatham*, 95; HMS *Chelmer*, 72, 94; HMS *Colne*, 72, 94; HMS *Endymion*, 94, 97; HMS *Hector*, 127, 232; HMS *Inflexible*, 142, 262n8; HMS *Jed*, 96; HMS *Jonquil*, 61–62, 77, 170, 203, 206–207; HMS *Majestic*, 7, 126; HMS *Manica*, 127, 232; HMS *Minerva*, 96; HMS *M30*, 100; HMS *Queen Elizabeth*, 5, 94; HMS *Renard*, 139; HMS *Talbot*, 77; HMS *Theseus*, 94, 97; HMS *Triad*, 98, 207; HMS *Triumph*, 7, 126; HMT *Aragon*, 131, 142, 145; HMT *Edenmore*, 164, 168, 172; HMT *Efi*, 164; HMT *Ikalia*, 172; HMT *Royal Edward*, 127, 232; planning, 106–107, 116–17; role in August Offensive, 232–36; 2nd Squadron, 25, 95; SS *Baron Jedburgh*, 133; SS *Cawdor Castle*, 132; SS *Pfalz*, 131; SS *River Clyde*, 139, 158; 3rd Squadron, 95. *See also* Navy; Submarines
Edmonds, Charles, 103
Edwards, Henry, 63
Egerton, Granville, 21–22, 248
Egypt, 48, 52, 55, 79–80, 128–29, 143, 184–86, 212, 293n41
Ejelmer Bay, 35
Ellison, Gerald, 124, 136, 143, 145–46, 166, 176, 179
Engineers. *See* Royal Engineers
Ewart, John, 30–31

Fanshaw, Edward, 212
Fatigues, 52, 135, 158–59, 165–68, 174, 187, 216, 225, 302n58
Feints, 6, 29–30, 70–71, 96, 173, 188–91, 198–201, 309n6
Field Service Regulations, 18–19, 23, 40, 59, 69, 140, 142–43, 157, 160–62, 173–74, 322n2. *See also* Doctrine
Fire support. *See* Artillery
Fisher, John, 13–15, 96, 113
Fisherman's Hut, 35, 318n69
Force size, 52–56, 58–59, 79, 82, 95, 140, 222, 239, 321n123, 321n134
Forster, Thomas, 55, 142
400 Plateau, 29, 190, 227, 258
Francis, Frederick, 239
French, John, 23, 31, 67
French forces, 7, 48, 52, 54, 79–80, 87, 114, 158, 189, 201; artillery, 70, 78, 79; Corps Expéditionnaire Français des Dardanelles, 31, 219; 1st French Division, 6; navy, 125, 262n8
Fuller, Richard, 72, 75–76, 87, 98, 101

Gaba Tepe, 25–27, 29, 38, 43–44, 159, 178, 190, 216–18, 221, 223, 230–31, 237–38, 309n13, 321n125
Gallipoli (town), 25, 104
Gallipoli Campaign: April landings, 5–7, 219; as a combined amphibious operation, 93–94; evacuation, 7; historical bias, 7–10; May counterattack, 6, 28; as a secondary theater, 54; second battle of Krithia, 7; strategic objective, 3, 5, 12, 15, 44, 236; support for, 16; third battle of Krithia, 7. *See also* August Offensive; Dardanelles Campaign
Gallipoli Peninsula, 5, 11; advance across, 6–7, 11–12, 15–16, 25–26, 29, 33, 36, 38, 43–44, 47,

Gallipoli Peninsula (*continued*) 50, 52, 56, 67–68, 80, 112, 116, 149, 155–56, 172, 176, 190, 197, 214–16, 220, 222–24, 230–32, 237–40, 243; decision to land on, 5, 113. *See also* Logistics; Terrain
Gamble, Douglas, 137
Gellibrand, John, 191
General Headquarters: administrative staff, 20–21, 120, 143, 145–46, 169–70, 184; communications, 60–63; concerns about ammunition expenditure, 84–85; during the August Offensive, 201, 204–206, 208; general staff, 72, 85, 106, 184; at Imbros Island, 60, 138; on logistics, 135, 161–62, 166–67, 169–71, 182, 186, 238; orders issued, 39–40, 48, 161, 175, 202, 211; planning, 8–9, 22, 26, 28–35, 37–39; position of inspector general of communications, 142–46, 161; relationship between general and administrative staffs, 146, 184; relationship with navy, 106; war establishment, 53
German Officers' Trench, 71, 198–99, 201
Ghazile Tepe, 35–36, 38
Gibraltar, 125, 141, 219
Gibson, Isham, 234
Godfrey, John, 108–109
Godfrey, William, 114, 116
Godley, Alexander, 27, 63–65, 98, 202, 207–208, 213, 215, 250
Gouraud, Henri, 31
Granet, Edward, 77
Green Hill, 197–98
Grey, Edward, 14
Gulf of Xeros, 49, 189
Gun Ridge. *See* Third Ridge

Haig, Douglas, 23, 45
Haldane, Richard Burdon, 13–14
Hall, William, 17
Hamilton, Ian, 5, 7, 11, 151; appeal of maneuver, 23–24, 45, 244; on Asiatic shore, 220, 235; bias, 7–8; on the August Offensive, 7–8, 35, 43, 223; and Birdwood, 27, 29; criticisms of, 92, 244–45; on cutting Ottoman lines of communication, 105; on Dardanelles defenses, 233, 235; on difficulty of the terrain, 65–66; experience, 5, 22; on failure of the August Offensive, 215, 218; and Kitchener, 121; on logistics, 82, 124, 130, 136, 140, 143–45, 157, 176, 179–80, 238; on Lone Pine, 190; on loss of Chunuk Bair, 210; on Mahon, 211; message to the troops, 188; operational commander, 33, 39; opinion of the enemy, 15–16, 24, 67; opinion of the navy, 108, 139, 147; penchant for secrecy, 47–50; on reinforcements, 15–16, 30, 32–33, 36, 52, 54–56, 244; relationship with de Robeck, 11, 108–12, 117, 243; removed from command, 115; on Skeen, 26; on Stopford, 31, 211–12; on subsequent phases, 40, 73, 218, 223, 226–27; on Suvla Bay, 41; visit to Suvla Bay, 206–207, 313n114
Hammersley, Frederick, 206–207, 211
Hankey, Maurice, 14, 41, 104–105, 113, 123, 132, 137–38, 166, 190, 229
Health, 9, 24, 45, 47, 56–58, 66, 68, 95–96, 112, 157, 203, 239, 243, 274n51
Helles sector. *See* Cape Helles
Hill 971, 25–27, 29, 33, 35, 38–39, 43, 57–58, 194–95, 205, 207, 216–17, 321n125
Hill Q, 26, 29, 58, 64, 195, 203, 206–208, 215

INDEX 357

Hill 60, 63, 100, 210, 213
Hill 10, 197–98, 203–204
Hill 305. *See* Hill 971
Historiography, 8–11, 44, 242
Hobbs, Joseph Talbot, 71, 178
Horses, 36, 96, 128, 174–75, 177, 224–25, 230, 238
Howse, Neville, 57
Hughes, Frederic, 201
Hughes, John, 194
Hulbert, Edward, 63
Hunter, Frederick, 86
Hunter-Weston, Aylmer, 6, 31, 230, 262n13

Imbros Island, 37, 58, 60–61, 97, 128, 138–39, 142, 158, 165, 182, 186, 204
Indian Mule Cart Train, 175–78, 304n118
Intelligence, 7, 9, 17–22, 25, 28–29, 37, 45, 47, 95, 104, 127, 182, 222, 235
Interservice cooperation, 14, 16–17, 69–70, 106, 108–12, 142, 146–47, 162–63, 187, 242
Ismail Oglu Tepe. *See* W Hills
Istanbul. *See* Constantinople

Jackson, Henry, 107, 113
Jackson, Robert, 145
Jellicoe, John, 114
Jephson's Post, 204
Joffre, Joseph, 17, 47
Johnston, George, 72–73, 75–77, 102, 223–25, 230
Johnston's Jolly, 29

Kalkmaz Dagh, 218
Kannengiesser, Hans, 117, 198, 202
Karachali, 189, 191
Kearns, Thomas, 136
Kemal, Mustafa, 208
Kephalos Harbour, 60, 128, 138–39, 142, 158
Kerr, Mark, 233
Keshan, 229

Keyes, Roger, 22, 105–107, 110–11, 145, 147, 159, 164–66, 207, 223, 235–36; proposal for a naval offensive, 107, 113–16
Kilia Liman, 26, 41, 218, 226, 258–59
Kilid Bahr, 103, 223, 226–27, 234
Kilid Bahr Plateau, 6, 103, 191, 218–19, 221, 224, 227, 230
Kiretch Tepe Ridge, 66, 74, 87, 198, 203–204, 206, 210, 212
Kitchener, Horatio Herbert: on Allied lines of communication, 238; on the August Offensive, 30–33, 36, 39, 55; influence, 12–14, 109; and Hamilton, 49, 67, 108, 121, 137, 143–44, 210–11, 221; and Maxwell, 128–29; on strategic potential of Dardanelles Campaign, 15
Kite balloons, 102–103
Koe, Frederick, 122–23, 145, 164, 167, 238
Koja Dere, 35, 43, 191, 227
Krithia, 7, 40, 223
Kuchuk Anafarta, 35, 206, 210
Kum Kale, 6, 235
Kum Keui, 35

Lala Baba, 87, 165, 197
Lambart, Lionel, 114
Lancashire Landing. *See* W Beach
Learning curve, 23, 245
Legge Valley, 217
Lemnos Island, 49, 55, 60, 79–80, 97–98, 104, 119, 125–36, 138–45, 152, 158, 165–66, 184, 186, 238
Light Horse: 1st Australian Light Horse Regiment, 199; 2nd Australian Light Horse Brigade, 201; 2nd Australian Light Horse Regiment, 199; 8th Australian Light Horse Regiment, 200; 10th Australian Light Horse Regiment, 200
Limpus, Arthur, 114, 125

Lindley, John, 211
Lines of communication. *See* Logistics
Lloyd George, David, 14–15
Logistics: acquisition, 11, 119, 120–23, 147–48; administration, 140–47; Allied lines of communication, 11, 48, 55, 119–20, 124–47, 229, 238, 293n47; ammunition supply, 16, 27, 32, 75–76, 79, 82–85, 92, 99–100, 105, 119, 127, 170–71, 173–74, 176, 178–80, 182, 224–25, 230–32, 237, 245, 303n94; at Anzac, 158–61, 164, 167–69, 171–81, 240–41; breakdown, 148, 157, 166, 172, 175–76, 178–83, 243; at Cape Helles, 158–61, 168–69, 171–72; comparison to Western Front, 120–21, 140–41, 148, 166, 168, 173–75; disembarkation, 11, 120, 128–29, 157–63, 165–69, 171, 173, 175–78, 183, 186, 204; distribution, 140, 143, 148, 157–58, 160–62, 166, 169, 170, 172–79, 182–83, 238; during subsequent phases, 236–41; floating depots, 132–33; forage, 164, 171–72, 177, 238–39; 40th Depot Unit of Supply, 168; impact of German submarines upon, 126–28, 139; impact of weather upon, 168–69; Indian Mule Cart Train, 175–78, 304n118; inspector general of communications, 121–22, 130, 142–46, 161, 164, 179, 184–85; loading of ships, 122–23; medical, 183–87; Ottoman lines of communication, 6, 18, 35, 43, 47, 103–105, 124, 226–30; piers, 36, 128, 130, 134, 139, 153, 158–59, 160, 162–63, 165–66, 169, 176, 187–88; pull/push system, 120–22; request process, 121–22; responsibility on the beaches, 160–63; role of army, 169–74; role of navy, 94, 106; shortage of labor, 135, 158–59, 165–68, 184, 302n58; shortage of small craft, 73, 130, 135–38, 163–65, 172, 184; stockpiling, 133, 153, 157–62, 164, 166, 169–73, 178, 187–88, 240; at Suvla, 37, 127, 129, 137–38, 155, 159, 161–70, 172, 174–78, 181–83, 204, 238–41, 282n98, 304n118, 305n125, 305n127; transhipping, 129, 131–34, 139, 158, 163–65, 168; transport, 173–78, 238; voyage to the peninsula, 123–29, 131, 139–41, 177, 183, 204; water supply, 27, 58, 106, 119, 126, 130, 165, 169, 172–76, 178–83, 184, 187, 205, 215, 237–39, 306n157; Zion Mule Corps, 175
London, 4, 12–17, 30–31, 33, 39, 45, 86, 92, 108–109, 114–15, 120–21, 143, 183, 190, 229
Lone Pine, 29, 70–71, 73, 89, 94, 98, 154, 189–91, 201, 204, 278n19, 309n13
Long, Sidney, 121
Loos. *See* Western Front

Machine guns, 18, 27, 70–72, 84, 101, 159, 165, 177, 180, 189, 199–202, 205, 208, 217
Mackenzie, Compton, 95
MacMunn, George, 122, 130–31, 140, 145
Mahon, Bryan, 30, 211–12, 248
Maidos, 25–26, 29, 33, 35, 38, 41, 43–44, 91, 140, 190, 216, 218, 221, 223–24, 226–27, 230–31, 237–40, 243
Malone, William, 26, 32, 56
Malta, 114, 125–27, 129, 141, 184–86
Mal Tepe, 6, 25, 35
Malthus, Cecil, 180, 216
Maneuver, 3, 21–24, 26–27, 29, 44–45, 47, 50–51, 54–55, 59,

66, 68, 188, 216, 221, 225, 227, 230, 243–44
Manual of Combined Naval and Military Operations, 19, 108, 116, 160, 166
Maps, 18, 21, 35–36, 48, 50, 65–66, 88, 90–92, 101, 202, 226–27, 245
Marseilles, 124
Maude, Frederick, 212
Maxwell, John, 55, 128, 144
McGrigor, Charles, 128, 143
Medical evacuation, 11, 132–33, 136, 158, 162, 183–87
Mediterranean Expeditionary Force. *See* Mediterranean Expeditionary Force battalions; Mediterranean Expeditionary Force brigades; Mediterranean Expeditionary Force corps; Mediterranean Expeditionary Force divisions
Mediterranean Expeditionary Force battalions: 1st Battalion, 5th Gurkha Rifles, 195, 212; 1st Battalion, 6th Gurkha Rifles, 64, 195, 203, 208; 2nd Battalion, 10th Gurkha Rifles, 195, 202, 212; 3rd Australian Battalion, 56; 4th Battalion, South Wales Borderers, 192; 5th Australian Battalion, 191; 5th Battalion, Connaught Rangers, 191, 212; 5th Battalion, Dorset Regiment, 198, 203; 5th Battalion, Wiltshire Regiment, 192, 195, 207–208; 6th Australian Battalion, 198–99; 6th Battalion, East Lancashire Regiment, 207; 6th Battalion, Lincolnshire Regiment, 204; 6th Battalion, Loyal North Lancashire Regiment, 180, 207–208; 6th Battalion, Royal Irish Rifles, 207; 6th Battalion, South Lancashire Regiment, 207–208; 6th Battalion, Yorkshire Regiment, 197; 6th Battalion, York and Lancashire Regiment, 198, 203; 7th Australian Battalion, 191; 7th Battalion, Gloucestershire Regiment, 202, 205; 8th (Pioneer) Battalion, Welch Regiment, 205; 8th Australian Battalion, 198–99; 8th Battalion, Royal Welch Fusiliers, 201; 9th Battalion, Lancashire Fusiliers, 198; 10th Battalion, Hampshire Regiment, 207, 212–13; 11th Battalion, Manchester Regiment, 165, 198; 12th Australian Battalion, 191; 13th Australian Battalion, 195; 14th Australian Battalion, 195; 14th Sikhs, 58, 195; Auckland Battalion, 194, 202; Auckland Mounted Rifles Regiment, 192, 205; Canterbury Battalion, 65, 194, 202, 250; Canterbury Mounted Rifles Regiment, 26, 192, 195, 251; Otago Battalion, 194, 205, 250; Otago Mounted Rifles Regiment, 32, 192, 251; Wellington Battalion, 26, 32, 56, 180, 194, 202, 205, 216, 250; Wellington Mounted Rifles Regiment, 192, 205, 251. *See also* Artillery; Force size; French forces; Logistics; other Mediterranean Expeditionary Force entries; Royal Engineers; Signal service
Mediterranean Expeditionary Force brigades: 1st Australian Brigade, 154, 190–91; 2nd Royal Naval Brigade, 50, 139; 4th Australian Brigade, 49, 58, 65, 194–96, 202–203, 205, 207, 212, 220; 29th Brigade, 191, 249; 29th Indian Brigade, 25, 27, 64–65, 194–95, 203, 205–206, 251; 30th Brigade, 198,

Mediterranean Expeditionary Force brigades (*continued*) 212; 31st Brigade, 198, 212; 32nd Brigade, 97, 197–98; 33rd Brigade, 97, 197; 34th Brigade, 50, 97, 197–98; 38th Brigade, 207; 40th Brigade, 191–92; 88th Brigade, 189; 125th Brigade, 189; 127th Brigade, 189; New Zealand Infantry Brigade, 56, 194–95, 202–203, 207–208; New Zealand Mounted Rifles Brigade, 63, 65, 72, 94, 191–93, 201, 212. *See also* Artillery; Force size; French forces; Logistics; other Mediterranean Expeditionary Force entries; Royal Engineers; Signal service

Mediterranean Expeditionary Force corps: Australian and New Zealand Army Corps, 5–6, 24–26, 30, 32, 53t, 56, 59–61, 65, 76–77, 96, 161, 167, 172, 176, 180–81, 188, 190, 197, 201, 226, 240, 262n11; VIII Corps, 21, 31, 40, 43, 76, 84–85, 171, 189, 219, 230; IX Corps, 9, 18, 30–31, 38–39, 50–51, 54, 57–59, 61–62, 73–74, 77, 94–97, 105, 127, 132, 135–36, 155, 159, 161–62, 165, 167, 172, 181–82, 197–98, 203–204, 206–207, 211, 219, 240. *See also* Artillery; Force size; French forces; Logistics; other Mediterranean Expeditionary Force entries; Royal Engineers; Signal service

Mediterranean Expeditionary Force divisions: 1st Australian Division, 43, 57, 176, 178, 190–91, 199, 250; 2nd Australian Division, 293n41; 2nd Mounted Division, 52, 55, 212; 10th Division, 30, 97, 191, 198, 248; 11th Division, 30, 50, 58, 97, 139, 204, 206–207, 212, 249; 13th Division, 30, 63, 65, 131, 181, 201, 212, 249, 275n76;

29th Division, 6, 53, 127, 189, 212, 262n14; 42nd Division, 53, 189, 280n66; 52nd Division, 22, 27, 248; 53rd Division, 36, 52, 54–56, 79, 135, 210–11, 252; 54th Division, 36, 52, 54–55, 79, 180–81, 210, 252; New Zealand and Australian Division, 27, 63, 98, 202, 275n76, 280n66; Royal Naval Division, 26, 50, 53, 79, 139, 167, 280n66. *See also* Artillery; Force size; French forces; Logistics; other Mediterranean Expeditionary Force entries; Royal Engineers; Signal service

Mercantile Marine, 124–25, 141
Miles, Sherman, 111, 219
Minefields, 5, 19, 44, 93, 114, 220, 231–34, 236
Minesweeping, 19, 44, 93, 114, 220, 233–34
Mitchell Report, 117, 125
Mobility, 3, 7, 9–11, 23–24, 47–68, 79, 150, 157, 214, 216–22, 230–31, 238, 241–43
Monash, John, 49, 57, 63, 65, 195, 203, 205, 220
Monash Valley, 173, 199, 201
Monro, Charles, 115
Morale, 17, 20, 22, 24, 28–29, 47, 57–58, 66, 99–100, 103, 126, 187, 243
Motor lighters, 96–97, 136–37, 139, 155, 163–64, 177
Mudros Harbour, 79–80, 97–98, 104, 119, 125–36, 138–45, 152, 158, 165–66, 184, 186, 238
Mule Gully, 173, 177
Mules, 73, 135, 153, 167, 173–79, 181–82, 187, 214–15, 225, 228–29, 238–39, 305n123, 305n125
Murray, Archibald, 9
Murray, James Wolfe, 13–14
Myth, 8–11, 44, 59, 65, 68, 118, 214–15, 222, 226, 230, 241–42, 244, 263n23, 263n24

Nagara, 19, 235
Narrows, 5–6, 19, 35, 41, 66, 103, 106, 112–14, 116–17, 215, 219, 227, 232, 235
Nasmith, Martin, 104
Naval gunfire support, 5, 11, 25, 72, 74–75, 94, 97–103, 106, 189, 191, 204, 218, 227, 223, 225, 227, 231–36, 243
Naval Transport Department, 124, 133, 141
Navy: administration, 146–47; during August Offensive, 44, 189, 204; during February–March, 3–5, 142, 234; during fourth phase, 44, 93, 231–37; on importance of Sari Bair Ridge, 43; supporting the MEF, 18–19, 69, 77, 94–101, 105–18, 124, 137, 139–42, 160–65, 177, 183–86. *See also* Combined operations; Eastern Mediterranean Squadron; Interservice cooperation; Naval gunfire support; Royal Naval Air Service
Neuve Chapelle. *See* Western Front
Nevinson, Henry, 64
New Army, 16, 30, 79, 265n25
Nibrunesi Point, 25–26, 60, 62, 197, 241, 268n93
Nicholas, Grand Duke, 3
Nicholson, Stuart, 95, 313n114
No. 1 Outpost, 27
No. 2 Outpost, 63, 173, 177, 194
North, John, 233, 263n21
North Beach, 159, 176–77, 225, 240

Old No. 3 Post, 28, 72, 94, 192
Oliver, Henry, 14, 236
Operational level of war, 9–10, 17, 19, 22, 93, 119, 242, 263n33, 264n34
Ottoman Army, 126, 191, 197, 199, 202, 208, 210, 215, 262n8; allied opinions of, 15, 21–24, 26, 28–29, 66–67; capabilities, 6, 47, 58, 66–67, 89, 181, 198,
200, 221–22, 236; casualties, 6–7, 28, 191, 208, 309n21; defenses, 3, 5, 19, 27, 28, 44, 66, 70–72, 93, 103, 112–13, 116–17, 159, 197, 200, 205, 217–22, 232–35; dispositions, 25, 37, 65, 197, 206–207, 212; 8th Division, 208; 15th Regiment, 191; 5th Division, 191, 212; 5th Ottoman Army, 49, 198, 204, 222; 14th Regiment, 202; General Staff, 104–105, 213, 236; knowledge of August Offensive, 48–49, 65, 94, 96, 188–89; 19th Division, 202; 9th Division, 191, 198; 72nd Arab Regiment, 202; 16th Division, 191; 16th Ottoman Army Corps, 206; 64th Regiment, 191; supply routes, 6, 18, 35, 43, 47, 104–105, 156, 158, 223, 226–30, 232; 13th Division, 208; 13th Regiment, 191; 25th Regiment, 191; 24th Regiment, 208; 26th Regiment, 208; 23rd Regiment, 208; use of terrain, 64, 66, 87, 91–92, 156, 180, 219; Ottoman artillery, 28, 33, 35, 37–39, 64, 71, 74, 80, 86, 90–91, 102, 114, 159, 168–69, 175, 178, 180, 186, 215, 229–31, 234, 238
Ottoman Empire, 3–4
Overton, Percy, 26–28, 195, 268n93

Paris, Archibald, 26
Parker, Walter, 163
Pasha, Esat, 191
Peyton, William, 55
Phillimore, Richard, 137, 142, 164
Piers, 36, 128, 130, 134, 139, 153, 158–59, 160, 162–63, 165–66, 169, 176, 187–88
Pincer movement, 29, 42
Plugge's Plateau, 179
Poett, Joseph, 162, 165, 169–70
Pope's Hill, 153, 199
Porter, James, 184–85
Port Iero, 97

362 INDEX

Prisoners of war, 6, 17, 20–21, 41, 49, 135, 157, 210

Quinn's Post, 43, 199

Rabbit Island, 99
Rawlinson, Henry, 30, 262n19, 281n74
Raynell, George, 164
Reconnaissance, 17–20, 26–29, 37, 106, 206, 208, 210, 212, 268n93
Reed, Hamilton, 18, 62, 66
Reinforcements, 14–16, 27–28, 30–33, 35–37, 45, 52, 54, 56, 58–59, 95, 133, 148, 171, 177, 179, 186, 188, 197–98, 211–12, 221
Reserve Gully, 173
Rettie, William, 88, 91, 131, 212
Rhododendron Ridge, 27–28, 65, 194–95, 202–203, 306n157
Rosenthal, Charles, 77
Royal Army Medical Corps, 127
Royal Artillery. *See* Artillery
Royal Australian Naval Bridging Train, 165
Royal Engineers: during August Offensive, 159, 165, 183, 192; 1st New Zealand Field Company, 194; 72nd Field Company, 192; 68th Field Company, 165; stores, 130, 169, 174
Royal Naval Air Service: air raids, 103, 105; intelligence, 18; observation, 5, 10, 75, 90–92, 99, 101–103, 227, 229, 232, 243; photography, 18, 90; reconnaissance, 17–19, 29, 206, 208, 210
Royal Naval Division. *See* Mediterranean Expeditionary Force divisions
Royal Navy. *See* Navy
Russell, Andrew, 192
Russell's Top, 27–28, 173, 199–200

Salonica, 49, 127
Salt Lake, 66, 89, 198, 204

Sari Bair Ridge, 194–96, 201–210; communications, 63; during August Offensive, 194–96, 199, 201–10; during subsequent phases, 27–29, 38, 41, 43, 47, 58, 68, 181, 214–32, 238–40; fire support, 72–73, 80–81, 86–87, 150, 204; foothills, 28, 30, 64, 72, 94, 150, 191–93, 196; logistics, 27, 41, 173, 176–77, 181, 238, 305n123, 305n127; as an observation post, 25–26, 103, 223; Ottomans, 26, 58; terrain, 64–66, 69, 83, 150; war establishment, 52. *See also* August Offensive; Chunuk Bair; Hill 971; Hill Q
Savory, Reginald, 58
Sazli Beit Dere, 27, 192, 194, 225
Scimitar Hill, 100, 206–207, 210, 212
Scrubby Knoll, 43, 217
Sea of Marmara, 5, 104, 112, 204, 229, 233, 235–36
Secrecy, 13, 18–19, 41, 45, 47–50, 73, 76, 221
Shaw, Frederick, 65, 131, 181, 208
Shell crisis, 15, 82–83
Shrapnel Gully, 200
Signal service, 59–60, 62–63; New Zealand and Australian Divisional Signals Company, 62–63; 13th Divisional Signal Company, 62–63
Signals personnel, 62–63
Simpson, Henry, 131, 133–34, 141–42, 146
Simpson-Baikie, Hugh, 76, 85–86, 90, 98
Skeen, Andrew, 26
Smith, Sydenham, 77
Stalemate, 3, 7–8, 22–24, 41, 54, 67, 69, 72, 114, 219, 221, 238, 244–45
Steele's Post, 198
Steevens, John, 121
Stocks, David, 104
Stodart, Robert, 199

Stopford, Frederick: on capability of his corps, 54; chosen for IX Corps command, 30–31; command experience, 197; and de Robeck, 127; during Hamilton's visit to Suvla, 207; issued plans for Suvla Bay, 38, 48, 161; lack of consultation, 170; remains on HMS *Jonquil*, 61–63, 77, 170, 203, 207; removed from command, 181, 210–12; scapegoat, 240; suggests alterations to plans, 38–39
Striedinger, Oscar, 174
Stuart-Wortley, Richard, 121–22
Submarines, 16, 41, 130; allied, 11, 19, 95, 103–105, 204, 228; German, 7, 19, 94–95, 98, 124–29, 138–39, 141, 232, 293n41
Supplies. *See* Logistics
Supply ships. *See* Eastern Mediterranean Squadron
Surprise, 19, 23, 28–29, 37, 47–49, 54, 65, 72, 90, 97, 114, 188, 190, 201, 215, 221
Suvla Bay: artillery at, 38, 54, 69, 73–74, 77–81, 86–88, 90–91, 213, 225–26, 234, 280n69, 281n81; after August Offensive, 210–13, 225; casualties, 315n167; communications, 60–63, 89–90, 203, 220; conditions at, 58, 181–83, 204; criticisms of plan, 9; fighting during August Offensive, 203–204, 206–207; Hamilton visits, 206–207; landings, 50, 94, 96–97, 105, 132, 136, 155, 165, 192, 196–98; logistics, 37, 127, 129, 137–38, 155, 159, 161–70, 172, 174–78, 181–83, 204, 238–41, 282n98, 304n118, 305n125, 305n127; as a logistic hub, 36, 38–41, 43, 66, 155, 159, 197, 237, 239–41; naval support, 69, 73, 95, 100–101, 110, 127; origins of plan, 25, 28, 34–37; Ottomans at, 74, 159, 197–98, 206, 212; planning process, 37–39, 48; reconnaissance of, 19, 25, 37, 210; significance of failure, 111, 239–40; terrain, 66, 89, 101, 150, 214, 234. *See also* Mediterranean Expeditionary Force entries; Stopford, Frederick
Su Yatagha, 43

Table Top, 192, 194
Taifur Keui, 25
Talbot, Henry, 161–62, 300n18
Taylor's Gap, 195
Tekke Tepe Ridge, 35–36, 38, 74, 181, 207
Terrain, 10, 17–20, 29, 35, 45, 47, 60, 64–66, 68–69, 75, 77, 83, 87–92, 99, 101, 150, 156–57, 169, 173, 175, 182, 187, 194, 214, 216–20, 222, 224–25, 230, 234, 238, 240, 242–43
The Apex, 27, 202, 208
The Cut, 198
The Dardanelles. *See* Dardanelles
The Farm, 195, 202–203, 206, 208
The Nek, 70–71, 98, 200–201, 311n66
The Pinnacle, 202, 208
The Straits. *See* Dardanelles
Third Ridge, 27–31, 33, 35, 43, 190, 216–17, 219, 224, 227, 321n125
Thompson, Julian, 183, 303n83
Thomson, Graeme, 121–22, 141
Thursby, Cecil, 24, 223
Transport. *See* Logistics
Transports. *See* Eastern Mediterranean Squadron
Travers, Jonas, 192
Travers, Tim, 79, 101, 182, 216
Trench warfare. *See* Stalemate

U-boat. *See* Submarines
United Kingdom, 11, 52, 57, 82, 95, 120–23, 124–25, 129–30, 132–33, 136, 140–42, 144, 147, 165, 184, 186, 188, 244
Unwin, Edwin, 163

V Beach, 6, 158, 168
Victoria Gully, 173
Vineyard, 189
Von Clausewitz, Carl, 23, 217–18, 222
Von Moltke, Helmuth, 40
Von Sanders, Liman, 49, 210

Walden Point, 192
Walker, Harold, 190, 199
Walker's Ridge, 28
Wallace, Alexander, 130, 143–45
War Cabinet, 16
War Council, 14–15
War establishment. *See* Force size
War Office, 9, 12–14, 17, 92, 120–24, 130, 135, 140, 143–44, 179, 183; relations with Admiralty, 108–109, 115, 137
War ships. *See* Eastern Mediterranean Squadron
Water supply. *See* Logistics
Watson, James, 160
W Beach, 6, 158, 168, 172
Weather, 18, 36, 39, 41, 103, 114, 124, 130, 134, 138, 168–69, 171–72, 178, 187, 204, 240–41
Wemyss, Rosslyn, 104, 110, 114, 130, 136, 142, 145, 147

Western, William, 162, 300n19
Western Front, 15–16, 45; comparisons with Gallipoli, 9–10, 52, 54, 60, 62, 64, 69, 75, 79–83, 101–102, 120–21, 140–41, 148, 157, 164, 166, 168, 173–75, 213, 220–22, 224, 242, 244–45; Loos, 81, 245, 281n79; Neuve Chapelle, 3, 23, 44–45, 67, 75, 79–81, 83, 89, 92, 224, 245, 281n74
W Hills, 28, 33, 35, 37–39, 100, 197–98, 204, 206, 210, 212
White, Alexander, 200
White's Valley, 173
Wigram, Clive, 8
Williams, Orlo, 32, 55, 201, 262n13
Willmer, Wilhelm, 197–98, 204, 206
Wilson, Henry, 82–83
Wine Glass Ridge, 43, 217, 227
Winter, Samuel, 121, 134, 143–45, 163
Wray, Fawcet, 95

Yilghin Burnu. *See* Green Hill
Young, Frederick, 160–61

Zion Mule Corps, 175

www.ingramcontent.com/pod-product-compliance
Lightning Source LLC
Chambersburg PA
CBHW022059150426
43195CB00008B/199